NARRATIVE
COMPREHENSION

For Andrew Mathews

NARRATIVE COMPREHENSION

A Discourse Perspective

Catherine Emmott

OXFORD
UNIVERSITY PRESS

OXFORD

UNIVERSITY PRESS

Great Clarendon Street, Oxford OX2 6DP

Oxford University Press is a department of the University of Oxford
and furthers the University's aim of excellence in research, scholarship,
and education by publishing worldwide in

Oxford New York

Athens Auckland Bangkok Bogotá Bombay Buenos Aires Calcutta
Cape Town Chennai Dar es Salaam Delhi Florence Hong Kong Istanbul
Karachi Kuala Lumpur Madras Melbourne Mexico City Mumbai
Nairobi Paris São Paulo Singapore Taipei Tokyo Toronto Warsaw

and associated companies in Berlin Ibadan

Oxford is a registered trade mark of Oxford University Press

Published in the United States
by Oxford University Press Inc., New York

British Library Cataloguing in Publication Data

Data available

Library of Congress Cataloging in Publication Data

Narrative comprehension: a discourse perspective
Catherine Emmott.
Based on the author's thesis (Ph.D.)
Includes bibliographical references and index.
1. Discourse analysis—Psychological aspects. 2. Discourse
analysis, Narrative. 3. Comprehension. I. Title.
P302.8.E47 1997   401'.41—dc20   96-34437
ISBN 0-19-823868-1

1 3 5 7 9 10 8 6 4 2

Typeset in Photina
by Joshua Associates Ltd., Oxford
Printed in Great Britain on acid-free paper by
Biddles Ltd., Guildford and King's Lynn

PREFACE

In a variety of ways, narratives provide evidence for the
nature of the mind. . . . I see narratives as overt manifestations
of the mind in action . . . windows to both the content of the
mind and its ongoing operations.[1]

(Chafe 1990: 79)

The human mind is a powerful and effective processor of written
and spoken text.[2] Although the mind does not have the memory
and processing capacity of a computer, it nevertheless performs a
task which artificial intelligence researchers are struggling to
replicate. Readers of narrative text, for example, manage to
create a richly represented fictional world from mere strings of
words. Stories can be interesting to the human reader, but
making a computer interested in what it reads is at present impossible.

Reading a story is an astonishing feat of information processing,
requiring the reader to perform complex operations at a number
of levels. For each sentence, the reader must decode the alphabet
letters, assign meanings to the words, and recognize the grammatical structure. The reader must also judge how a sentence is
linked to the previous text, often by making inferences based on
general knowledge or stored information about the fictional

---

[1] Most of Chafe's work describes the production of spoken text, whereas this book
discusses the comprehension of written text. The expression 'overt manifestation'
is particularly relevant to oral narration, since the hesitations of the speaker are a
direct reflection of the mental effort involved in communicating a story. Nevertheless, studying written narratives provides an indication of the demands which
texts place on their interpreters and thereby provides insight into some of the factors which need to be taken into account in a cognitive model.

[2] In this book I use the terms 'text' and 'discourse' interchangeably to mean a
stretch of language which is (generally) longer than a sentence and which has its
own structure over and above sentence-level syntactic structure. My use of these
terms also implies that the language is 'natural' or 'real', meaning that it has
occurred in actual usage (e.g. in a conversation or a novel) rather than as a 'constructed' example created by the researcher specifically for the purpose of experimental testing or linguistic analysis. This will be discussed further in Ch. 3.

world. The significance of a sentence has to be assessed and the reader's model of the fictional world altered accordingly. A single sentence can perform a number of functions. It might describe one action in a chain of events, yield information about one or more of the characters, signal a shift to a new location or context, add to the overall plot, and contribute to one of the themes of the book. In addition, the reader invariably has some awareness of the style of the text, particularly for literary works. The speed and ease with which experienced readers carry out all these operations when processing a text is remarkable.

Researchers in a variety of disciplines are currently working on the mental processing of text, including artificial intelligence researchers, educationalists, linguists, literary theorists, and psychologists. Obviously, the vast scope of the subject means that no individual research project can discuss in detail every aspect of text processing.[3] The aim of this particular study is to hypothesize about the mental stores and inferences that are necessary to create and keep track of characters and contexts in a narrative text. More specifically, I examine how such information may be utilized to interpret 'shorthand' linguistic forms such as pronouns. As a discourse analyst (from within linguistics), I am particularly interested in how information gathered from all over a text is needed to interpret grammatical items and how a reader's sensitivity to the hierarchical structure of discourse plays an important role in grammatical interpretation. Shifts from one context[4] to another, such as from flashback to main narrative, can

[3] Ch. 2 provides a summary of work on inference-making. In this book I focus on discourse-level interpretation, not on how isolated sentences or sentence pairs are understood. As far as sentence-level processing is concerned, there are many accounts available of how readers recognize words and letters (e.g. Gibson 1985*a*, *b*; Laberge and Samuels 1985; McClelland and Rumelhart 1985; Carroll 1985; Samuels 1985; Seymour 1987) and how they utilize their knowledge of semantics (e.g. R. C. Anderson and Freebody 1985) and syntax (e.g. D. C. Mitchell 1987). Elsewhere, psychologists have also examined eye movements (Carpenter and Just 1977; Just and Carpenter 1978), the constraints of working memory on text processing (e.g. Daneman 1987), and the formation of propositional constructs (e.g. van Dijk and Kintsch 1983). Other common topics of research are individual differences in comprehension (see Ch. 2), the acquisition of reading skills in childhood (e.g. Beech and Colley 1987), and reading disabilities (e.g. Hulme 1987; Temple 1987). Useful introductions to many of these aspects of text comprehension can be found in a number of books (e.g. Smith 1985; Garnham 1985; J. Greene 1986; Smyth *et al.* 1987: ch. 1; Eysenck and Keane 1990: ch. 9).

[4] By 'context', I mean that a narrative portrays a group of participants as being together in the same physical location at a particular point in time. This type of

have the effect of automatically altering the pool of potential referents for a pronoun and may mean that a pronoun can be interpreted without an antecedent. This has implications for
grammatical theory, throwing a question-mark over the role of
the antecedent in anaphoric theory and over the borderline
between anaphora and deixis. At the same time, there are implications for text theory, since a reader constantly needs to be aware
of contextual information, making inferences about how long particular contextual facts remain valid and about when contextual
information needs to be updated. In real life, speakers are surrounded by their context, but for narrative fiction the reader
needs to create and maintain a mental model of the context
which has been described by the preceding text. For each sentence
of a text, the reader's knowledge of the fictional context will contribute to the meaning of the sentence and, conversely, the content
of the sentence will force the reader to update his/her mental
representation of the fictional world.

As the topics of pronoun interpretation and context representation are important to cognitive researchers in a number of disciplines, this book addresses a broad audience. Experiments on text
processing show that readers respond to a text in radically different ways depending on their own knowledge and interests. This
observation is particularly true of experts reading an interdisciplinary work, especially when the subject matter crosses from the
arts to the sciences, through the social sciences. For this reason,
the remainder of this Preface discusses the problem of addressing
such a wide-ranging audience (which is a problem for cognitive
science as a whole and not just for this work) and gives an indication of the relevance of the book to each discipline.[5]

Although sharing an interest in the mind, cognitive researchers
have very diverse perspectives due to their different technical

context is, therefore, part of the fictional (or non-fictional) world created from a
text and represented within the mind of the reader. This is different from the real-
world contexts which the writer and reader inhabit. The topic of context representation will be discussed in detail in Chs. 4 to 6.

[5] In addition to differences in perspective, each discipline also has its own bibliographical interests. It is almost impossible for a researcher to be familiar with everything that has been published in one discipline, let alone the five (or more) which
this study draws on. Readers from each discipline will no doubt have additions
which they would wish to make to my bibliography, but I hope that the breadth
across the disciplines will provide some compensation for this.

knowledge, different research objectives, and different theoretical backgrounds. One illustration of this is provided by cognitive psychology and literary theory. Cognitive psychology takes the role of the reader for granted—after all, it is the science of the human mind. By contrast, the major contribution of literary theory's 'reader response' work is to argue this very fact. It could be said that literary theory is simply stating the obvious, but this ignores the paradigm shift in a discipline which had previously focused almost exclusively on either the author or the text. Similarly, psychology findings will not always be directly relevant to major problems in the arts. For example, although literary researchers have an interest, in broad terms, in how a text is interpreted, it seems unlikely that many of them would require detailed information about experiments which determine at exactly which point in a sentence an inference is made. Such differences in academic perspective are multiplied once a number of disciplines are considered. Hence, it is necessary for any interdisciplinary study to make clear the framework within which it is based and what it has to offer both to its own discipline and beyond.

A major aim of this book is to highlight the importance of mental processing to discourse analysts and text theorists. Psychologists and artificial intelligence researchers take such mental processing for granted, but it is a relatively new development in linguistics for text to be viewed from a cognitive perspective. Until recently, many discourse analysts have concentrated simply on the text itself, rather than attempting to produce process models. Moreover, when a cognitive standpoint is taken it can take different forms. Some researchers might, therefore, go little further than seeing mental representations as mental copies of antecedents, rather than as stores of information that are built up as the whole text is read. Other researchers might postulate fuller mental representations, but might not consider the mental effort involved in maintaining and updating these representations to match the dynamic development of the discourse. This work aims to show how readers must make inferences about continuity and change in order to keep track of the mentally stored information that is relevant at any particular point in the discourse.

This book should also be of relevance to literary theorists working on reader response. Literary research often stresses inferences which have significance to the overall interpretation of the work, particularly so far as literary value is concerned. There is, never-theless, a significant amount of inferencing involved simply in making sense of which characters are being referred to, keeping track of spatial and temporal information, and establishing causal links between events. Although this level of textual under-standing may not be relevant to literature study in the standard sense, it is important as far as literacy is concerned, as discussed below, and must presumably be taken into account in any model of the relationship between the reader and the text.[6] In addition to inference-making, my interest is also in narrative structure, the province of narratologists. Narratives are generally regarded as being, by definition, 'event sequences': I argue that another important factor is that some of these events occur in a particular context. This study looks at the mechanisms of context change and of switching from specific contexts to broader generalizations.

Educationalists are an important part of my audience, since they use linguistic information about narratives in order to develop techniques for teaching reading. Research in educational psychology has shown that 10 per cent of children who can read a text aloud cannot make sense of what they are reading.[7] The ability to decode individual words is there, but there is difficulty forming a coherent overall representation and one result of this is that there are problems interpreting pronouns. A major debate in Education is over the matter of whether children need to be exposed to 'real books' as well as being taught basic decoding skills. Narrative is an important text type in Education because it is the medium through which children learn to read,[8] as well as

[6] In fact, Chatman (1978: 31) makes this point too: 'The drawing of narrative inferences by the reader is a low-level kind of interpretation. Perhaps it doesn't even deserve the name, since "interpretation" is so well established as a synonym for "exegesis" in literary criticism. This narrative filling-in is all too easily forgotten or assumed to be of no interest, a mere reflex action of the reading mind. But to neglect it is a critical mistake . . .'

[7] See Oakhill and Garnham (1988); Yuill and Oakhill (1991); and Oakhill and Yuill (1995).

[8] Narrative is important in the education of young children both in terms of the amount of contact they have with this genre and the type of mental activity it encourages (Britton and Pellegrini 1990; McCabe and Peterson 1991). The ability to 'displace' in time and space, including seeing things from another's perspective, is thought to be a key factor in linguistic and cognitive development—indeed, argu-ably, 'displacement' is one of the defining characteristics of human intelligence (e.g. Hockett 1963; Piaget 1955). Also, incidents from our own 'life stories' provide a central contribution to social interaction (Schank 1982; Linde 1993; Polanyi

giving insight into the skills required for advanced adult literacy. This study emphasizes the fact that in adult texts, at least, mental representations have to be maintained over lengthy stretches of text and the reader needs to be responsive to the overall structure of the narrative. At some time in their education, children need to acquire the skills necessary to do this, which involves exposing them to texts which are long and complex enough to have a hierarchical organization.

Psychologists (and psycholinguists) obviously do not require any convincing about the importance of mental representations. There is, however, a need for some psychology researchers to be more aware of the significance of discourse structure in their text-processing models.[9] Seminal studies, such as Johnson-Laird's (1983) *Mental Models*, are often difficult to apply to full-length texts because they account for static scenarios in which context shifts do not occur.[10] Even within psychology, there has begun to be a questioning of the traditional 'sentence pairs' used in experimental work, but moves towards 'ecological validity' in text-processing work have not generally been particularly successful due to a lack of insight into the properties of natural discourse.[11] What is needed is cooperation between psychologists and discourse analysts at the stage of experimental design. This book might serve as a prelude to this, since it describes, on the basis of textual evidence, some of the demands which texts place on their readers in respect of shifting from one hierarchical level to another.

The objectives of this book should be most familiar to artificial intelligence researchers, since their discipline has already made a substantial contribution to the study of discourse hierarchy and cognitive modelling.[12] Much of this research has, however, been

---

1985*a*) and, more controversially, narrative may be instrumental in creating the human 'self' (Dennett 1991; Flanagan 1992). The importance of narrative as a key to the workings of the human mind is shown by the fact that when normal thought processes are disrupted, as in schizophrenia, the ability to produce and understand narratives can be lost (Rochester and Martin 1979).

[9] Ch. 3 provides a discussion of this topic.

[10] Johnson-Laird's work is discussed further in Ch. 2.

[11] 'Ecological validity' in psychology work is discussed further in Ch. 3.

[12] Some of the main artificial intelligence work on text processing (e.g. Grosz 1977; Sidner 1979*a*; Reichman 1985) is discussed in Chs. 5 and 7. Other chapters draw more generally on artificial intelligence insights, such as 'the frame problem' from robotics research (see Ch. 4).

on topic shifts in spoken non-narrative, whereas this book focuses instead on context changes in written narratives. Although the overall principles might be similar, the discourse organization of each text type needs separate study. Moreover, contexts are rather different in nature from topics. Contexts have a spatial and temporal orientation which is maintained over a stretch of text, as well as forcing the reader to make assumptions about participant continuity. In addition, narrative flashback needs special consideration because it creates different versions of the same character in past and present contexts.

Overall, therefore, this book aims to make a contribution to the growing body of interdisciplinary work in cognitive science. One of my main aims is to show that the mind plays an important role in reading full-length texts. This is an obvious truism, but it is surprising how many models of language have managed either to ignore cognitive processing altogether or to avoid looking at inference-making beyond a two-sentence span. As a discourse analyst, I stress the properties that language has beyond sentence-level structure and argue that mental representations explain how information is amalgamated from different parts of a text. The subtitle of the book, *A Discourse Perspective*, highlights how my approach differs from that of psychologists. My emphasis is on what discourse can tell us about the human mind. In this book I am not examining the act of reading directly (for this would require psychological testing), but, by looking at the texts which experienced readers process, I am hypothesizing about the demands which texts place on their readers in terms of inference-making and the mental storage of information. Reading involves the interaction of the mind with the text. If linguists do not adequately account for the mind and if psychologists ignore the properties of real[13] texts, there is little prospect for fully understanding the mechanisms underlying reading.

C.E.

Glasgow
January 1996

---

[13] It should be emphasized that by words such as 'real' and 'natural' I mean authentic texts, not the so-called 'realistic' or 'naturalistic' samples sometimes constructed by psychologists.

ACKNOWLEDGEMENTS

A number of people have had an important influence on this work either because of specific comments that they have made about my research or because they have given me the benefit of their opinions on some of the topics discussed.

I am particularly grateful to Michael Hoey, who supervised the Ph.D. work from which the current book originated. His tremendous enthusiasm for text analysis and his thoroughness and insight will continue to influence me throughout my career as a linguist.

I am also grateful to John Sinclair and Malcolm Coulthard, who were my teachers, both as an undergraduate and a postgraduate. They have continued since then to encourage me and to comment on my work. Although my subject matter is very different from their seminal work on spoken discourse, their approach to language should be evident throughout my research.

The final draft of this book was produced with the support of a Research Fellowship from the Leverhulme Trust, during study leave in 1994/5 funded jointly by both that organization and the University of Glasgow. During this time I was a Visiting Scholar based at the University of California, Santa Barbara. This provided a most stimulating working environment and enabled me to meet some of the linguists who have been a formative influence on my ideas about narrative, consciousness, and anaphora. I am especially grateful to Wallace Chafe for many useful discussions, for reading and commenting on the manuscript, and for allowing me to attend his insightful seminars on 'discourse and grammar'. I am also very grateful to Patricia Clancy, who likewise read and commented in detail on the manuscript, giving me the benefit of her specialist knowledge of pronominal anaphora. Sandra Thompson, John Du Bois, and Susanna Cumming also made many helpful suggestions during my year in Santa Barbara and gave me much encouragement. In addition, I was able in 1995 to visit the Center for Cognitive Science at the State University of

New York at Buffalo and would particularly like to thank Erwin Segal, David Zubin, and Len Talmy for their willingness to exchange ideas about narrative processing and their hospitality during my visit.

The late Paul Werth, from the University of Amsterdam, provided useful feedback on an earlier draft of this book. I am fortunate to have had the opportunity to see advance copies of his related work on 'text worlds', which has allowed me to explore connections and provided me with a great deal to think about in the future. Several of my Glasgow colleagues, Christian Kay, Des O'Brien, and Jeremy Smith, also provided detailed comments on a previous draft of the book. I have also benefited greatly from the suggestions of the three anonymous reviewers who read the text on behalf of Oxford University Press and from the guidance of my editors, Frances Morphy, Hilary Walford, and Leonie Hayler. In addition, I would like to thank a number of other people for either general advice and discussions or for specific comments on related articles or conference papers: Jamal Ardehali, Ruth Berman, Tony Bex, Teresa Bridgeman, Maquela Brizuela, John Corbett, Jonathan Culpeper, Florence Davies, Martin Davies, Nils Erik Enkvist, Nigel Fabb, Monika Fludernik, Margaret Freeman, Gordon Fulton, Keith Green, Peter Jones, Robert Longacre, Michael MacMahon, Martin Montgomery, Walter Nash, Beata Ozieblowska, Louise Ravelli, Elena Semino, Mick Short, Paul Simpson, Peter Stockwell, and Katie Wales. Many of these people have become known to me through the annual meetings of the Poetics and Linguistics Association (PALA), which provides a most stimulating forum for literary and non-literary text analysis. I have also learnt a lot from Susan Stuart's interesting and useful seminar course on consciousness at the University of Glasgow.

Finally, I would like to thank both Paul Emmott and Andrew Mathews for their patience, encouragement, and practical support throughout the writing of this book. I owe a great debt to Andrew Mathews, since he has read the book at every stage of development, commenting extensively on the style, structure, and presentation of the text and assisting in the preparation of the bibliography and index.

The author and publisher are grateful to the following for permission to reproduce extracts from copyright material: Hughes

Massie Ltd., London, and Putnam Publishing Group, New York, for *Sleeping Murder* by Agatha Christie, © Agatha Christie Ltd. 1976 and Agatha Christie Mallowan 1977.

CONTENTS

PART ONE: COGNITION AND DISCOURSE

1. Narrative Comprehension: Text, Knowledge,
   and Inference-Making   3

2. Key Topics in Text-Processing Research   21

3. A Discourse Perspective: Understanding Full, Real Texts 74

PART TWO: NARRATIVE STRUCTURE
AND PROCESSING

4. Creating Fictional Contexts   103

5. Modifying, Switching, and Recalling Contexts   133

6. Characters and Contexts   175

PART THREE: IMPLICATIONS:
LINGUISTIC THEORY AND NARRATIVE THEORY

7. Mental Representations, Inference-Making,
   and Reference Theory   197

8. Distinguishing Narrative Text Types   236

9. Summary   267

Suggested Further Reading for Students   276

Bibliography   278

Author Index   313

Subject Index   317

PART ONE

Cognition and Discourse

I

Narrative Comprehension: Text, Knowledge, and Inference-Making

> ... although we rarely notice it, we are all the time engaged in constructing hypotheses about the meaning of the text. The reader makes implicit connections, fills in gaps, draws inferences and tests out hunches; and to do this means drawing on a tacit knowledge of the world in general and of literary conventions in particular. The text itself is really no more than a series of 'cues' to the reader, invitations to construct a piece of language into meaning.
>
> (Eagleton 1983: 76)

Communication is made efficient by language producers assuming that their readers or listeners will draw on knowledge that is 'stored away'[1] within the mind and that a large amount of information can therefore be left unstated. For a written text, the words on the page are like the dots in a gestalt figure or a child's drawing book—the connections are often obvious, but they still need to be made. To do this, readers use their knowledge stores to make inferences. These inferences often lack the certainty of logical deduction and can be best described as reasonable assumptions. Such assumptions may vary amongst readers, since different textual clues may be responded to and the knowledge of readers may differ. There is, however, within a given speech community, a certain amount of shared 'general' knowledge which is taken for granted. In addition to this, a writer can expect the reader to know certain facts because they have been stated earlier in the text that is being processed.[2]

---

[1] The notion of mental 'stores' is a convenient one, but it may be more appropriate to view this storage as a network. Parallel distributed processing is discussed in Ch. 2.

[2] As discussed later in this chapter and in Ch. 2, readers only retain a small portion of the information that they read, but writers nevertheless have to assume that certain highly salient facts are remembered.

Particular genres may rely more heavily than others on certain types of knowledge. In everyday speech, for example, a major factor is 'mutual knowledge' (H. H. Clark and Marshall 1978, 1981; H. H. Clark 1992) arising from the shared prior experiences of the speaker and listener. Textbooks may demand expert knowledge from their readers and in instructional dialogue (e.g. Grosz 1977; Suchman 1987) there may be an assumption of knowledge of the immediate physical context. Narrative fiction also requires additional input from the reader, assuming, for example, a knowledge of the norms of behaviour in a particular culture, common situations, everyday objects, and social relations. In addition to this general knowledge, readers of narrative must accumulate knowledge that is specific to the fictional world, such as facts about particular characters and the situations they are placed in.

Although this book looks in detail at narrative data, it is (unlike much work within linguistics and literary studies) not a book about literary style or about literary themes, nor is it about specific texts. This research deals with issues that concern artificial intelligence researchers (and cognitive scientists in general), setting these topics within a linguistic framework. My aim is to present a hypothesis about how people read narratives, focusing on some of the most basic aspects of story comprehension. The objective is to answer questions such as 'How do readers accumulate and store information about characters?', 'How do they know which characters are involved in the action at any particular point in a story?', and 'How do they monitor the location and time of the action?' The need to describe a reader's ability to process these elementary facts should be obvious to those with a cognitive background, but may not be so obvious to those from outside cognitive disciplines. Questions which seem ridiculously simple are by no means simple[3] for artificial intelligence researchers trying to replicate the brain's ability to process texts or for educational psychologists attempting to explain why certain children have literacy problems. As Johnson-Laird (1983: p. x) points out: 'That is the nature of many problems about the mind: we are so familiar with the outcome of its operations, which are for the most part highly successful, that we fail to see the mystery.'

[3] For similar observations, see Charniak and McDermott (1985: 6, 21); McTear (1987: 35); Boden (1987: 4, 147, 179–80); Johnson-Laird (1988: 8); and Eysenck and Keane (1990: 62).

This failure can be seen most obviously in research on vision. Object recognition is something that in everyday life we take for granted, but it is extremely difficult to describe the process in sufficient detail for an engineer to replicate.[4] In these circumstances, artificial intelligence researchers working on vision are not yet in a position to go beyond trying to explain basic perception and so are not ready to begin studying the even greater complexities of, for example, how people appreciate works of art. Likewise, most artificial intelligence researchers working in the field of Natural Language Processing are still at the preliminary stages of examining how readers understand the basic storyline of a narrative, rather than looking yet at how literary value is recognized.

For those unfamiliar with research on these basic 'nuts and bolts' inferences, a good illustration of their importance and pervasiveness is provided by Meehan's *Talespin* project (cited in Schank 1984). Meehan programmed a computer with a certain amount of information about the world and then instructed it to tell a story. Since the computer had a lack of general knowledge the result was as follows:

> One day Joe Bear was hungry. He asked his friend Irving Bird where some honey was. Irving told him there was a beehive in the oak tree. Joe threatened to hit Irving if he didn't tell him where some honey was.   (Schank 1984: 83)

Clearly, neither the computer nor Joe Bear are aware of the link between beehives and honey. When programmed with this information, however, the computer still misses the point:

> One day Joe Bear was hungry. He asked his friend Irving Bird where some honey was. Irving told him there was a beehive in the oak tree. Joe walked to the oak tree. He ate the beehive.

> (ibid.)

In this case, the computer has gone to the opposite extreme and equated the beehive with the honey, rather than regarding it as a container for the food. Meehan shows here that although

---

[4] Similar comments can be found throughout the cognitive science literature (e.g. Marr 1985: 108; Boden 1987: 180, 409; Johnson-Laird 1988: 58; Eysenck and Keane 1990: 43). There is general agreement about the current limitations of computers, but much debate about whether complete replication is possible in the future (as discussed in Ch. 2).

common sense often suggests an easy solution to such problems, it is not so straightforward to specify a complete set of rules that work unambiguously in all circumstances. Meehan's work analyses story production rather than comprehension,[5] but it serves as a demonstration of what inferences are by showing what happens when 'taken for granted' information is not 'taken for granted'. A human reader would not normally fail to make the inference in the way that Joe Bear does and so the text becomes amusing.[6]

Much of the research that has been done on inference-making is characterized by the fact that the listener/reader draws on general knowledge. A couple of examples of this type of work are provided here, with a more detailed survey being presented in Chapter 2. General knowledge often enables readers to infer a causal link between two events. So sentences such as 'Dark clouds appeared overhead. The children ran inside' (see Charniak 1972, 1986 for similar examples) can be interpreted by assuming that rain is anticipated and that the children do not want to get wet. In addition to showing the relation between two sentences, general knowledge can also assist in the interpretation of 'shorthand' forms such as pronouns. In sentences such as 'John hit Henry. He fell to the ground', the causal link leads us to assume that the person who has been hit has fallen and since it is Henry that has been hit, we can assume that the pronoun 'He' refers to Henry rather than to John.

For written text, it might be assumed that, because a writer and reader are often unknown to each other, a writer would only be able to call on the reader's general knowledge. This is rather different from a conversation where two participants know each other and can rely also on mutual knowledge, such as the awareness of previous shared experiences. Nevertheless, even for written text there is a pool of shared knowledge, of a special type, over and above general knowledge.[7] Shared knowledge is established between a writer and reader by virtue of the fact that a reader can be assumed to have retained some of the information presented

---

[5] However, Graesser (1981: 135) uses materials from Meehan's work in his experiments on story comprehension.

[6] In fact, this technique is sometimes used in literature to portray a special 'mind-style' of a character. See Ch. 2 for references to the stylistics literature on this topic.

[7] Chafe (1994: 275) gives a good example of shared general knowledge in written text.

earlier in the text that is being read. For example, facts about the characters, such as their professions, ages, and relations to others in the story, may be taken for granted after being stated and a text may require the reader to draw on this information to assist in the interpretation of subsequent sentences. I use the term **text-specific** to describe this type of knowledge, since the information is usually gathered from a specific text and drawn on for the interpretation of that text.

The major potential problem with a writer assuming that the reader has text-specific knowledge is that readers only remember a fraction of what they read and, moreover, different readers remember different things. Since texts do, however, make such assumptions (as will be illustrated throughout this book), it seems that for many writers the gains in efficiency of communication outweigh any difficulty in assessing how much a reader knows. Presumably, there is a certain minimum threshold of information which the average reader might be expected to retain, such as key facts about the major characters and the locus of a particular stretch of action. Conversation provides a parallel to this since speakers are constantly assuming a basic general knowledge and memory for the preceding conversation, there being a level of elementary assumption-making beyond which no listener would be expected to sink without good reason. In sociology, Garfinkel's (1967) classic ethnomethodological 'experiments' show that when a listener deliberately and consistently challenges 'common sense' assumptions, communication breaks down completely and the speaker is either outraged or makes adverse judgements about the listener's mental capacity and/or personality. At the heart of modern linguistics lies the pragmatic assumption of 'cooperation' between the language producer and the language receiver (Grice 1975, 1978). The producer attempts to provide language which is tailored to the needs of the receiver, on the assumption that the receiver will supplement the text with basic inference-making where necessary (H. H. Clark and Haviland 1977).[8] Of course, for written (and spoken) text there may be a vast gap between the 'implied reader' (Iser 1978) or 'ideal

---

[8] Chafe (1994: 278) makes this point clearly about spoken language: '. . . the shape of language emerges from an ongoing interaction of what is happening in the speaker's mind with the speaker's assessment of what is happening in the listener's mind.'

reader' (Fillmore 1982) (i.e. the person with the exact amount of knowledge that the text demands) and the 'actual reader' (i.e. the particular individual who reads a book on a specific occasion). It is nevertheless essential to attempt to assess the demands placed on readers by texts because an understanding of such demands is fundamental to an understanding of literacy.

Sometimes, as literary theorists have argued, it may be virtually impossible to assess exactly what the text does require of its readers. In this book I am not, however, writing about such open-ended and difficult matters as 'literary interpretation' but about linguistic items of the text which do have the specific function of demanding a reasonably clear-cut input from the reader. These items are pronouns. A whole text may, perhaps, be interpreted in numerous ways, but a pronoun requires the reader to provide a referent and there are rarely more than two potential antecedents denoting referents.[9] Pronouns are interesting to the cognitive researcher because they are 'shorthand' forms used at points at which a writer seems to assume that a reader has enough knowledge to identify the intended referent. Studying these linguistic items provides some insight into the demands placed on readers not only to draw on their general knowledge but to retain, in memory, key textually presented information for decoding purposes. This explains why pronouns are a central topic in artificial intelligence and psychology work.[10] In his seminal work on story understanding, Charniak (1972: 56) comments that: 'Most of the processes which we would call "understanding" seem to be necessary to decide reference. Hence, reference can be viewed as a paradigm of "understanding".'

Psychologists also stress the importance of an understanding of reference theory. Sanford and Garrod (1981: 89), for example, argue that:

. . . reference resolution in all its forms constitutes the cornerstone of successful comprehension in terms of the reader's task of building an appropriate mental model of what is being said. If one can understand how

---

[9] The inferences involved in reaching a decision may be many and various, but the end result is that the reader must supply a referent.

[10] See, for example, Winograd (1972: 32–3, 69, 158–63); Charniak (1972); Grosz (1977); Webber (1979); Sidner (1979*b*); Sanford and Garrod (1981); Reichman (1985); and Grosz and Sidner (1986).

reference is resolved, then an understanding of other parts of the general comprehension process will follow automatically.

The present study looks particularly at third-person pronouns denoting the central characters in narratives. References to these characters usually span substantial stretches of text, the reference chains stretching like a 'backbone' (Chafe 1980b: 18; Bernardo 1980: 295) to the narrative. To interpret pronoun references, information may be required from much earlier in the text, giving an indication of how the previous narrative needs to be mentally represented if such 'shorthand' forms are to be understood. The information required in such cases indicates that in order to establish basic 'textual coherence', a reader must build up and utilize stores of knowledge about the characters and the context.

For artificial intelligence researchers and cognitive psychologists, observations about the need to form mental representations (i.e. mental stores of information) are so integral to their research that they may wonder why I spend time throughout this book arguing that representations play an important role in language processing. In response to such comments, it has to be pointed out that within discourse analysis the idea of the cognitive effort involved in processing a text is a remarkably new addition to accepted thought. Part of the reason for this is due to the history of the subject. Generative linguists have largely abhorred textual study, focusing instead on speakers' supposed 'competence' with regard to the syntactic structure of individual sentences. Text, from this point of view, has sometimes been regarded as a degenerate instantiation of a mental knowledge of language.[11] Discourse analysis has developed partly in reaction to these generative ideas,[12] arguing that the act of communication is what language is all about, rather than an abstract knowledge of the rules underlying it. For many text linguists this rejection of the notion of syntactic 'competence' has also led, in the 1970s and 1980s at least,

[11] Their objection to textual analysis is a theoretical one rather than just being a question of practicalities. This is made all too clear in the following excerpt from Chomsky (1965: 4): '... linguistic theory is mentalistic, since it is concerned with discovering a mental reality underlying actual behaviour. Observed use of language or hypothesized dispositions to respond, habits, and so on, may provide evidence as to the nature of this mental reality, but surely cannot constitute the actual subject matter of linguistics, if this is to be a serious discipline.'

[12] Sinclair and Coulthard (1975: 2) say that the two schools are 'diametrically opposed'.

to a wholesale dismissal of cognitive work.[13] The mistake in this was that 'competence' and cognition are not synonymous. Without needing to accept or even contemplate ideas of innate universal structures, text linguists can speculate about both acquired textual-processing strategies and the mind's role, on particular occasions, of making information derived from one part of a text available when another part of the same text is read. Text linguists have in the past simply viewed information as being present in the surrounding text, rather than considering the mental storage and assumption-making involved in supplying this information during the reading process. Of course, there are certain linguists who have been pioneers in cognitive discourse analysis,[14] but it is only in the last decade that there has been a tremendous surge of interest in cognitive work from outside a generative framework. Moreover, a fair amount of the seminal material in the new 'cognitive linguistics' movement concentrates on sentence-level phenomena rather than text.[15] For many linguists, therefore (with the exception of psycholinguists), the notion of including mental representations in text theory is either completely new or sufficiently new to merit consideration of how such notions might be assimilated into existing models of language.

Inference-making has, of course, been studied in linguistics within the field of pragmatics, but the pragmaticists have been traditionally occupied with isolated utterances or, at most, pairs of utterances.[16] In such work, it is common simply to imagine the circumstances in which an utterance might occur. As far as the prior text is concerned, a preceding sentence might be imagined, but the fact that sentences usually occur within larger stretches of text is generally ignored. In order to produce controlled experimental conditions, psychologists also tend to prefer to use de-contextualized sentence pairs. In this book, I argue that in cer-

[13] See Cook (1990: 12) for a discussion of this.

[14] For example, Chafe's earlier work (1973, 1974, 1976, 1980*a*, 1987).

[15] For example, Langacker (1987, 1992); Lakoff and Johnson (1980); Lakoff (1987); and Fauconnier (1994).

[16] Schiffrin's (1994) book on discourse includes the suggestion that discourse analysts might use real text to question the boundaries of pragmatic theory. She argues that such an analysis is guided by ' . . . an effort to resolve problems that stem from concrete observations about language use' (p. 203) and that this ' . . . shift in data can have far-reaching effects on Gricean pragmatics itself' (ibid.). More detailed arguments for the potential impact on pragmatic theory are presented in Schiffrin (1987*b*).

tain cases linguistic forms cannot be interpreted without information from much earlier in a text and that there therefore needs to be some mechanism for maintaining this information in memory until it is needed again. These 'long-distance links', which are illustrated below, can be contrasted with the processing involved in examples of the 'John hit Henry. He fell to the ground' type discussed earlier, where the referent of the pronoun has been recently mentioned and the appropriate individual is selected by means of a cohesive link ('hit'/'fell', in this case) which spans only the two-sentence example.

The following text extract[17] illustrates how information needed to understand a pronoun may not be present within close range of that pronoun:

EXAMPLE 1.1

and Clark Mulligan, who had been showing two weeks of science-fiction and horror pictures and had a full head of lurid images—*you can show it, man, but nobody makes you watch it*—walked out of the Rialto for the fresh air in the middle of a reel and thought he saw in the sudden black-out a man who was a wolf lope across the street, on a fierce errand, in an evil hurry to get somewhere (*nobody makes you watch the stuff, man*).

8

Housebreaking, Part Two

Jim stopped the car half a block away from the house. 'If only the god-damned lights didn't go off.' They were both looking at the building's blank façade, the curtainless windows behind which no figure moved, no candle shone.

(Peter Straub, *Ghost Story* (1979), 279;[18]
Straub's italics, my emphasis in the final paragraph)

What is interesting about this example is that, from this extract alone, we cannot fully interpret the pronoun 'They'. One of the two participants is Jim, but there is no recent mention of the other character. To understand the text at this point it is necessary to have some knowledge of the overall structure of the text,

---

[17] This example was discussed briefly in Emmott (1994).
[18] The original text begins mid-sentence with the words 'and Clark Mulligan'. The number '8' signals a new section.

as someone reading the whole novel would presumably have. Before this extract begins, the reader has been reading about two characters, Jim and Peter, who are driving towards a house which they intend to break into. This is an important point in the story because the house is occupied by a supernatural being who is responsible for a number of murders in the town where Jim and Peter live. As the two approach the house, the narrative breaks off from this scene and begins to describe events currently happening elsewhere in the town. The description of Clark Mulligan, at the beginning of Example 1.1, is the last of a series of such descriptions, showing how citizens in the town are being troubled by supernatural occurrences. This break in the action serves to reinforce the importance of the 'housebreaking' which Jim and Peter are about to engage in, as well as heightening the sense of danger. It is also a classic device for increasing suspense, since the action is temporarily halted as it reaches an exciting point. When the main action resumes, halfway through Example 1.1, there can be little doubt that 'They' refers to Jim and Peter, even though Peter is not mentioned. A reader who did not make this assumption would not be following the main action, thereby defeating the whole purpose of reading the novel. Of course, psychologists would want to test this, but I am basing this hypothesis on the common-sense position that since a major motive for reading is to know 'What happens next?',[19] a reader who is successfully engaging with the text must have some idea of what events are in progress, particularly at a climactic moment in the plot.

If we accept the hypothesis that a reader would be able to interpret the pronoun 'They', then there are a number of implications from the point of view of text-processing theory and linguistic theory. As far as text processing is concerned, the main point is that the interpretation of this pronoun depends on an ability to handle the transition from one discourse unit to another, in this case the break from the action in the main context and the switch to the descriptions of subsidiary events occurring elsewhere at the same time. The 'sentence pair' fragments traditionally analysed in text-processing research are too short to have any dis-

---

[19] Forster (1963) is one of the most often-quoted proponents of this view. Lodge (1992: 31) suggests that '... an effect of suspense ("what will happen?")' is a question that is one of '... the mainsprings of narrative interest and as old as storytelling itself'.

course structure of this type, so the ability to handle shifts in discourse structure is either completely ignored or its significance is underplayed. To interpret this pronoun, the reader needs to have built a representation of a context in which Jim and Peter are travelling together in their car with the intention of housebreaking. This contextual information then needs to be held in mind whilst the subsidiary events occurring in the town are described. The reader then needs to reactivate this context at the appropriate point and make the inference that the pronoun refers to Peter as well as Jim. In this particular example, there is a very blatant signal of the return to the main context (the heading 'Housebreaking, Part Two'), but the signalling is usually more subtle than this, relying on the mention of one aspect of the context (one of the participants or a detail from the location) to reintroduce the full context. This example demonstrates how the reader can manage to access the right context to make an inference, but there is also assumption-making involved in building and maintaining the context in the first place.

From a linguistic point of view, a recognition of discourse structure provides a radical new perspective on grammatical theory. Traditionally, grammarians have worked at sentence level. Even when the preceding sentence has been considered (as a source of potential antecedents, in the case of reference resolution), the focus has been on a very narrow stretch of text. The 'tunnel vision' of the traditional analyst is, however, very different from the reader's knowledge and expectations about a text which he/she is in the process of reading. Apart from the need to explain how a pronoun can be interpreted when an antecedent is missing, a discourse perspective on grammar throws new light on some of the fundamental assumptions of grammatical theory.[20] Example 1.1 therefore raises questions about the role of the antecedent in pronoun interpretation. Even in cases where a full antecedent is present, it may be that 'long-distance' information is still necessary to determine which of two potential antecedents is the appropriate one. Example 1.1 also raises questions about the dividing line between anaphora and deixis, since it is a knowledge of the fictional context which enables the reader to decode the pronoun

[20] I am not, of course, the first person to point this out. See Chs. 3 and 5, in particular, for discussions of related work on a range of text types in linguistics and artificial intelligence.

here, not a preceding antecedent. These topics will be discussed in detail later in the book.[21] The main point at this stage is that looking at this type of data not only forces researchers to provide an explanation of how the language actually operates, but also provides a contribution to theoretical debates.

Discourse analysts and artificial intelligence researchers have already begun to point out the importance of a discourse perspective on grammar but it will be a long time before such observations will be adequately reflected in grammar textbooks or grammar teaching. Sentence-level grammatical theory has nearly two thousand years of tradition and does not yield easily to discourse observations (Emmott 1996). Even reasonably comprehensive studies of grammar, such as Quirk *et al.* (1985), include discourse as an add-on chapter at the end rather than as a basis for their theory. Ironically, too, corpus linguistics, which is one of the major recent developments in discourse-based grammar, generally focuses on small quantities of text around particular keywords, rather than tracking reference chains across a stretch of text. Although computer concordances[22] are very useful for making generalizations about usage for purposes such as dictionary compilation, concordance packages are not normally sensitive to information flow within a text and are not therefore able to provide a full picture of how grammatical items such as pronouns and determiners are used. Concordance-based approaches to grammatical analysis, therefore, need to be supplemented by types of discourse grammar which reflect the hierarchical structure and dynamic unfolding of particular texts (Emmott 1995*b*, 1996, forthcoming *b*).

In discussing Example 1.1, I have emphasized the extent to which information from much earlier in the text needs to be

---

[21] Similar examples are examined in Ch. 5 and the implications for reference theory are discussed in Ch. 7.

[22] Quirk *et al.* (1985) do, of course, make some use of a corpus, but I am thinking here of projects such as the COBUILD dictionary (Sinclair 1987*a*) (see also Sinclair 1987*b*, 1990). Such projects have been revolutionary in terms of analysing large numbers of instances of words, both from the lexical and grammatical point of view. Their object, however, is not to study lexical and grammatical choices as a text develops. Of course, concordances are frequently used to study stylistic options in particular texts (e.g. Emmott 1985), but they are a fairly 'rough and ready' tool as they do not usually recognize discourse units or distinguish between referents referred to by the same linguistic form (see Emmott 1995*b*, forthcoming *b*, *d* for a discussion of this).

drawn on to interpret a pronoun. I am hypothesizing that the reader of the novel would know about the 'Peter and Jim context' before they began reading this extract, since a continuation of events in this context is essential to the plot. In such cases, information needs to be held in a mental representation (i.e. a mental store) whilst the intervening text is read. Up to a point, this type of link is not qualitatively different than those local links where the clues to decoding are in the preceding sentence. When we read 'John hit Henry', in the constructed example discussed earlier, I would argue that we update our mental representations for each character as we read about the action. This means that we can then go on to interpret 'He fell to the ground' using our knowledge that one character has been assaulted, rather than searching back in the text for an explanation. One advantage of looking at a longer example is simply to highlight the need to postulate mental representations. When the clues for decoding are all present in a two-sentence span, linguists are liable to overlook the fact that readers will read one sentence first and then carry this information in their minds as the second sentence is read. It is very easy in linguistic models just to say that the information is there in the text and to ignore the sequential process of reading and the mind's contribution. In Example 1.1 it becomes more obvious that the mind is needed to 'bridge[23] the gap' because the information required to decode the pronoun is not even on the same page as the pronoun in the original text (and in many examples this information may have appeared many pages earlier). Apart from the need to include mental representations in linguistic models, this example gives an indication of the mental work involved, since information must be held in the mind whilst large stretches of intervening text are read.

There is a qualitative difference, too, between Example 1.1 and the 'constructed' example. It is not just a question of the distance between the pronoun and the earlier relevant information (which in Example 1.1 is the earlier mention of the character in this particular context). It is also a matter of an intervening layer

---

[23] This is a useful metaphor, originally from H. H. Clark (1977). However, in Clark's work it carries the connotation of a backward inference, whereas my own work argues that many such inferences are anticipatory. Ch. 2 discusses the difference between backward and forward inferences. Clark's work is examined further in Ch. 7.

of linguistic organization, a shifting from one level in the discourse
structure to another which is more likely to occur in lengthier
texts. This is too often ignored in the analysis of short constructed
examples, but it is important because the resulting antecedentless
pronouns create a different type of inferencing. Contextual information needs to be drawn on as well as information about the
referent. This necessitates there being some mechanism for accessing the appropriate context, but also for forming the representation of the context in the first place and for keeping it constantly
updated as the text is read (see Chapters 4 and 5). Even when
text-processing models recognize discourse shifts, the creation
and maintenance of the mental representations may often be
ignored, perhaps because this is not quite such an obvious issue
when topic shifts are considered as opposed to context shifts.

Many of the examples in this book explore the interpretation of
pronouns occurring after shifts from one discourse unit to another.
This includes looking at shifts between flashback and main narrative, as well as between two different locations at the same point
in time. Less obviously, narratives also involve regular shifts from
the events occurring in a specific context to stretches of text
which give general background information (see Chapter 8). However, the book is not just about these types of examples, for mental
representations of contexts and characters are needed to interpret
every sentence that we read. Apart from making information
available for decoding pronouns, these representations enable us
to make real sense of what we are reading at every point in the
text. The problem with discussions of constructed examples is
that they never force us to ask questions such as 'Who is John?',
'Who is Henry?', 'Why are they fighting?', and 'Who else is present?' More importantly, such examples do not force the analyst
to account for how a reader keeps track of this information and utilizes it. Of course, it could be argued that this is missing the point
of constructed examples, since they are designed for the specific
purpose of testing one particular aspect of comprehension. Nevertheless, if analysts look solely at such examples, there is the
danger that they will themselves miss the point, losing sight of
what reading is all about. Reading is about empathizing with characters, about understanding their motivations, and about judging
the effect of the actions of one character on other characters in the
context. Reading a story involves building dynamic, complex

mental representations which are capable of creating our interest in the text, this being the primary purpose of reading.

Overview of the Book

The purpose of this chapter has been to provide an overview of the relationship between the text and the reader's knowledge, showing how inference-making enables the two to interact. This has included a brief introduction to how cognitive scientists study the most basic 'taken for granted' level of textual interpretation. I have also drawn a distinction between the study of general knowledge, which has received a lot of attention in the cognitive literature, and text-specific knowledge, which has not been studied to the same extent and which is particularly interesting to discourse analysts. I have emphasized the need for a discussion of the role of mental representations in discourse studies, since cognitive work is an exciting new mode of thinking to those whose primary interest is in the text. I have also argued that, conversely, the study of inference-making can be enriched by an awareness of discourse structure and can lead to text-processing and linguistic models which more fully account for the textual data.

Chapter 2 presents an overview of some of the key issues in text-processing work in order to set my own work in the context of what is being done in the field as a whole and to enable me to draw on this body of ideas throughout the rest of the book. This chapter begins with a discussion of different types of mental representation of knowledge, looking at general knowledge and text-specific knowledge and examining how both complement each other. I then consider the debate over how information is stored in the mind, looking at Johnson-Laird's work on 'mental models' and the current move towards a parallel distributed processing approach to the study of cognition. The final sections of the chapter discuss how human readers differ from computer readers. I look briefly at the tremendous surge of interest in consciousness that has occurred across a range of disciplines in recent years and, more specifically, consider the contribution of Chafe's work on consciousness to text linguistics. I also discuss the importance of the topic of 'forgetting' in cognitive work and give an indication of the extent to which readers process a text differently because of their different backgrounds.

Chapter 3 stresses the importance of the study of 'real discourse' to text-processing work. It should be clear from Chapter 2 that my main criticism of much of the research on cognition is that it ignores aspects of the dynamic development of a text, such as the need to switch from one discourse unit to another. This chapter begins with a consideration of why discourse analysts believe that full-length texts have properties over and above those of the individual sentences or sentence pairs so often examined in cognitive research. A full-length text is not just longer, it often has additional layers of structure which merit study in their own right. By contrast, I then look at the type of materials used in traditional experimental work in psychology and comment on the problems of studying reading in the laboratory. This chapter concludes with a discussion of my own methodology, arguing that the study of written discourse can give insight into the extent to which a text demands input from its readers.

Chapter 4 begins to explore the topic of fictional context, which I then continue to discuss throughout the remainder of the book. I consider why it is important that narrative is seen not just as a sequence of events but as events in context. From the point of view of cognitive modelling, I argue that it is not simply a question of readers establishing a causal link between two adjacent sentences, but of connecting each new sentence with the 'global representation' of the text. Even when researchers do look at longer texts, this type of connection is not always modelled, as I illustrate with reference to de Beaugrande's work. I then discuss the extent to which maintaining a context involves the mental effort of making inferences about continuity and change, drawing a parallel with the artificial intelligence work on 'the frame problem' within robotics. My aim is to show that a context is not just there in ready-made form for the reader whenever the reader needs to draw on it, but that the reader is actively involved in constructing and updating contextual knowledge at the same time as focusing on the events which are happening within that context. I also aim to provide an indication of how this contextual knowledge is necessary not only to interpret particular linguistic items such as pronouns but to make any real sense of the narrative at all.

Having discussed how a context is created, Chapter 5 looks specifically at context changes. Modifications to a context, such as the departure of a participant, have little effect on the reader's assumptions about the rest of the context. By contrast, when there is a switch from one context to another, a reader has to revise more radically his/her assumptions. From a linguistic point of view, what is most interesting is when an earlier context is reactivated. In such cases, there only needs to be linguistic mention of part of the context for all the participants to be automatically reintroduced and this can lead to characters being referred to with pronouns with no antecedents. The implications of this for reference theory are considered further in Chapter 7.

In Chapter 6, I suggest that context is also an important factor in determining the subset of the information that we know about a character that is relevant at any one time. Narrative flashbacks, in particular, require a reader to be able to differentiate between past and present versions of a character and this involves recognizing the linguistic cues of a hierarchical shift. This has implications for cognitive work, since it means that information must be stored in the mental representation of a character in such a way that it can be separately accessed. It also has implications for reference theory, since it means that identifying the character is not just a matter of accessing the appropriate mental representation, but of accessing a subset of information within this representation.

Chapter 7 is the most overtly 'linguistic' chapter of the book, serving to set the observations of the previous chapters within the framework of a general discussion of reference theory. I present a number of arguments to show that contextual knowledge plays an essential role in the decoding of pronouns in narrative. I also show how my own notions of contextual assumption-making complement artificial intelligence work on 'focusing'.

In Chapter 8, I consider some of the implications of my work for narrative theory. Narratives are typically viewed as event sequences, but this notion needs to be supplemented with the notion that a core property of narrative is also the fact that certain events occur in a specific context. Linguistic researchers have observed that narrative has a 'foreground' and a 'background' and my aim here is to explain this phenomenon in terms of context rather than the usual notion of an 'event-line'. The hierarchical shifts between specific contexts and more general observations are as important in decoding pronouns as are shifts from one context to another, so discourse structure is again important in grammatical interpretation. This chapter ends with a discussion of narrative text types in texts other than fictional narrative, such as autobiographies and sociology textbooks.

Chapter 9 provides a summary of the book, examining the implications of the work for text-processing theory and for a linguistic model of reference and including a discussion of how the research might be extended.

2

Key Topics in Text-Processing Research

This chapter provides an overview of the main areas of study in text-processing research and discusses some of the current controversies about how information is held in the mind. This review aims both to set my research in the context of the field as a whole and to introduce key notions which will be drawn on throughout the book.

Chapter 1 explained that the focus of this book is on text-specific mental representations, which, for narrative, are stores of knowledge about a particular fictional world. There are, however, other important types of knowledge, particularly general knowledge, which first need to be discussed to provide a more comprehensive picture of text-processing research as a whole. In Section 1 of this chapter, therefore, I give an overview of four major types of mental representation: general knowledge; knowledge of typical text structures; text-specific knowledge of a particular fictional world; and knowledge of the style of a particular text. In this discussion, I differentiate between these knowledge types, which are all necessary for text processing and are heavily interdependent.

Any study of mental representations of knowledge must take account of controversies over the precise form in which the knowledge is 'stored' in the mind. Section 2 examines the debate over the nature of mental representations, looking particularly at whether they are propositional (e.g. Kintsch and van Dijk 1978) or in the form of 'mental models' (e.g. Johnson-Laird 1983), and at the separate question of whether mental representations are clusters of information or neural networks.

Sections 3 and 4 summarize characteristics of the human mind which make it different from computer processors and which therefore need to be taken into account if text-processing models are to be psychologically realistic. Section 3 discusses human consciousness, about which there is currently much general debate in philosophy, artificial intelligence, and science, as well as some specific work on consciousness and language in linguistics. My own research draws on this research on consciousness, since my model is based on the assumption that readers often have a continued awareness of characters even when the text is not referring to an individual in a particular sentence.

Section 4 explains that, in addition to consciousness, two other key factors which differentiate humans from computers are the brain's limited memory capacity and each individual's set of unique personal experiences. As a result, readers process texts in distinct ways, a topic which I discuss with reference to both psychology studies and literary theory ideas about 'reader response'. Although my work is not in itself an exploration of individual response, my model nevertheless acknowledges that people read differently.

I. TYPES OF MENTAL REPRESENTATION

As discussed in Chapter 1, a key feature of comprehension is that knowledge is used by readers (and listeners) to make sense of the text. Published written text does not normally have a particular addressee (although the writer may have a type of reader in mind) and so mutual knowledge and the reader's personal knowledge are not really at issue as far as the basic inferences necessary for textual coherence are concerned (although personal knowledge undoubtedly plays a role in reading, as discussed in Section 4). Research on the processing of written text has, therefore, focused particularly on general knowledge (in 'schemata') and information about typical text structures (e.g. in 'story schemata'). Readers also need to retain information about entities and situations in the particular text that is being read (in what I term 'text-specific representations' (Emmott 1994)) and stylistic information about that text (in 'text-specific stylistic representations'). These different types of knowledge representation are outlined below.

(a) General Knowledge Representations

Although this book concentrates mainly on text-specific knowledge, research on general knowledge is so central to text-processing work that a discussion of it is necessary to give an overall picture of the field. This discussion summarizes some of the seminal work on general knowledge, also considering how it needs to be supplemented by text-specific knowledge for a reader to make complete sense of a text.

(i) Seminal Studies of General Knowledge

The term 'general knowledge' is used in everyday parlance to mean an awareness of key facts from subjects such as history, geography, and science. Whilst such information is undoubtedly important in reading texts, there is a more basic type of knowledge which is also important but which is usually taken for granted because it is learnt through experience with the world rather than by school instruction. This is a knowledge of entities in the world (e.g. tables and chairs), typical scenarios (e.g. a kitchen), and typical event sequences (e.g. what usually happens in a restaurant).

Artificial intelligence researchers and psychologists have begun to study this basic general knowledge, formulating theories about how the information is stored in the brain and how it is utilized in reading texts. Traditionally, general knowledge of this type was viewed as being so abstract that individuals would no longer be able to remember the original incidents that gave rise to the knowledge. General knowledge of an entity, such as a chair, can be regarded as an abstraction based on many previous experiences of chairs. We expect, therefore, that the majority of chairs have a back, four legs, and a seat, even though this is not always the case in practice (e.g. Rosch 1977). The term 'frame' (Minsky 1977)[1] is sometimes used to describe our general knowledge of entities, although the term is used in a completely different sense in this book (see Chapter 4). More complex general knowledge structures are normally called schemata (Bartlett 1932; Schank 1972). One type of schema is the scenario (Minsky 1977; Brewer and Treyens 1981) which stores information about a stereotypical

---

[1] See Shapiro (1987) for a useful summary.

location. A scenario for a modern kitchen, for example, would lead
to the expectation of a refrigerator and a cooker. Other forms of
schemata are scripts (Schank and Abelson 1977a, b; Bower,
Black, and Turner 1979), which represent our general knowledge
of stereotypical sequences of events, many of which may be based
in stereotyped locations and have stereotyped participants. One
well-known example in artificial intelligence is the script for a
visit to a restaurant (Schank and Abelson 1977a, b) which suggests that diners will normally be given a menu by a waiter, have
their order taken, be brought food, be given a bill, and be expected
to pay before they leave.[2] General knowledge constructs enable
the reader to make inferences over and above what is read in a
text.[3] So if the text mentions that 'the bill arrived' (Eysenck and
Keane 1990: 277, based on Schank and Abelson 1977a, b), the
reader can assume that a waiter brought it, this usually being the
case in real life.

   This early work in artificial intelligence viewed general knowledge of this type as being 'semantic' rather than 'episodic'. These
psychology terms were used by Tulving (1972, 1983) (the former
term originating from Quillian (1968)) to describe different types
of knowledge utilized during psychology tests. Semantic memory
is described by Tulving (1972: 386) as:

. . . a mental thesaurus, organized knowledge a person possesses about
words and other verbal symbols, their meaning and referents, about relations among them, and about rules, formulas and algorithms for the
manipulation of these symbols, concepts, and relations.

Cohen (1983: 18) interprets this as: '. . . a store of more or less permanent knowledge, of facts that are true independently of context,
such as that cats are animals, that leopards have spots, that roses
are red, and that two and two make four'.

   What Tulving means by episodic memory is best seen by his contrast of the two types of memory in psychology recall tests. In
these tests, the experimenter asks the subject to remember pairs
of words. There may be no inherent relation between these pairs,
as in the examples 'tree' and 'ice-cream', or 'fish' and 'telephone'.

---

   [2] See Mandler (1984) and J. Greene (1986: 33–50) for useful surveys of schemata, scripts, and scenes.
   [3] See Pitrat (1988) for a general introduction and also a useful discussion in
Werth (MS b: ch. 4).

This information is stored in episodic memory, so when the subject has to recall which word occurred with which, he/she must remember back to a specific occasion, since on another occasion the word may have a different pairing. Tulving points out that the subject would be justified, on being asked 'What word occurred with ice-cream?' to ask 'When?' or 'Where?' Conversely, free association tests may utilize semantic memory, for then the subject is not shown a word list, but simply asked a question like 'Think of a word connected with eagle' and expected to produce a word like 'large' or 'bird', since these words can be used to describe eagles. This is an answer that would generally be true, so Tulving argues that the question 'Where?' would be meaningless here as the originating episode is not important.

Although the original artificial intelligence research followed this distinction,[4] later research (e.g. Schank 1982) argued that general knowledge did contain a fair amount of episodic information. This is not surprising, since semantic knowledge is formed from an accumulation of specific occasions. If, for example, an individual has only flown on an aeroplane once, his/her script for air flights will be coloured by this one experience. Even when he/she has flown dozens of times, with many of the details having become condensed together, salient deviations from the standard script are likely to be retained distinctly, alongside the standard information. Schank (1982) argues that this is an essential part of schema formation, since it allows individuals to cope with the unexpected by drawing on their experience of previous unexpected happenings. Schank's (1982) work also highlights the fact that semantic memory is 'dynamic', constantly changing to meet new circumstances, particularly in an age of rapid technological development. Entities such as computers have changed radically over the last twenty years, altering our 'frame' conception of them and we have also had to develop scripts for dealing with these machines and other new equipment such as telephone answering machines and fax machines. Our scenarios are also subject to change—in the developed world, our default expectations for offices and kitchens probably include more equipment than ten years ago.

---

[4] Morton and Bekerian (1986: 65) summarize this by saying that general knowledge representations 'do not ... map directly on to any single event, i.e. schemata represent generic concepts and are types rather than tokens'.

Early artificial intelligence research on scripts and scenarios drew on very specific situations, such as restaurants. Later work looks at features which are common to many situations, such as the script for payment which will be a subcomponent of many other scripts. There is also, however, a need for detailed research on our most basic assumptions about how the world works. We know, for example, that people cannot be in two places at one time and cannot instantaneously materialize in a location. We also have expectations about how long everyday events are likely to take, such as travelling from one location to another by different forms of transport. These very basic assumptions are essential for processing narrative fiction, in addition to text-specific information about the individuals and locations involved. Of course, in specific genres, such as science fiction (see Chapter 5), the world may work in different ways, but we assume these rules to hold unless there is evidence to the contrary.

(ii) *Utilization of General Knowledge in Text Processing: Basic Inferences*

Psychology experiments have confirmed that general knowledge inferences are made during reading, showing that subjects are often unable to distinguish between what they have actually read and what they have inferred (de Beaugrande 1980: 168, 175, 220–41). This confusion of original input and subsequent inference can be disturbing where very precise accuracy of recall is required (as in eyewitness accounts (Loftus 1975; Loftus, Miller, and Burns 1978)), but the interplay between stored knowledge and the text seems nevertheless to be a natural part of reading.

Much research on the utilization of general knowledge during reading has focused on how the reader uses this knowledge to make basic inferences. As already mentioned, one use is to 'fill in' unstated but obvious information about script-based actions, as in the 'restaurant script'. This is similar to the gestalt-like nature of vision where although we may not see all of an object which is hidden by another object, we still assume it to be there in its entirety and are probably unaware most of the time that we are making these inferences. General knowledge may also enable us to infer links between objects. For example, if a car is mentioned in a text, we may infer a subsequent mention of 'the wheels' to relate to car wheels even though this is not explicitly stated. This particular observation has greatly interested both linguists and psychologists because the general knowledge link explains the use of the definite article in front of the word 'wheels', even though the wheels have not previously been lexically mentioned.[5]

General knowledge may be used not only to 'fill in' missing parts of a script or to show the links between objects, but to deduce connections such as cause and effect. If, for example, we read that 'John heard the ice-cream van. He rushed for his piggy bank' (see Charniak 1972, 1973, 1978, 1983, 1986 for similar examples), we can assume that the second event is a consequence of the first. The connection is made by inferring John's intentions (i.e. that he wants to buy an ice-cream from the ice-cream van) and also from our knowledge of monetary exchange for goods (i.e. John needs money to buy the ice-cream) and of the relationship between objects (ice-cream vans are a source of ice-cream, piggy banks are a source of money).

Psychology researchers have investigated whether readers make backward or forward inferences on the basis of their general knowledge, an issue which I will also consider in Chapter 7 in relation to text-specific knowledge. In an example incorporating the words 'a car . . . the wheels', it could be argued that we read 'the wheels', look for an antecedent for the definite article, and find the related word 'car' (a backward inference). Alternatively, on reading about the car we might automatically assume it has wheels, so that when we see the expression 'the wheels', the definite article is then a signal that the wheels are already in our consciousness (a forward inference). Early work on inferencing suggested the former (e.g. H. H. Clark's 1977 bridging inferences), but Sanford and Garrod (1981) have argued that forward inferences are more likely. Sanford and Garrod test the reaction times of subjects reading these types of sentence pairs and find that there is no increase in reading time at the point that the definite article is encountered, suggesting that no bridging inference is made at that point. I will return to this topic in Chapter 7 and argue there that some text-specific inferences are forward-oriented.

---

[5] This has been discussed extensively in the text-processing literature (e.g. Haviland and Clark 1974; Rieger 1974: 117; Bolinger 1979; Du Bois 1980; Sanford and Garrod 1981; E. F. Prince 1981; Yule 1982; G. Brown and Yule 1983; A. Anderson, Garrod, and Sanford 1983; Cornish 1986; Givón 1989: 207; Gundel, Hedberg, and Zacharski 1993).

One counter-argument to the idea of forward inferencing has been put forward by Rieger (1975, 1977). Rieger suggests that a reader cannot know in advance which inferences will be required by the subsequent text and that therefore forward inferencing would lead to a lot of unnecessary inferences being drawn, a 'computational explosion' as he terms it. Whilst there is some truth in this, it is still possible to assume that inferences about highly probable events or relations will be made. Indeed some psychologists make a distinction between different degrees of likelihood associated with causality (e.g. Myers and Duffy 1990: 160) suggesting that forward inferences occur only if a consequence is virtually inevitable. If, for example, someone is murdered, the reader can infer with certainty that they are dead. Likewise, the reader can infer that it is highly probable that a car will have wheels.

Inferencing on a probability basis is a rather different matter when text-specific knowledge is available in addition to general knowledge. In the above example about John and the ice-cream van, we know nothing about who John is or what his current situation is. The sentences have no context and the reader can only therefore make a judgement based on a stereotyped script. If, however, the reader has text-specific knowledge available, judging the probability of an event is a less open-ended matter. Clearly, there would be a 'computational explosion' if we assumed that every time a character saw a restaurant they would eat there. If, however, we knew from our text-specific knowledge that the character was either looking for somewhere to eat or, conversely, was engaged on some other activity that left him/her no time to eat, inference-making becomes a matter of assessing the situation. Likewise, text-specific knowledge about the character's personality and predispositions can influence our judgement, narrowing down the possibilities. In everyday life, people make many inferences about known individuals in specific circumstances, just as in reading a fictional narrative, inferences are made on the basis of text-specific information accumulated about the fictional world.

(iii) *Utilization of General Knowledge in Text Processing: Overall Interpretation*

The previous section described how general knowledge inferences may help to establish the basic coherence of a text. A narrative text may also encourage the reader to draw on his/her general knowledge to create certain special effects or to contribute to the overall plot or themes of a book. As will be discussed in Section 1c below, text-specific inferences can, by parallel, contribute both to the overall interpretation of a work and to the 'nuts and bolts' level of identifying characters and contexts.

A text which describes a character's failure to make normal general knowledge inferences can highlight how that character differs from the reader, giving us an insight into what stylisticians have termed the 'mind-style' of the character (Fowler 1977, 1986). In such cases, the reader often has to draw on his/her general knowledge to solve the 'problem' of what the character is actually perceiving. In the following example, the reader needs to work out that the 'hrududu' is a car and that it moves so quickly and smoothly through the fields because it is on a road, even though the rabbit, Hazel, perceives the 'hrududu' as a predator. Moreover, unlike Hazel, the reader can draw on general knowledge of cars to see that it is unlikely that the 'hrududu' will leave the road and hunt down the rabbits in the field.

EXAMPLE 2.1

> When he was half-way across the field, Hazel became aware of a hrududu approaching very fast on the other side of the further hedge. It was small and less noisy than the farm tractor which he had sometimes watched from the edge of the primrose wood at home. It passed in a flash of man-made, unnatural colour, glittering here and there and brighter than a winter holly tree. A few moments later came the smell of petrol and exhaust. Hazel stared, twitching his nose. He could not understand how the hrududu could move so quickly and smoothly through the fields. Would it return? Would it come through the fields faster than they could run, and hunt them down?

> (Richard Adams, *Watership Down* (1973), 57–8)

In fact, in this particular case, it might be argued that the 'mind-style' of the character is merely 'gestured at' rather than coherently represented, for it seems rather incongruous that Hazel has a special word for a car, but not for a tractor, petrol, or exhaust. The problem in writing such texts is that in giving the reader enough information to make intelligent guesses about what is going on, the representation becomes a rather unrealistic fusion of interpreted and uninterpreted information.[6] Texts which do present a more thorough representation of the character's thoughts—such as the often-discussed presentation of a Neanderthal man, Lok, in Golding's *The Inheritors* (Halliday 1971)[7] and a mentally subnormal individual, Benjy, in Faulkner's *The Sound and the Fury* (Leech and Short 1981: 202–8)—may require more processing effort by readers. The portrayal of a particular mind-style can often be a major objective of a literary work (probably *the* major objective in some of the novels mentioned above), so is important for the reader's overall interpretation of the work.

Rather than focusing our attention on specific characters, our general knowledge can also help us to evaluate a text by judging the overall relation of the fictional world to the real world. In texts based on historical events or situations, such as John Steinbeck's *The Grapes of Wrath* or Harper Lee's *To Kill a Mockingbird*, our knowledge of the historical background adds to the social comment. Conversely, our knowledge that certain fictional events are unlikely or impossible, such as the total rebuilding of the human body in Fay Weldon's *The Lives and Loves of a She Devil*, enable us to view a story as black humour rather than tragedy.

Providing information from general knowledge at a relatively late point in a story can force us to re-evaluate everything that we have read up until that point. Roald Dahl's 'Genesis and Catastrophe: A True Story' (1990), for example, opens with a lengthy discussion between a doctor and a young woman who has just given birth. The woman asks continually for the doctor's reassurance that the child will not die, as her three previous children have done. Towards the end of this conversation, the doctor suddenly refers to her as 'Frau Hitler'. It is unusual to name a character at such a late stage in an episode, but here our general knowledge adds an extra dimension to the story. The story is, arguably, more powerful than if the historical link had been made at the start, for it allows us to form a dual perspective, viewing events from the standpoint of the characters at the time and with the knowledge of hindsight.

---

[6] The same problem occurs when novelists attempt to represent the speech of characters speaking foreign languages or having foreign accents or 'strong' regional dialects. Realism often has to be sacrificed to intelligibility (Page 1973).

[7] See also Leech and Short (1981: 31–8).

General knowledge may also lead us to make inferences about the overall plot of a story. Detective stories are interesting to look at from this point of view because they require us to solve a puzzle as we read. The text may be presented in such a way that a reader is invited to make a seemingly obvious inference, only for this to be revoked at a later stage and a less obvious inference suggested. A reader of Agatha Christie's *Murder on the Orient Express* (1959) may not initially infer that because the victim has a large number of different stab wounds, some deep and some barely scratches, that a large group of people have committed the crime. This, however, is a plausible inference once it is pointed out. Much of the skill of writing detective stories lies in trying to prevent the reader from making crucial inferences at the outset (either by making these inferences seem too unlikely or by distracting the reader with other suggestions) so that the puzzle can be solved at a later stage by the detective. From the point of view of inference-making, this is just a matter of encouraging inferences at different stages in a story, but the technique has particular significance in terms of the overall development of the plot.

These examples of how general knowledge might be used to contribute to the overall meaning of a text are by no means comprehensive. They do, however, give some idea of the way in which our ideas of how general knowledge schemata are utilized may need to be extended beyond basic level gap-filling of the 'restaurant script' type to inference-making which may be less 'automatic', but may have greater consequences for the interpretation of larger stretches of text. Some preliminary work of this type has already been undertaken in relation to poems (e.g. Semino 1995), newspaper articles (Werth MS *a*: ch. 4), advertisements (Cook 1994), and narrative text extracts (Werth 1995: 55–8; Werth MS *a*: ch. 5; Hicks 1995). There is, nevertheless, still a need for schema theorists to examine how general knowledge is utilized during the course of reading a full novel or short story. Of course, the type of analysis suggested in this section is only too obvious to stylisticians and literary critics, so it is, for the most part, more a matter of researchers fusing observations from artificial intelligence and literary work than of beginning from the start. Similar observations will be made about the utilization of text-specific knowledge in Section 1c below and in subsequent chapters.

(b) *Text Schemata*

A second type of knowledge is a reader's awareness of typical text structures. This is different from text-specific knowledge, described in Section 1c below, because it is not information about a particular fictional world, but about the conventions of storytelling. Artificial intelligence researchers and psychologists examining texts which are longer than a couple of sentences have often concentrated on this type of analysis.

In artificial intelligence and psychology, the best-known work is on story schemata (e.g. Rumelhart 1975; Mandler and Johnson 1977; Thorndyke 1976, 1977). This research followed on from the recognition of story structure by literary theorists (e.g. Propp 1968; Greimas 1971; G. Prince 1973), anthropologists (e.g. Lévi-Strauss 1968/1977; Colby 1973), and linguists (e.g. Lakoff 1972). Rumelhart proposed that stories are comprised of units which are structurally connected in the same way as the units of sentences and that therefore grammars of stories could be produced using phrase structure rewrite rules. At the highest level, a story would therefore always be made up of a setting and an episode, with the episode comprising an event and a reaction. Rumelhart argued that detailed structural knowledge of this type could be used by readers to recognize key points in a story and thereby facilitate summarization after the story had been read. Rumelhart also suggested that story schemata might be utilized during the reading process itself to facilitate comprehension, but did not make clear how this might happen in practice.

There has been much criticism of story schemata, with writers such as J. B. Black and R. Wilensky (1979) arguing that the notion should be abandoned. Black and Wilensky question the psychological validity of story schemata, stating that their own experimental work does not produce the summaries that would have resulted from the rewrite rules of the story grammarians and pointing out that the use of story schemata in comprehension had not been specified by researchers like Rumelhart. Black and Wilensky's main criticism, however, resulted from the fact that story schemata had been viewed as being grammatical in nature at a time when the dominant view of grammar, following Chomsky (1957, 1965, 1972), was that it should account for all the sentences of a language and only those sentences. It was clearly not true of stories that they could all be accounted for by the schemata proposed and it was also evident that these schemata described other types of text (for example, Black and Wilensky used them to analyse a procedural text). Nowadays, Chomsky's notion of a strict dividing line between grammaticality and ungrammaticality at sentence level is not an issue for all linguists, particularly linguists who work with text, and there is a recognition by discourse analysts that it can be worthwhile to describe common text structures occurring across genres. Winter (1982), Hoey (1979, 1983), and Jordan (1984) have, therefore, described in detail the 'problem-solution' pattern (which is very similar to Rumelhart's 'setting-event–reaction' schema), underlying a whole range of texts, including some stories, but also 'everyday' texts such as advertisements, letters, etc. Although this problem–solution pattern is seen as a common structure of texts, it is not the only structure (Hoey 1983) and is in fact just one choice from a range of possible structures built from what Winter and Hoey term 'clause relations' (although they might more appropriately be termed 'discourse relations' as they link units both at and above clause level). Similar work, which also recognizes common structures across genres, has been carried out independently by Mann and Thompson (1987, 1988; Mann, Matthiessen, and Thompson 1992) and has been termed Rhetorical Structure Theory. These discourse 'building blocks' can be used to describe overall structure, but do not commit the analyst to finding just one simple structure in the text as a whole. The theory can also be used to identify relations at a more local level, such as the relationship between a pair, or a small group, of sentences within a lengthy text. This means that this work is not limited to very simple texts in the way that the early 'story grammar' studies were.

One question, though, is whether these discourse relations are actually just a sub-set of general knowledge and are not specific to text organization. Black and Wilensky (1979) make this point about the cause–effect relations in story schema and such relations do play a major role in both Clause Relational Theory and Rhetorical Structure Theory. There are, nevertheless, other relations, such as 'generalization–example', which are more specific to textual presentation of an argument rather than to life in general. The other question about such work is the extent to which readers have a knowledge of these patterns and whether they make use of this knowledge when reading. Hoey and Jordan's work on how readers can make assumptions about elided parts of typical structure suggests that this is the case, but there is a need for more work on this topic. Although the linguistics work on clause relations and rhetorical structure is parallel to the story schema work, these types of analysis have tended to concentrate more on non-narrative than on narrative.

There is a need for more research on how our knowledge of typical story structures helps us to read specific stories, particularly for narratives which do not follow the traditional storylines of myths and fairytales. One way in which story structure knowledge can be useful is that it enables the reader to anticipate complications or resolutions, depending on the stage that has been reached in the action. This can enable us to judge, for example, that a character is going into danger before the character is aware of any danger, hence increasing the suspense. Often, the fact that the narrative tells us an apparently trivial fact can lead us to read plot-relevance into it. In Dick Francis's *Whip Hand* (1981: 211), for example, the text mentions that a van is parked next to the hero's car. The hero thinks little of this, but the mention of the van would be trivial unless it was going to lead to some complication. In fact, two men jump out of the van, threaten the hero, and abduct him. Text-specific knowledge is also useful here, however, since the reader knows that the same thing has happened to the hero previously (p. 87) and that there are violent men in this particular fictional world who have reason to abduct the hero.[8]

It may be that one of the main things that we draw on from our knowledge of other stories is not typical structures, but storytelling conventions. Some of these storytelling conventions may just be a subset of textual conventions in general. Recognizing that there may be some significance in a narrator dwelling on a trivial fact, is really just responding according to Grice's (1975, 1978) maxim of relevance. Story readers may, however, need to become attuned to signalling in narrative, recognizing, for example, how flashbacks are linguistically indicated, how major and minor

---

[8] It may also be necessary to postulate a level of knowledge between schemata knowledge and text-specific knowledge. In reading a Dick Francis novel, for example, 'author-specific' knowledge will tell a reader familiar with this author's work that a violent scene is likely at the climax of the novel, usually involving the abduction of the hero.

characters are distinguished, and how background information differs from the narration of events. These conventions differ from language to language, explaining why children and foreign speakers may have difficulty with them (see Section 4 for a discussion of reading differences). This book assumes that textual knowledge of this type plays an important role in the formation, tracking, and utilization of 'text-specific' representations of characters and contexts.

(c) *Text-Specific Knowledge*

The reader is usually in possession of relevant general knowledge and text schemata knowledge before starting to process a particular text (although obviously there will be occasions when a particular text introduces a new fact or a new genre to the reader for the first time). By contrast, text-specific knowledge, the major focus of this book, is information which applies only within a particular text (or a related group of texts), such as accumulated knowledge about specific characters, about which characters are related to each other, and about which characters live in a particular place, as well as a record of the events that have occurred.

For comprehending fictional narrative, the distinction between general knowledge and text-specific knowledge is particularly important because readers must, to a certain extent, keep the facts of a fictional world distinct from the real world. We do not expect to meet fictional characters in real life and we do not expect everything that is true of a fictional world to be true in reality. When individuals fail to make these distinctions, they may become the subject of psychologists' case studies. In Luria's (1987) study, for example, the individual concerned found it difficult to remember where one world started and another finished, so would import people from real life or characters from other stories into a story that he was reading. (This rather unusual case study is discussed in more detail in Section 4a.) Of course, the division between a work of fiction and reality is not always clear. Characters from stories sometimes become part of popular culture (e.g. Dracula), hence entering our general knowledge, and on occasions a real-life person or place is referred to in a story. The problematic status of unauthorized portrayals of real-life individuals reflects this difficult area, particularly when facts are changed for artistic effect (as in the television film *Tumbledown* (Charles Wood, 1988, UK, BBC), portraying one of the British soldiers injured in the Falklands war).

It is also difficult to draw an absolute dividing line between general knowledge and text-specific knowledge, because the creation and tracking of 'text-specific' representations may itself utilize general knowledge. Although mental representations of characters may be built up from explicit descriptions in the text, we may also learn some facts about them by inference. We may, therefore, be told that a character is a doctor or we may just infer this information because we see this individual treating a patient in a surgery (see Chapter 7, Example 7.2). In both cases the representation is text-specific, but general knowledge is used in constructing the representation in the latter case. Likewise, although knowledge of who is in a particular context at any particular time is 'text-specific', we may only learn such facts from the text by drawing on our general knowledge of time and space (as discussed in Chapters 4 and 5).

Despite the problems of drawing a clear dividing line between general knowledge and text-specific knowledge, the division seems to be a useful one, at least while the study of knowledge representation is still in its early stages. As already indicated, readers do generally need to draw certain distinctions between the fictional world and the real world. It is also interesting to see how much textual information a reader needs to retain in order to make sense of a particular text, both from the point of view of how memory operates and to see how much the language of a text needs to be supplemented by drawing on what has been previously read. Chapter 3 gives examples of how text-specific mental representations may explain the actions of characters and may provide clues for the interpretation of pronouns. Also, from a practical point of view, dividing knowledge stores up in this way draws attention to the fact that a lot of work has been done on general knowledge but relatively little on text-specific knowledge.

It is convenient to regard text-specific information as being held in a number of distinct representations, such as representations for each character and for each location, since this allows researchers to 'map out' the types of knowledge involved. There are nevertheless a lot of connections between these representations. For example, the actions of one character may indirectly affect other characters and information about a place may tell us as much about the personality and background of the individual that lives there. Also, although it is convenient to speak of these representations as stores, this does underplay the extent to which readers may be actively aware of text-specific knowledge and the possibility that knowledge may be held in neural networks (as discussed in Section 2b).

Many researchers have recognized that there needs to be a way of reflecting how the mind collects together information about particular entities, so most references in the cognitive science literature can be found to entity representations. In cognitive psychology, mental representations of characters and other entities may be included in theoretical models (e.g. van Dijk and Kintsch 1983: 163, 338–9), but they are rarely discussed in any great detail in the text-processing literature. Social psychologists and sociologists have, however, explored such mental representations in rather more detail, looking particularly at how first impressions of people are arrived at and exploring the extent to which our memories are affected by schemata (e.g. Warr and Knapper 1968; Clifford and Bull 1978; Hastie *et al.* 1980; Woll and Graesser 1982). Artificial intelligence researchers often work with database representations of characters which can be equated with mental representations (e.g. Rieger 1974; Sidner 1979*b*; Rieger 1979) or these researchers talk directly about mental representations of characters (J. R. Anderson 1978; Webber 1978, 1979, 1983; Schuster 1989). Some linguists also use this notion (e.g. Karttunen 1976; G. Brown and Yule 1983; Clancy 1980; Du Bois 1980; Bernado 1980). Mental stores have also been suggested by logicians such as Kamp (1979, 1981) as part of 'Discourse Representation Theory' (DRT).

Much of the above-mentioned work simply recognizes the need to have entity representations to gather together information about a character and to fulfil the role of a referent in cases where there is no real-life referent.[9] G. Brown and Yule's (1983) work is interesting because it shows how entity representations fit into a linguistic theory of reference and recognizes the need to update these representations (see Chapter 7). However, little detailed work has been done on how an entity changes over time, although

---

[9] Of course, real-life referents may also be mediated by mental representations.

Dale (1992) does provide a model for recipes. In recipes, not only do entities need to be updated as food materials radically alter their properties (i.e. they are cooked, grated, etc.), but there is a major problem of whether identity of reference is retained. An egg may be split into the yolk and the white, for example, and then each part may play a quite independent role in the remainder of the recipe. Conversely, ingredients may be added together and from then on be treated as a single mixture. Dale's work highlights the extent to which mental representations need to be updated and indicates the problems of modelling this particular genre. A parallel model is needed for narrative, as Brown and Yule (1983: 202–3) point out:

> ... we need some model of processing which allows entities to accumulate properties or to change states as the discourse progresses. (It would be a poor reader of *David Copperfield* who failed to realise at the end that the hero was no longer the infant whom he was introduced to at the beginning.)

As far as the updating of entity representations is concerned, however, narrative text is likely to make rather different demands on a reader than recipes. In some respects there may be fewer problems for the analyst, since characters in narratives do not usually lose their identity in the way that eggs do when the yolks and whites are separated (although groups of people may split or assemble). However, characters require more complex representations in view of the fact that they have intentions and awareness, as well as past histories and personalities and relations to other characters (as discussed in Chapters 3, 4, and 6). Readers must also form representations of objects and locations, although a lot of detailed information about such entities is likely to be forgotten.

Readers also need to have an awareness of configurations of entity representations in specific locations. Chapters 4 and 5 introduce the term 'contextual frame' to indicate the monitoring of a group of characters in a particular place at a particular time. This is important for narrative comprehension because an action within a context is likely to have some effect on the other people present, even if it is only that they witness what occurs (Chapter 4). Obviously this is not generally a factor in Dale's recipe contexts, since the entities are inanimate. Narrative also differs from recipes as a result of context shifts such as flashbacks. There must be some method of determining which is the current context (and recalling any information which has been given about that context at an earlier point). Flashback shifts also affect entity representations, since different information needs to be activated depending on whether an entity is located in the past or present context (as discussed in Chapter 6).

Obviously, a reader must also maintain some record of events that occur in a story. Although I have focused in this study primarily on characters and contexts rather than events, all of these types of knowledge are interlinked. Events cause entities and contexts to change and so the appropriate representations have to be updated. Conversely, entity representations explain why certain actions occur (for example, by providing information about the motives and personality of the person performing the action). The reader must, however, also have some mental record of the events themselves, not just of the determining factors and the results, since there is a need to monitor on-going actions.

A number of other text-specific factors must also be monitored by the reader. A reader must, for example, be aware of whose point of view the action is seen from. This topic has been studied extensively by narratologists and linguists (e.g. Uspensky 1973; Booth 1983; Banfield 1982; P. Simpson 1993; Fludernik 1993; Chafe 1994) but has only recently attracted the attention of cognitive scientists (e.g. Bruder *et al.* 1986; Wiebe and Rapaport 1988; Duchan, Bruder, and Hewitt 1995). Linked to this is the related notion of whether situations and event sequences are real or hypothetical (Werth MS *a*: *passim*; 1995), since text segments which have the status of intentions, beliefs, conditionals, etc. require readers to increment their mental knowledge in a different way than when information is presented in a factual manner (see Bruce 1980; J. Allen 1983). In addition, the reader must retain an awareness of which character is the current focus of attention (Sidner 1979*b*). A reader must also retain an overview of what is happening in the book as a whole. It is necessary to remain aware of the overall goals of the characters and the obstacles they face. In many types of stories, the reader must also keep track of problems they themselves are trying to solve, awaiting information that will fill the gaps in their knowledge of the fictional world. Furthermore, some researchers (e.g. Schank 1982; Lehnert 1981, Dyer 1983*a*, *b*) have suggested that readers need to recognize the overall message of a text, i.e. the theme or moral. These topics will be discussed in this book whenever they are relevant to the examples discussed, but each topic would merit a full-length study in its own right.

Keeping track of all the salient information presented about entities, contexts, events, and these other factors is a complex information-processing task. This complexity has not always been noted in models of text processing because many studies have looked at simplified texts that have been constructed by the researcher rather than having occurred naturally. The nature of 'real' discourse is described in detail in Chapter 3, so at this stage I will only indicate briefly one of its main features, its length. Obviously, not all texts are long—a text can consist of a single word written on a signpost, such as 'Danger!'—but they are usually longer than a couple of sentences or even a couple of paragraphs, particularly where the text concerned is a narrative. Many studies, however (particularly in psychology), focus on examples such as the following:

> Bill lost a tennis match to John.
> Accepting the defeat, he walked slowly towards the showers.
> (Gernsbacher 1989: 121)

This particular example shows a classic problem of reference resolution, since the reader needs to work out who is the 'he' that has been defeated. Nevertheless, examples such as this one overlook important factors in 'real' narratives. The hierarchical structure of text is missing—the reader needs to have strategies for handling shifts from one narrative unit to another and for monitoring his/ her position in the discourse hierarchy at any one time. Length also enables a writer to create the characters and contexts which are lacking in the made-up sentences above. Although the individuals Bill and John are mentioned, these are just names and there is no preceding discourse presenting a description of these characters or the circumstances they find themselves in. Studying only these made-up sentences ignores the large amount of information from the previous text which readers hold in memory (even allowing for the large proportion of detail that is forgotten). Apart from creating rather more interesting reading material than that of made-up sentences (which may well have some effect on how the sentences are read), this data gives no opportunity to study how realistic amounts of prior information are drawn on and the extent to which the information base needs to be updated. This is discussed further in Chapter 3 and subsequent chapters.

The discussion of general knowledge inferences, in Section 1a above, made a distinction between inferences that made sense of a narrative at a basic level (e.g. establishing a causal relationship between two sentences) and inferences that contributed to the overall interpretation of a work. Although much of this book is concerned with basic level text-specific inferences, text-specific knowledge can also contribute to the overall interpretation of a story. At the basic level, I look mainly at how a reader knows that a pronoun refers to a particular character or how the reader keeps track of the locus and time of a stretch of the action. Sometimes, however, such factors can be manipulated for the purposes of the story as a whole. In particular, uncertainty over identity is often crucial to a plot. Chapter 5 contains some examples of this. Example 5.17 shows how a detective novel creates such uncertainty in order to draw the reader's attention away from identifying the murderer, and Example 5.16 illustrates how parallel strategies are used to create a plot reversal in a literary work.

(d) Text-Specific Stylistic Knowledge

Readers not only need to remember details about the content of a text, they also need to retain some knowledge of the way in which a text was worded. Although this book focuses specifically on text-specific content, it is necessary to look briefly at the reader's awareness of the style of a work in order to provide a more complete overview.

Although psychological tests have shown that memory for the surface form of a text decays rapidly (J. S. Sachs 1967), most readers do retain some general awareness of style. On occasions this may consist of fragments of the original wording, but even if the actual words are forgotten, factors such as the overall tone may be remembered. We can, therefore, often recall whether an essay was well written or badly written or whether a textbook was easy or difficult to read, despite the fact that the exact words have long been forgotten.

Therefore, in addition to text-specific mental representations of content, readers must also have representations which monitor the style of specific texts (and, by parallel, they must presumably accumulate some schematic knowledge of common styles). In many models of text processing there is no provision for such representations.[10] Psychologists, nevertheless, have shown that this sort of store does exist (e.g. Hjelmquist 1984). In some cases readers may, for example, have a vague recollection of where on a page they encountered information (Lovelace and Southall 1983), although they may not remember which page it was. Memory of words generally decays rapidly so that most of the time it is the gist that is recalled rather than the precise details.[11]

In literary text, in particular, the wording is often an important part of the text. Although psychologists have often avoided using literary text in their experiments (as it is viewed as too problematic (László 1987)), a recent study by Zwaan (1993) indicates that readers pay greater attention to the surface form of literary material than to the surface form of other genres such as newspaper articles.

Obviously an awareness of the surface form can enable us to recall techniques such as irony, where there is a discrepancy between what is said and what is meant (Zwaan 1993: 156). Stylistic foregrounding, the heavy accumulation of particular stylistic features at key points, would also have little effect on the reader if there were no memory at all for the surface form. From the point of view of linguistic theory, stylistic representations are needed to account for metalinguistic references in texts. This can be seen from the following example:

EXAMPLE 2.2

'There is a young Mrs Repton?'
'There is indeed—the decorative Scilla! One of the things I haven't discovered is whether she spells i̱t like the flower, or in the classical manner like Scylla and Charybdis.'

(Patricia Wentworth, *Poison in the Pen* (1977), 12; my emphasis)

[10] For example, van Dijk and Kintsch (1983); see the discussion of this point in Zwaan (1993).
[11] This has been found repeatedly in experimental work (e.g. Sachs 1967; Bransford and Franks 1971; Johnson-Laird and Stevenson 1970; Bransford, Barclay, and Franks 1972; Le Ny 1980; Gernsbacher 1985; R. E. Johnson 1986; Johnson-Laird 1988: 342).

In a subsequent discussion of the role of mental representations in reference theory (Chapter 7), I suggest that a noun or pronoun normally refers to an entity representation rather than to an earlier word. This is not, however, the case for 'it' in the above example. Here the pronoun refers either to the actual word 'Scilla' or to the memory of the actual word rather than to the entity representation of Scilla. Although Scilla is female, the pronoun 'it' is the appropriate pronoun in this sentence because it denotes the name not the person. These metalinguistic pronouns[12] are comparatively rare, but they require the reader either to search the preceding text or to hold a mental representation of the words of text (as opposed to the meaning denoted by these words).

Text-specific stylistic representations are not examined further in this book, but the fact that there is some awareness of the original wording of a text (at least whilst it is being read) is important. This is obvious to the analyst of literary narrative texts, but is too often overlooked in models which look only at short artificial examples or non-literary texts.

2. THE NATURE OF MENTAL REPRESENTATIONS

(a) *Propositions or Mental Models*

Section 1 of this chapter has outlined some of the different types of knowledge that are needed to read a text. One major debate in cognitive science has been over the form in which information about specific entities, contexts, and events extracted from a particular text is stored in the mind. Since this book focuses on text-specific knowledge, this debate is particularly relevant to subsequent chapters. The controversy arose because some models of text processing, such as Kintsch and van Dijk (1978) and van Dijk and Kintsch (1983), have viewed the information as being stored in the mind only or mainly in propositional form, whereas Johnson-Laird (1983)[13] has argued that the human mind creates

[12] Lyons (1977: ii. 667–8) refers to this phenomenon as 'textual deixis', distinguishing it from anaphora.

[13] I will use the best-known term 'mental models' (Johnson-Laird and Garnham 1980; Garnham 1981; Johnson-Laird 1981, 1983) to summarize the research by Johnson-Laird and his associates, although a variety of labels are in fact used (for example, 'mental representations of spatial descriptions' in Mani and Johnson-Laird (1982) and 'spatial descriptions' in K. Ehrlich and Johnson-Laird (1982)). Brewer (1987: 189) provides a useful definition of mental models which contrasts

analogical forms which he terms 'mental models'.[14] In my own model, I assume that information is integrated in a similar fashion to mental models, but I suggest later in this discussion that Johnson-Laird's approach needs to be adapted to take account of naturally occurring discourse.

Much of van Dijk and Kintsch's work concerns propositional representations. In their (1983) book, for example, they argue for a 'textbase' which is created from propositions and is, therefore, 'the semantic representation of the input discourse in episodic memory' (p. 11). A central component of van Dijk and Kintsch's model is the notion that the major propositions obtained from a text can be connected into a sequence to create a 'macrostructure' representing 'the gist, the upshot, the theme, or the topic, of a text' (p. 15)[15] and that this 'macrostructure' can be used for summarizing the text. By contrast, Johnson-Laird (1980, 1983, 1993) argues that it is not appropriate to adopt a propositional approach, since meaning is not lodged exclusively in the words making up propositions and readers do not generally reason using the rules of formal logic. Johnson-Laird demonstrates this by pointing out that the conclusion drawn from sentence pairs such as 'John is on the right of Henry, Bill is on the right of John' can vary depending on whether these individuals are seated in a straight line, a small circle, or a large circle. So meaning depends on context and has to be determined by reference to a spatial model rather than a decontextualized deduction. Johnson-Laird argues that even when drawing a conclusion from sentences such as 'Mary is taller than Jane, Jane is taller than Ann', the reader will produce and use a spatial model (of the three different heights) rather than relying on the abstract logical transitivity operation. Although having visual elements, mental models are not necessarily images. Johnson-Laird (1983: 146–66) draws a

them with schemata: 'In *schemas* the molar knowledge structures are old generic information while in *mental models* the global knowledge structures are constructed at the time of input. In other words, schemas are precompiled generic knowledge structures, while mental models are specific knowledge structures that are constructed to represent a new situation through the use of generic knowledge of space, time, causality and human intentionality.'

[14] Chafe, too (1980a: p. xi), suggests that information derived from a text '. . . is stored in the mind in part analogically, and not only propositionally' (see also Chafe 1972: 42; Sag and Hankamer 1984: 333; Rumelhart and Norman 1983).
[15] See also Graesser (1981: 5–13).

distinction between the two, although he does not give much explanation of exactly how they differ. It may be the case that there are degrees of visual detail depending on the reader, the type of text being read, and the purpose that it is being read for. When solving a problem such as who is taller, readers may imagine three figures representing three individuals or might just produce a schematic visual representation similar to plotting their heights on a graph. When reading fictional narrative, many readers seem to have images of the characters, but presumably these are not as specific as when we are thinking of a person we know in real life.

Johnson-Laird's notion of mental models has been widely accepted within cognitive science. Even van Dijk and Kintsch in their (1983) book add in a 'situation model' which is the 'cognitive representation of the events, actions, persons, and in general the situation, a text is about' (pp. 11–12).[16] A great deal of their research is, nevertheless, focused on propositions. Conversely, although much of Johnson-Laird's work argues against 'pure logic', he does sometimes acknowledge that there might be different 'levels' of mental processing and that propositional representations might be appropriate to account for certain types of processing (1983: 156–65).

In many respects, Johnson-Laird's mental models seem to be useful for describing narrative processing, although this is not a topic he discusses in any detail. Most of Johnson-Laird's examples are of the type:

The knife is in front of the spoon.
The spoon is on the left of the glass.
The glass is behind the dish.   (Johnson-Laird 1983: 374)

The reason for concentrating on such examples is partly the practical need to produce carefully controlled psychological experiments, but also because Johnson-Laird's main interest is in processing strategies for the types of premises used in logic problems.

When Johnson-Laird does briefly discuss narrative, it seems only as a contrast to this type of problem-solving. I will quote the relevant passage from Johnson-Laird (1980: 103–4) in its entirety

---

[16] See Ch. 4 for a discussion of van Dijk and Kintsch's work.

because I find some of his statements (towards the end of this quotation) about narrative rather odd:

Ordinary discourse is often indeterminate. If you were to come across the following passage in a story, then you would probably form only a rather vague idea of the actual spatial lay-out:

> I opened the door and went in. The room was at the corner of the building and on my right there was a long window overlooking the bay. A plain but tasteful table ran the length of the room and there were chairs on either side. A large colour television set stood flickering on one side of the table beneath the window, and on the other side there was a small safe, its door ajar. At the head of the table facing the door, Willis sat deep in thought, or so it seemed. The room was very quiet. And Willis was very quiet, frozen in a posture of unnatural stillness.

A few details would stand out—the open safe, the TV, and the corpselike appearance of the man—but you would be unlikely to have gone beyond the description to have figured out whether the safe was on the right hand side or the left hand side of the room from where the narrator viewed it. Yet, if you read the passage again with the aim of determining the answer to this question, then you can form a very much more complete mental picture of the room. There accordingly appear to be different levels of representation, and the hypothesis that I wish to advance is that they differ in kind. The result of a superficial understanding is a propositional representation: a fairly immediate translation of the discourse into a mental language. A more profound understanding leads to the construction of a mental model which is based on the propositional representation, but which can rely on general knowledge and other relevant representations in order to go beyond what is explicitly asserted.

The first part of this passage seems reasonable and Johnson-Laird informally tests this out in later work by giving students a passage from a Sherlock Holmes story to read normally and subsequently asking how much spatial detail they remember about the series of rooms that the characters walk through as they attempt to burgle a blackmailer's house (Johnson-Laird 1983: 158–9). Occasionally, one reader in a hundred could draw a picture of the building lay-out, but most readers just remembered salient details of the overall atmosphere of the building, such as the darkness, the hushed voices of Holmes and Watson, the smell of cigar smoke in the rooms, and the way in which Watson is surprised by a cat which rushes towards him. It is also not surprising that if the readers are told in advance that spatial detail is going to be tested, or are asked to read the passage again for this detail, they would remember more about the lay-out. What is disputable, however, is Johnson-Laird's equation of natural story-reading with 'a superficial understanding' which yields a propositional representation. The labels 'profound' and 'superficial'[17] are in fact technical terms in psychology denoting the level of processing, but the connotations are unfortunate when applied to a literary text. More puzzling is the notion that natural story-reading is purely propositional which, if true, would seem to limit the usefulness of Johnson-Laird's mental models.

Although I do not disagree that we forget or fail fully to process spatial details, I would still argue that mental modelling is important for explaining how people read narrative. To apply Johnson-Laird's ideas to narrative processing, it is necessary to take account of salience and reading purpose. The majority of readers may not be concerned about the precise positions of objects in a room because this is generally not the main point of reading a passage like this. Experienced readers of the Sherlock Holmes story are more likely to be concentrating on factors such as whether the characters are going to be caught as they raid a criminal's house, what incriminating evidence they are going to find, what will happen to them if they are caught, the skill of Sherlock Holmes, and the relationship between Holmes and Watson. In other words, the actions of the central characters and an overall impression of the location will normally be of most importance. Likewise, in the above-cited passage about the corpse-like man, a reader is more likely to be puzzling over whether Willis is dead or alive and making inferences from the fact that the safe door is open, than worrying about whether the safe is on the left or the right. An image of the room can still be formed, with the reader placing the safe anywhere they wish (as they might do if no spatial detail had been given).

A reader is presumably more likely to remember spatial details when they are of importance to the plot as a whole or the specific actions being described. If, for example, the hero/heroine is hiding behind a curtain and there are killers looking for him/her, the exact position of the curtain might be important. Similarly, if

---

[17] These words have disappeared by the time of Johnson-Laird's (1983) discussion of Sherlock Holmes, but the notion that normal reading of narrative text creates 'propositional' representations still remains.

a child is between a gunman and the hero/heroine, the relative positions become important (even if we do not know their absolute locations). Readers also need to have the ability to 'move' the characters 'around' in mental space. If a group of characters are in a location and two of them split off from the main group to talk, we need to keep track of who is where (to understand, for example, who hears a conversation in one of the parties). This seems quite similar to the mental grouping of participants which Johnson-Laird describes as necessary to draw conclusions from premises like 'None of the authors are burglars. Some of the chefs are burglars' (Johnson-Laird 1983: 95). This is not a matter of putting the characters in any particular place, but of keeping some characters separate from others and noting characters who are in similar circumstances or have similar properties.

Although Johnson-Laird's mental models do offer some important insights into how the mind reasons, his work contains little consideration of how mental modelling would apply to story-reading. Most of his examples, like the knife/spoon/glass example above, contain static descriptions, not event sequences. This is not surprising as Johnson-Laird's examples are designed primarily as critiques of the standard three-line examples of premises and conclusion in logic. The examples do not contain entities that we might empathize with and there is no distinction between major and minor facts. Furthermore, entities do not change in any way and there is no regrouping of entities.

An attempt to extend Johnson-Laird's work to narrative has been made within psychology by Morrow, Bower, and Greenspan (1990). Their experimental texts, unlike the materials used by Johnson-Laird, do consist of sequences of events and do involve characters moving from one location to another, for example:

> Kathy finished drinking coffee in the kitchen.
> Then she remembered that she had promised Bill to wash the windows.
> She didn't think he had cleaned up the house, so she didn't want to do her work.
> Instead, she looked for something else to do.
> **She was walking from the kitchen to the bedroom.**
> She noticed **the rug** was dirty.   (Morrow, Bower, and Greenspan 1990: 129; their line breaks and emphasis)

The series of experiments described in Morrow, Bower, and Greenspan (1990) aim to prove the usefulness of a 'mental modelling' approach for processing this type of data. Their overall point, which is also the main point that I am making in this book, is that information that the reader already knows about the fictional world is used in making inferences as each new sentence is read. For Morrow, Bower, and Greenspan, however, 'situation' means specific spatial information about a location which is different from my own term 'context' denoting a reader's knowledge about the overall configuration of the participants, the time, and the location at any particular point in a text (see Chapter 4). In Morrow, Bower, and Greenspan's experiment with the above passage, the readers acquire knowledge about the situation by memorizing a diagram of the apartment in advance. The diagram shows that the room between the kitchen and the bedroom is the hallway and that this is where the rug is located. As a result of this knowledge, the readers of the passage manage to make the inference that at the point at which Kathy notices the rug, she is in the hallway, even though this is not explicitly stated in the text.[18]

Although Morrow, Bower, and Greenspan's theory appears reasonable, I would suggest that the methodology raises one key question. They draw conclusions from this experiment about how people read narratives, but they do not even comment in this article on the fact that readers do not normally gain their knowledge of a fictional world from memorizing spatial diagrams in advance of reading.[19] This is not a trivial criticism, since Johnson-Laird's informal test of readers of the Sherlock Holmes story showed that when a real story was read, most readers did not recall such details from the text that they had only recently processed. If the conclusions from Johnson-Laird's informal tests are correct, this experiment may tell us little about how a real narrative is read because there is no guarantee that the readers would have had the appropriate information available to make the

---

[18] It might be argued here that the reader could draw on general knowledge, since hallways usually provide a link between rooms. In the other experiments in this article, however, the intermediate rooms presented are a library and a living room.

[19] Occasionally novels do include lay-out drawings and maps, but presumably readers consult these diagrams when necessary rather than memorize them. The fact that these diagrams are deemed necessary in such cases perhaps indicates that the narrative text itself is not a good means of conveying this information.

inference, or that the readers would have even needed to make the inference if something interesting had been happening in the plot at that time.

Morrow, Bower, and Greenspan (1990) have at least made an attempt to go beyond the traditional decontextualized sentence pairs, with their work showing a recognition that prior knowledge of the fictional world is useful for inference-making. However, not only is their method of supplying 'situational' information unrealistic, the type of knowledge that they consider is likely to be of low relevance for a reader of narrative. Readers are more likely to be interested in who else is present and overall information about the time and place, rather than being concerned with trivial spatial details.[20] What is needed for this type of investigation is a recognition of what people read in real life, why they read it, and how they read it, not just an uncritical attempt to apply Johnson-Laird's theory to pseudo-narratives. This discussion of experimental and natural data is continued in Chapter 3 and my study of fictional context begins in Chapter 4.

(b) Parallel Distributed Processing or Serial Processing

In this book it is convenient to refer to mental representations as 'stores', a term which may suggest that information is regarded as being held in a particular location of the brain. In fact, it is possible that this 'storage' of information may instead be in the form of networks of connections. Although the 'hardware' instantiation of mental representations is not of direct relevance to the arguments put forward in this book, it is such a topical issue that it merits brief consideration here.

Recently, cognitive scientists have begun to consider whether to view mental processing in terms of the operations of a traditional (von Neumann design) computer or whether to adopt a model which better reflects observed facts about the neurology of

---

[20] Linde and Labov's (1975) 'spatial networks' are stores of information about individuals' apartments. Since this is a topic that is of real interest to the subjects of Linde and Labov's experiments, the experiments are described as being 'well-motivated' (p. 925). However, unless the subject has only on one occasion seen the flat, these 'spatial networks', although describing a specific context, are a fusion of information derived from many occasions. They are, therefore, best regarded as forms of 'scenario' representing personal schemata rather than as 'mental models'.

the human brain. This new model has been variously called connectionism, neural networks, and parallel distributed processing (McClelland, Rumelhart, and Hinton 1986).[21] Parallel distributed processing is still highly controversial, but offers a reasonable explanation of certain low-level cognitive processes, such as visual pattern recognition and understanding of verb suffixes. This does not, however, mean that parallelism underlies all cognitive processes or that, if it does, it functions alone. Basically, parallel distributed processing theories view knowledge as being distributed throughout the brain rather than in clearly defined stores. Furthermore, brain activity is seen not as a single 'train of thought', but as neural activity occurring in many parts of the brain at any one time (Dennett 1991; Flanagan 1992) and the connections between items of information are regarded as being as important as the information itself. The brain is viewed as more likely to make connections that it has made many times before, with the links being 'excitatory'. So 'lawyer' and 'rich' might be connected in this way, whereas the connection between 'student' and 'rich' might be the converse, 'inhibitory' (although this of course depends on cultural experience). If this is the case, it would explain how we stereotype people and how we automatically perform certain operations, such as linguistic and visual pattern recognition.

There does, however, seem to be a vast difference between automatic operations such as verb-suffix recognition (automatic for native speakers, at least) and the type of thought involved in problem-solving and our everyday stream of consciousness, where we can give some account of the stages we have been through. Many people have suggested that these differences may correspond to different levels of processing. There may be parallel and serial thought, or parallelism may underlie serialism like machine code underlies an operating system, but we do not yet know. If parallel distributed processing does underlie higher cognition, it may mean that regarding mental representations, such as entity and contextual representations, as 'stores' of information is a notional concept rather than a description of how information is actually held in the brain. The main point is, though, that items of information are viewed as being connected to each

---

[21] See A. Clark (1989) for a useful summary.

other or not connected (e.g. John is tall (connection), John is not
tall (no connection), John and Henry are currently in the same
location (connection), John and Henry are not currently in the
same location (no connection)), regardless of whether this is neu-
rologically realized by the information being held in one place.
For ease of description I will continue to speak as if 'gathering
together' of information occurs, but it is possible that each representation is actually a network. A connectionist approach
might, moreover, be more in line with the 'activation' model that
I am proposing here, rather than the usual 'access from storage
model' (see Chapter 7).

3. THE SIGNIFICANCE OF CONSCIOUSNESS

Consciousness is currently a major topic in artificial intelligence,
since it is a major property of the human mind which it is at present
proving impossible to replicate on computers. Sections 3a and 3b
look at this problem in artificial intelligence as a whole, drawing
on observations made by both scientists and philosophers. This
general discussion is followed in Section 3c by a summary of
some of the major work within discourse analysis on consciousness and text production/processing, including a comparison
with my own ideas and approach.

(a) Computers and Consciousness

Traditionally, artificial intelligence research on text has concentrated exclusively on knowledge representation and how this
knowledge is utilized in processing. However, some scientists and
philosophers believe that we will never be able to create real intelligence because we have no adequate understanding of human
consciousness (W. James 1890), the ability to be aware of what is
going on around us.[22] Consciousness is difficult to define, but is
illustrated by Penrose's (1989: 530) contrast between a video
camera, which is able to record visual images, and a human
being, who is able to perceive these images. The best-known pro-
ponent of this latter view is Searle, whose argument is illustrated

[22] There is much debate on this topic (e.g. Scriven 1963; Searle 1984: 15–16;
Blakemore and Greenfield 1987: 205–91, 307–20, 361–402; Johnson-Laird
1988: 353–92; Dennett 1991; Flanagan 1992; Crick and Koch 1992).

by his famous 'Chinese room' example (Searle 1980, 1984: 31–8).[23] Searle imagines that he is a man locked in a room who receives sets of Chinese symbols from people outside the room and, in accordance with rules specified in a rule-book written in English, sends out of the room another combination of Chinese symbols. Unknown to the man in the room, the incoming symbols are questions in Chinese about a story in Chinese (which he has also been given) and the outgoing symbols are appropriate answers in Chinese. The man appears to understand the story, although in fact he has no real understanding at all, as he has no knowledge of the language. In this respect, Searle compares the man to a computer. Interestingly, this 'thought experiment' was originally intended by Searle as a critique of Schank and Abelson's (1977a, b) work on scripts in story comprehension (discussed in Section 1a above).

Consciousness has recently become a key area of research,[24] both amongst scientists and philosophers of mind, but we are still a long way from understanding what consciousness is. Penrose (1987, 1989, 1995) has argued that consciousness is a fundamental law of physics of which we are not yet in possession and without which we will never fully understand the human mind. Dennett (1991), by contrast, argues that an understanding of consciousness is possible within our current scientific framework, but only if we adopt radically different ways of thinking about the human mind. He cites experiments which suggest that consciousness may be a device that the brain has developed for broadcasting information from one part of its parallel system to another.[25]

Whether or not scientists discover the mechanics of consciousness, there is little dispute that it exists and we can still observe its effects and make provision for it in cognitive models. One reason, though, that consciousness has not been taken into account is that computer programs sometimes appear to work reasonably effectively without it. The famous Turing test (Turing 1963) works on the principle that if we are unable to distinguish between a person and a machine performing the same tasks, then the

---

[23] See also Searle (1987) for a summary and Boden (1988: 238–51) for a discussion of Searle's work.

[24] See Davidson (1993) for a summary.

[25] Crick and Koch (1990: 272) have hypothesized that the point at which we become conscious of a stimulus is when neurons oscillate at a frequency of 40Hz.

machine is as intelligent as a human.[26] Even in the early stages of
artificial intelligence research, programs were developed which
could fool people into believing they were communicating with
another person rather than a machine (Weizenbaum 1966,
1984). However there is obviously something wrong with judging
performance in this way. By analogy, there have been cases
where an ordinary member of the public can pose as a doctor and
remain undiscovered for a number of years, but such impostors
are often discovered eventually because they do not have the skill
of a real doctor. Similarly, a computer program would have to be
judged over a period of time and, even if it appeared to function as
a human, there might still be something missing. In simulations
of story-reading, a machine may be very effective at summarizing
and answering questions, but still not function in a psychologically realistic way. People enjoy different types of texts depending
on their interests, they can get bored or thoroughly immersed in
what they read and they know when they have read a story
before. Computers do not do this and yet interest in a story is the
chief motive for reading in the first place.

(b) Simulating Human Experience

Consciousness may be viewed as just being synonymous with
awareness or it can also encompass the specific experiences we
have through senses such as sight and touch (Flanagan 1992:
23). Although a fair amount of work has been done on simulating
vision and movement, there is still a lot that is not understood.
However successful artificial intelligence researchers become in
modelling visual recognition, this does not explain how humans
can think (without visual stimulus) of an imaginary thing such
as a purple cow (Flanagan 1992; Dennett 1991). Likewise,
although robots can be programmed to move objects around,
they cannot really feel these objects in the same way that we
can. There are many thought experiments in philosophy of mind
which stress these differences. One famous one features a blind
scientist, called Mary, who knows everything there is to know
about the physics of vision, but is still surprised when she sees
for the first time because the actual experience of vision is quite

---

[26] See Sharkey and Brown (1986) and Sharkey and Pfeifer (1984) for critical discussions of the Turing Test.

different from a textbook description (Jackson 1982, 1986). There is some debate over whether the experience of the senses (the phenomenology) is crucial to the cognitive processes or just an accompanying 'sideshow' (i.e. epiphenomenal, see Flanagan 1992: 130), but it seems reasonable to take these experiences seriously until we know more about them. In research on reading, this would mean taking account of the reader's tendency to form visual images, as these might give some clues to the underlying representations and processing.

Our ability both to experience and imagine physical and emotional experiences makes us very different from computers (Dreyfus 1979; Searle 1980; Abelson 1987; Alexsander and Burnet 1987: 95, 118). Whereas a computer only has definitions of, for example, the words 'fear', 'love', 'anger', 'thirst', 'cold', 'heat', 'red', and 'yellow', the human reader has a full understanding of what these words mean, having actually experienced what is denoted by the word.[27] Some people may argue against this, pointing out, for example, that we can understand a story about skiing even if we have never been skiing ourselves (Wilks 1982: 505). Clearly a non-skier's reading of such a text may be different from a skier's, but a non-skier will generally have a store of general knowledge about the sport from sources such as television. A non-skier can also draw on their own experiences of snow, speed, excitement, fear, competitiveness, cold, glare, injury, and other potentially relevant factors.

Many artificial intelligence researchers would claim that we will eventually be able to program a computer with all this general knowledge. However, if this is ever going to be possible, we will first need to understand how the mind stores and utilizes a lifetime's experiences (Dreyfus 1979: 281). It can also be argued that we would need to create not only artificial minds but artificial human beings in order to understand experiences of the emotions and senses.[28] Although we are a long way from achieving this, models of language processing can at least be sympathetic to the nature of human experience, recognizing that our emotions,

---

[27] See discussion in Schank (1984: 22–58) (also Alexsander and Burnet 1987: 18; Boden 1987: 138, 205; Boden 1988: 247; Johnson-Laird 1988: 388; Tulving cited in Campbell 1989: 307–8; Eysenck and Keane 1990: 508).

[28] Dreyfus (1979: 10, 235–55, 281); see also Boden (1987: 434–44) for counterarguments.

sensations, and physical placement in the world are important. Recent developments in 'cognitive linguistics', such as 'cognitive grammar' (Langacker 1986, 1987, 1991), 'mental spaces' (Fauconnier 1994), 'force dynamics' (Talmy 1978, 1988), and metaphor theory (Lakoff and Johnson 1980; M. Johnson 1987; Lakoff 1987), recognize that the body exerts an influence on our language. For example, abstract ideas are often anthropomorphized and the language reflects the fact that events are generally seen from a particular spatial perspective (with the possibility of alternative hypothetical perspectives).

'Cognitive linguistic' theory offers important insights at word, phrase, and sentence level, but has not tended to handle discourse to any great extent.[29] There is, however, a body of research which has grown out of an analysis of texts and which looks at the human ability to construct mental representations of 'worlds' which are held in place while stretches of text are processed. Recent work by Werth (MS *a*, *b*; 1995) distinguishes between a 'discourse world', which is the immediate situational context 'shared' by a speaker and listener, and a 'text world' which is created in a reader's mind from a text. The text world is peopled by characters and has its own spatio-temporal parameters, meaning that a reader experiencing this world must reset his/her deictic orientation by responding to 'world builders' provided in the text. A text world may be split into a number of sub-worlds, some of which may involve temporal or spatial shifts and some of which may require the reader to enter the minds of characters and experience their hopes, beliefs, intentions, etc.

Although Werth's work has obvious parallels with the philosophical notion of possible worlds, there are some important differences. Werth stresses that his worlds are 'rich worlds' unlike those of traditional logic. The characters in them are not just names but people with human minds, relations to other characters and a physical connection with their environment. To understand a text denoting them, a reader must make assumptions about human behaviour rather than simply manipulating symbols.

---

[29] There are, however, some recent exceptions to this generalization (e.g. Werth 1994, 1995, MS *a*, *b*; D. C. Freeman 1992, 1993, 1995; M. H. Freeman 1995; Redeker 1995; Sanders 1994, 1995). This may reflect a growing trend, particularly in view of Fauconnier's recent (1995) observations about extending 'mental space theory' to discourse.

Werth's work is linked to that of the cognitive linguists, since it argues for an 'embodied' and 'experiential' response to language, but his own work accounts for how whole texts are read. Werth suggests that reading must take account of information presented in the whole of the preceding text, the 'Common Ground' as he terms it, and argues that this would require a radical re-evaluation of traditional philosophical notions such as presupposition (Werth 1993).

Gerrig (1993) also discusses worlds, using the term 'narrative worlds'. He aims to account for readers' reports that they experience a feeling of departing from their immediate context and being 'transported' to a narrative world. His explanation of a reader's involvement goes beyond basic inference-making to reflect the excitement felt as suspense develops in a story. He suggests a set of 'participatory responses' which include readers' hopes and fears with regard to the central characters. Readers might, therefore, feel like crying out 'Watch out!' when a character moves into danger, hypothesize about possible escape routes when a character is in danger, or, conversely, hope that an evil character gets caught. Such responses require the reader to postulate alternative narrative worlds, resulting not from direct mentions of such worlds in the text but from readers' empathy or lack of empathy for particular characters. Participatory responses seem to engender significant feelings of fear, sadness, and happiness. Their relationship to real-life responses is arguable, as is their effect on our everyday lives. Gerrig points out that however afraid we are when we watch a fictional horror film, we do not usually (as adults, at least) run away from the screen to warn our family of the danger. Nevertheless, Gerrig also points out that viewing a horror film such as *Jaws* can subsequently have a material effect on our desire to swim in coastal waters. Hence the borderline between the real world and a narrative world is not clear-cut. Gerrig compares this to a journey in which we return from the place we have visited but are 'somewhat changed' as a result.

A recent volume (Duchan, Bruder, and Hewitt 1995b) by a group of cognitive science researchers from State University of New York at Buffalo presents a number of papers which provide an interdisciplinary approach to the topic of reader involvement. Like Werth (MS *a*, *b*, 1995), these researchers regard narrative as a means of relocating the reader's deictic centre, so that a reader enters the spatio-temporal world of the narrative and moves around in it (e.g. Segal 1995*a*; Zubin and Hewitt 1995). They term this 'Deictic Shift Theory' and illustrate how the reader's 'cognitive stance' is reflected in deictic verbs, with 'come' and 'go', for example, indicating the point at which the reader is currently located in the narrative world (e.g. Duchan, Bruder, and Hewitt 1995*a*; Bruder 1995). These researchers put particular emphasis on how readers often take on the subjective perspectives of characters within the narrative world, suggesting that this has an effect on the form of anaphoric items such as pronouns and articles (e.g. Zubin and Hewitt 1995; Wiebe 1995; Hewitt 1995; Bruder and Wiebe 1995). Like Gerrig (1993), these researchers use the metaphors of being 'transported' and going on a journey,[30] as well as speaking of 'vicarious' and 'mimetic' experience (e.g. Segal 1995*a*, *b*; Galbraith 1995).

My own work on narrative contexts is in line with the general approach of these projects (see Chapters 4–6, 8). Although originating in different disciplines, all of this work recognizes that responding to language is not just a matter of decoding individual words and applying rules to understand syntactic structures. Just as speech involves relating utterances to a real-world context, so narrative sentences need to be viewed in relation to mentally represented contexts created from the texts themselves. In reading narrative texts, we imagine worlds inhabited by individuals who can be assumed to behave, physically and psychologically, in ways which reflect our real-life experiences of being situated in the real world. In real life we are always rooted in a specific physical context, so context-building simulates our need for orientation and our continuing awareness of our spatial-temporal co-ordinates. This book looks primarily at how the illusion of situatedness and embodiment in specific contexts within a fictional world is achieved. In line with the other work mentioned in this section, I regard readers as imagining situations in which the characters appear to be 'present' to the extent that the reader seems to 'witness' the actions occurring (Emmott 1989, 1992, 1994, 1995*a*, forthcoming *a*). I focus particularly on the way that information presented at earlier stages in the text, such as details of the spatio-temporal co-ordinates and the co-present

---

[30] See also Pavel (1986: 85) for use of this metaphor.

participants, needs to be held in consciousness whilst lengthy stretches of text are read. The reader also needs to be able to recognize textual cues which signal when to stop assuming that contextual factors are still relevant and to be able to maintain an awareness of other contexts at varying levels of consciousness. This topic is explored in detail in subsequent chapters and the following section of this chapter discusses the linguistic background to these ideas.

(c) Consciousness and Text Linguistics

In text linguistics, the topic of consciousness has been discussed extensively by Chafe (e.g. 1980*b*, 1994), together with his collaborators (Tannen 1980; Downing 1980; Clancy 1980; Du Bois 1980; and Bernado 1980). Chafe's work is a development of the linguistic interest in 'given' and 'new' information in the sentence. Halliday (1967) first drew attention to the fact that the clause is generally organized so as to give prominence to 'new' information, by placing it in clause-final position where it has more impact. Links with the preceding text are also reflected, with 'given' information often being placed in the clause-initial subject position and frequently being expressed by 'attenuating' elements such as pronouns and unmarked intonation.[31]

E. F. Prince (1981) points out that there have been very different approaches to the study of the 'given/new' distinction and that not all of the accounts are overtly cognitive. Given information, can, for example, be viewed simply as information that has already been mentioned previously in the text, or it can be viewed as information that is currently in the consciousness of the reader or listener (or information that the speaker or writer thinks is in the consciousness of the other party). Chafe has pioneered the latter, cognitive, approach.[32] For Chafe (1994: 72), 'given' means 'already active at this point', 'new' means 'newly activated at this

---

[31] Chafe often draws (e.g. Chafe 1972, 1974, 1976, 1980*b*), on the literature on given and new information and on theme and rheme (e.g. Halliday 1967, see also Halliday 1985), also making links (Chafe 1974, 1976) with work by the Prague school linguist Firbas on 'communicative dynamism' (see Firbas 1986 and 1992*a*, *b* for recent work). Chafe suggests that items that are 'already in the minds of the participants in the discourse' (1972: 51) are most likely to be pronominalized or mentioned with lower pitch and amplitude.

[32] For example, Chafe (1974, 1976, 1979, 1980*a*, 1980*b*, 1990, 1994).

point' and there is also a possibility that information may be 'semi-active' and therefore 'accessible'.

Other researchers have added more levels to the list. Prince's (1981) 'given–new hierarchy', Ariel's (1990) 'accessibility scale', and Gundel, Hedberg, and Zacharski's (1993) 'givenness hierarchy' are all attempts to show a correlation between different degrees of linguistic explicitness and different degrees of cognitive 'givenness'. Gundel, Hedberg, and Zacharski (1993: 275), for example, give the following scale (as summarized in Chafe 1994: 179):

Type identifiable	*a* + Noun
Referential	indefinite *this* + Noun
Uniquely identifiable	*the* + Noun
Familiar	*that* + Noun
Activated	*that, this, this* + Noun
In focus	*it*

Here, the least explicit form 'it' is linked with the information which is at the forefront of consciousness, whilst increasingly more explicit forms are used to denote less available information. Some writers suggest that an analysis with a large number of categories of 'givenness' is more 'rigorous'[33] than an analysis with only 'given/new' or 'given/accessible/new'. Unfortunately, this ignores the fact that Chafe's work has a number of other distinctions in addition to givenness, such as 'identifiability' and 'contrastiveness', yielding a more sophisticated analysis which is better able to describe real data. Indeed, Chafe himself comments that Gundel, Hedberg, and Zacharski, and Ariel ' . . . have forced into a single dimension several aspects of discourse that it would be more profitable to keep apart' (1994: 179). For Chafe, 'givenness' options reflect the speaker's assumptions about the 'flow' of information through the listener's mind during a specific discourse, 'identifiability' relates to mutual knowledge of a referent and 'contrastiveness' places special emphasis on one referent rather than another. It is 'givenness' therefore that is linked with consciousness, but identifiability and contrastiveness also have a competing influence on the linguistic form used.

Chafe (1994: 105) distinguishes between 'givenness' and 'identifiability' with the example 'I talked to Larry last night'. Here, we can assume that Larry is a person who is known to both the

---

[33] Gordon, Grosz, and Gillion (1993: 342).

speaker and the listener prior to the conversation, otherwise an expression such as 'my lawyer' or 'a friend called Larry' would have been used. Hence Larry is 'identifiable'. Since this is, however, the first time that Larry has been mentioned in the conversation, he is being 'activated' in the discussion for the first time and is therefore also a 'new entity'. There is, therefore, a link between form and function, but two distinct factors are competing to create the form at this particular point in the discourse.

In the above example, the linguistic form 'settles' at a 'middle' level of linguistic explicitness, not using the inexplicit form 'he' and not using a highly explicit form such as 'a friend called Larry'. Sometimes, however, two quite different signals are given within the linguistic form. One of Chafe's major contributions has been to distinguish between 'givenness' and 'contrastiveness'. In one example that Chafe gives (1994: 77), a speaker puts primary intonation stress on the word 'I'. As a participant in the conversation, the speaker is 'given', as reflected by the choice of a pronoun. The stress, however, reflects contrastiveness, since the speaker is differentiating himself from other speakers who might have answered the question.

Chafe's work shows that there are competing factors which make it impossible to link one particular form with one particular function (in English, at least), although a statistical analysis can indicate a tendency in the language. In fact, when Chafe uses statistics himself, he is careful only to try to establish very broad form–function links, such as the likelihood that a subject will express either 'given' or 'accessible' information. Whilst it might be possible to show statistically that pronouns are generally used for items in focus, a raw statistic will miss all the complexity of usage. In an earlier study (Emmott 1985), for example, I showed that over long stretches of text, references to a character in focus might sometimes be lexical if there is a need for a stylistic variant or if a literary theme is being conveyed.[34] In such cases, the

---

[34] This study was of a literary text in which there is only one major female character who is in focus for most of the narrative. Despite the lack of ambiguity of the pronoun form, there is re-lexicalization at frequent intervals. This is, arguably, a device to introduce stylistic variants, since continued use of the same form would become tedious. In addition, there are certain points at which re-lexicalizations cluster. These points appear to correlate with moments at which a literary theme is being conveyed or there is a key development in the plot. See Emmott (1985, 1995*b*, and forthcoming *d*) for further details.

inexplicit form is being overridden, even though it would be interpretable by the reader. Conversely, as Example 1.1 showed, a pronoun can be used when a context is reinstated, even though a
character has not been mentioned for some time (and is presumably not, therefore, at the forefront of consciousness).

In addition to looking at the 'given–new' structure of sentences
and the use of explicit or inexplicit forms, Chafe and his collaborators hypothesize that the length of intonation units and the
pauses between them reflect how the mind focuses on small
chunks of information at any one time[35] (Chafe 1980a, 1994:
53–70). Moreover, the cognitive effort of articulating new ideas
can be measured by comparing pause times, with a major cognitive reorientation—such as a change of scene or topic—normally
being accompanied by a longer pause. In this way, Chafe is using
the text as a key to what is going on in the mind, talking about
mental effort and occasionally hinting at accompanying imagery.

The research described in this book is in line with Chafe's seminal work on consciousness, but there are differences in the type of
data studied and the methodology. Chafe mainly examines oral
production rather than the comprehension of written text.
Although he is studying the discourse rather than the reader, the
pauses he observes provide evidence of the cognitive work being
undertaken, just as psychologists (in controlled experiments)
hypothesize about inference-making by timing how long subjects
take to read sentence pairs (e.g. Sanford and Garrod 1981). My
own work models comprehension of written texts by looking at
the complexity of the text and the linguistic clues available,
rather than studying particular readers in action (although this
is a possible extension of the work described here).[36] This is com-
parable to Chafe's assumption that the information structure of a
sentence and the linguistic form of references reflects what is
active in the consciousness of the speaker and listener. The language is not direct proof of mental processes, but it can be assumed
to give some indication of what is going on in the mind.

[35] Although concentrating on focal information, Chafe and his collaborators do
also look at background information held in peripheral consciousness. Clancy
(one of the contributors to Chafe 1980a) has suggested that, at any one time, the
speaker is not only concentrating on articulating the current intonation unit but
also planning the next one and monitoring the prior one (either consciously or
unconsciously) (Clancy, personal communication).
[36] See Ch. 3 for further discussion of my methodology.

There is also a difference in emphasis between my own work and Chafe's. His exploration of 'intonation units' (which often correlate with clauses) means that his main emphasis is on the focus of consciousness, although he does make clear that consciousness has a periphery too (1980*b*: 12, 40). In this book I am more concerned with hypothesizing about information that is in the 'background' of awareness (see Chapters 4 to 6), although I do also discuss focal consciousness briefly (Chapter 7) to provide a more complete picture. In narrative text, the fictional context does not surround the reader (or listener) as in the case of a real-life context: it has to be constructed by making text-specific assumptions about the continued presence of the participants and about the place and time of the action. This 'background' information may not be referred to in every sentence. My own approach does not, therefore, involve just looking at explicit or inexplicit linguistic forms, since I am also interested in cases where there is no linguistic expression of information at all for long stretches of text. This 'background' information can, nevertheless, be assumed to be held 'in mind' both because the text would make no sense without it and because at intervals the text will demand this information for the interpretation of a linguistic item such as a pronoun. My emphasis is on how a reader can interpret an inexplicit form, hypothesizing about the inference process and about how information about a context is made available to do this. This approach gives emphasis to the different levels of processing and highlights the extent to which information is held in peripheral awareness over long periods, showing how the human mind compensates for the short focal attention span that Chafe has demonstrated.

4. SUBJECTIVE READINGS: MEMORY LIMITS AND PERSONAL EXPERIENCE

There is a great deal of evidence to show that different individuals read and remember texts differently. The nature and quantity of information retained will vary according to memory capacity and interest. Readers are also likely to 'filter' the text through their own personal experience, 'reconstructing' both as they read and as they try subsequently to recollect the material. This section examines some of the psychological evidence for these differences and gives a survey of the theoretical debate within literary

theory. Although my own work does not explore individual readings (since I am examining texts rather than particular readings
of texts), the topics discussed in this section are of importance to
an overall understanding of how the human mind processes text.

(a) Memory Limits

Very few people have a perfect memory for what they have read
and the amount that is remembered will vary from person to
person.[37] Although commonly viewed as a problem, forgetting[38]
is in fact a key characteristic of how the human mind operates for
it enables us to distinguish between important and unimportant
information (Smyth *et al.* 1987: 237).

The problems of having 'perfect' recall are recorded by Luria
(1987) in his study of a mnemonist, an individual who became a
professional 'memory man'. Luria's testing of the mnemonist
revealed that 'it was impossible to establish a point of limit to the
capacity or the duration of his memory' (p. 61). Although there
were advantages to having such a memory, the mnemonist had
difficulty creating schemata, since in order to formulate generalizations it is necessary to forget many of the precise details of specific instances.[39] The mnemonist's reading skills were also affected
by his memory. The mnemonist had a particular interest in textual
detail, often spotting contradictions in the text. On one occasion,
for example, the mnemonist noticed that one of Chekov's characters (in 'The Malefactor') had appeared in a *'shinel'* (Russian:
'greatcoat') and then subsequently taken off a different type of
coat, a *'pal'to'* (Russian: 'overcoat') (p. 97). In general, however,
the mnemonist found reading problematic. The vivid way in
which he visualized imaginary scenes (which appeared to be
linked to his vivid memory of past events) meant that he would

[37] See, for example, summaries of the psychological research in Garnham (1985:
134–82); Smyth *et al.* (1987: 207–37); and Eysenck and Keane (1990: 15–169).

[38] Some psychologists, as Eysenck and Keane (1990) point out, argue that no
information is totally lost, since even long forgotten facts can be retrieved by hyp-
nosis or neurological stimulation with electricity (although see Eysenck and Keane's counter-arguments, pp. 157–8). The terms 'forgetting' and 'memory loss' are
used in the current study in their everyday senses to refer to information which is
not readily accessible to the conscious brain.

[39] This may not, however, apply to incidents which break schema expectations.
As discussed earlier, Schank (1982) has suggested that in such cases there is an
'episodic memory' of an incident.

often become side-tracked. The following extract is the mnemonist's own account of one such problem:

> ... I was read this phrase: 'N. was leaning up against a tree ...' I saw a slim young man dressed in a dark blue suit (N., you know, is so elegant). He was standing near a big linden tree with grass and woods all around . . . But then the sentence went on: 'and was peering into a shop window.' Now how do you like that! It means the scene isn't set in the woods, or in a garden, but he's standing on the street. And I have to start the whole sentence over from the beginning ...
>
> (Luria 1987: 112–13; Luria's omission marks)

Luria's study concentrates on how the mnemonist suffered from not being able to forget information which was not important or no longer important. It seems, though, that the mnemonist also had the problem of not being able to treat memories as being more or less active depending on the circumstances. A reader does not want to forget everything that has been previously read but must be able to set these previous reading experiences to one side as each new text is encountered. The mnemonist was unable to do this and often brought scenes and characters from other books (and from real life) into play as he was reading (Luria 1987: 114).

Even amongst 'normal' readers, there may be individuals who pay more attention to detail than others, as illustrated by Johnson-Laird's informal tests of students who had read a Sherlock Holmes story (discussed earlier). Although most students forgot (or did not register) spatial details, one student in a hundred could draw a detailed plan of the building mentioned in the story. In evaluating these results, it is easy simply to assume that the person who can draw the map of the house is the best reader and has the best memory. This is not necessarily a valid assumption, since this person's all-round memory for detail may not be so impressive. We know from everyday life that, whilst some people have a good memory for directions and place names, others have a much better memory for other things such as names, and faces, or details of conversations (e.g. Herrmann and Neisser 1978; Martin 1978). More importantly, having a good all-round memory does not mean that an individual understands a story any better or enjoys it more. Luria's study of the mnemonist shows that good recall is not necessarily synonymous with good comprehension. If good comprehension of narrative means the reader's understanding of the main events and themes of a book plus an appreciation of the text, comprehension is not easy to explain or, in an educational setting, to teach and test.

Nevertheless, although a degree of forgetting is normal and useful, some individuals obviously suffer from undue memory loss and their reading (and production of language) may be affected accordingly. There are plenty of case studies in the psychology literature of individuals who have so much damage to their brains that they cannot hold information from one minute to the next. Clearly there will be problems for these people in integrating information from different parts of a text into mental representations (see Luria's (1975) study of *The Man with a Shattered World* and Sacks's 'The Lost Mariner' (O. Sacks 1985)). These studies consider general linguistic ability but rarely look in detail at interpretation/production of specific items such as pronouns. Within linguistics, however, Rochester and Martin (1979) provide an account of how schizophrenics use pronouns without providing any antecedents (as if they expect the listener to know, without adequate clues, who they are thinking of). Also, Knuf (1994) has given an interesting example in which an elderly Alzheimer's patient tells of an incident from her childhood involving an encounter with one of her teachers. Although she describes a specific person on a specific occasion, the gender of the teacher fluctuates from female to male, as if the patient is unable to maintain a coherent mental representation of the person for any length of time.

(b) Personal Experience

Readers not only forget details from the original text, they also add inferences from general knowledge (as described in Section 1a) and 'filter' the text through their own personal viewpoint.

When reading stories, additions to a text may also result from a desire to create in the mind an image of a scene or person. If, for example, a text describes a fictional character as beautiful, readers may superimpose their own notion of beauty onto the text, regardless of whether detailed information about the character's appearance is given. The images readers create of fictional people, scenes, and events may often depend partly on their previous experiences of similar people, scenes, and events from real life and fiction. Obviously these experiences will differ from reader to reader.

There is ample evidence to show that readers not only add their own images as they read, but may more radically reconstruct a text in memory. This is demonstrated by Holland (1975) in his psychoanalytic study 5 *Readers Reading,* in which he asked five different readers to reproduce a story that they had read. He noted transformations of the original text, which varied from reader to reader, such as changes to the positions of characters (e.g. sitting, standing, sprawling), their positions in relation to each other (e.g. in front, behind, above, below) and the colour of their clothes (e.g. a white dress changing to a black one). Whether or not we accept Holland's attempts to correlate these reconstructions with the personalities of the readers, there is little doubt that different readings do occur.

People read differently because of their own idiosyncratic experiences, but they also read differently because of factors such as cultural background, the era they are born, education, social class, age, etc. Reconstructions are particularly likely when a reader is presented with a text from another culture[40] and is puzzled by unfamiliar entities and events which make little sense because the reader lacks the appropriate general knowledge. Bartlett (1932: 63–94) describes English-speaking subjects who, having read in translation a North American Indian folk-tale *The War of the Ghosts,* attempted on recall to rationalize anything which could not be explained by their own cultural assumptions. In particular, the mention of 'something black' (p. 65) coming out of the mouth of a dead Indian was sometimes viewed as the soul by readers from a Christian background, even though there was no suggestion of this in the original text. De Beaugrande (1980: 220–41) found similar 'reconstructions' occurred when subjects were presented with disorganized or misleading text.

Another major difference in individual comprehension of text

---

[40] Many researchers have shown that the interpretation and production of a text can also vary across cultures (e.g. Tannen 1980; Polanyi 1985a; Berman and Slobin 1994). Luria (1979), for example, shows that syllogistic reasoning is affected by cultural assumptions.

will result from whether the reader is an adult or a child (P. L. Harris 1978; A. L. Brown and Campione 1978; Appleyard 1991). Children not only have less experience of the world to bring to texts than adults, they may also have difficulty in deciding how to apply their general knowledge when reading. Yuill and Oakhill (1991: 93), for example, found that certain less-skilled 7-year-old readers who were asked about when an event in a story took place, selected the day of the interview, the real-world time, rather than the day mentioned clearly in the text. Children will also often have less experience of the conventions of written discourse (e.g. Tucker 1981). In addition to age, comprehension may also be affected by factors such as mood (Alexander and Guenther 1986), time of day (Oakhill 1986; Petros, Beckworth, and Anderson 1990), and the reader's perspective (R. C. Anderson and Pichert 1978; Lee-Sammons and Whitney 1991).

Much of the detailed study of differences in interpretation has been conducted by psychologists, but literary theorists have also played their part in emphasizing the importance of these diverse readings, as discussed in the following section. Artificial intelligence researchers have not studied this topic in any detail, but some of their work does acknowledge that it is a factor. As mentioned earlier in this chapter, Schank (1982) acknowledges in his study of 'reminding' that our general knowledge scripts may contain a certain amount of information about specific 'episodic' experiences, particularly where these do not match normal expectations. Although Schank's interest is primarily in how we recognize the underlying similarities between two different stories or real-life incidents, his work also highlights the storehouse of individual experiences which each of us maintains and which presumably must have some effect on reading text.

(c) Reader Response: A Literary Theory Perspective

In recent years, one of the major contributions of literary theory has been to draw attention to the importance of the reader of a text. Literary theorists have argued this in Reception Theory and Reader Response Theory.[41] More specifically, some studies have

---

[41] For example, Iser (1978); Eco (1979); Suleiman and Crosman (1980); Tompkins (1980); Holub (1984); and Freund (1987). See Eagleton (1983: ch. 2); Maclean (1986); and Selden (1989: ch. 5) for useful introductions.

looked for reasons for differences and have provided examples of individual readings of the same text. Psychoanalytic criticism is of particular relevance in this respect.[42] Based on Freud's theories, psychoanalytic criticism assumes that as we read 'We recast the work to discover our own characteristic strategies for coping with the deep fears and wishes that shape our psychic lives' (Selden 1989: 129). Holland's work, discussed above, provides a typical example.

Although literary theory's emphasis on the reader is in line with the psychology work described in this section, it should be remembered that literary theory has its own agenda. The subject has been dominated earlier this century by the notion that the meaning of a text resides either with the author (e.g. Leavis 1962) or in the text itself (e.g. Russian formalism, structuralism). The emphasis on the reader is in part a reaction against these positions, so in some works there may be a tendency to downplay other factors such as the contribution of the text. An interest in the structure of a text and in the role of the reader, however, should not necessarily be viewed as mutually exclusive options.

Literary theory also seems to be generally more concerned with interpretation after the event rather than the details of on-line processing. In psychology, too, this is sometimes the case, as experiments can focus on a subject's memory for a text already read (e.g. Bartlett 1932). However, much modern experimental work examines the inferences made whilst comprehending specific sentences (e.g. Sanford and Garrod 1981). Most literary critics and theorists are unlikely to be unduly interested in the mechanics of basic inference-making, although Eagleton (1983: 74–7) does acknowledge the importance of such inferences. Eagleton examines two opening sentences of a novel picked at random and considers the assumptions a reader might make about how many characters are present, how they are related to each other, and who is speaking to whom (pp. 74–5). He comments (as cited at the beginning of Chapter 1):

... although we rarely notice it, we are all the time engaged in constructing hypotheses about the meaning of the text. The reader makes implicit connections, fills in gaps, draws inferences and tests out hunches; and to

---

[42] For example, Holland (1975); Bleich (1978); see also summaries in Eagleton (1983: ch. 5) and Wright (1986).

do this means drawing on a tacit knowledge of the world in general and of literary conventions in particular. The text itself is really no more than a series of 'cues' to the reader, invitations to construct a piece of language into meaning. (1983: 76)

These particular sentences sound almost as if they could have been written by an artificial intelligence researcher, but it is not literary theory's aim to investigate knowledge representation and inference-making in any detail. Moreover, for most literary theorists, the word 'meaning' often has connotations of 'value', for literary researchers are interested in what makes a literary text a work of art.

Literary theorists are particularly interested in the role of the literary critic. There is the realization (and, in some cases, the fear) that if any reading of a text becomes just as valid as any other, then the literary critic and the classroom teacher of literature may no longer have any role at all (Fish 1980). This debate over the skilled literary reader is not a question which has so far been pursued to any great extent in psychology and artificial intelligence.

Literary theory has made some important contributions to the philosophy of reading, particularly in assessing the relationship between the author, the reader, and the text, in examining the various types of readers, and in its practical demonstrations of how interpretations differ. Nevertheless, the division of the subject into categories such as structuralism, reader response, etc. does sometimes seem to encourage theorists to place themselves in particular camps, either 'for' or 'against' the text. Yet although the theoretical position of structuralism (the notion that meaning resides solely in the text) has been effectively challenged, many of the practical observations about the structure of texts are still very useful.

Although reader response and reception work vary in the role they attribute to the reader, their arguments have sometimes resulted in an over-emphasis on subjective interpretation. In extreme cases this can lead to the text dropping out of the equation completely, leading to a chaos of interpretations. More generally, the text is seen as a framework around which different types of readers can build their own edifice. Often the resulting meaning is described in terms of particular social or psychological theories such as Marxism, feminism, and psychoanalysis. Although such influences are no doubt important, the tendency to view readers along these lines can both under- and overestimate differences between readers. The general knowledge representations described earlier in this chapter suggest some unity, at least within a particular culture. There is, therefore, likely to be some reasonable consensus about everyday objects such as chairs, the relationship between objects such as cars and wheels, the anticipated sequence of events in a restaurant which has waiters, and basic facts about the world such as a person not appearing in two places at one time. This type of general knowledge is usually taken for granted regardless of the social orientation of the readers or the childhood traumas they have undergone. Artificial intelligence research has shown that a fair amount of inference-making uses these sorts of assumptions. Nevertheless, in certain respects, reading is also very ad hoc, a fact which may also be obscured by grouping readers by class, sex, etc. As discussed earlier in this chapter, our personal experiences may lead us to have particular associations, which may also lead to the formation of highly specific images as we read, and this type of experience might only adequately be explained by a catalogue of all the chance encounters that we have had with objects and scenarios during our lifetime. Schank's discussion of 'reminding' emphasizes this store of idiosyncratic memories which are harnessed in conversational story swapping.

Summary

This chapter has provided an overview of text-processing work, summarizing the main topic areas in the subject as a whole and highlighting key issues which will be returned to and elaborated on in subsequent chapters.

The chapter began by outlining the different types of knowledge needed to read texts, indicating that general knowledge and text schemata have received most attention from researchers. Rather less attention has been directed towards the need to model how information from specific texts is stored and utilized, such as details about the characters, locations, contexts, and events, as well as some awareness of the style that a text is written in. The need to take account of text-specific information becomes evident once naturally occurring texts are considered rather than decontextualized sentence pairs that have been made up by the researcher. The properties of 'real' discourse will be discussed further in Chapter 3.

There has been particular dispute about the nature of mental representations. Propositional models have been criticized because they view each proposition as being interpreted in isolation rather than taking meaning from the reader's knowledge of the situation. Mental models, by contrast, provide information about the situation, having produced an image-like 'map' in memory. The research on mental models provides a useful base on which to hypothesize about text-specific representations, but needs to be supplemented by a study of the properties of real texts, as discussed in Chapter 3. Another debate, which is beyond resolution until neurological research has progressed further, is whether information is held in particular areas of the brain or is distributed in networks.

Computers can collect information together in representations, but humans have processing characteristics which are not yet found in machines. An explanation of consciousness is the most obvious stumbling block at present to the development of truly intelligent computers. Artificial intelligence researchers have used computers both as a metaphor for how the mind works and as a practical means of testing processing theories. This emphasis on the computer may have led these researchers to underestimate the role of human consciousness in reading. Chafe's work within linguistics has emphasized the importance of consciousness in language production. My own research hypothesizes that an ongoing awareness of certain text-specific information is essential for the processing of a story. This is a major theme of this book, particularly in Chapters 4 and 7.

Psychologically realistic models of text processing cannot ignore the fact that information decays in memory or that people read differently as a result of their prior experiences. Although not all of these aspects of human intelligence can so far be replicated on machines, it is still worth considering that some of these characteristics may play an essential role in reading (such as providing the motive for reading a book in the first place), rather than simply being epiphenomenal extras. Although my own work does not investigate individual differences (since I do not study individual readers), I acknowledge that such differences are important. This book studies the demands which texts place on their readers: when a text is actually read, individuals will attempt to meet these demands in many different ways.

3

A Discourse Perspective: Understanding Full, Real Texts

We are interested in the strategies people use when they read a text—a book chapter for an exam, or a story for their entertainment . . . [In the laboratory] the usual redundancies on which these strategies rely have been removed from the text. Hence, the subject falls back on general problem-solving strategies and devises on the spot some procedure that works. The trouble is that this procedure may be entirely task specific and of no general interest as far as normal discourse processing is concerned . . . We might be left with quite the wrong conclusions from such experiments (and give quite the wrong advice to educators, textbook writers, etc.). . . . Studying sentences in isolation may tell us something, but it is also possible that it will mislead us.

(van Dijk and Kintsch 1983: 32)

The unnaturalness of the data on which so much of psychology and linguistics relies can be highly disturbing to anyone who is sensitive to what language is really like. To find examples one need only attend any psychology, linguistics, or computer science conference or open any journal from these fields. . . . It is as if one tried to study birds by building airplanes that were rather like birds in certain ways, and then studied the airplanes, just because they were easier to control than the birds themselves. I suspect that ornithologists have come to understand birds more successfully by examining them as they really are. There is much to be gained from examining language as it really is too.

(Chafe 1994: 16–17)

One of the major arguments of this book is that research on text comprehension must take account of full, real texts, since these are fundamentally different from the artificially constructed sentence pairs and 'text' fragments that are often used in work on inference-making. This chapter opens with a discussion of the properties of naturally occurring discourse in Section 1, focusing particularly on the hierarchical organization of texts and arguing that cognitive models must take account of this high-level structure. I then look, by way of contrast, at some of the 'texts' typically used by experimental psychologists, explaining why such materials are used and pointing out how these materials differ from natural discourse. Section 2 then explains how text analysis can play a role in cognitive research, arguing that such research can reveal the complexity of the processing task and can contribute to the formation of hypotheses about how processing is performed. This approach is then utilized in the discussion of fictional context in Chapter 4 and in the rest of the book.

1. THE PROPERTIES OF REAL TEXT

(a) Overview

The properties of naturally occurring discourse have already been discussed briefly in Chapters 1 and 2. This section looks in more detail at some of the points so far introduced and broadens the discussion to examine other properties. The main purpose of this discussion is to show how real discourse differs from the short made-up 'texts' illustrated in Chapter 2, looking particularly at the following features:

- Real text often has a hierarchical structure. A reader needs to be able to recognize this structure in order to be able to 'orientate' him/herself, but also to interpret certain linguistic items at sentence level, such as pronouns.
- In real text, the meaning of an individual sentence is derived partly from the surrounding sentences, the textual context.
- Real text requires the reader to be able to draw on stored information from the preceding text (and general knowledge).
- Stored information from the preceding text may also be used to assist interpretation by narrowing down the possibilities, such as when a reference item could in theory denote several referents.
- Real text has 'connectivity'. Sentences are organized so that they flow on from each other and this connection is often signalled linguistically.

Of course, if we look at genres such as conversation, there are
other key properties such as knowledge of the immediate real-
world context, the mutual knowledge of the participants, and
their social relationship. The above list is simply a list of properties
that are particularly important for the type of text studied here,
narrative text, as well as being common to other text types as
well. A comprehensive model of text processing needs to take
account of these features of real discourse. This is not just a
matter of looking at discourse-level features once a model has
been provided at sentence-level, for discourse factors must be
taken into account to interpret sentences in the first place
(Emmott 1996).

(b) Hierarchy

One of the major aims of discourse study (by discourse analysts
and those in related fields such as artificial intelligence) has been
to recognize units of structure and meaning above the level of the
sentence. Previously, only sentences were seen as having structure, and texts, if studied at all, were regarded simply as a conjoin-
ing of sentences. Discourse study, however, has shown that
larger structural units do exist, with texts consisting of a series of
groups of sentences, with each group cohering together as a unit
and having its own internal structure. The discussion in Chapter
2 of clause relational analysis and Rhetorical Structure Theory
provided some examples of research which sees text as being segmented in this way. A section of a text may, for example, be devoted
to explaining a problem, whereas another section may have the
function of offering a solution (Winter 1982; Hoey 1979, 1983;
Jordan 1984). Elsewhere, one section may have a function such
as generalization and be followed by a section which give exemplification of this generalization (e.g. Winter 1982; Hoey 1983;
Mann and Thompson 1988). Within any particular discourse segment, certain sentences may be of more central importance than
others and there may be a typical ordering of components (see
Mann and Thompson's (1988) discussion of nuclei and satellites).
The ordering of the segments themselves is also important and if
the order is untypical, it is generally signalled (Hoey 1979,
1983). Segments often have characteristic lexical keywords and
syntactic linkers such as conjuncts (Jordan 1984; Hoey 1979,

1983, 1991). This type of analysis has been applied mainly to non-narrative texts such as discursive writing, letters, advertisements, etc.

Some of the most interesting examples of text segmentation involve the embedding of one discourse segment (often of 'lesser' importance) into another, to create a hierarchical structure. Examples of hierarchy can be found throughout the discourse literature, including in the above-mentioned works (e.g. Hoey 1979, 1983, 1991; Mann and Thompson 1987, 1988; Mann, Matthiessen, and Thompson 1992). Embedding is interesting because it allows us to observe not only a shift to another segment, but also a subsequent resumption of the first segment. Often this resumption is marked linguistically and this provides evidence that the speaker/writer recognizes the structure and the processing needs of the listener.

One seminal view of hierarchical structure in discourse is that of conversation analysts such as H. Sacks, Schegloff, and Jefferson.[1] Although these researchers use the term 'adjacency pair' (e.g. H. Sacks 1992*b*: 32–43, 521–69; Schegloff and Sacks 1973; H. Sacks, Schegloff, and Jefferson 1974: 716) for utterances which belong together, there can be embedding of other utterances between the adjacency items. Embedding may be signalled by 'misplacement markers' such as 'by the way' or 'oh!' (Schegloff and Sacks 1973: 310; Schegloff 1978: 88–9), if there is an unexpected change of topic. An example of embedding is the insertion sequence (Schegloff 1972) which often elaborates on the current topic, such as the request for more information in the following extract from Merritt (1976: 333):

[A:] May I have a bottle of Mich?
[B:] Are you twenty-one?
[A:] No
[B:] No

---

[1] The conversation analysts have looked at narratives, particularly oral narratives, but the main emphasis here is usually on how a story is embedded within a conversation (i.e. the connection of the story to the preceding talk; interaction between the storyteller and listener during storytelling; and the return to turn-by-turn talk after the story) (e.g. H. Sacks 1992*a*: 236–66, 1992*b*: 3–31, 222–303, 453–89; Jefferson 1978; Goodwin 1984; H. Sacks 1989; Schegloff 1992; Polanyi 1985*a, b*) rather than on how it is internally segmented.

Here, the middle two utterances form an adjacency pair embedded within the main question–answer pair, formed from the first and last utterances. In this particular example, there are no overt indicators of embedding. The embedding seems instead to be signalled by the fact that a question is answered by another question rather than by the second part of the adjacency pair. General knowledge of the need to be a particular age in order to buy alcohol shows how the insertion relates to the main question and accounts for the embedding at this point. Sometimes, as Sperber and Wilson (1986: 140) point out, a lack of 'relevance' to the current 'context' can force us to assume that a new 'context' (in the sense of topic or sub-topic) has been introduced. This is particularly the case with side sequences (Jefferson 1972) which consist of embedded utterances on a quite unconnected topic. An interruption of this type depends on the circumstances at the moment of speaking. In the case of '. . . a mildly relevant but pressing question, or . . . some moderately interesting incident in the landscape' (Sperber and Wilson 1986: 160), a side sequence may be worthy of the attention of the participants because of the short-term nature of the stimulus (p. 160), but will generally be followed by a resumption of the previous conversation.

Conversation analysis provides many other examples of such discourse units and similar patterns have been found in interaction in professional settings such as teaching, medicine, and law (e.g. Sinclair and Coulthard 1975; Coulthard 1985; Atkinson and Drew 1979). There has been a lot of work by artificial intelligence researchers on spoken discourse. Grosz (1977), for example, examines how instructional dialogue is subdivided into segments which correlate with the sub-tasks being performed. Grosz looks particularly at how the main task in the hierarchy can be returned to with minimal linguistic signalling. This artificial intelligence work (and other similar research by Linde 1979; Reichman 1985; Fox 1987*a*, *b*) is particularly relevant to the topic of context shift, which is examined in Chapter 5 and so discussed further at that point.

Like written non-narrative and conversation, narrative text is also segmented into different units. The locus of narrative action may shift from one place to another, as well as encompassing temporal shifts (i.e. flashbacks and flashforwards). In narrative text, there are also shifts between the action itself and passages giving background detail. Often units of the narrative may interrupt each other, resuming at later points in the text. The hierarchical structure of narrative will be examined in detail in Chapters 5, 7, and 8. The main point being made in this section is simply that hierarchy is an important feature of naturally occurring texts which is often completely missing in the materials used in experimental psychology. This can lead researchers to underestimate the importance of the reader recognizing discourse units, drawing on the background information provided by a particular unit and being able to switch from one unit to another. A study of naturally occurring discourse can indicate the complexity of the task, particularly with regard to the linguistic signalling which needs to be interpreted.

(c) Textual Context

In addition to hierarchical organization, another property of real discourse is that the meaning of an individual sentence or clause is often influenced by the surrounding text. To a certain extent, this can be demonstrated even by made-up sentences. Toolan (1988: 148–9), drawing on Labov and Waletzky (1967), provides the following example (see also Hoey (1979, 1983) for a similar discussion of the ordering of narrative clauses):

> John fell in the river,
> got very cold,
> and had two large whiskies.   (p. 148)

As Toolan points out, if these clauses are rearranged, the 'story' changes radically:

> John had two large whiskies,
> fell in the river,
> and got very cold.   (p. 149)

Although the individual clauses are still the same, the meaning of two of them has changed as their textual context has changed (assuming that the reader has drawn some fairly standard inferences about alcohol). In the first 'story', if the whiskies are to be 'relevant' (in Grice's (1975, 1978) sense of the term), it seems that they are being drunk as a reaction to the accident. We do not know whether this is to alleviate any physical pain, to warm John up, or to calm his nerves, but readers can make their own more specific inferences. By contrast, the 'whiskies' clause in the second example has none of these connotations. The 'falling in the river' clause can also be viewed from different perspectives depending on the context. In the second example, it is possible to infer that John was perhaps slightly drunk, that he lost his balance, and that this caused him to fall. The text encourages us to make this inference because, if we assume a 'cause–consequence' relation (see Hoey 1979, 1983), each clause is 'relevant' and the text has maximal coherence. Conversely, in the first example we have no idea why John has fallen and there is nothing to suggest whether he was drunk or sober prior to his fall.

To read the different versions of each story, readers need to create distinct mental representations of John at specific stages in the story. In the first example he is probably not drunk when he falls, whereas in the second he probably is. Likewise, in the first example, his drinking occurs when he is suffering the after effects of his fall (whatever the individual reader infers these to be), whereas in the second example there is no suggestion of this sort. If readers employ mental imagery for such short examples, then we might hypothesize that the images would be rather different in each case, reflecting the different mental representations created (though obviously this would need to be tested empirically by psychologists).

Whilst these 'context effects' can be observed, the difference from real text is that whilst the second and third clauses have some minimal context, the first one does not. Obviously this is also generally true of the first sentence of a novel, but the norm in real text is for there to be preceding context. This lack of context means that for the first clause we may be reading quite differently than if we were immersed in a real story, since we are starting with a void of explanatory information. In the second example, we have no idea whether John is drinking at home or in a bar and whether he is with friends or on his own. His drinking is abstract rather than contextualized and it is possible that this might lead to a different type of reading than for real text.

Moreover, it is only by looking at real discourse that we can understand the different ways in which a sentence may change in context and the different types of context that influence it. In a number of examples that I have examined, some of which will be discussed in Chapter 8, there are no syntactic indicators to show whether an action occurs once or habitually, or to show whether a description is true always or just on a particular occasion. The clues that are available to help us decide may vary greatly. A sentence such as 'She talked in a high-pitched voice' (see Example 8.18 for a real text example) may mean that this person always talks like this or that on a particular occasion her voice has become high-pitched for a particular reason, such as fear (i.e. a 'cause–consequence relation' in Hoey's (1979, 1983) terms). The reader's decision may be influenced by whether the sentence occurs during the 'setting' part of the story or the 'climax', since the reader can utilize knowledge of the convention that 'permanent' descriptive features are more likely to be given at the start of a narrative. A parallel example is a sentence such as 'She painted' (see Example 8.17 for a real text example), which could be habitual, as she is a painter, or could describe a single event. Often, the meaning of a verb seems to be influenced by the types of verbs occurring in preceding sentences—so if the preceding text has been habitual, there is more likelihood that a sentence like 'She painted' is habitual (see Chapter 8). These contextual clues to the meaning of a sentence are of several types—knowledge of overall 'story schemata', knowledge of cause–consequence relations, awareness of previous verb types—and they seem to work together in complex ways. Unless we have some such knowledge of how a sentence is tied to its context, we cannot begin to offer explanations of the amount of work involved in reading a text.

(d) Mental Representations: Adding Meaning

Although it is necessary to postulate mental representations even for short made-up 'texts', such as Toolan's 'whiskies' examples above, the longer the text is, the greater the likelihood that complex mental representations are formed. Entity representations, for example, are likely to be formed which contain information about the central characters, which enable us to view them as personalities and empathize with them. In particular, the death of a character can have an impact on us, even though that character does not exist (see discussion in Schank 1984: 22–58).

It would, moreover, be difficult on occasions to understand the text at all if we did not have these mental stores of information to draw on. The past history of the characters and their personalities may explain behaviour that would otherwise be puzzling to the reader, as illustrated by the example below. This approach is rather different from the research which looks at the plans and actions of individuals in stereotyped situations which they respond to in predictable ways.

EXAMPLE 3.1

At the top end of the room, where a small bar had been set up, Don saw Lewis Benedikt, wearing a khaki jacket and carrying a bottle of beer. He was talking to a gray-suited old man with sunken cheeks and bright, tragic eyes who must have been Dr John Jaffrey.

'Your son must be here,' Don guessed.

'Shelby? Indeed he is ... We're all here for the entertainment, which promises to be very exciting.'

'And you were waiting for me.'

'Well, Donald, without you none of this could have been arranged.'

'I'm getting out of here.'

(Peter Straub, *Ghost Story* (1979), 399)

Out of context of the rest of the novel, Don's final utterance seems rather rude. In context, it is quite appropriate and the whole passage has a sinister feel to it, for a reader who has built entity representations will know that everyone here except Don is dead. A knowledge of previous events will also tell the reader that these particular ghosts are dangerous.

Even in ordinary situations mental representations can help to explain the behaviour of the characters, as shown below:

EXAMPLE 3.2

Carrying two large shopping bags, he emerged from Treasure Island and turned in the direction that was downtown. Diesel fumes drifted toward him, cars with *Keep the Southland Great* bumper stickers rolled by. Men in short-sleeved shirts and short gray crewcuts moved along the sidewalks. When he saw a uniformed cop trying to eat an ice-cream cone while writing out a parking ticket, he dodged between a pickup truck and a

Trailways van and crossed the street. A rivulet of sweat issued from his left eyebrow and ran into his eye ...

(Peter Straub, *Ghost Story* (1979), 24; Straub's italics)

It can probably be inferred from general knowledge that Don is dodging behind the pick-up truck and sweating because he has committed an offence. The reader of the novel, however, has more precise information to hand than this, knowing that Don has kidnapped a young girl. Indeed, once the policeman is mentioned, the reader may even anticipate Don's reaction.

Although obvious, these observations are important because they suggest that the mind must have the capacity to hold salient textually presented information and be able to draw on it to interpret later text. This emphasizes the importance of meaning beyond sentence level, which has not always been viewed as important in linguistics. Studying the information needed to explain the text in this way also gives some idea of the minimum amount of detail that needs to be mentally stored if the text is to be understood.

(e) *Mental Representations: Reducing Possibilities*

In addition to adding meaning, stored information from the preceding text may also be used to assist interpretation by narrowing down the possible interpretations. Entity representations can, for example, hold information which can be drawn on to resolve what would otherwise be ambiguous. In Chapters 4 and 5, a number of examples will be given to demonstrate that the reader needs information about the set of characters present in a situation in order to interpret pronouns. Sometimes, for instance, a shift from a flashback back to main-level narrative will automatically replace one set of referents with another set. Contextual information of this type means that the reference pool is limited to a subset of the total number of referents in a story, often to just one or two referents. This will be discussed in more detail in Chapter 7.

Information held about individual characters, in entity representations, can also be useful for narrowing down options. If the following extract is read out of context, there is ambiguity over who 'the older man' is, since it could denote Stanley, Tom, Harry, or possibly some fourth person.

EXAMPLE 3.3

> Stanley whistled again. Then he began stamping with his feet, and whistled and yelled and screamed at the woman, his face getting scarlet. He seemed quite mad, as he stamped and whistled, while the woman did not move, she did not move a muscle.
>
>   'Barmy,' said Tom.
>
>   'Yes,' said Harry, disapproving.
>
>   Suddenly <u>the older man</u> came to a decision.
>
> (Doris Lessing, 'A Woman on a Roof', in *Collected Short Stories I: To Room Nineteen* (1979), 255; my emphasis)

A reader of the whole story, will know that 'the older man' is Harry, for he has at the outset been described as 'Harry, the oldest, a man of about forty-five'. At this earlier point the reader can make the equation, store it away in the mind in the appropriate entity representation and then draw on it when necessary. Knowledge that there are only three male characters involved in this episode also reduces the possibilities. It would be unlikely that a new character would be introduced at this stage, particularly not with the definite article.

Knowledge about the characters can also help in the interpretation of pronouns. Often pronouns are understood by some clue in the previous sentence (such as the verbal cohesion in 'John shot Henry. He killed him'). Sometimes, however, the clue lies in the entity representation we have formed of the character from information presented much earlier in the text.

EXAMPLE 3.4

> <u>Esther</u> had forced herself to stay cheerful and strong, to go to <u>Debby's</u> room always with a smile. <u>She</u> was pregnant again and worried because of the earlier stillbirth of twin sons, but to the hospital staff, the family, and Deborah, her surface never varied, and she took pride in the strength she showed.
>
> (Hannah Green, *I Never Promised You a Rose Garden* (1985), 33; my emphasis)

The statement 'She was pregnant' is, from this extract alone, ambiguous until later in the sentence in which it occurs. Once the text mentions this pregnant woman's attitude to the hospital staff, the family, and Deborah, we know that the pregnant woman cannot be 'Debby' (assuming that Deborah is 'Debby') and so must be Esther. This would be a cataphoric interpretation, for it involves waiting for the antecedent or other disambiguating information. If the passage is taken in the context of the rest of the novel, 'She was pregnant' can, however, be interpreted as it occurs. If someone has been reading the novel, they know Deborah to be a small child and so she cannot be the referent in 'She was pregnant'. By a process of elimination the referent must, therefore, be Esther and hence the pronoun can be viewed as anaphoric (see further discussion in Chapter 7).

(f) Overt Connectivity

From a linguistic point of view, one of the most important features of real text is that it has 'overt connectivity'. By this I mean that most sentences contain signals to show that they flow on from one another. Halliday and Hasan's seminal work on cohesion (1976) has been responsible for highlighting how conjunctions, pronouns, lexical reiteration, and many other linguistic features signal connection in this way. The literature on 'given–new' (e.g. Halliday 1967; Chafe 1976, 1994; E. F. Prince 1981), which is discussed in Chapters 2 and 7, also emphasizes this 'connectivity', as exhibited in the structuring of a sentence (and intonation contouring, in speech), as well as specific items such as pronouns.

Much experimental research aims to investigate such connectivity, but the danger is that the made-up sentences used may not reflect the complexity of cohesive and structural patterning in real text and, even more worrying, that they may on occasions misrepresent this patterning. If such sentences are being used to demonstrate how a reader responds to cohesive items it is important that the data contains either real or realistic examples. However, 'connective' patterning is sufficiently complex that we do not know enough to replicate it accurately. Chafe (1994: 108) has pointed to the fact that made-up sentence pairs rarely reflect the given–new patterning that he has observed in examining real text. Indeed, it is particularly doubtful whether people who use made-up 'sentence pairs' are in a good position to simulate cohesive patterning and given–new information structure realistically, since such researchers do not usually make a detailed study of real text prior to creating their own data.

Whether a referent is referred to by a name, lexical noun phrase, or pronoun is one aspect of text patterning which we are still learning about (Emmott 1985, 1995*b*; Jones 1994). Psychologists occasionally make assertions about this patterning, extrapolating from their sentence-pair work, and these assertions are not always backed up by text data. Sanford and Garrod (1981: 12, 163), for example, state that repeating a name across two sentences (rather than pronominalizing) 'seems to violate some rule' (p. 12) and that if this does happen it 'reflect[s] some sort of strain imposed on the reader' (ibid.). To back this up, Sanford and Garrod discuss the following made-up sentence pair, which their subjects found 'strange'.

> Mary went to meet John at the station. Mary took the green Ford.   (ibid.)

Without any context or communicative purpose, reiteration of the name Mary, rather than pronominalization, does sound strange here. But in real text, such patterning often provides emphasis at key points in the discourse, as has been demonstrated repeatedly by linguists using real text examples. Longacre (1974, 1983), for example, shows that lexical reiteration may occur at the climax of a story or at other key points, such as when there is conflict. In Emmott (1985), I discussed examples in which reiteration of the noun phrase 'the woman', when there was only one woman present, occurred at a point of conflict and also had thematic significance since male/female oppositions were important in the story (see also Emmott 1995*b*). Fox (1987*a*: 134) and Tannen (1989) give examples where speakers repeat all or most of what a previous speaker has said, to express emotions such as surprise and anger, and these repetitions may include the same lexical items for referents, even though a pronoun would have been clear (see also de Beaugrande 1980: 134–7).

Of course, lexical reiteration of this type is stylistically marked and pronominalization is the norm, but texts exhibit more diverse types of patterning, for more diverse reasons, than is suggested by this decontextualized data (Emmott 1995*b*, 1996). We need to recognize the complexity of linguistic patterning and the communicative purpose behind it if we are to give full credit to the sophistication of both language and language processing.

2. EXPERIMENTAL DATA AND 'ECOLOGICAL VALIDITY'

The first section of this chapter has pointed to some of the significant features of naturally occurring discourse, arguing that it is not possible to give a full account of text processing unless the properties of natural discourse are understood. My main aim is to justify the study of natural discourse, such as the narratives examined in this book, as an important part of hypothesizing about how the mind works.

This section continues this discussion by looking in more detail at the work of experimental psychologists. Whilst this chapter is fairly critical of the data traditionally used in this type of research, I am of the opinion that what is needed is a balanced approach, rather than that the work of either discipline—experimental psychology or discourse analysis—should be discounted. I would argue, therefore, that experimental work should be informed by a recognition of the nature of natural discourse, even if it is not practical for experimenters to use this type of data in their work. Conversely, I recognize that many of the theoretical claims made in my own work need empirical testing and feel that this should be done by those experienced in empirical work rather than linguists such as myself (although linguists may be able to assist at the experimental design stage).

This section begins by examining why many psychologists prefer to handle made-up data and explains the type of research that they are doing.[2] I then look at attempts that have been

---

[2] Artificial intelligence researchers, like experimental psychologists, have traditionally used short made-up material (e.g. Charniak 1972; Charniak and McDermott 1985: 556). Increasingly, though, there have been calls within artificial intelligence for real texts to be used (e.g. Riesbeck (1982: 37) comments that 'It is becoming increasingly obvious [in artificial intelligence] that we have to deal with real texts, texts that were originally generated to communicate, not to test parsers. The days when we can compare programs by how well they handle "Max went to the store" have passed.' A fair amount of work has been carried out using real data, either spoken (e.g. Grosz 1977; Riesbeck 1982; Reichman 1985) or written (e.g. Nakhimovsky and Rapaport 1989; Caenepeel and Mellor 1992). Nevertheless, the artificial intelligence term Natural Language Processing still incorporates research on made-up sentences.

made within empirical psychology to encompass real discourse or observations about real discourse, although I argue that these attempts have not always been particularly successful. The final section will then turn to a consideration of my own data and the pros and cons of studying natural discourse in cognitive research.

(a) Controlled Data and Experimental Research on Human Subjects

Psychologists are obviously more interested in the mind than the text, and therefore concentrate on experiments which test the comprehension of human subjects. As psychologists cannot look directly into the mind, they test their subjects at the point of reading (i.e. on input) and on subsequent recall (i.e. when accessing stored information). Therefore, whilst an individual reads a text, it is possible to measure the time taken to process particular words or clauses,[3] to observe eye movements,[4] to obtain verbal protocols (i.e. explanations from the subjects of their thought processes),[5] and even to monitor brainwave activity or cerebral blood flow.[6] To access the information that has been read, the subject may simply be told to retell the story[7] or be asked questions about the content of the passage (such as who performed a particular action).[8] Subjects may also be asked about the degree of difficulty of reading passages[9] or be required to provide a plausible continuation of a story.[10] Another common technique is to provide the subject with key words and to ask if the key words have appeared in the text or are linked to the content of the passage.[11] When being tested for memory of the linguistic form of a sentence

[3] For example, Graesser (1981: ch. 2); Murphy (1984); K. Ehrlich (1980); and O'Brien, Plewes, and Albrecht (1990).

[4] For example, Kennedy (1987); O'Brien *et al.* (1988); and Garrod (1990).

[5] For example Ericsson and Simon (1985) and R. E. Johnson (1986).

[6] See Temple (1993: 32–5, 151–84) for a summary of these techniques.

[7] For example, Goldman and Varnhagen (1986); Yussen *et al.* (1988); Oakhill and Davies (1991); and Lee-Sammons and Whitney (1991).

[8] For example, Graesser, Robertson, and Anderson (1981); Garnham and Oakhill (1985); Singer *et al.* (1992).

[9] For example, A. Black, Freeman, and Johnson-Laird (1986).

[10] For example, Duffy (1986).

[11] For example, McKoon and Ratcliff (1980, 1981); O'Brien, Duffy, and Myers (1986); Macdonald and MacWhinney (1990); Speelman and Kirsner (1990).

(e.g. whether it was active or passive),[12] the individual may be asked to choose from several options.[13]

The data used by psychologists, even in recent years, is generally very short, often consisting of just one or two sentences[14] or a brief paragraph.[15] Although psychologists frequently use the words 'text' and 'discourse' to describe their data,[16] they often mean something which is not what a discourse analyst would regard as discourse, as Garnham (1985: 134) points out:

> The distinction between sentence meaning and text meaning has rarely been drawn by psychologists, since psycholinguistics is the study of language use, and when a sentence is *used* it assumes the properties of a monologue or text. Psycholinguistic experiments with single sentences are therefore experiments on *discourse* comprehension. (Garnham's italics)

Although discourse analysts do recognize single-sentence texts, such as notices and street signs, much naturally occurring discourse is longer than a sentence in length. This is particularly true of narrative text which much psycholinguistic data is attempting to replicate. Moreover, sentences given to a subject in the course of an experiment do not constitute 'language use' as understood by discourse analysts.

Nevertheless, the 'texts' used in psychology experiments are designed for a particular purpose.[17] Made-up sentence pairs will focus attention on one particular aspect of interpretation, with the subject's response reflecting the time taken to make an inference. So, in Sanford and Garrod's (1981: 154; their italics) work,[18] sentences such as:

Mary dressed the baby. *The clothes* were made of pink wool.

---

[12] For example, Johnson-Laird and Stevenson (1970).
[13] See Graesser (1981); Cohen, Eysenck, and Le Voi (1986); Sanford and Garrod (1989); Gernsbacher (1990); and Eysenck and Keane (1990) for summaries of these techniques.
[14] For example, Caramazza *et al.* (1977); Fletcher (1984); Bharucha, Olney, and Schnurr (1985); Till, Mross, and Kintsch (1988); Macleod (1989); Lucas, Tanenhaus, and Carlson (1990); and Macdonald and MacWhinney (1990).
[15] For example, O'Brien (1987); Speelman and Kirsner (1990), Garrod (1990); Graesser, Lang, and Roberts (1991); and Singer *et al.* (1992).
[16] For example, Fletcher (1984); Murphy (1984); Till, Mross, and Kintsch (1988); Oakhill, Garnham, and Vonk (1989); and Lucas, Tanenhaus, and Carlson (1990).
[17] See Ziman (1991) for a general discussion of scientific methodology.
[18] Sanford and Garrod's work is discussed in Ch. 7.

are designed to test the amount of inferencing involved in interpreting the definite noun phrase 'the clothes'. Timing of the subject reading these sentences can therefore be taken as an
indication of the mental effort involved in understanding this particular linguistic feature (see Chapter 7 for a more detailed discussion of this work). Finding naturally occurring sentence pairs
which exhibited the required feature and no other complicating
factors would require a large amount of searching, so it is more
straightforward for investigators to create their own data. Apart
from focusing on one linguistic relation, made-up sentence pairs
allow the investigator to provide experimental controls by altering one or two words in the 'text'—it would be difficult to find two
samples of natural discourse which were identical apart from just
one feature. Furthermore, made-up sentences are self-contained
enough to allow an inference to be drawn simply from the 'text'
provided—there is no requirement to have knowledge of entities
over and above the information provided in the test data itself.

Psychology experiments have the advantage that they can
allow a statistical analysis of the processing of linguistic features
at sentence level, testing readers' responses rather than simply
hypothesizing about them. The problem, though, is that the data
may sometimes be so different from naturally occurring data that
it may misrepresent the work involved in processing natural discourse, under-representing factors such as the need to hold and
utilize information from much earlier in a text and the need to
recognize signals of hierarchical shifts, such as to or from a flashback.

There is also the question of whether subjects read made-up
'text' using everyday processing strategies. The experience of
reading made-up sentences cannot be equated with the interest
of reading an exciting story (de Beaugrande 1980: 220; Cohen,
Eysenck, and Le Voi 1986: 19), as made-up sentences contain
only names, not 'developed characters'. A reader knows that nothing has happened before the events described in the made-up sentences and that nothing will happen afterwards and so their
imagination has no base on which to begin working (although Allbritton and Gerrig (1991) provide one attempt within psychology
to simulate prior context). If a reader's attention is not fully
engaged, it is unlikely that they will read with their usual degree
of concentration, but also their mental processes may be different.

László (1987) demonstrated this by showing that certain standard psychology tests were unworkable with literary data because the subjects got 'too' interested in what they were reading. If this is the case, then the problem may lie not with the subjects but with the tests.

Laboratory reading may also be unlike 'real' reading because of the experimental situation itself. In general, people often act differently when under observation (Labov 1972b: 209; Baxter et al. 1990). As far as text processing is concerned, some individuals find it difficult to read a passage in their usual manner when someone is watching them read (Cohen, Eysenck, and Le Voi 1986: 19). In such situations it can be hard to concentrate on the text. Also, rather than reading the passage for its own sake, it is natural for the reader to start wondering why the text has been chosen or, in the case of a psychology test, to start memorizing it (d'Ydewalle and Rosselle 1978; Oakhill and Davies 1991). Johnson-Laird's (1980, 1983) work on memory for spatial details, discussed in the previous chapter, suggests that mental representation of a text is different if it is seen as just a story or as a prelude to a test on spatial organization. This sometimes seems to be forgotten in psychology tests. For example, Chapter 2 (Section 2a) discussed how Morrow, Bower, and Greenspan (1990) draw conclusions about mental models in narrative comprehension on the basis of subjects having memorized the lay-out of a location beforehand. They observe their subjects being able to draw spatial inferences and comment that previous experiments may not have yielded the same results because subjects may have read the texts too 'superficially'. I would argue that this type of experiment tells us nothing about how narratives are read naturally, since readers do not usually memorize spatial plans beforehand (see discussion of Johnson-Laird's work in Chapter 2).

When investigating human responses to real-life situations, psychologists have been particularly aware of the need to avoid experimental bias. For example, in one well-known experiment (Brewer and Treyens 1981), subjects who had been invited to participate in a test were asked to wait for the experimenter to arrive. Unknown to the subjects, this waiting period was part of the test itself, since they were subsequently asked questions about what they had observed during this time. It would of course be difficult to perform detailed text comprehension tests on readers without them being aware that they were being tested, but when experiments are conducted the possibility of bias should at least be considered. Experimental bias can, after all, completely change both results and conclusions.[19] One experimental strategy is to disguise the exact purpose of the test from the subject (e.g. Murphy 1984; Macleod 1989), but this does not wholly overcome the problems of the experimental setting.

Tests which show how people read sentences in laboratories, therefore, may not reveal how people read real texts in real situations (Baddeley 1985: 209). Indeed, there has been criticism of traditional laboratory data by psychologists themselves. There have been calls for more realistic experimental work in real contexts, under the headings of 'ecological validity' (Neisser 1976, 1978)[20] and 'contextualism' (e.g. Jaeger and Rosnow 1988). Such work, however, often tends to focus on topics such as face recognition, absent-mindedness, and eyewitness testimony rather than on reading.[21] There are, nevertheless, researchers who do use real data in reading research, such as Kintsch, Mandel, and Kozminsky (1977), Einstein *et al.* (1990), and Feldman *et al.* (1990), and real data is strongly argued for by van Dijk and Kintsch (1983), as shown in the extract cited at the beginning of this chapter. Nevertheless, although van Dijk and Kintsch do make extensive reference to a real news article from the magazine *Newsweek*, their experimental work in *Strategies of Discourse Comprehension* uses more traditional materials. Their tests on pronoun comprehension, in particular, use isolated made-up sentences (1983: 173–80). Other psychologists who take some account of the need for ecological validity may be apprehensive of working

---

[19] McGarrigle (cited in Donaldson 1978: 43–50), for example, performed experiments which reworked some of Piaget's experiments on children, using toy bears and chairs rather than abstract counters, and found that children were able to perform mental operations which Piaget had thought impossible at their age (see also Johnson-Laird, Legrenzi, and Sonino-Legrenzi (1972); Johnson-Laird and Wason (1977); Adler (1984); Boden (1987: 335); and Bruner and Kenney (1974) for similar differences in tests involving abstract and concrete data).

[20] For example, Brewer and Treyens (1981), Baddeley (1981, 1985); Gardner (1985: 124); Graesser, Millis, and Long (1986: 128); Smyth *et al.* (1987); J. R. Anderson (1987); and Eysenck and Keane (1990: 501–2).

[21] The effect of alcohol levels on task performance (e.g. Baddeley 1981) is often cited in the 'ecological validity' literature, in addition to face-recognition (e.g. Young, Hay, and Ellis 1985), absent-mindedness (e.g. Reason and Mycielska 1982; Rabbitt and Abson 1990; Pollina *et al.* 1992), and eyewitness testimony (e.g. Loftus 1975 and Loftus, Miller, and Burns 1978).

with real texts. Yuill and Oakhill (1991: 85), for example, comment about their own work:

... both experiments could be criticized for using very short and unnatural texts to investigate children's understanding of pronouns ... we decided to look at their understanding of anaphoric expressions more generally, using more naturalistic materials.

Yuill and Oakhill (1991: 87–95) go on to use a 'naturalistic' text in their tests (a seven-hundred word 'constructed' story), but later put forward their doubts about longer texts:

... use of this method for natural texts, as opposed to the carefully constructed sentences we used in the pronoun studies, is open to the criticism that correct answers can sometimes be obtained without really understanding the anaphors. For example, there might only be one plausible referent ... or clues might be given from other parts of the text ...   (p. 87)

Far from distorting the picture, I would see the decision about who is a plausible referent and the identification and use of clues from other parts of the text as being a complex task which is fundamental to pronoun resolution. Jaeger and Rosnow (1988: 71–2), in writing about psychological research in general, advocate recognition of the richness of psychological phenomena in experimental testing: 'Although the notion of contextual dependence is not new, contextualism would require a shift from viewing "context" as something external, merely impinging on behaviour, to viewing context as integrated within the phenomenon itself.'

This section has, up to this point, focused on the type of 'text' used by experimental psychologists in controlled experiments. Natural texts are, however, more likely to be used by psychologists adopting the technique called 'protocol analysis' (e.g. Bruner 1986). In this type of work, the subject is usually asked to read natural discourse, being interrupted at specific points to 'talk through' the inferences they have made. There have also been occasional attempts by experimental psychologists to take into account observations made by discourse analysts and artificial intelligence researchers about the hierarchical structure of extended discourse. Malt (1985), for example, in a paper entitled 'The Role of Discourse Structure in Understanding Anaphora' cites discourse analysis research.[22] Malt's aim is to investigate

[22] Schegloff and Sacks (1973); Grosz (1977); Sidner (1978); and Hopper and Thompson (1980).

whether there is likely to be less referential cohesion between a line of dialogue and a line of narrative, which Malt suggests may be 'distinct sub-discourses' (p. 274), than there is between two lines of dialogue. Malt's experimental strategy is to present her subjects with the following 'text':

> Deanna and her friends were at a barbecue.
> 'Someone drank Herb's lemonade,' Deanna remarked.
> He had only drunk half of it when it disappeared.
> 'Indeed, someone did,' Annie agreed.   (p. 274).

Malt asks her subjects to interpret the ellipsis in 'someone did' and then presents them with the identical passage except that quotation marks have been put round the third line to turn it into direct speech. Malt describes this as 'content-free manipulation for comparison' (p. 275). However, the idea that main narrative can be simply transformed into dialogue by adding quotation marks seems rather odd and fails to take account of the large amount of research that has been done on speech representation in the novel (e.g. Leech and Short 1981). Malt does not comment on the authenticity of her data, except to suggest that her sentences 'sound plausible' (1985: 277).

Clearly, the aim of Malt's 'content-free manipulation' is to produce a controlled experiment and had she chosen real discourse she would not be able to achieve the same level of control. There is no real solution to this dilemma. However, it would be useful if discourse work was not only drawn on as a possible source of hypotheses about text processing, but was also used as a means of assessing experimental data. This might either suggest ways in which the data could be made more realistic or allow some discussion of whether experimental data misrepresents essential characteristics of real discourse.

(b) Hypothesizing about Narrative Comprehension

Having discussed the methodology of experimental psychologists, this section offers justification for my own method of analysis. This book and a fair amount of other research on discourse (in discourse analysis and artificial intelligence) hypothesizes about text comprehension by looking at the text rather than the reader. Examining texts reveals characteristics (e.g. hierarchical structuring and linguistic patterning) which, if we assume the text to be interpretable (by at least some readers), need to be taken into account in a cognitive model. In particular, this involves looking at places in the text where an inference must be made if textual coherence is to be established, such as the inferencing necessary to assign referents to pronouns. In such cases, by looking at what the text leaves inexplicit, it is possible to hypothesize about the amount of work that the reader needs to do to make basic sense of a text.

When discourse analysts (and others studying discourse) do not test readers' responses, their models of text comprehension have the status of a hypothesis rather than a theory for which experimental evidence has been produced. Without testing, we can only say that it seems likely that a particular mental representation is formed, if the reader is to make sense of a piece of text, not that a mental representation definitely is formed. However, hypotheses are useful and can form the basis of future testing. Moreover, even if a hypothesis is empirically tested, many competing theories can arise to explain the same experimental results. No one is able to look directly into the mind. Neurophysiologists can observe brainwave activity, but this does not automatically reveal the workings of the mind. All research on the mind depends on inference-making by the researcher.[23] Psychologists can accurately measure the speed of reading, but they still have to infer the processes being performed.[24] They can also investigate the type and amount of information retained in memory, but they must nevertheless infer the structure of mental representations from this data.

Even if discourse analysts only hypothesize about comprehension, they can offer evidence of text structure. If someone argues that, for example, pronouns are never used on a return from a flashback and if, by contrast, a discourse analyst can find examples to show that pronouns are used in this way, then the discourse analyst has produced evidence about text structure which counters the other person's suggestion. For discourse analysts, producing

---

[23] The methodology of inferring the structure and processing strategies of the mind from the tasks it can perform has parallels in pure science. As Sterelny (1990: 4–5) points out, before the structure of DNA was discovered, the existence and nature of genes was in part inferred from observing their function, the passing on of traits from one generation to another.

[24] As observed by Johnson-Laird (1983: 2, 148); Boden (1987: 408); and Oakhill and Garnham (1988: 147).

examples as evidence of language use has always been important. Chapter 1 explained that discourse analysis has developed partly in opposition to generative work in which analysts speculate about what they themselves regard as acceptable, even though sociological research suggests that there is a substantial discrepancy between what people think is acceptable and what they actually say. For discourse analysts, language is what people actually do say or write and the best way to study this is to look at texts that have actually been produced. Since texts are one part of the equation in text comprehension, evidence of their characteristics is important.

Nevertheless, cognitive discourse analysis (and non-cognitive discourse analysis) does go beyond observing linguistic patterning to speculate about what language means.[25] The problem with this is, as any literary theorist will point out, what is meaning? Some discourse analysts acknowledge that there is a problem about simply saying that a text means something. Mann and Thompson (1988: 246), for example, say that all their judgements are 'plausibility judgements', a term they use to stress that 'all judgements of the reader's comprehension of the text are made on the basis of the text rather than the analyst's direct knowledge of the reader' (i.e. 'every judgement of the completed analysis is of the form, "It is plausible to the analyst that. . . ."'). Mann and Thompson are following the traditional arts approach of suggesting their own interpretation and waiting to see whether their readers disagree, an approach which has been referred to as 'inter-subjectivity' by literary stylisticians (see P. Simpson 1993 for a discussion of stylistic methodology).

Hypothesizing about comprehension on the basis of examining textual characteristics is possible for the sort of 'nuts and bolts'

---

[25] Chafe (1994: 14–15) makes this point about linguistics in general: '. . . a great deal of modern linguistics is built on introspective data. Only in the subfield of phonetics and those areas of psycholinguistics dominated by the psychological tradition has an exclusive commitment to public data been maintained. Most of linguistics differs radically from psychology in this respect. To take a simple example, linguists are happy to talk about a past-tense morpheme, a plural morpheme, or the like. But pastness and plurality are based squarely on introspective evidence. . . . Without an awareness of what one "has in mind" when one uses a past tense or plural form, semantics, for example, could hardly be practiced at all, and without semantics, linguistics would surely have diminished interest and significance. [One of my goals] is to show how the study of discourse is equally dependent on introspective insights.'

inferences that establish basic coherence. Of course, a text may not always be understood by a particular reader, but if 'shorthand' forms such as pronouns were never understood, it seems unlikely that they would be such a prominent feature of the language. Writers and speakers have a communicative obligation to produce discourse which they reasonably anticipate can be understood.

Moreover, research which hypothesizes about these basic mechanisms of text processing often makes assumptions that are difficult to argue against without completely ignoring common sense. G. Brown and Yule's (1983: 202) research provides an example (which is discussed further in Chapter 7):

Kill an active, plump chicken. Prepare it for the oven.

Although Brown and Yule do not attempt to prove empirically that 'it' means 'a dead, plump chicken', it would be rather pedantic to start arguing about this. Although some readers may not make the inference because they are inexperienced readers, or inattentive, the deadness of the chicken derives from the fact that it has been killed. Whatever Reader Response Theory says about a multiplicity of interpretations, some inferences are demanded by the text (although what happens after the information has entered the reader's memory is another matter).[26] In fact, psychologists make a distinction between different types of inferences (e.g. recognizing degrees of causality (Myers and Duffy 1990; Gerrig 1993) and distinguishing between bridging and elaborative inferences (e.g. Long *et al.* 1990)). Moreover, psychologists themselves often take the nature of the inference for granted and aim instead to study at exactly what point an inference is made (e.g. Sanford and Garrod 1981).

The approach used here, therefore, is to cite examples from text as evidence of how texts are organized and then, assuming that a

[26] Readers, for example, make what Gernsbacher (1990: 80) terms coherence inferences which ' . . . tie together the events of a story and thereby improve the story's cohesion'. Gernsbacher argues that if we read that 'Joan put a full can of white paint on the top step of the ladder', and later read that 'Joan looked down to the ground and saw the empty can and a big splotch of white', it can be inferred that the paint pot has fallen. A great deal of work has been carried out on 'reconstruction' of a text's meaning by inference-making by psychologists (e.g. Bartlett 1932; Bransford and Franks 1971; Bransford, Barclay, and Franks 1972; M. K. Johnson, Bransford, and Solomon 1973; Sanford and Garrod 1981), by linguists (e.g. Haviland and Clark 1974; H. H. Clark 1977) and by artificial intelligence researchers (e.g. Rieger 1974: 155–8; Rieger 1976).

reader can understand the text, to hypothesize about how this might be explained in a cognitive model and in linguistic theory. Artificial intelligence often works in this way too. Schank's (1982) work on dynamic memory, for example, presents a cognitive model based on the observation that people often see an underlying theme or moral point to a story and can produce their own stories which, although they look very different on the surface, have the same underlying point to them. Even though this hypothesis has subsequently been extensively tested both by psychologists and artificial intelligence researchers, the original study was based largely on casual observations of storytelling. Likewise, Grosz's (1977) work on instructional dialogues (discussed in Chapter 5) relies heavily on observations made about the transcripts of the conversations between an instructor and an apprentice, which then suggests a possible way of programming a computer to interpret such conversations.

By looking at the form and structure of a text and by observing people managing to interpret such texts, therefore, researchers hypothesize about how readers understand. In experimental testing, the nature of textual organization is often overlooked and yet is an important factor if we are to explain how readers comprehend real texts. An important feature of this book is that it discusses the inferences required to make sense of complete novels and short stories, examining over forty texts by a range of authors, including Douglas Adams, Agatha Christie, Doris Lessing, and Iris Murdoch. The complexity of text structuring and linguistic patterning in even the most non-literary narrative texts (such as Agatha Christie) needs to be acknowledged in cognitive models of narrative comprehension.

Summary

This chapter has discussed how naturally occurring discourse has properties which are not usually present in short made-up examples. Of particular importance is the hierarchical structure of text, the way in which sentences take their meaning from the prior text and the linguistic patterning which reflects given and new information.

Psychologists often use made-up examples to enable 'reader response' testing to be controlled. The problem is that much of the complexity of real texts is ignored when such materials are used, so the research may not adequately reflect the complexity of processing required to make sense of real texts. Sometimes, too, the purpose of reading stories seems to be forgotten in psychological tests and the experimental subject may be responding to a problem-solving task rather than becoming immersed in a fictional world. For these reasons, a study of real, full texts can supplement empirical research on subjects. Whilst textual analysis cannot prove what goes on in a reader's mind, it can reveal the complexity of texts and can thereby indicate the nature of the task to be undertaken.

PART TWO

Narrative Structure and Processing

4

Creating Fictional Contexts

In Chapter 2, I suggested that one important and under-investigated type of knowledge is 'text-specific' knowledge. To make sense of full, real texts, such as novels, a reader must have background information about specific entities and about the configurations of entities which occur in specific situations. This chapter describes how the reader needs to create mental representations of the fictional context, collecting information from the text and maintaining an awareness of these facts whilst the subsequent text is read. Chapter 5 continues the discussion with regard to multiple contexts and Chapter 6 considers the implications of this discussion of context for mental representations of characters.

By fictional **context**, I mean that whenever the text describes an event in the fictional world, the reader generally needs orientational information which may not be stated explicitly in the text at that particular point. At the very least, the reader must usually know:

   (i) Which characters are present in the physical environment?
  (ii) Where is the action located?
 (iii) What is the approximate time of the action?

This information is required for the following reasons:

(i) The actions of one character will affect other characters in a context. For example, the speech of one character will often change the knowledge or beliefs of other characters present. Likewise, a physical action by one individual might either have a direct physical effect on another character or might change that other character's opinion of the first individual. To judge the effects of an action on other characters, the reader needs to have a continuing awareness of who is present in the context. This is discussed throughout this chapter.

(ii) Whether or not precise details of the time and location are necessary to read a particular story, the reader needs enough information to make orientational judgements such as 'Is the action occurring in the main narrative "present time" or a flashback "past time"?' Narratives often switch suddenly from one location to another or from one time to another and, therefore, to make sense of the story the reader needs to be able to recognize such switches. This topic is introduced in this chapter and explored in more detail in Chapter 5.

It should be clear from this brief introductory explanation (developed further in this chapter and in subsequent chapters), that by 'context', I do not mean the detailed spatial 'maps' of a particular location that have been postulated by psychology researchers such as Morrow, Bower, and Greenspan (1990) (see Chapter 2). Whatever specific information the reader remembers about a location would be stored in an 'entity representation' for that location (or, more specifically, a 'location representation'), just as detailed information about a particular character needs to be held in an 'entity representation' (or, more specifically, a 'character representation'). By contrast, contextual information, which I view as being stored in mental representations termed **contextual frames**, provides 'episodic' information about a configuration of characters, location, and time at any point in a narrative, rather than details about individual people and places.

The aim of this chapter is to introduce this notion of contextual frames. Section 1 provides a general discussion of context, examining previous work and presenting my own arguments for the importance of a continued awareness of contextual information on the part of a reader. This section evaluates van Dijk and Kintsch's (1983) situation model and the 'textual worlds' of de Beaugrande (1980). I also draw on artificial intelligence discussions of 'the frame problem', which has arisen due to the problems of modelling contextual knowledge within robotics. I argue that a reader needs to monitor contextual information in order to keep track of continuity and change within a fictional world. I also suggest that a reader needs to be actively conscious of contextual information all the time, rather than having to stop and access information when each new sentence is read. In this chapter, I appeal mainly to my reader's intuitions about what reading a story entails, but Chapters 5, 6, and 8 give textual evidence to show that contextual knowledge is necessary to follow the hierarchical structure of a narrative and Chapter 7 places these observations within a linguistic model of reference theory. Section 2 of this chapter builds on these general observations about context, introducing my own term 'contextual frames' and other terminology necessary to draw distinctions between main and subsidiary contexts and between what a text explicitly mentions in a particular sentence and what has to be inferred by a reader. These ideas and terms are then drawn on in all the subsequent chapters of the book. Finally, Section 2 demonstrates how contextual information is necessary to make sense of actions and descriptions in a narrative and discusses some of the problems of deciding the boundaries of a specific context.

I. THE IMPORTANCE OF CONTEXT

(a) Overview: Event Sequences and Events in Context

Narratologists[1] generally define narrative as events in sequence, often with a causal link between them.[2] E. M. Forster (1963: 93) gives the well-known example 'The king died, and then the queen died of grief' which fits these criteria, whereas 'Roses are red, violets are blue' does not count as narrative, since it describes states rather than actions (Chatman 1978: 30; G. Prince 1982: 1–2). The fact that events are central to storytelling means that the text often explicitly mentions these events. To understand a story fully, however, the reader needs to make inferences about what is not mentioned. These inferences account for much of the cognitive effort involved in understanding stories.

Much of the standard work on event sequences has concentrated on stereotyped settings. In Schank and Abelson's (1977a, b) restaurant script (discussed in Chapter 2), certain unstated events in the sequence can be inferred because we know from general knowledge that they always happen in these circumstances. Real adult narrative is often not so stereotyped, though, and

---

[1] See also linguistic work such as Hopper (1979, 1991, 1995); Hopper and Thompson (1980); Tomlin (1987a); and Berman and Slobin (1994).

[2] For example, Forster (1963); Chatman (1978); G. Prince (1982); Labov and Waletzky (1967); Labov (1972a); and Rimmon-Kenan (1983).

many assumptions have to be made based on the textual world itself.

In real adult narrative, people are usually important within the textual world. In Chapter 2, I suggested that 'entity representations', cognitive stores which hold information about characters (and locations and objects), can explain the significance of events and enable readers to empathize with the participants. Conversely, readers must respond to events by updating their knowledge and opinions of the characters. Often, the text does not make these links explicit, but readers cannot really understand and appreciate a narrative without supplementing the text in this way.

In addition to the reader's knowledge of characters, another important factor in real adult narratives is the grouping of characters on particular occasions. In stereotyped scripts this is not important. In the restaurant script, the waiter, the meal, and the bill arrive regardless of whether there are one or more characters at the table and regardless of who these characters are. In real narratives, by contrast, the restaurant will often just be a backcloth for gathering particular characters together. When a character speaks or acts it is usually essential to know who else is there. This is most evident in detective stories, where being in a place at a particular point can make a difference to the overall plot. A character who has been present when a murder is committed or who has overheard an incriminating fact is usually in some danger from the murderer. This is an extreme example, but it is usually true to say that it matters who (if anyone) hears what a character says and who (if anyone) sees the actions that a character performs. It also matters who has not been present and who therefore has not heard or seen an event.

The reader's awareness of the grouping of particular characters in a particular place at a particular time is what I refer to in this chapter as 'contextual monitoring'.[3] Knowledge of a specific fic-

---

[3] The importance of tracking place and time has been highlighted by Frederiksen (1986). He uses the term 'frame', apparently taking the term from those who study general knowledge schemata and extending its use to text-related structures. His frames are of a number of different kinds, one of which is 'narrative frames'. These are composed of 'event structures' and 'scene structures'. 'Event structures' chart whether events described in a narrative occur in sequence, together or at different times. 'Scene structures' provide a 'map' of all the locations in a narrative, providing information about whether locations are distant, close, adjacent, or contained within each other. The 'narrative frame' itself shows the relationship between par-

tional context is built up from reading the text rather than from general knowledge. The reader is given information about each new context as it occurs (i.e. who is present, where, and when) but must hold this information 'in mind' as specific events are described. Each time an event occurs, it must be viewed within this fictional context even if the full context is not mentioned for some time. This is important for discourse studies because it emphasizes the extent to which a sentence does not have meaning in isolation from the rest of the text. It is also important for cognitive studies because context building and monitoring requires the reader to supplement each sentence of a narrative with knowledge derived from earlier in the text and stored within the mind whilst substantial stretches of text are read.

(b) Context: Previous Work in Text Linguistics

In this section, I concentrate on some of the work which has attempted to model how a context is created by a text. There is also, of course, a considerable amount of general theoretical work which stresses the importance of contextual information without necessarily discussing the complexities of context representation. In philosophy (e.g. Peirce 1932: 170–2; Bühler 1990; Bar-Hillel 1954) and pragmatics (e.g. Barwise and Perry 1983; Levinson 1983; Leech 1983; G. M. Green 1989), context is of particular importance, since it allows indexical expressions to be interpreted. This work has been utilized in fields such as artificial intelligence, ethnomethodology, and conversation analysis (e.g. Garfinkel 1967; Garfinkel and Sacks 1970; H. Sacks 1976; Schegloff 1988a,

---

ticular events at particular times and the locations in which they occur. Frederiksen's emphasis is on the location of events and he does not consider the monitoring of participants within a particular location nor does he discuss reference theory. His work shows what mental representations might be formed from narrative text but does not indicate how these representations can be used to fill gaps in the subsequent text.

Recent work by Duchan, Bruder, and Hewitt (1995b) and Werth (MS a, b) is also similar to the notion of contextual monitoring that I am putting forward in this book. Werth looks mainly at how 'sub-worlds' are created through the beliefs, intentions, and dreams of characters, but does also discuss 'sub-worlds' created by changes in the place and time parameters of a context. Duchan, Bruder, and Hewitt (1995b) likewise concentrate particularly on information mediated through the subjective perspective of characters, but also study the tracking of contextual information about people, places, and time. (See Ch. 2 for further details.)

1992; H. Sacks 1992*a*, *b*; see also Suchman 1987: 58–62 for a summary). Indexical expressions are items which require information from the context to be interpreted. As Givón (1989: 1; Givón's bold typeface and italics) explains:

> Pragmatics as a method may be first likened to the way one goes about constructing a **description**. The reason why I've chosen 'description' as my first metaphor for pragmatics may trace back to dimly recalled times in military reconnaissance. When one was sent to draw a panoramic view of some Godforsaken hill, the resulting sketch-cum-commentary had to always specify the **map coordinates** of one's vantage point; that is where one stood when drawing the picture. Your description—pictorial-cum-verbal, you were told—was *useless* without those coordinates.

In discussing Garfinkel's ethnomethodological work, Heritage (1984: 143–59, see also Suchman 1987: 59) gives the example of the expression 'That's a nice one'. He explains that this can mean quite different things depending on whether it is uttered by a visitor admiring a host's photographs, a girl pointing her boyfriend's attention to a ring in a jeweller's window, or a customer choosing a lettuce in a greengrocer's. Heritage argues that it is not just the pronouns ('that', 'one') that can have different meanings here but also the adjective 'nice', which describes different properties when applied to a ring than to a lettuce (p. 143). The intent of the message may also be different, with the comment about the photograph being a compliment and the remark about the ring perhaps being a hint about marriage (p. 151), as is made clear in speech act theory (Austin 1975; Searle 1969). Heritage concludes (1984: 152; Heritage's italics) that:

> Our original utterance . . . is now triply indexical. Its *referent* could not be determined without a physical (or verbal) context. The *sense of particular expressions* (in this case 'nice') could not be made out without the use of context. Finally the *sense of the utterance*—now, unavoidably, construed as an action—could not be made out without invoking a social context which was co-ordinated with the sense of the particular descriptive terms.

In Heritage's examples, as in speech act theory, the emphasis is on the interpretation of indexicals by drawing on the extra-linguistic context and, perhaps, shared knowledge. The conversation analysts have also drawn attention to the importance of context created by means of the preceding text, the 'sequential context' in

Schegloff's terms (Schegloff 1988*a*: 61, see also Schegloff 1982, 1987*b*, 1988*b* and similar comments in literary theory by Bakhtin 1981: 340).

In the current work, I seek to explore how a context is monitored whilst reading narrative, and how it is utilized both in the interpretation of indexical expressions and to give an overall impression of a situation even when it is not referred to in a particular sentence. There are some well-known attempts within linguistics and psychology to model textually presented context, such as van Dijk and Kintsch (1983) and de Beaugrande (1980), which I will outline and evaluate in this section. In the following section, I will introduce artificial intelligence research on the representation of context, looking particularly at discussions of 'the frame problem' within robotics.

The work of van Dijk and Kintsch (1983) has already been referred to in Chapter 2 and, as explained, the situation model is 'the cognitive representation of the events, actions, persons, and in general the situation, a text is about' (pp. 11–12), in contrast with the 'textbase' (propositional representation), which is more closely connected with the text itself. Most of van Dijk and Kintsch's book discusses the 'textbase', with the explanations of the 'situation model' being rather sparse (pp. 11–12, 106, 163, 172, 336–48) in comparison. Indeed this component was not present in earlier versions of their model, such as Kintsch and van Dijk (1978), and may have arisen in part in response to the 'mental models' of Johnson-Laird (1980) and Johnson-Laird and Garnham (1980) (as discussed in Chapter 2).

Van Dijk and Kintsch (1983) offer little exemplification to show how their 'situation model' might work in practice. Their discussion is more useful as a theoretical justification of mental representations of entities and contexts than as a demonstration of how such representations might be constructed and managed. Moreover, the model seems to reflect properties of the particular genre of texts that van Dijk and Kintsch studied in this book, since they examined one particular news article in detail.[4] News articles rely very heavily on real-world knowledge, presupposing

---

[4] Earlier work (e.g. Kintsch, Mandel, and Kozminsky 1977) does look specifically at stories. However, the situation model appears to be a new addition in van Dijk and Kintsch (1983) and is particularly concerned with the link between the real world and the text world, as discussed here.

a pre-textual acquaintance with the places and people discussed. News articles also serve to update our knowledge of the real world. This is very different from fictional texts where entities are created within the text itself and where the events which occur in the textual world must be kept distinct from events in the real world. As a result of examining this genre, van Dijk and Kintsch stress the importance of supplementing a text with general knowledge. Their situation model does not give much indication of how a reader may gather together information from the text itself to create fictional contexts. This type of information is only discussed in detail in the 'textbase' description, but the 'textbase' is simply a propositional representation (as discussed in Chapter 2).

The 'textual worlds' of de Beaugrande (1980: 79–102) (see also de Beaugrande and Dressler 1981: 94–110) are extremely detailed models of everything that is remembered both from the information presented in the text and from general knowledge inferences made whilst reading the text. De Beaugrande's model shows both how information is collected from each sentence and how this is integrated to create representations of the entities, the location, and their relation.

De Beaugrande (1980: 90) looks particularly at the following paragraphs:

A great black and yellow V-2 rocket 46 feet long stood in a New Mexico desert. Empty, it weighed five tons. For fuel it carried eight tons of alcohol and liquid oxygen.

Everything was ready. Scientists and generals withdrew to some distance and crouched behind earth mounds. Two red flares rose as a signal to fire the rocket.

De Beaugrande shows how all the information about the rocket is held together, being gathered from different sentences of the text once co-reference has been established. This includes the physical characteristics of the rocket as well as the events it participates in. All this information is categorized in terms of its relation to the entity. For example, the rocket's yellowness is labelled by de Beaugrande as an 'attribute' and its take-off as 'motion' (p. 95). Presumably this would enable a reader to answer questions such as 'What did the rocket look like?' and 'What did the rocket do?'. General knowledge is used both to establish co-reference (e.g. 'it weighed five tons' must describe the rocket not the desert) and to add extra information about the referents to explain their behaviour (e.g. when the scientists and generals withdraw from the rocket, we can infer that this is because of the danger from the launch blast) (p. 98).

De Beaugrande's model provides a useful basis for anyone wanting to account for how information about characters and objects is extracted from naturally occurring discourse. In addition to forming representations of each entity, the model also shows certain relations between entities and the contextual links between entities and their locations. De Beaugrande's model, for example, records the fact that the rocket is located in the desert and also shows the inference that the scientists are watching the rocket (p. 98).

De Beaugrande states that his model is just a 'starting point' (p. 99). One factor that de Beaugrande does not discuss is mental imagery (although he mentions it as a factor which might be included in a more complete model (p. 99)). Imagery may just be epiphenomenal, in which case it can be handled as an 'add-on extra', but it might instead be either a signal to how information is stored or part of the storage process (see Flanagan 1992). This is something that Johnson-Laird's 'mental models' approach takes into account, for it includes quasi-visual images of entities and locations. Although relations such as 'left and right' are not relevant to de Beaugrande's text, what is relevant is that the people and the rocket are both in the desert and that they are at some distance from each other. A visual representation can show all this information in one or two images, keeping it active in consciousness. In de Beaugrande's model, however, some of this information is not recorded at all (even in the form that de Beaugrande uses for inferred information). There is no connection labelled between the scientists/generals and the desert (p. 98), even though de Beaugrande himself takes this for granted when including in his model (in his diagram of the stages of text processing) the inference that the scientists are watching the rocket (p. 94). Apart from providing the setting for the scientists/ generals, the inference about the location needs to be made in order to make the inference about the scientists and generals seeing the rocket.

Later in this chapter, I will suggest that salient entities in a location and the location itself are all viewed as 'contextually connected' and are held in the same mental working space (which may take the form of full or partial images or may be more like just 'plotting' items onto a graph). Once the working space is set up this would automatically allow context-based inferences to be made (such as the inference that the scientists observe the rocket because both the scientists and the rocket are in the same location). This mental grouping would also allow contexts to be switched and subsequently retrieved, as described in Chapter 5.

In his model, de Beaugrande concentrates on how general knowledge is used to make a connection between each incoming proposition and the previous discourse, but this is sometimes at the expense of creating a coherent contextual representation from the salient textual details. Indeed, de Beaugrande states that his aim (in this preliminary model, at least) is to establish '*at least one* connection between all nodes of the model', stating that 'a gap in connectivity is construed as a problem ... and a "problem-occasioned" inference must be done' (p. 95). This suggests that it is sufficient simply to 'cement' the new information on somewhere, rather than 'wiring it up' to all the appropriate connection points. One problem with this is that there is no provision for updating information held within the cognitive stores (although de Beaugrande does recognize that this is an important and difficult task (p. 96)). Another problem is that de Beaugrande's model does not take any account of time—as he points out, he ignores the tense of verbs (p. 99)—and does not make provision for context shifts. The following section discusses updating and Chapter 5 explores time shifts.

(c) *Contextual Monitoring: Change and Continuity*

Some of the most useful research on context has been carried out by artificial intelligence researchers working on robotics problems. The main concern of these researchers is to examine how each new action affects the context it occurs in. This work is both practical and philosophical, since it aims to produce robots which act in a meaningful way on their context and also hypothesizes about the mental assumptions involved in performing and understanding simple actions.

The title given to this work is 'the frame problem', a term originally used by J. McCarthy (1968)[5] in his study of liquids, but now used more broadly to describe the study of the effects of actions on their contexts (e.g. Pylyshyn 1987; F. M. Brown 1987). Garnham (1988: 129) summarizes[6] this research as follows:

This problem takes its name from an analogy between successive states of the world and frames in an animated cartoon. To describe any frame completely requires a large number of statements. However, most of these statements remain the same from frame to frame. Only a few change. The frame problem is to specify which ones change as a result of an action being performed.

The frame problem also accounts for what does not change as a result of the action. If a person moves a saucer and teacup across a table, the two objects move relative to the table, but they do not necessarily change position relative to each other (Hayes 1971). Moreover, the context does not change in other respects. For example, the person pushing the cup and saucer does not disappear, their hair does not turn purple and the wallpaper does not come off.[7] A certain amount of continuity can be assumed.

The robotics models discussed by 'frame problem' researchers generally involve a robot creating a contextual representation of the real world (or a simplified world containing a small number of objects). A reader's creation of a fictional world is parallel to this. For the reader, the fictional world is presented through the medium of the text, which can only present a limited amount of information at any one time. The human mind must compensate for this by bringing isolated statements together into a connected whole, assuming the continued existence of entities even when they are not actually being referred to. Du Bois (1980: 204), for example, argues that an object must:

. . . be first introduced into the discourse as a discrete entity, and then traced through the evolving narrative. The continuity of the object's identity must be established. This continuity of the real object with itself runs as a continuous thread in the real world, but in discourse the continuity can be expressed only intermittently, through phrases which appear at intervals in the narration.

---

[5] See also J. McCarthy and Hayes (1969).
[6] See also Lormand (1990) for a summary of 'the frame problem'.
[7] For similar observations, see Pylyshyn (1987).

In the same volume, Chafe (1980*b*: 41–2, see also 1990: 93–6), makes a similar point about other types of information, such as details of the setting:

... [information about the setting] needs to be placed at the beginning of a narrative ... Once established in that manner, it can be retained in peripheral consciousness as background orientation for the particular, localized events which may then be focused on.   (p. 42)

The intermittent nature of text can be seen by looking at any text extract and noticing how much each sentence omits to tell us about the context as a whole. By 'context', I mean here not just the physical location, but details of the participants present in that location and any other salient information about the context.

EXAMPLE 4.1

   'Speaking professionally,' said Doctor Prunesquallor, 'I should say the face was irregular.'
   'Do you mean it's ugly?' said Lord Groan.
   'It is unnatural,' said Prunesquallor.

                            (Mervyn Peake, *Titus Groan* (1985), 50)

The last sentence of this extract refers only to Prunesquallor. This last sentence makes no mention of Lord Groan and were this one sentence quoted in isolation to someone who had not read the previous text, they would not be aware of Lord Groan at all. The reader of this passage nevertheless assumes the presence of both Lord Groan and Doctor Prunesquallor throughout the extract. If, moreover, they were in the process of reading the whole novel, they would, on the basis of previous text mentions, also know the location to be a landing and know that a third character, Steerpike, is secretly listening to the conversation.

   Were the text to be explicit in each sentence about all of this contextual information, the extract would read something like this:

   'Speaking professionally,' said Doctor Prunesquallor to Lord Groan, on the landing, overheard by Steerpike, 'I should say the face was irregular.'
   'Do you mean it's ugly?' said Lord Groan to Doctor Prunesquallor, on the landing, overheard by Steerpike.
   'It is unnatural' said Prunesquallor to Lord Groan, on the landing, overheard by Steerpike.

This form of presentation would probably make reading more difficult, rather than easier (Smyth *et al.* 1987: 182), as well as being quite unnecessary. Readers do not need to be reminded of the fictional context in every sentence if, as they read, they monitor this context mentally. Of course, readers of a narrative will not need to remember every detail from the previous text, but they do generally need to remember important details such as who is present and where the action is taking place. These details can usually be assumed to stay constant, unless there is some indication to the contrary.

(d) *Contextual Consciousness*

Robotics researchers (e.g. Haugeland 1987: 84) sometimes use the expression 'sleeping dogs' (as in 'let sleeping dogs lie') to describe the heuristic of assuming everything to remain the same unless there is explicit mention otherwise. This expression, however, seems to downplay the importance of contextual information. It suggests that the background is either ignored altogether or 'hidden away' in memory where it can be accessed only if needed.

My own view is that reading is a much more active process than this and that the reader's consciousness must be taken into account (see discussion of Chafe's work in Chapter 2). Many readers form images[8] as they read, not just of isolated actions but of a fuller context which includes other participants and the setting. This seems to reflect a continued awareness of background information, which presumably must involve some mental effort.

Contextual monitoring is a form of memory, but an active form. The existence of different types of memory can be seen from the fact that in everyday speech the word 'remember' is used in different senses. If an individual is told: 'Remember the last time you went to a restaurant', they will search their minds for a mental store of information created on a previous occasion. If, on the other hand, a person is shown a tray of objects and at that point told: 'Remember everything that is on the tray', they are expected

---

[8] There have been many summaries of imagery in psychology, although in the majority of these, experimenters simply instruct their subjects to think of an object, rather than studying how images are created in response to texts such as narratives. See e.g. Kosslyn (1975, 1980) and Pylyshyn (1973).

to create a new mental store there and then, keeping the information activated. Although the word 'storage' is useful for showing how information is gathered together, it underplays the extent to which this information may still be in consciousness (albeit in peripheral consciousness, as Chafe 1980*b* suggests).

In everyday life, a parallel to this contextual monitoring is the need for individuals to keep track of their intentions in order to make sense of the world. For example, if a person decides to walk to the local shops, he/she needs to be able to keep in mind this intention, recognizing when the destination has and has not been achieved. Individuals do not, as they take each footstep, wonder what they are doing and have to remember back to when they formulated the intention. They keep their intention active, carrying it forward.

Of course individuals do sometimes get distracted and temporarily 'forget what they are doing' (see Reason and Mycielska 1982 for a discussion of absent-mindedness). A person may, for example, walk into another room to get a pair of scissors and then, on arrival, forget what object was required. This may happen with fairly trivial tasks in familiar surroundings, but if it occurred all the time a person would hardly achieve anything and would be suffering from a very serious disability. Amnesia can occasionally take this form. O. Sacks (1985: 25), for example, describes an unusual case of a patient suffering from Korsakov's syndrome (caused by excessive intake of alcohol) who has:

... an extreme and extraordinary loss of recent memory—so that whatever was said or shown or down [*sic*] to him was apt to be forgotten in a few seconds' time. Thus I laid out my watch, my tie, and my glasses on the desk, covered them, and asked him to remember these. Then, after a minute's chat, I asked him what I had put under the cover. He remembered none of them—or indeed that I had even asked him to remember.

Campbell (1989: 321–38) cites similar cases. Sacks refers to his patient as 'the lost mariner' (p. 22) for the man is ' . . . isolated in a single moment of being, with a moat or lacuna of forgetting all round him . . . He is man without a past (or future), stuck in a constantly changing, meaningless moment' (p. 28; Sacks's omission marks).

People generally have the capacity to remember, as well as the ability to make assumptions that what was recently true often continues to be true. Piaget (1966) suggested that our assumptions about continuity are basic reasoning operations which we must learn as children. Adults know that if an object is placed behind their back it is still there, but, according to Piaget, young babies cease to grasp for the object when they cannot see it. Likewise, adults know that if water is poured from a tall thin beaker into a large wide one, although the volume may look less, there cannot be any change in volume unless some water has been spilled. Young children, however, according to Piaget, are misled by their perceptions and fail to make the assumption of consistency of quantity.

In some respects, reading a text seems to be more demanding[9] in terms of contextual monitoring than responding to the real-world context which physically surrounds us.[10] Textual presentation may give some information (such as the location) only once at the outset. Characters are only mentioned at intervals, sometimes quite long intervals. By contrast, when we have a context around us, we can see a reasonable number of entities at one time (in focal or peripheral vision) and our eyes can move from item to item at will. Nevertheless, we still make certain assumptions to supplement the evidence of our eyes. Sight can provide a lot of information at once about a context, but it does not always reveal everything. If a person turns their back on someone who is in the same room, the first person will still be aware of the second person even if that second person makes no noise. This awareness

---

[9] Recent psychology research by Katzenberger (1994) suggests that children need to learn to make assumptions about participant continuity when relating stories based on picture sequences (see also Berman, forthcoming). Presumably different tasks have their own demands but there must always be a need for such assumptions in both story telling and story comprehension. (I am grateful to Ruth Berman for drawing Katzenberger's work to my attention. My comments are based on the English summary of this Hebrew thesis.)

[10] Psychologists (e.g. Cohen, Eysenck, and Le Voi 1986; M. K. Johnson and Raye 1981; M. K. Johnson 1988; Koriat, Ben-Zur, and Sheffner 1988) use the term 'reality monitoring' to describe our ability to distinguish between a past event which actually happened and one which we only imagined to happen. Ellis and Hunt (1989: 112) give the example of people not being able to remember whether they actually locked a door or just thought they did. This type of monitoring keeps track of our beliefs about fairly automatic actions.

The idea of 'co-participant-tracking' suggested by H. Sacks (1992e, f) is closer to the notion of contextual monitoring discussed in this book. Sacks observes how conversational participants track who is present at any point in a conversation in order to assess mutual knowledge for subsequent utterances.

comes not from the senses but from mental monitoring of the current context. Individuals can be assumed to have this awareness because they behave differently when other people are around, even if they cannot see them. We also make similar assumptions about objects. If our view of a chair is partly obscured by a table, we assume that the hidden part of the chair still exists even though we cannot see it.

Contextual monitoring is, of course, also necessary during telephone conversations, since the participants are not visible to each other. Verbal feedback provides each person with intermittent reassurance that the other party is still there, but for some of the time they must simply assume this to be the case. A blind person in a room[11] with a group of sighted and blind people has a more difficult task to perform because of the need to monitor a number of participants. There may be occasions when no one is speaking and so the only auditory signals of presence will be noises of movement, which are often not in themselves enough to identify any particular participant. When one person speaks the others can give verbal feedback but such sounds may be drowned out by background noise, may be difficult to attribute to specific people, and may not be forthcoming from all participants. It is easier to monitor who is in the room and, regardless of whether they make any noise, assume them to be there until there is some indication that they leave. The reader of fiction is in this respect similar to a blind person for the reader receives only intermittent signals of the presence of the characters from the text and must therefore monitor the fictional context mentally. Of course, in constructing a representation of the fictional world in their heads, some readers may form a quasi-visual image (Eysenck and Keane 1990: 207–35). This is, however, only parallel to a non-congenitally blind person (or a sighted person with their eyes shut) receiving auditory input and translating this into quasi-visual form in their imagination. Visual terms like 'point of view'[12] are useful

---

[11] Comments on blindness both in this section and throughout the book are based on my own informal observations from 1986–1988 at Queen Alexandra College for the Blind, Birmingham; The Commercial Training College (Royal National Institute for the Blind), London (now in Loughborough); and The City and Hackney Talking Newspaper for the Blind, London.

[12] 'Point of view' in the novel is sometimes compared to our interpretation of a painting (e.g. Uspensky 1973; S. Ehrlich 1990: 1) or our view through a camera lens or window (e.g. Zubin and Hewitt 1995: 132–3). Fowler (1986: 127–8) sug-

expressions to describe what is going on in 'the mind's eye' once a context has been built.[13] In terms of building the context in the first place, however, blindness may be a more appropriate metaphor than vision.

(e) Contextual Monitoring: Inferring Change

'Assuming continuity unless stated otherwise' is a reasonable heuristic for much of context monitoring, but it ignores a certain type of change. In addition to stated changes and unstated continuity, there is often some inferred change. This is the lesson of the 'frame problem' in robotics research.[14] If we push a saucer and a cup is positioned on top of it, the cup and its contents move too (Hayes 1971). Dennett (1987) presents us with a scenario in which a hypothetical robot R1 is given the task of saving its spare power pack from a bomb in a room. Since the power pack is on a small wagon, R1 pulls the wagon out of the room, overlooking the fact that the bomb is on the wagon too. R1 has failed to model the whole context. Many actions have indirect consequences within their context and an awareness of the context is necessary to take account of these indirect consequences.

In narrative text, this means that a stated action may have unstated side effects. Most of the robotics problems involve objects being moved from one location to another, but where there are people in the context we need to think of the psychological effects as well as the physical ones. For example, when the text describes someone speaking, we must not only assume the continued presence of any listeners, we must also assume that the listeners hear and that their knowledge changes accordingly. Therefore,

gests that 'Just as a painting is composed structurally so that the viewer seems to see some objects close up, some in the distance, some focused, and some less clear; so that the eye moves from one part of the painting to another in an apparently natural succession—in the same way, someone who reads a novel which represents objects, people, buildings, landscapes, etc., is led by the organization of the language to imagine them as existing in certain spatial relationships to one another and to the viewing position which he feels himself to occupy.' The term 'point of view' does not of course just refer to vision, for it can also encompass access to one particular character's psychological and ideological perspective (Uspensky 1973; Fowler 1986: 128).

[13] Chafe (1980*b*: 12, 42) compares different levels of consciousness with focal and peripheral vision (see Ch. 2 for a discussion of Chafe's work).

[14] See Dennett (1990) for a summary.

although our knowledge of the context often provides an unchanging backcloth for the action, we must also be aware that if two things are in the same context they can have an inferred effect on each other.

Inferred changes will generally be limited to other entities that are in the context or are connected in some other way (as discussed later in this chapter). The 'communicative contract' between a writer and reader limits possible inferences because, in accordance with Grice's maxim of quantity (1975, 1978), a reader can expect to be told if anything extraordinary occurs. Although this maxim is sometimes breached (as in Agatha Christie's *The Murder of Roger Ackroyd* (1957), when the narrator fails to tell us that he is the murderer), much communication depends on it.

Context monitoring is, however, complicated for the reader of fictional narrative by the fact that the whole context may suddenly change. In everyday life, we cannot suddenly be transported back or forwards several years in time and we cannot be instantaneously relocated miles away. In fiction this does not usually happen to the characters themselves (except in science fiction), but the reader's focus of attention may be suddenly shifted from context to context in this way. This means that although there is a general expectation of continuity within a context, there also has to be a readiness to respond to signals of total change, as discussed in Chapter 5.

2. DESCRIBING NARRATIVE CONTEXTS: INITIAL NOTIONS AND TERMINOLOGY

In the remainder of this chapter I outline the basic elements of my model for describing a reader's monitoring of narrative contexts, introducing some terminology which will be used throughout the book. This chapter concentrates mainly on single contexts, but Chapter 5 looks in detail at switches between contexts and at retrieval of previously activated contexts.

I am not aiming to look at every detail that the reader processes, although obviously a comprehensive account would need to do this. My main interest is in 'core' facts about the context, such as where the action is located, the people involved, the time of the action. Without this information the reader would find it impossible to interpret 'shorthand' linguistic forms such as pronouns or to make sense of the events that occur. The demands of the subsequent text for contextual information suggest that writers assume that experienced readers have this textually presented information available in memory and that they can access this. Readers may hold more contextual information than that required to interpret the subsequent text, but my emphasis here is on trying to ascertain the minimum amount of textually presented information needed for the text to make sense.

(a) Contextual Frames

I use the term 'contextual frame' (or 'frame')[15] to describe a mental store of information about the current context, built up from the text itself and from inferences made from the text. Contextual frames carry facts which are 'episodic' (to use Tulving's (1972, 1983) term discussed in Chapter 2) within the fictional world. This means that information may be true on a particular occasion within a story, but may not be relevant beyond this. So, on one occasion X and Y may be together in Location L1, but on another occasion X and Y may be together in Location L2. Although there may be no inherent link between these entities, I am suggesting that each contextual configuration needs to be retained in memory, at least temporarily. Without this, we could not create a context from the fragments of information provided in individual sentences. Also, as will be discussed in Chapter 5, we need to assume that this information is held in memory if we are to account for the recall of previously activated contexts on occasions when the text mentions one or two elements of the context but does not re-specify the full configuration.

In addition to these basic 'episodic' relations, frames can also be assumed to hold salient details about the situation (e.g. the purpose of the encounter) and must, for a short period at least, retain some details of the descriptions and events that have been recently referred to. Much anaphoric decoding relies on readers being aware of actions or states mentioned in the previous sentence or sentences (e.g. in 'John shot Henry He fell to the ground', the reader needs to be aware of who has been shot in order to judge who has fallen). Some of this stored information may be fairly

---

[15] See Emmott (1989, 1992, 1994, forthcoming *a*) for other discussions of this notion.

trivial (e.g. John is currently seated, but Henry is standing) and is unlikely to be remembered for any length of time, but may be needed to make sense of events in the short term.

In addition to the 'episodic' information stored in contextual frames (such as the fact that John happened to be in a restaurant with Henry at a particular time), there is also 'non-episodic' information which is true beyond the immediate context, such as the fact that John is tall or the restaurant is expensive. This is the type of information that would be stored in entity representations (which can be subdivided into classes such as character representations and location representations). The frames would simply contain the information that brings all these entities together on a particular occasion, providing the contexts in which events occur.

It is, of course, impossible to say at this stage that particular groups of neurons hold contextual information and that others hold entity information (and quite possibly the information is held in distributed networks rather than actual 'stores'). Scientists do not know yet how neurological activity relates to the complex cognitive processing that takes place during activities such as reading. My aim here is simply to indicate the type of text-derived information that needs to be drawn on if the text is to be understood. In particular, I am drawing attention to links which need to be made (e.g. participants and places on a particular occasion) and information which needs to be kept separate (e.g. a description of one character does not necessarily apply to another character), using the notion of mental representations to signal how this information is handled. Somehow the brain must be able to make these distinctions, but until we have some proper understanding of the mind–brain connection, we can only provide models of how information processing might be achieved. Although I may on occasions refer to mental representations as if they are a psychological reality, these representations are simply part of a hypothesis about how information must be managed if the text is to be understood.

(b) Building and Activating Fictional Contexts

This section provides some basic terminology which will be drawn on throughout the book to describe the information-processing tasks which are necessary if fictional contexts are to be created and managed. The terminology will also be used to signal the amount of information the mind needs to be aware of over and above the explicit content of the sentence being processed at any particular point in time.

Let us assume that the reader can hold information about more than one context at once, but that the reader's attention is usually concentrated on one context in particular. To make this distinction, I use the terms 'binding' and 'priming', as described below.

Binding means simply that 'episodic' links between entities (people and places) are established, thereby creating a context which is monitored by the mind. The term 'frame' describes the mechanism by which the mind makes and retains these links. For fictional narrative, therefore, 'binding' means the reader's awareness that one or more fictional characters are in one particular fictional place at one particular time. Characters are bound in to a mental frame at the point at which the text mentions that they enter a place, and they remain bound there until there is an indication that they leave and therefore need to be bound out. At any one point in the novel one or more frames may be set up. For example, in one chapter of Douglas Adams's *Dirk Gently's Holistic Detective Agency* (1988), a reader needs to know that Reg and Richard are present together in Reg's sitting room (p. 63), whilst simultaneously a horse is upstairs in the bathroom. Reg, Richard, and the sitting room can, therefore, be regarded as all bound into one context, monitored by one frame, and the horse and the bathroom can be regarded as bound into another context, monitored by another frame.

Priming, by contrast, is used in this study to describe the process by which one particular contextual frame becomes the main focus of attention for the reader. Since any one sentence of a narrative will normally only follow events in one context, the reader processing that sentence will concentrate on the action occurring in that particular place. The context which is currently 'the reader's main context' is the primed context and the characters and location are then both bound and primed. In the example given above, the reader of Adams's novel is, at this particular point, following the action in the sitting room. Reg, Richard, and the sitting room are, therefore, primed as well as bound, whereas the horse and the bathroom are just bound.

The terms 'priming' and 'binding' both describe types of monitoring and, like the term 'frame', are therefore expressions which relate to the representational level in the mind, although they are set up by mentions of the characters and context in the text. When characters are primed, the mind remains aware of characters whether or not the text mentions them in any particular sentence. I will use the terms **textually-overt** and **textually-covert**, abbreviated to **overt** and **covert**, to describe whether a primed character is being referred to or not by a sentence. These expressions refer to the input or lack of input from the text at any one point. Mentally, readers are continually aware of primed characters, whether they are overt or covert.

Characters, therefore, are overt if, in the sentence concerned, there is a mention of them by a name, common noun, or pronoun, or if there is a grammatical elision or some other indication at the textual level that a character is present. In the following sentence, both Richard and Reg are overt participants even though Richard is mentioned only by pronouns.

E X A M P L E 4 . 2

He [Richard] poured some for himself, and then some for Reg, who was quietly contemplating the fire and was in need of a refill.

(Douglas Adams, *Dirk Gently's Holistic Detective Agency* (1988), 63)

Shortly after this sentence there follows a paragraph of direct speech which is untagged and therefore not directly attributed to anyone. A reader knows, however, that someone in the frame must be saying the words and can deduce that the speaker is Reg. Reg is, therefore, an overt participant during the course of this direct speech, even though he is not mentioned by either a noun or a pronoun. He is overt because the text is at this point drawing the reader's attention towards him. The sentence requires the reader to find a referent for the speaker role.

Example 4.1 illustrated the fact that not all sentences contain 'traces' of every participant who is present. In the final sentence of that example, Prunesquallor is overt but there is no trace of the other characters, no signal of their presence. Lord Groan and Steerpike are, therefore, covert participants while Prunesquallor speaks. The reader knows these characters to be there not because the text at that point signals their presence but because they have been mentioned earlier and so can be assumed still to be there. Covert means that the participant is temporarily 'hidden' as far as the text is concerned, although the character is nevertheless present in the reader's mind in the primed frame.

Characters who are not in the primed frame, the frame that is being actively monitored by the reader, are neither overt nor covert. They are not present in 'the reader's main context'. During Example 4.2, the horse remains bound into a different frame. The horse is, therefore, unprimed and so is neither overt nor covert.

The complete set of characters who have been introduced into a story at any one point form the **central directory**.[16] The central directory includes not only primed characters and bound unprimed characters but also unbound unprimed characters. These unbound characters are those who exist within the fictional world but are not known to be in any particular context at that particular point. Since they are unprimed they are neither overt nor covert. These different levels of knowledge are summarized in Figure 4.1 and are discussed further in Chapter 7.

<u>central directory</u>

| unbound and unprimed | bound and unprimed | bound and primed −overt |
| | | bound and primed −covert |

FIG. 4.1. Different levels of knowledge about characters in a fictional world

---

[16] Artificial intelligence programs may likewise include a 'history list' of objects that have been mentioned in the discourse (Mellish 1985: 21–2).

The overt and covert participant sets will often change from sentence to sentence; the primed participant set will, unless the make-up of the frame is modified (as described in Chapter 5), remain the same. This can be seen by turning again to Example 4.1, reproduced below:

> 'Speaking professionally,' said Doctor Prunesquallor, 'I should say the face was irregular.'
> 'Do you mean it's ugly?' said Lord Groan.
> 'It is unnatural,' said Prunesquallor.
>
> (Mervyn Peake, *Titus Groan* (1985), 50)

The primed participant set is the same for both sentences of this extract (Dr Prunesquallor, Lord Groan, Steerpike). In the first sentence, however, it is Dr Prunesquallor who is mentioned by the text and hence it is Dr Prunesquallor who is overt and the rest covert. In the second sentence Lord Groan is overt in the main narrative and Prunesquallor is overt within the direct speech (because of the pronoun 'you'), but Steerpike is still covert. In the third sentence, Prunesquallor is again overt and the others are covert. The location remains covert throughout the extract, as does Steerpike.

The terminology used in this section can also be applied to real-world situations. For a blind person monitoring a real-world context, the people in that context at any one time are primed. Those people who are at any moment evident to the blind person's senses due to hearing, touch, etc. are, at that moment, overt. Those who are assumed to be present, but are not at that point evident to the senses are covert. Anyone who is assumed to be in another location at that particular point in time is bound into that other location but is unprimed and is, therefore, neither overt nor covert. Despite these similarities, the blind person does, however, differ from the reader because the blind person is physically part of the context that they are monitoring, being bound in to it.

(c) *Inferring Continuity and Change within Fictional Contexts*

Once a configuration of character(s) and a location is established within a contextual frame, the reader can expect the character(s) to remain there (until there is some signal to the contrary). In the following example, for instance, the character is still there even in sentences when only the setting is mentioned, such as sentences 2 and 4:

EXAMPLE 4.3

(1) <u>She</u> [Stella] left London at midday by train, armed with food unobtainable in Essex: salamis, cheeses, spices, wine. (2) The sun shone, but it wasn't particularly warm. (3) <u>She</u> hoped there would be heating in the cottage, July or not.

(4) The train was empty.

(Doris Lessing, 'A Man and Two Women', in *A Man and Two Women* (1965), 90; my emphasis and numbering)

In the first sentence of this example the text describes a context in which Stella is on the train. She is at this point an overt participant. In the second sentence the reader must still remain aware of Stella, although she is now textually-covert. When the text tells us that it isn't 'particularly warm', this presumably means that Stella isn't particularly warm. This inference, if made, can be added to the entity representation for Stella. This then makes sense of the fact that Stella is hoping that there will be heating in the cottage. In the final sentence, Stella is again covert, but we can assume Stella's presence on the train, interpreting the sentence to mean that the train is relatively uncrowded or that there is no one else on it.[17]

The above example shows the 'episodic' link created between a character and a context. Similar links are established between characters in the same context. A reader can also make inferences about these characters because they are together. The equivalent to this in robotics was the assumption that pushing the saucer would move the cup too. In narrative text, for example, when one

[17] It might, perhaps, be argued that sentence 4 is a continuation of Stella's thoughts and that the train is empty as seen from her perspective. Whether or not this is true of this example, it raises the question of the need to track point of view (see Duchan, Bruder, and Hewitt 1995*b* for recent work on this). Whilst I would agree that it is often necessary to track point of view, the reader also needs to retain an awareness of the context beyond the focalizer and focalized (and, in many cases, to have an awareness of other contexts). This becomes more evident in contexts which have multiple participants, not all of whom may fit into the categories of focalized or focalizer at any one point in a narrative. (See Emmott (forthcoming *a*) for further discussion of the interplay between contextual monitoring and the tracking of a subjective perspective.)

character in a frame speaks, the reader not only assumes the presence of the others in the frame, but can also assume them to hear what is said. Likewise, when a character performs an action, the other characters present can be assumed to see what occurs. If this were not the case, we would expect to be told (see the discussion of 'restricted contexts' below).

Links within a context also exist between characters and objects. If a character is in a car and the car veers off the road, the character can usually be assumed to go off the road too (see Example 7.8). If a bomb explodes in a room, it probably injures the people in the room. If a group of people are watching the television and one person turns it off, the others are no longer watching it. Many of these inferences are probabilities rather than certainties, made on the basis of assumptions about cause and effect in circumstances of physical proximity. The judgements are made on the basis of our general knowledge about what happens in real contexts in such circumstances, but the links result from text-derived knowledge of the contextual configuration.

Unless we assume readers make these type of inferences, it is impossible to explain how people read the texts that they do. The cognitive work involved in assuming both continuity and change must be included in cognitive models. As each new statement is encountered, readers need to assess the effect of events on the rest of the context, drawing on their general knowledge, and if necessary updating their entity representations of both overt and covert characters.

In addition to contextual links that are true within a specific context, readers also need to be aware of 'non-episodic'[18] relations between characters. These are facts which are true beyond specific contexts, such as about relationships. The text may only overtly mention the relationship from one point of view, so further inferences often have to be made. For example, if we read that A is B's uncle we need also to store the information that B is A's nephew. Likewise, if C goes to a certain school and D goes to that school, then the reader can deduce that C and D both go to the same school.

'Non-episodic' links between characters can result in inferences being made on the basis of the relation, even when two characters

---

[18] I am using the converse of Tulving's term 'episodic' here (see Ch. 2). The information is not, however, 'semantic', as it is not part of our general knowledge and is not true beyond this particular fictional world.

are not contextually co-present. In the following example, the reader's knowledge that Guy and Gertrude are married enables the entity representation of Gertrude to be updated as soon as Guy is mentioned, regardless of whether they are in the same context or not.

EXAMPLE 4.4

Time had passed and Guy Openshaw was dead. He lived longer than had been expected, but obliged the doctor's prediction by dying on Christmas Eve. His ashes had been scattered in an anonymous garden. It was now early April in the following year, and Gertrude Openshaw, *née* McCluskie, was looking out of a window at a cool cloudy sunlit scene.

(Iris Murdoch, *Nuns and Soldiers* (1981), 103; Murdoch's italics)

As soon as the text states that Guy is dead, the reader can automatically add to Gertrude's entity representation the fact that she is a widow. Subsequently, when Gertrude is mentioned, this information explains why Gertrude's maiden name is provided as well as her married name. Inferences are constantly being made on the basis of non-contextual links such as relationships, in addition to inferences resulting from the juxtaposition of two unrelated characters in the same context.

(d) *Real-World Assumptions about Fictional Contexts*

To make judgements about the effect of actions in a fictional context, readers need to draw on their general knowledge of the physical constraints of real-world contexts, assuming similar constraints to operate in the fictional world (unless there is some indication to the contrary). For example, although the participants may be in the same physical location there may be factors mentioned which we know will prevent them hearing or seeing each others' actions, such as distance or additional noise. In this case, the context can be described as a 'restricted' context because there are restrictions on the inferences we would normally draw about characters in the same location. The same restrictions apply when characters are in different locations but can still hear each other, as when they are on the telephone or in different rooms. It is arguable whether these circumstances should be regarded as one restricted context or two overlapping restricted contexts.

Sometimes the existence of a restricted context or restricted overlapping contexts must be inferred from the behaviour of the characters. For example, in Alan Ayckbourn's television play *Way Upstream* (Terry Johnson, 1988, UK) four characters sit on the deck of a riverboat, two at one end and two at the other. From the angle of the camera, they are all in view and appear to be quite close together. The subject matter of the conversation makes it clear, however, that the two characters nearest to the camera know that they cannot be overheard. All four characters are overt to the viewer (all can be seen), but each end of the boat forms a separate context in terms of sound, although the characters can all see each other.

Our real-world knowledge of spatial constraints also controls our assumptions about how likely it is that other characters will enter the context. Sometimes it will be impossible for characters to enter the current context because they are bound into a frame set in a distant physical location. Sometimes characters may be sufficiently near that they can be assumed to be able to enter a context easily. In such cases a close context may become an overlapping restricted context, because although the characters may not normally be able to hear each other, it may be possible to hear screams, shouts, and other loud noises. This type of inferencing may be used in interpreting the following example. Gwenda and Dr Kennedy are in the hall of Gwenda's house. The danger to Gwenda is increased because, to her knowledge and to the reader's knowledge, there is no one else either in or close by the house.

EXAMPLE 4.5

   Gwenda retreated before him, slowly, the scream frozen in her throat. She had screamed once. She could not scream again. And if she did scream no-one would hear.
   Because there was no-one in the house—not Giles, and not Mrs Cocker, not even Miss Marple in the garden. Nobody. And the house next door was too far away to hear if she screamed. And anyway, she couldn't scream . . . Because she was too frightened to scream. Frightened of those horrible reaching hands . . .
   She could back away to the nursery door and then—and then—those hands would fasten round her throat . . .

A pitiful little stifled whimper came from between her lips.

And then, suddenly, Dr Kennedy stopped and reeled back as a jet of soapy water struck him between the eyes. He gasped and blinked and his hands went to his face.

'So fortunate,' said Miss Marple's voice, rather breathless, for she had run violently up the back stairs, 'that I was just syringing the greenfly off your roses.'

(Agatha Christie, *Sleeping Murder* (1977), 184)

From the second paragraph of this example, it seems that Gwenda and Dr Kennedy are completely alone. Subsequently, this paragraph can be seen to represent the erroneous beliefs of Gwenda, the passage being from her subjective point of view rather than being a statement by an omniscient narrator. On first reading, however, Miss Marple seems to be appearing from nowhere as she comes to the rescue. She is not mentioned until after she attacks Dr Kennedy, which means that there is some temporary uncertainty about who performs the attack (see the discussion of 'frame participant ambiguity' in Chapter 7). Even when the identity of Dr Kennedy's assailant is revealed, some explanation of how Miss Marple has managed to get there is required. This comes partly from the statement in Example 4.5 that she has run up the back stairs and also from an additional statement in the next chapter of the novel:

EXAMPLE 4.6

'But, of course, dear Gwenda, I should never have dreamed of going away and leaving you alone in the house,' said Miss Marple. 'I knew there was a very dangerous person at large, and I was keeping an unobtrusive watch from the garden.'

(Agatha Christie, *Sleeping Murder* (1977), 185)

So, unknown to the reader and the other characters, Miss Marple has been in an overlapping, restricted context which, presumably, has allowed her to hear Gwenda's scream even though she could not see what was going on. The reader can only set up this 'Miss-Marple-in-the-garden context' in retrospect. In general, this means that a reader must monitor not only which frames are in existence at any one time, but also the relationship of these frames to each other in terms of physical distance.

Summary

This chapter has argued that events cannot simply be viewed in isolation, but must be judged in terms of their relation to the context in which they occur within the fictional world. Contextual information may be needed to interpret a sentence: to give meaning to 'shorthand' forms such as pronouns; to give fuller meaning to lexical forms; or to make the significance of new information clear. Many events may also be inferred to have an effect on entities which are not mentioned in a sentence but are present in the same physical location. This means that information about the current context must be available 'in mind' as each new sentence is read.

I use the term *'contextual frame'* to suggest a mental store of information about a particular context. Entities within a location are *bound* within that location—'episodically' connected to the place and the other people and objects there. When the narrative describes a particular context, that particular context is *primed*. When characters within the primed context are referred to in a sentence they are *overt*. For the rest of the time the characters in the primed frame are still assumed to be present, albeit *covert*.

The assumption that covert characters are present allows inferences to be made about these characters even when they are not mentioned, with the result that their entity representations can be updated accordingly. In addition to these 'episodic' contextual links, 'non-episodic' links may also have to be taken into account when assessing the impact of an event. For example, if two characters are related, the action of one may affect the other, even if they are not co-present in a location at the same time. In judging the effects of an event, readers must also draw on their real-world knowledge of spatial restrictions, such as whether two characters can hear each other in a 'restricted' context or in two nearby contexts.

This chapter has looked mainly at how a single contextual frame is created, with the reader needing to make assumptions about the continued presence of the characters in the context until there is some suggestion that the context has changed. The following chapter looks at how a context may be altered and also at how one context may be completely replaced by another.

5

Modifying, Switching, and Recalling Contexts

Judging contextual continuity and change requires inference-making on the part of the reader. Chapter 4 suggested that narrative events may require the updating of overt and covert entity representations, yet, in a particular context, the reader must also assume some contextual continuity. These assumptions of continuity are necessary, but readers also need to recognize that contexts can change. Characters may move in and out of a location or, alternatively, the narrative may shift to a completely new context. This chapter explores these different types of context change and examines the mechanisms by which a context which has previously been activated may be reinstated.

Section 1 summarizes related research, looking particularly at some of the seminal artificial intelligence work on discourse structure (e.g. Grosz 1977; Linde 1979; Reichman 1985). Section 2 continues my discussion of contextual frames. Sections 2a–c examine *frame modification*, which means that the same contextual frame remains primed but that the frame must be altered to take account of a change to the participant group. Sections 2d–e examine *frame switch*, in which one contextual frame is replaced by another. Section 2f discusses *frame recall*, where a previously primed frame is reinstated, sometimes with an antecedentless pronoun and only minimal linguistic signalling. Section 2g distinguishes between *instantaneous* and *progressive* frame switch and frame recall.

Section 3 broadens the discussion to look at related issues. Section 3a considers the applicability of the model to texts such as science-fiction stories, in which contexts and entities may have different properties from the real world. Section 3b argues that a 'repair mechanism' is needed, for occasions when readers miss or misinterpret signals of a context change and need to revise their contextual assumptions accordingly. Section 3c compares frame switches with readers' re-evaluations of their beliefs about the truth or falsity of situations. Section 3d examines the role that probability plays in textual interpretation, giving examples of participant identification and frame switches.

I. CONTEXT CHANGE: RELATED RESEARCH

As explained in Chapter 3, one of the main achievements of discourse studies—within discourse analysis and related fields such as artificial intelligence—has been to recognize the overall structure of texts. Within non-narrative texts, new units generally either introduce new topics or provide embedded discussion about the current topic. Narrative has its own parallel hierarchical structure. Story schemata researchers, as discussed in Chapter 2, have devised models of narrative structure which identify the main units that develop the storyline, such as 'event' and 'reaction' (Rumelhart 1975). In addition to this type of approach, it is possible to divide narrative into units which relate to contexts. By 'context', I mean the physical placing of individuals in time and space. Contextual units are important because readers need to recognize the context in order to orientate themselves, interpret events, and assess the effects of events on the characters present.

The research that will be discussed in this section comes from a number of distinct disciplines and contributes to our understanding of narrative comprehension in different ways. One type of research has involved recognizing narrative sub-units and attempting to categorize them in a systematic way. Some of this work has involved examining the linguistic items which signal these units and there have also been attempts to assess the cognitive effort involved in switching from one unit to another. In particular, I will discuss work which has studied the return from an embedded stretch of discourse to the main text, much of which relates to genres other than narrative. At the end of the section, I also consider research which examines the mental representations and basic-level general knowledge needed to make inferences about continuity, change, and movement in time and space.

Narrative structure has been examined extensively by narratologists, particularly in terms of breaks in the time line of a narrative. From a theoretical point of view, these time shifts have interested narratologists because they highlight the distinction between the story itself and its realization in text form (see Rimmon-Kenan 1983: 1–5, 133 for a summary). As far as practical analysis is concerned, Genette's (1980, 1988) work has been particularly influential. He has studied the different types of flashback (*analepsis*) and flashforward (*prolepsis*), analysing them in terms of their duration (*extent*), whether they extend back (or forward) beyond the boundaries of the story (*internal* or *external reach*), and whether they involve the same characters (*homodiegesis*) or different characters (*heterodiegesis*). This type of analysis is very useful, but it does not look at the mechanics of how one context is replaced by another. Most narratologists take for granted the linguistic signals and cognitive effort which underlie basic reading operations.

Within linguistics, context shifts have also been examined by linguists working on narrative. Researchers from the Summer Institute of Linguistics (e.g. Grimes 1975, 1978a) have performed analyses of oral narratives in languages other than English. Much of this work focuses on topics that have relevance to the current study, such as the location, size, and composition of participant groups in particular episodes,[1] time and place indicators,[2] and context shifts.[3] The Summer Institute of Linguistics work offers detailed descriptions of the linguistic signals, such as morphological indicators, involved in participant identification and context presentation. The research of Grimes and his associates does not, however, give much insight into the cognitive processing of narrative. Chafe's work (e.g. 1980a)[4] is more promising in this respect, although it should be stressed that his main focus is on the mental effort involved in producing rather than understanding narrative text. Much of Chafe's work describes how events within particular contexts are verbalized (as discussed in Chapters 2 and 3), but Chafe is also interested in switches between contexts. In analysing the production of oral narratives, he notes

[1] For example, Grimes (1975: 185); Leal (1978: 191); Newman (1978: 97); and Krusi (1978: 269).
[2] For example, Grimes (1975: chs. 2 and 6, p. 102); Watters (1978: 8–11); Flik (1978: 48); and Schottelndreyer (1978: 255).
[3] For example, Grimes (1975: 96); Marchese (1978: 73); and Leal (1978: 195).
[4] For example, Chafe (1972: 52, 1974: 127–32, 1976: 33, 1979: 176–80, 1980b: 43–5, 1990: 94–5, 1994).

that context shifts are usually accompanied by hesitations by the speaker which are lengthier than the pauses which usually occur at the end of intonation units. This seems to suggest that the speaker needs time to readjust the context in his/her mind. In fact, the longest pauses were found when the speaker moved from discussing the fictional world to interaction in the real world, an observation which is particularly relevant to oral storytelling embedded within conversation. Within the description of the fictional world itself, though, time–space reorientations represent the major boundaries. Chafe's work is particularly useful because of the combination of detailed linguistic analysis of real narratives with a cognitive account of the effort involved in processing every new event. The measuring of the pauses between intonation units provides a rough index to this effort, although the nature of the inferences being made must still be inferred from the text (or from questioning readers). It is also difficult to assess how much of the effort is due to speakers reorientating their thoughts and how much is due to the task of articulating this reorientation in a suitable form for the listener. Although Chafe's work is more empirical than that of most linguists, he still stresses the extent to which his observations must be accompanied by common-sense introspection on the nature of reading (Chafe 1994).

As far as hierarchical shifts are concerned, one topic which has particularly interested linguists and artificial intelligence researchers is that of resumptions of earlier text units. Later in this chapter and in Chapter 6, I discuss my own work on resumptions after narrative flashbacks and in Chapter 8 I look at resumptions to the main narrative after 'background' information had been provided. Before considering research that has been done by others on narrative, I will discuss here some of the work on resumptions in genres other than narrative. Within artificial intelligence, Grosz's (1977; see also Grosz 1978, 1981, 1986 and Grosz and Sidner 1986) work on instructional dialogue provides an excellent study of how a text resumes after an embedding. Grosz studies transcripts of experts instructing novices to perform tasks, in this case without the two being able to see each others' actions:

> E: Good morning. I would like for you to reassemble the compressor.

E: I suggest you begin by attaching the pump to the platform.

. . . (Other subtasks)

E: Good. All that remains then is to attach the belt housing cover to the belt housing frame.

A: All right. I assume the hole in the housing cover opens to the pump pulley rather than to the motor pulley.

E: Yes that is correct. The pump pulley also acts as a fan to cool the pump.

A: Fine. Thank you.

A: All right the belt housing cover is on and tightened down.

(30 minutes + 60 utterances after beginning)

E: Fine. Now let's see if it works.

(Grosz 1977: 30; Grosz's annotations)

In the final utterance, the speaker is returning from the sub-task to the overall purpose of the exchange, which Grosz argues has been kept broadly in mind, in 'global focus', throughout the whole discussion. Grosz notes that the completion of a sub-task is often marked linguistically by words like 'okay' (or, in this case, 'Fine'), which indicate that a new unit of the discourse is about to begin (p. 37). Since the overall task has been kept in 'global focus', it is pronominalizable. As Grosz points out, the 'it' of the final utterance refers not to the recently mentioned belt housing cover but to the compressor mentioned thirty minutes earlier.

Grosz's work shows the subdivision of a discourse into units and how the first utterance of a resumption may have more coherence with the last stretch of discussion about the topic than with the immediately adjacent sentence. Grosz notes the signalling which rounds off the previous sub-topic (the 'Fine'), but also points to a lack of explicit references to the newly resumed context. Presumably, the listener's understanding of the need to continue discussion of the main task means that he/she can comprehend a pronominal rather than lexical reference to the object being assembled in the main task. In analysing spoken discourse, comprehension can be inferred from the transcript if the analyst observes that the listener does not query the use of 'shorthand forms' such as pronouns (although obviously this does not mean conclusively that the listener has understood).

Linde uses Grosz's notion of global focus to account for pronoun use in oral descriptions of apartment lay-outs, extending the analysis of data first examined in Linde (1974). For example:

> You walk into my apartment and you walk down a long thin hall full of garbage. Actually that's a lie. It's not full of garbage any more.   (Linde 1979: 344)

In the second utterance, the speaker expresses an opinion about her first utterance. The second utterance is, therefore, a metastatement and as such is distinct from the rest of the discourse. This explains how the pronoun 'It' in the last utterance refers not to the lie mentioned in the second utterance but to the hall mentioned earlier. The structure of the discourse influences the interpretation of the pronoun. Linde (1979: 350–2) also gives examples in which the distinction is not between statement and metastatement, but between units of discourse describing parts of the apartment and units of discourse describing the whole apartment. Linde's work has some relevance to the narratives discussed in this book, since she deals with descriptions of physical locations which, although not fictional, still have to be imagined by both the speaker and the listener because they are not themselves physically present in the location specified (unlike Grosz's tasks where the items to be assembled were in front of at least one of the participants). Linde's locations, involving overt spatial relations, are rather like Johnson-Laird's mental models. If, on hearing the above example, the listener creates a quasi-visual image of the hall, then it may be that this image is retained whilst the metalinguistic comment is made. These descriptions do not, however, involve participant groups and are general accounts of a location rather than being set at a particular point in time. They are descriptions of a person's apartment, projected into narrative, rather than stories. These accounts are interesting as far as the borderline between narrative and non-narrative is concerned (see Chapter 8), but are different from the participant group/time/location configurations described in Chapters 4 and 5.

Much of the research on non-narrative has involved studies of switches of topic. Reichman (1985) uses the term 'context spaces' to describe everyday conversation, but she means rhetorical units (of the type discussed in Clause Relational Theory and Rhetorical Structure Theory), rather than descriptions of physical co-presence. Like Grosz and Linde, she also observed examples (e.g. pp. 83–4, 87–8) in which there was pronominalization on return to an earlier mentioned 'context space', providing this earlier 'space' was still 'open' (i.e. more discussion on the topic is anticipated). Like Grosz, she notes that resumptions are often not very explicitly marked. Although there are usually some indicators that the context is being changed, such as 'incidentally', 'okay', 'so', and 'now' (p. 36), Reichman (p. 6) comments that:

... we do not continually interrupt ourselves to say things like, 'Now, I'm going back a minute to what you said about . . .', or 'I'm going to change the subject here and we'll get back to what you're talking about in a minute.' If such verbalizing were necessary, there would be little time for substantive discussion—only time for metadiscussion. Effective, efficient communication occurs because participants share implicit knowledge about the shifting of conversational reference frames.

Like Reichman, Fox (1987a) uses a rhetorical framework, giving examples (pp. 20–40, 45–62, 144–8) of pronouns from conversation and expository written text that are used after what she calls a 'return pop', a resumption of a previous topic of the discourse. Fox observes that in speech, the resumption is often signalled by an exact lexical repetition of key words or phrases from the earlier discussion of the topic (p. 32). She also observes that resumptions can occur with pronominalized referents, but that this depends partly on the nature of the intervening material (e.g. whether an embedded unit is a sub-topic or a quite separate topic) and whether this intervening material has been explicitly closed off. Fox found that pronominalized resumptions were common if the referent of the intervening material was of a different gender, but still possible if the referents of the two stretches of text were of the same sex.

These examples from non-narrative genres show how a resumption can be made without re-specifying the referents lexically, even when the pronoun used in the resumption could in theory refer to a character mentioned in the embedded discourse. When speculating about narrative not all of these researchers have thought that this would be possible in narrative. Sidner hypothesizes about this when considering an example from a story by Potok (see Sidner 1979b: 196–7 for the text). Potok describes an old woman, then switches to telling of an earlier incident involving himself and a male schoolteacher, then returns to the

description of the old woman with the words 'She had worn . . .'
Sidner comments that: 'If Potok had told of a discussion between
[himself] and a female teacher, it would no longer have been possible [to interpret a pronoun]' (p. 197). Sidner calls this a 'stacked
focus constraint'. In fact, the frame recall examples that I present
later in this chapter show that a pronoun can be used in such circumstances and that it is possible for the reader to interpret the
pronoun if there are adequate clues as to which context is
intended. Sidner acknowledges that the 'stacked focus constraint'
is 'overridden' in Grosz's examples from instructional text, but
the examples given in the current chapter show that this is also
possible in narrative.

Some preliminary work on narrative has been done by Fox
(1987*b*, 1988), extending her previous analysis of non-narrative
(1987*a*) to examples from popular fiction, noting pronoun
resumptions after embedded sections. Her analysis concentrates
more on shifts from the main 'event-line', as she terms it, to background generalizations, rather than from one context to another.
This type of shift is discussed in detail in Chapter 8, so Fox's work
is considered further at that point. Although Fox does mention
the reader's attention at points in her analysis, her main interest
is in the 'rhetorical structure' of the text (which she analyses with
Mann and Thompson's Rhetorical Structure Theory (see Chapter
3)) rather than in hypothesizing about the cognitive demands on
the reader.

Within artificial intelligence, Charniak (1972: 23, 145–9,
212ff., 234; 1986), who is often cited within the artificial intelligence literature, uses the term 'bookkeeping', which is similar to
contextual monitoring by frames. Charniak's overall aim, in fact,
is to construct a theory of general knowledge, looking particularly
at how we use this general knowledge to fill gaps in the text of children's stories (see also Charniak 1973, 1978, 1983). Charniak
(1986: 333) discusses, for example, the sentences:

Jack was in the house. Sometime later he was at the store.

and:

Jack was in the house. Sometime later he was in the kitchen.

Charniak is interested in how to model computationally a human
reader's knowledge about whether Jack is still in the house in the

second sentence of each example. By 'bookkeeping', the reader keeps track of Jack's whereabouts. The important point for Charniak, however, is that in the first sentence our general knowledge tells us that if Jack is in the store he is no longer in the house, whereas in the second sentence we assume that Jack is still in the house, because houses contain kitchens. Charniak's work shows that context-building and monitoring depend partly on our general knowledge representations. The contexts which he examines are, however, largely derived from constructed sentences such as those cited above, which lack the complexity of full, adult narratives. Moreover, Charniak's emphasis is more on general knowledge than on the contexts themselves and he does not take his analysis further than this as far as context shifts are concerned.

Much of the work discussed in this section has focused on non-narratives. Narrative is interesting to study in its own right because it has its own reasons for embedding text (e.g. flashbacks, background generalizations) and its own system of signalling switches and resumptions. The contexts described by narrative text are different from the topics or tasks identified by much of the artificial intelligence work. As discussed in Chapter 4, narratives establish configurations of participants and places, the convention being when a particular context is in force, the whole configuration is assumed to be there even if unmentioned at a particular point. This physical co-presence has implications for updating the entity representations of covert characters, as outlined in Chapter 4. It also means, as will be discussed in Section 2f of this chapter, that a hierarchical resumption can be achieved by mentioning just one part of the context and automatically recalling the rest. These physical contexts, therefore, make narrative different from non-narrative and, in consequence, I would suggest that the assumption-making involved in recognizing hierarchical shifts in the different genres may be different. Although my own work has focused almost exclusively on narrative, I briefly discuss the implications of my work for non-narrative texts in Chapter 8.

2. EXPLORING CONTEXT CHANGE

This section continues the discussion of Chapter 4 about fictional contexts, looking particularly at context change. The previous chapter examined how events occurred against a general background of continuity in a context. Although characters take part in the action and other characters are directly or indirectly affected by it, many things can be assumed to remain the same. If one speaks or moves around the room, for example, this does not affect our assumptions about the presence of the other characters. The contextual configuration—who is present in a location at a particular time—is not affected. Although it is necessary to make assumptions about contextual continuity much of the time, readers must also be responsive to signals that the overall context does change. These different types of change are discussed in this section.

(a) *Frame Modification of the Primed Frame*

The most obvious type of change to the overall context is if the text explicitly states that a character enters or leaves the location. I term this **frame modification**, for although there is a change to the contextual configuration, monitored by a particular frame, the reader's assumptions about the rest of the frame must remain intact.

EXAMPLE 5.1

> Giles stood poised to leave. 'You okay, then?' He watched Jim with suspicion.
> 'Yes, love.' Amy reassured him.
> 'Some of us are going to the beach for driftwood, it's low tide.'
> 'Have fun.'
> 'Bye, then.' Giles sprang away, his trainers going thud thud thud on the stairs.
> 'So Hebe was selling things at one time.' Jim tried to place her. Camden Passage? Some antique shop in the provinces? Portobello Road?

> (Mary Wesley, *Harnessing Peacocks* (1986), 145–6)

In this example Giles is bound out of the frame because, at the point at which he says goodbye and goes down the stairs, he leaves the physical location and the other characters. As this is the primed frame, Giles is also primed out. Once primed out, he cannot be classed as a covert participant for the reader must have ceased to monitor his presence. In this situation the reader's assumptions about the other characters must remain the same. The other characters are still primed, for there is no indication that they too have been bound out. So whether or not Jim and Amy are mentioned again immediately, the reader knows them still to be there. In the same way, a blind person who knows that one person has left the room continues to assume the presence of others that are being monitored, whether or not these other people in some way reaffirm their presence.

A frame may be modified by adding or removing characters. After modification, the same frame remains in force even though the participant set has changed. It is the same frame because our monitoring assumptions about the other characters continue despite the change. Likewise, an extension may be built on to a house or the roof replaced, yet the building would still be classed as the same house.

In some cases, there may be so many modifications to a frame that we may find that the opening and closing participant sets are quite different. This can still be regarded as the same frame, since there has been some continuity of assumption after each change, either about the characters who have remained behind or, if they all leave the room at once, about the location.

(b) Frame Modification of an Unprimed Frame

Characters are bound in and out of the primed frame by overt references to them entering or leaving. If a character was said to enter or leave an unprimed frame, this would normally prime that frame automatically, for it would switch the reader's attention to it. It is possible, however, to modify a frame whilst it remains unprimed, as illustrated below:

EXAMPLE 5.2

> She [Isbel] dared not acknowledge to herself that she was *waiting* for that door to open, and yet perhaps she was.
>
> She uttered a faint cry, and half-rose from the couch. The door was opening. . . . Her terrified eyes met those of Judge!
>
> (David Lindsay, The Haunted Woman (1987), 85;
Lindsay's italics and omission marks)

At the opening of this example, the text focuses on Isbel in one room of an old house, this context forming the primed frame.

Judge and two other characters (Roger and Blanche) can be assumed to be elsewhere in the house together, this group forming an unprimed frame. As Judge enters, he is not only bound (and therefore primed) into the primed frame but can be inferred to have been bound out of the unprimed frame. His entry into the primed frame is overt but his exit from the unprimed frame is covert. The reverse process is similar. If characters leave the primed frame with the intention of joining an unprimed frame it can be assumed that they are bound into the unprimed frame, although the reader cannot normally be completely sure that this has happened because the characters may never have actually arrived there.

It may also be possible to infer that an unprimed frame has altered because of the passage of time. In the following example, while Gwenda lies on her bed, the reader can assume that the other characters have either left or will shortly leave the theatre, for the play was just finishing when Gwenda ran out. The longer the period of time, the greater is the assumption that the other characters have been bound out of the now unprimed theatre frame.

EXAMPLE 5.3

At the theatre ... Gwenda sat in the middle of the row between Raymond and the barrister.

The lights went down and the play began.

It was superbly acted and Gwenda enjoyed it very much. She had not seen very many first-rate theatrical productions.

The play drew to a close, came to that supreme moment of horror. The actor's voice came over the footlights filled with the tragedy of a warped and perverted mentality.

'Cover her face. Mine eyes dazzle, she died young...'

Gwenda screamed.

She sprang up from her seat, pushed blindly past the others out into the aisle, through the exit and up the stairs and so to the street ...

With fumbling fingers she got out money, paid the taxi and went up the steps. The servant who let her in glanced at her in surprise.

'You've come back early, miss. Didn't you feel well?'

... She ran up the stairs to avoid further questions.

She pulled off her clothes, left them on the floor in a heap and got into bed. She lay there shivering, her heart pounding, her eyes staring at the ceiling.

(Agatha Christie, *Sleeping Murder* (1977), 23–4)

(c) Frame Modification: Retrospective Binding and Priming

Example 5.2 provides an example of retrospective binding out, for the binding out can be inferred to have taken place prior to the reference to Judge being bound into the primed frame. Unprimed frames are particularly subject to retrospective binding in and out, for the reader is not witnessing the action in these frames.

Iris Murdoch's *The Good Apprentice* provides a further example of retrospective binding out of an unprimed frame:

EXAMPLE 5.4

Edward panted up the narrow flight of stairs. Putting his key in the door he realised that he was drunk. The key skidded over the painted surface seeking the hole. He found it and opened the door, entered and closed the door. The darkened room with its one shaded lamp was curiously cold. Edward saw at once that the newspaper he had put over the lamp was brown and scorched. He quickly removed it, then turned to the divan. The divan was empty. Edward looked quickly about the room, there was nowhere to hide, nowhere to go. There was no one there. Mark was gone. Then he saw the chair drawn up beside the window and the window wide open.

(Iris Murdoch, *The Good Apprentice* (1986), 7)

Here, the retrospective binding out is central to the plot of the novel. Edward has tricked his friend Mark into taking drugs and then has left him asleep whilst he visits Sarah. The reader's attention has been centred on the 'Edward/Sarah' frame, this being the primed frame. Meanwhile, Mark is alone in Edward's room, the text stating that 'Such sleeps could last a long while' (p. 3). When Edward returns he finds that Mark has committed suicide. At some point during Edward's absence Mark has jumped out of the window, so binding himself out of the unprimed frame. The reader does not know exactly when this happened, but it is obviously prior to the point at which Edward discovers that Mark is missing, so the binding out is retrospective. The fact that Mark jumped out of the window whilst Edward was with Sarah heightens Edward's sense of guilt, affecting his behaviour throughout the whole novel.

The examples so far have been of retrospective binding out of an unprimed frame. The following example illustrates retrospective binding and priming into the primed frame:

EXAMPLE 5.5

There seemed to be a great eruption of emotion in the air near to him [Dirk]. A wave of something surged through the room, causing the furniture to flutter in its wake . . . the whole phone leapt into the air and hurtled across the room. The receiver cord wrapped itself round an Anglepoise lamp on the way and brought it crashing down in a tangle of cables, coffee cups and floppy disks. A pile of books erupted off the desk and on to the floor.

The figure of Sergeant Gilks stood stony-faced in the doorway.

'I'm going to come in again,' he said, 'and when I do, I don't want to see anything of that kind going on whatsoever. Is that understood?'

(Douglas Adams, *Dirk Gently's Holistic Detective Agency* (1988), 165–6)

Presumably, if Sergeant Gilks has witnessed the scene in the room, he must have been standing in the doorway prior to the point at which there is an overt reference to him. We therefore assume him to have been both bound and primed in at an earlier point. This means that he can be retrospectively inferred to have been a covert participant in the primed frame. The reader does not, however, know exactly how much of the scene he has witnessed for there is no indication of the precise point at which he was bound into the primed frame. Presumably, Dirk, too, only becomes aware of Sergeant Gilks when the sergeant is overtly referred to.

Retrospective binding and priming also happen in real life. A blind person may miss hearing someone enter the room if there is a lot of background noise. If, at a later stage, that person speaks, the blind person will have to update retrospectively his or her mental frame, wondering exactly how long that person has been there. Conversely, a blind person may miss hearing someone leave and will, if they subsequently learn that this has happened, retrospectively have to bind and prime the other person out. This may also happen when a sighted person misses someone entering or leaving outside of their range of vision.

(d) Frame Switch: Change of Place

Frame modification meant that one particular frame was altered by adding or removing a character. **Frame switch**, on the other hand, means that the reader ceases to directly monitor one frame and starts monitoring another frame. The following example demonstrates both frame modification and frame switch:

Example 5.6: Frame Modification and Frame Switch

'Thank you.' Hebe edged Hannah towards the door, closed it after her. Oh, the joy of being alone! The telephone pealed, shattering with its intrusion the welcome quiet. The cat leapt bristling on to the windowsill. Hebe picked up the instrument.

'Hello.'

''Allo, 'allo, vot colour knickers you wear?' A thick French accent.

'Wrong number.' Hebe put the telephone back in its cradle.

Higher up the street Jim Huxtable sat on the seat a town councillor had given in memory of aged parents who had lived in the street when it was first built.

(Mary Wesley, *Harnessing Peacocks* (1986), 23)

At the beginning of this example Hannah and Hebe are together in Hebe's house. Hannah then leaves, the frame being modified as a result. The reader, however, can still continue to assume Hebe's presence. Frame modification has changed the composition of the frame but has not removed the frame altogether.

Frame switch is quite different from this. After Hebe has put the telephone down, we read that 'Higher up the street Jim Huxtable sat . . .' Jim Huxtable is not being added into the 'Hebe frame', he is not joining Hebe in her house. Instead of changing the existing frame, the new location signals a switch to a quite different frame which replaces the 'Hebe frame'.

As already indicated, the major difference between frame modification and frame switch is that a frame switch can create a new frame. In doing so, frame switch generally leaves the original frame intact. So in Example 5.6, Hebe was in the house alone before the switch to Jim and she is still in the house alone after the switch. The binding of the original frame has not altered, but it is no longer primed. The characters have not moved, it is the reader's perspective which has shifted.

As a result of a frame switch, characters can be primed out without the text overtly referring to them. By contrast, when a primed frame is modified, the text must overtly refer to every character who is primed in or out and must also use a binding marker such as 'came in' or 'left'. No binding marker is necessary when the switch is to a new frame because the characters are not normally entering the new frame. They are already there and the reader is the one who, in his or her imagination, is entering the context.

The frame switch in Example 5.6 is signalled by a reference to the location of the new frame, 'Higher up the street'. Frame switches are often accompanied by an orthographic break in the text created by starting a new chapter or section, as illustrated below, or by simply leaving a gap of a few lines.

E x a m p l e 5 . 7

Abigail lay on her side, well tucked in, the teddy bear she was too young for sitting in the corner by her feet. Adam stood watching her, listening to her silent sleep.

7

With the specialist's contempt for the layman's ignorance, Rufus read accounts of the inquest in two newspapers.

(Barbara Vine, *A Fatal Inversion* (1987), 78)

Orthographic breaks do not always herald a new frame, but they do alert the reader to the possibility of one. In the above example, the gap in the text and the chapter heading ('7') are followed by a frame switch. Rufus has not been present in the previous frame in which Adam is with his young daughter, Abigail, in her bedroom. If this were a frame modification and Rufus was entering the bedroom, some sort of binding marker, such as the words 'Rufus came in', would be expected. Instead this can be assumed to be a frame switch, with the frame containing Adam and Abigail having been primed out. If, from the mention of the newspapers, the reader also assumes that the time is now the following morning, then it would seem unlikely that Adam and Abigail are still together in the bedroom. In these circumstances, the bedroom frame has been retrospectively bound out.

The frame switches that have been discussed so far involve a change from one context in the fictional world to another. The switch may also be from the fictional world into the fictional imagination of one of the characters:

EXAMPLE 5.8

>Eilís put her free hand to her mouth.
>
>—O God, my uncle. The boat is his. He'll be wondering why I'm not back. But he hasn't a phone.
>
>—I'll ring the police, said Delia. They'll get word to him. He may have contacted them already.
>
>Eilís could see her uncle opening his door to some large policeman . . .
>
>(Jeremy Leland, 'The Lake', in *The Last Sandcastle* (1983), 16–17; my emphasis)

The words 'Eilís could see her uncle' mark a frame switch. The verb 'see' is, in theory, ambiguous. It could indicate frame modification if the uncle is entering the 'Eilís/Delia' context and Eilís can physically see him. However, this is unlikely, since the text has mentioned earlier that Eilís's uncle has no idea of where she is. The mention of her uncle 'opening his door' confirms that he is at a distant location rather than joining the 'Eilís/Delia' frame. 'See' in this context must, therefore, mean that Eilís imagines her uncle and in doing so creates a new frame. This type of switch creates a hypothetical context contingent on the thoughts of a character, corresponding to what Werth (MS *a, b*) has termed a 'sub-world'.

(e) Time, Frames, and Frame Switch

Frames are needed not only to monitor participants and their location, but also to monitor time. Monitoring of time is more complex than the reader's other assumptions because time is usually moving inexorably onwards as events are described.

Within a frame, time may move at different speeds. It will normally appear to move relatively slowly during the course of a conversation. On the other hand, in Example 5.3 above, time appears to move much more quickly, since a whole play opens and draws to a close with only two sentences between. These are common observations about narrative text (Genette 1980, 1988) but the important point here is that, in the case of both the conversation and the play, the presence of the characters can be assumed until the text mentions their departure, despite the different speeds at which time moves. For practical purposes, then, this can be classed as a single temporal setting (Grimes 1975: 102).

Sometimes, however, time will move in such a way that the reader cannot expect the same grouping of characters to be there any longer. The narrative may move backwards in time or there may be a leap into the future (e.g. the following day, week, month, or year) which suggests that the frame that has been being monitored may no longer be primed and that it is necessary to switch to a new frame. What constitutes 'a substantial leap in time' will depend on a culture's expectations of how long people will remain together in particular locations. Psychologists (Sanford and Garrod 1981; A. Anderson, Garrod, and Sanford 1983) have tested these expectations empirically, by asking people how long they think such everyday occurrences as a restaurant meal or a visit to the theatre are likely to last, and have suggested that such expectations are applied to models of text comprehension (see also artificial intelligence work by Rieger 1974: 82, 274, 284).

Time must be regarded as a constituent of frames and has only been omitted so far for simplicity and because the reader often only becomes aware of time when there is a frame switch. Examples 5.9 and 5.10, which will be presented and discussed in the following section, give no indication of the precise day or year in which the events in the main narrative occur (although we can assume that it is an evening). However, the reader does know that the time is different from the flashback time, the flashback taking us to the evening before.

(f) *Frame Recall*

In the above examples of frame switch, the switch has resulted in the priming of a completely new frame. We have seen that one of the consequences of this is that characters are left bound into the unprimed frame (unless such a considerable period of time has elapsed that the reader has to infer that they would have left this context). Since the characters are still bound, there is the possibility that the frame can be re-primed. This is termed **frame recall** in this study.

The switch to an unprimed frame is illustrated in Examples 5.9 and 5.10, below, which are from the first chapter of Winston Graham's *After the Act* (1965). Before turning to these examples, some background information is needed about the frames in this chapter of the novel, for without such information it would be difficult to interpret the extracts given. The following summary of the relevant frames provides an indication of the facts that a reader needs to carry in their mind as they process the text. It also indicates how much information is lost when quotations are given 'out of context', or, in other words, how much is lost when no consideration is given to the on-going mental monitoring of context by readers.

The narrator is at home in London and is at dinner with his wife (Harriet) and four guests (Tim Dickinson, Isabel Chokra, Ralph Diary, and Mary Arlett). This will be referred to as the 'dinner party frame'. The narrator's thoughts begin to wander and there is a frame switch to another frame, the 'cocktail party frame'. This involves the narrator remembering the events of the previous evening which he spent at a cocktail party in Paris without Harriet. At this cocktail party there was a girl (later named as 'Alexandra') and a Countess, together with a roomful of other people. The four guests at the dinner party were not at the cocktail party.[5]

The frame switch described above involves setting up a new frame, the cocktail party frame. Subsequently, however, the narrator's thoughts return to the present. Here, in switching to the present, the reader is not switching to a new frame but recalling the dinner party frame. Later still, the narrator again starts to daydream about the previous night and so the cocktail party frame is recalled, these switches continuing to occur throughout the chapter.

---

[5] i.e. <u>Dinner party frame</u>: London (home), main narrative time, narrator, Harriet, Tim Dickinson, Isabel Chokra, Ralph Diary, Mary Arlett.
<u>Cocktail party frame</u>: Paris, flashback time, narrator, girl (Alexandra), Countess.

When a frame is re-primed, it is not necessary to mention each element of the frame again. A mention of one element means that the others, being bound to it, can be re-primed automatically. In this novel, one frame recall is signalled by the words 'Tim Dickinson had asked me something' (p. 9), the name 'Tim Dickinson' being enough to re-prime the whole dinner party frame. Only Tim Dickinson (and the narrator) are overtly referred to at the point of re-priming and the rest of the characters in the frame, and the time and place, are re-primed automatically.

Example 5.9 shows another occasion when the dinner party frame is recalled. At the beginning of the example the action is set at the cocktail party, the re-priming of the dinner party occurring in the final paragraph:

EXAMPLE 5.9

Alexandra had gone across to a short square-built man with freckled hair and a stance as if he was going to block an escaping enemy.

'I hadn't thought of it that way,' I said.

'They bring back memories, of course. I was in Nassau when *Oklahoma* first broke.' The Countess coughed throatily. 'Fishing from glass-bottomed boats. Memories . . . they're as difficult to deal with as indigestion. You're too young yet, Mr Scott. *Forsan et haec* . . . what is that old Latin tag?'

'It's strange,' said Harriet when our four guests had gone, 'to hear you whistling that tune? What's it *called*? . . .'

(Winston Graham, *After the Act* (1965), 13; Graham's omission marks and italics)

The mention of Harriet is sufficient to return the reader to the dinner party frame. The Countess and Alexandra are automatically primed out and the dinner party guests would be automatically primed in were it not for the explicit reference to their departure in the last paragraph (which retrospectively primes them out). Only the mention of Harriet alerts the reader to this switch to the stored frame, for there is no corresponding switch of aspect. The above extract is difficult to read out of context without some form of explanation. In context, however, there is no difficulty as the reader of the novel is aware of both the primed and unprimed frames. In addition, whilst reading about the cocktail party, the reader is anticipating a return to the dinner party frame, for that is where the main action is centred.

The notion of frame recall provides an explanation of how pronouns can be decoded which lack a recent co-referential antecedent.[6] In the following example, the 'she' of the second paragraph is not the same person as the 'she' (Isabel Chokra) in the first paragraph, and yet there is no intervening lexicalization to bring about this shift of referent.

EXAMPLE 5.10

> Isabel Chokra, whom I had known longer than any of the others, took him up on my likeness to Anouilh, which she didn't see, and my mind slipped away again.
>
> I can't remember even now exactly how we met, with what degree of interest the move was made, whether she came to meet me, but when I spoke to her we were some way from the piano. I asked her in French if I could get her more champagne, and she said thank you the waiter is bringing me some.
>
> (Winston Graham, *After the Act* (1965), 10; my emphasis)

From this extract alone, the 'she' pronouns might be wrongly inferred to be co-referential. The reader of the extract knows, from the words 'my mind slipped away again', that the paragraph boundary marks a switch from main frame to flashback. It would be possible to interpret this flashback as an account of how Isabel Chokra and the narrator first met. This would mean that there would be continuity of reference. The reader of the whole novel, however, knows that this may be the recall of the cocktail party frame. At the last mention of the cocktail party, the narrator had just noticed across the crowded room an as yet unnamed girl (Alexandra) to whom he is attracted. The reader, therefore, is expecting to hear more about this strand of the story. In such situations, in fiction, the two are likely to meet. That this is imminent is reinforced by the fact that the stored frame was first introduced with the words 'It could hardly have been more trite, the way I met her . . .' (p. 8). The first words of the novel, too, are 'The day after I met her I flew back to London' (p. 7). In this context the words 'I can't remember even now exactly how we met'

---

[6] Gerrig (1986: 33) calls such pronouns 'unheralded' pronouns.

of Example 5.10 appear to be a natural continuation of the cocktail party frame. The mention of 'the piano' reinforces this interpretation, since the unnamed girl was standing by a piano when last seen.

(g) Progressive Frame Switch and Recall

The type of frame switches and frame recalls that have been discussed so far can be termed **instantaneous**. They involve the reader in a sudden leap in time and/or space which causes the participant set to be primed out, unless there is some indication that one or more of the participants is to be in both frames. **Progressive** frame switch and frame recall have the same effect on the participant set, but do not involve a sudden leap:

EXAMPLE 5.11

[1] 'I've got a better idea,' Meg said, putting on her anorak. 'The Bereland graveyard. Why the Little Wood when we've already got an animal cemetery? Oh, do let's, Alec. It seems so *right*. It's been a traditional burying place for pets for so long. I'd like Fred to be there, I really would.'
[2] 'Why not?'
[3] 'I know I'm a fool. I'm a sentimental idiot but I'd sort of like to think of him with those others. With Alexander and Pinto and Blaze. I am a fool, aren't I?'
[4] 'That makes two of us,' said Alec.
[5] He went across to the old stable block where they kept the tractor and the wood that was stacked for winter and came back with a wheelbarrow and a couple of spades.
[6] 'We'll mark the grave with a wooden plaque, I think. I could make one out of a sycamore log, that's a nice white wood, and you could do the lettering on it.'
[7] 'All right. But we'll do that later.' Meg bent to lift up the parcel ...'

(Barbara Vine, *A Fatal Inversion* (1987), 7;
Vine's italics, my numbering)

This extract begins with Meg and Alec talking in the gunroom. A progressive frame switch occurs with the words 'He went across to the old stable block', as the reader follows Alec, leaving Meg

TABLE 5.1. *Frame progression*

Paragraph number	Status of participant	Linguistic form
1	primed overt participant	name 'Meg', pronoun 'I'
2	primed covert participant	no mention
3	primed overt participant	pronoun 'I'
4	primed overt participant	pronoun 'us'
5 (initial clause)	unprimed participant	no mention
5 (last clause)	primed covert participant	no mention
6	primed overt participant	pronouns 'we' and 'you'
7	primed overt participant	name 'Meg', pronoun 'we'

behind in the gunroom. The 'Meg/gunroom' frame ceases to be primed and an additional frame, the 'Alec/stable' frame, is created and primed instead. During the time that Alec is in the stable we no longer assume the covert presence of Meg. A progressive frame recall then occurs. However when Alec returns to the gunroom location (with the words 'came back') Meg is automatically re-primed because she is bound into the gunroom frame. So Alec's statement 'We'll mark the grave with a wooden plaque' can be assumed to be addressed to Meg even before she is again mentioned and the 'We' can be assumed to refer both to Alec and to Meg. During the course of the extract, Meg's status, therefore, changes as shown in Table 5.1. Progressive frame recall can, like instantaneous frame recall, allow the interpretation of a pronoun without a recent antecedent, as illustrated in the following examples. Example 5.12a, below, shows a frame being created and this frame is then recalled progressively in Example 5.12b. The recall is unusual because the frame has never been presented to the reader before (in other words, the frame has never been primed before): the reader has only been told of its possible existence.

EXAMPLE 5.12A

'Slagg!' shouted the Doctor, 'keep Titus near the keyhole. See that she does, Fuchsia.'

'Yes,' whispered Fuchsia; and went in search of Mrs Slagg.

(Mervyn Peake, *Titus Groan* (1985), 310–11; my emphasis)

At this point in the novel, the characters are trapped in a large building in a fire, split off from each other by the smoke. Mrs Slagg is supposed to be protecting the infant Titus by placing him near to the air coming through the keyhole of the outer door. Having read the above passage, the reader may subsequently assume that Fuchsia has managed to find Mrs Slagg and is now in the same frame as her. However, the reader does not know this for certain, because the action stays with the Doctor, Fuchsia being primed out. Subsequently, the Doctor sets off to find Fuchsia and Mrs Slagg. He moves progressively from one physical context to another, through the smoky building, in order to find them.

EXAMPLE 5.12B

The Doctor was gone from her [the Countess] in a flash and when he judged himself to be a few feet from the door—'Are you there, Fuchsia?' he trilled.

Fuchsia was just below him, and he was startled to hear her voice come up jerkily through the smoke.

'She's ill. Very ill. Quick, Dr Prune, quick! Do something for her.' The Doctor felt his knees being clutched. 'She's down here, Dr Prune. I'm holding her.'

Prunesquallor hitched up his trousers and knelt down at once.

(Mervyn Peake, *Titus Groan* (1985), 314; my emphasis)

With the mention of Fuchsia in the vicinity of the door, the reader can also assume the presence of Mrs Slagg. The reader expects her to be by the door and so she is the obvious person to be referred to by Fuchsia's 'She' pronoun. The pronoun can, therefore, be interpreted without an antecedent. The new frame supplies the referent (as in the earlier examples of instantaneous frame switch: Examples 5.6, 5.7, and 5.8) and it eliminates the Countess from the Doctor's (and hence the reader's) context.

Instantaneous frame switches, as described in the previous section, are not possible for those monitoring real life. Chapter 4 indicated that a blind person differed from the reader in that the blind person is bound into the real-world context that they are monitoring, the primed context. People in the real world, whether blind or sighted, cannot instantaneously switch to priming a distant location, for they cannot instantaneously move to a distant loca-

tion. An instantaneous frame switch is like a spliced film recording. The camera which makes the recording is itself bound to its
real-world context, as is the blind person. The viewer of the film
is, however, like the reader, not bound to any of the contexts in
the film and so can observe instantaneous frame switch in the
edited film.

Progressive frame switch is, however, possible for the blind
person. The blind person can move progressively to the boundaries of the current frame location and into a physically adjacent
frame location, leaving behind the participants of the first frame,
by, for example, walking into another room. On moving, the
blind person cannot any longer assume these other people still to
be present around him or her, unless there is evidence that those
from the first frame move too. The blind person will, however, be
aware that the others are still bound into the frame which he or
she has just left.

A frame can also be progressively recalled by a blind person. For
example, a blind person may leave a colleague in a room and
walk down the corridor to obtain some information. On returning
to the room, the blind person may address the colleague without
first checking whether they are still there. When the blind person
left the room they would have assumed that the colleague was
still present there and so not present in the new context, the corridor. The colleague is, therefore, no longer primed for the blind
person, but they are still assumed to be bound to the context of
the room. If only a short time has elapsed and there is no reason
to think that the colleague would have left the room, the colleague
will be automatically re-primed on the blind person's return.

3. TEXT TYPES AND READING STRATEGIES

The remainder of this chapter looks beyond a categorization of
context shifts to show how a reader's assumptions about contexts
and his/her management of context changes may be affected by
different text types and reading strategies. I look first at how the
theory of frames would need to be adjusted to take account of
genres such as science fiction and ghost stories, where the norms
of the real world may not hold. I then return to fiction in general
and focus on reading strategies. I consider how a model of text
processing needs to take account of readers 'miscueing' on frame

switches and thereby having to subsequently 'repair' their reading. This leads on to a discussion of a particular type of assumption-making, which I term 'belief frames', that may result in the reader re-evaluating stretches of the narrative that have already been read or holding different views on how the narrative should be interpreted. Finally, I discuss the extent to which narrative processing is a matter of judging possibilities rather than deducing certainties, showing how this can be capitalized on for stylistic effect within a narrative.

(a) Different Worlds, Different Conventions?

Contextual monitoring of fictional contexts has been compared in this book to our monitoring of the real world around us. In science fiction and in stories about the supernatural, though, the fictional world may be rather different from the real world. This study has not looked specifically at these types of text, but this section aims to give some indication of the extent to which 'contextual frame theory' would need to be modified in order to take account of these genres.

In science fiction, characters may sometimes appear 'from nowhere' in the middle of a context. One obvious example of this is the television programme *Star Trek* in which characters are 'beamed' from the star ship to other locations such as the surface of planets. This alters the way in which a character is bound into a frame. The television viewers can, however, still work on the general assumption that until they see the character, he or she is not in the frame, although retrospective priming may sometimes be necessary. In stories of the supernatural, ghosts may also suddenly appear and disappear. Moreover, a ghost may be present but invisible. If this occurs in a film or television programme, the viewer becomes like the reader or the blind person, judging the character to be present by assumption, by clues such as sounds or moving props, or by the reaction of other characters. The main problem with monitoring ghosts is, of course, judging whether a character is still present but invisible or whether the character has left the context completely. The viewer may have to alter their assumptions, priming out retrospectively (if the ghost has gone without the audience realizing, for example) or re-priming retrospectively (if the audience had thought the ghost had gone,

but it is still present although invisible). One example is the television programme *Randall and Hopkirk (Deceased)*, in which the
dead Hopkirk assists his partner Randall in detective work. Hopkirk is, however, visible to the audience and to Randall. In this
case, the audience needs to monitor the fact that although they
and one of the characters can see the ghost, no one else can. The
closest parallel to this is the restricted overlapping context
described earlier in this chapter, where only a subset of characters
present in a location may be able to hear something that is said
either within that location (because of physical proximity) or
from a distant context (by means of a link such as the telephone)
(see discussion of 'restricted' contexts in Chapter 4).

Character constructs may also be rather different in science fiction and stories of the supernatural than in other types of text. In
Stevenson's *Jekyll and Hyde* (1979), for example, one referent has
two sides to his character, one good, one evil. This could be
handled in the same way as for enactors (see Chapter 7), although
we would have to take into account that there may be a gradual
transition from one personality to the other, as in traditional were-
wolf stories.

Ghosts may also force us to build more complex character constructs. In Straub's *Ghost Story*, for example, when characters
die, they become evil (Example 3.1). In this particular novel, the
problem for the reader and for the characters is that of trying to
determine whether a character is still alive or whether a character
has died and become a ghost. Once a character has been established as being dead, the reader still needs to remember the live
character in order to understand the response to the ghost by his/
her friends and relatives. Interestingly, the reader may be making
inferences about the ghosts on the basis of assumed facts about
the overall fictional world. In Straub's novel, we can assume individual ghosts to be evil, as all other ghosts that we have encountered in this fictional world are evil. This is a type of inferencing
referred to as 'abduction' (e.g. Charniak and McDermott 1985:
453–556; Givón 1989: 20). Clearly, though, this depends on
building a model of the fictional world of a particular novel, since
in other stories ghosts may generally be benign.

It seems, from this brief examination, that in science fiction and
stories about the supernatural, readers and viewers will still
attempt to build and maintain frames. Indeed in some cases,

monitoring of contexts and characters may be a more complex task than for other types of text. 'Contextual frame theory' is not, therefore, invalid for these stories, although it may need to be developed further. Without contextual monitoring by means of frames, the reader of a story would be disorientated. Although it might be possible to construct a text in which there was no continuity of space, time, or participants, causing complete disorientation to the reader, it would be very unusual to have no contextual continuity at all.

(b) Repairing Contextual Monitoring

So far in this chapter, I have been describing frame switch and frame recall as if readers always respond to the text's signals to move to a different context. Although I am assuming that this happens a fair amount of the time, it is possible that readers may occasionally 'miscue' on these signals and fail to change context. This may be due to inattentive reading but on occasions it might be because the signals to change context are not clear or because there are conflicting signals. If this happens, the reader needs a mechanism for 'repairing' (e.g. H. Sacks, Schegloff, and Jefferson 1974; Schegloff, Jefferson, and Sacks 1977; Schegloff 1979, 1987a)[7] his/her assumptions about the contextual frame.

Obviously this aspect of textual interpretation demands psychological testing, since it concerns each individual reader's response to a particular piece of text. As an example, I provide here an account of my own 'miscueing' on a particular text, Lynne Reid Banks's book *An End to Running*. Other readers will not necessarily read this text in the same way, but there will presumably be parallel occasions when they need to employ repair strategies themselves. The first half of this novel ends with Martha falling asleep beside Aaron: Martha being the 'I'-narrator.

EXAMPLE 5.13A

But as I lay there holding him, my arm numb from the weight of his head, I thought that, after all, I would be getting off easily.

---

[7] The term 'repair' is normally applied to the rectification of conversational communication problems. Here, I use it to mean a reader's rereading of a stretch of text to locate the point at which they have misunderstood or been confused by the text.

The impossible difficulties would follow if what he asked me for was love.

(Lynne Reid Banks, *An End to Running* (1966), 135)

The second half of the novel opens with the same scene the next morning.

EXAMPLE 5.13B

God, what a sleep! Like the sleep of the dead—or the unborn. No dreams; no starting violently awake in the empty darkness, expecting to find some unspeakable threat hanging over you. Just warm, padded depths, a lightness in the throat, and peace.

Waking up was good, too—like waking from the first healthy sleep after a long, feverish illness. It was slow enough to savour each stage: the awareness of nameless happiness first, then up through the layers of drowsiness to the knowledge of satisfaction and safety, and at last the detailed remembrance, the warm, soft, sleeping flesh in my arms.

I lay quite still, with my eyes closed, and let my hands and arms and body enjoy her closeness.

(Lynne Reid Banks, *An End to Running* (1966), 139)

When reading this new chapter, my initial assumption was that the 'I'-narrator was still Martha, as Martha has been the narrator since the beginning of the novel and this passage appears to be a straightforward continuation of the previous chapter. The mention of the 'I'-narrator enjoying 'her closeness', however, showed that this interpretation was wrong. Looking back, I found that the first half of the novel had been prefaced by a separate page with the heading 'Part One: Martha' and that between the two extracts cited above was another page with the title 'Part Two: Aaron'. I had either failed to notice these section headings or not interpreted them as indicating a change of point of view. Other readers might read the book differently, anticipating this change from the heading. The main point is, having on this occasion mis-cued, I began to read the new chapter with an inappropriate frame but then was forced by the text to change this assumption. My representation of the context (Martha describing Aaron) was incompatible with the text I was reading (Aaron apparently being referred to by a feminine pronoun) and so I 'repaired' my representation (having reread the text in search of an explanation).

This particular text is unusual because of the sudden change of narrator and the way this change is achieved. Elsewhere, I give examples of miscueing where there was a failure to realize immediately that a flashback had ended and that the text had signalled a return to the main narrative (Examples 6.2 and 6.8). In some of these examples, the flashback and main narrative frames were very similar in terms of the location and the characters involved. Miscueing may be more likely in such circumstances, but other potential factors are the attentiveness of the reader and individual interpretations of textual cues to switch frames.

Repairs force readers not only to replace the 'erroneous' frame when they discover the problem, but to reread or reinterpret the text with the 'correct' frame from the point at which the switch should have taken place. The real-life correlate of this is when we fail to realize that a person has entered the room and carry on talking as if they were not there. When we discover our mistake, we have to re-evaluate what we have been saying in the light of this person having heard us. As mentioned in Chapter 4, the behaviour of blind people sometimes indicates that they are temporarily working with an inaccurate model of the real-world context, as when they fail to realize that someone has entered or left or they mistake the identity of one of the people present. These real-life examples of repairs are for frame modification rather than frame switch, since in real life instantaneous switches of time and place do not occur. In narrative, frame switch repairs may be more likely, since the cues can be rather subtle, particularly on frame recall. Frame modification of the primed frame is usually clearly signalled in the text, since without explicit statements like 'he left' we would not be able to tell that this had happened. Retrospective priming (mentioned earlier in this chapter) requires a reappraisal of the current context, but it is due to late signalling of the change rather than to a repair necessitated by the reader missing or misinterpreting a cue.

The ability not only to make assumptions about a context but to realize that these assumptions may need adjusting is an important feature of human cognition. Within artificial intelligence, Suchman (1987) has studied how machines often lack the ability to do this. Suchman explains that, in the early days of robotics, scientists built robots that merely carried out a pre-specified plan, without making adequate allowance for the need to monitor the execution of the plan in a specific context and to respond to feedback from that context (Suchman 1987: 29–33; see also Boden 1987: 282 for an ethological parallel). These early robots had no input whatsoever from the senses and simply acted on their own internal representations and their hypotheses about what might be happening in the context. Subsequently, the importance of contextual feedback was recognized in the more advanced robotics programs, with the problem becoming how to provide sufficient input from the situation by means of the senses and how to create a model of the world from this input (Johnson-Laird 1988: 361–3). However, in less sophisticated computer systems (for example, the type of equipment which is currently most likely to be found in homes or offices) contextual monitoring may not be a feature of the software.

Suchman (1987: 118–77) explores in detail one particular scenario in which human users battle with a pre-programmed photocopying and document-binding machine. The machine issues stage-by-stage instructions to its users about how to produce bound documents, but, in the specific context of use, the users are often unable to identify the correct button or machine part. The machine, however, assumes that its instructions have been carried out and continues to issue further instructions. The inability to monitor the current situation means that the machine is giving commands which are relevant to the stage which it believes the users have reached, rather than the stage the users actually have reached.

This computer program lacks 'robustness', the ability to rectify its mental model by means of repair strategies if a mismatch with the context is identified (Suchman 1987: 12, 25–6, 56). Human beings, by contrast, have this ability. For example, a blind person may assume that someone who has been standing near them is still there, but will update their model if the person fails to respond when addressed. Repairs provide proof that contextual models are created and acted upon, as well as being the mechanism which replaces an 'erroneous' frame with the 'correct' one.

(c) Switching Belief Frames

The repairs mentioned in the previous section are likely to be realized as soon as the reader notices an incompatibility between the frame that he/she is utilizing and the context which has been cued by the text. At that point, the reader realizes that something is wrong and is likely to search for the overlooked cues by looking back over the preceding text. The portion of text which was read with the 'wrong' frame is reread using the 'correct' frame and the misread text is regarded as unimportant.

In this section, I look at ways in which, instead of the reader misreading the text, the text may force a reader to reinterpret a stretch of narrative or to hold two different interpretations simultaneously. The frames discussed so far have been monitors of the physical context—who is present, where and when—but this section examines a different type of frame, discussed in Goffman (1975) which, for clarity, I will refer to as 'belief frames' (although Goffman himself simply uses the term 'frame'(originating from Bateson 1955)).

Goffman, as a philosopher and sociologist, is primarily interested in the borderline between truth and falsehood or reality and non-reality (or, alternatively, in different types of reality). Goffman looks extensively at confidence tricks and looks at how the victims have to radically reassess the situation when they realize that something is wrong. He is also interested in the theatre and, using many 'theatre of the absurd' examples, discusses cases in which the audience believe they are witnessing real-life events but subsequently find out that these events are part of the play. Goffman does not himself look at narrative text in any detail, but there has been a lot of interest within literary studies in reversals of this type. Recently, literary theorists have adopted the philosophy notion of 'possible worlds' to describe a reader's different assessment of the truth or falsity of a situation (e.g. Ryan 1991).

Julian Barnes's *A History of the World in 10½ Chapters* (1990) provides an example of a story which forces the reader to reassess his/her beliefs about the whole fictional world. In Chapter 4 of this novel, a woman leaves the civilized world and sails away to a desert island where she has nightmares about strange men. Eventually these men tell her that she is actually in a mental hospital, that they are doctors and that the island is just an hallucination. A single stretch of narrative, therefore, has two possible interpretations, only one of which can be 'real' within the fictional world. In general terms, this is a matter of what Givón (1989: xvii, 1, 4, 19, 89), citing Kant, has termed 'perspective', 'point of view', or 'framing': 'At [the] core [of pragmatics] lies the notion of *context*, and the axiom that reality and/or experience are not absolute fixed entities, but rather *frame-dependent*, contingent upon the observer's *perspective*' (Givón 1989: xvii; Givón's italics).

In many stories, we only discover that there is a second reading at a later stage, the classic case being when we find that part of the preceding action has been merely a dream, usually signalled by the dreamer waking up. Alternatively, the narrative may signal that there are different readings as events are described. One of the best-known examples of this is Henry James's *The Turn of the Screw* (1967) in which we are never sure whether there is a ghost in the house or whether the heroine is hallucinating. 'Belief frames' may sometimes provide a comment on the personalities of the characters involved. In *The Turn of the Screw* we are unsure whether the heroine is neurotically imagining a ghost or whether she is surrounded by people who are deceiving her about the existence of the ghost. A switch of 'belief frames' can also negate a stretch of action which has occurred. If a narrative describes a character dying and we then discover the whole stretch of narrative to be simply a dream, we can assume that the character has not actually died.

'Belief frames' often encompass the truth or falsity of events occurring in several physical contexts, whereas the 'frames' in this book are monitors of particular physical contexts. One similarity, though, is that the elements of both types of frame are interlinked. In the discussion of frame recall, it was seen that mentioning one element of a frame can recall the whole context. Conversely, mentioning someone or something that is not in the current frame can prompt the reader to replace that frame and set up a new one. 'Belief frames' also depend on each element of a situation fitting into the perspective that has been established. Confidence tricksters know that one small slip can alert the victim to the fact that there is something false about the situation. Dick Francis's *Decider* (1994: 179–80) provides an example from narrative fiction. In this novel, the leader of a group of animal rights protesters at the scene of the crime is challenged when their leader is discovered eating a hamburger. This one action throws doubts on the authenticity of the protest. The leader is found to be an actor who has been paid to occupy this position. On discovering this, the reader needs not only to alter the entity representation for this individual, but to assess the effect on a whole network of assumptions that have been made, particularly since the protesters have been establishing alibis for some of the main characters in the story.

'Belief frames' are rather different from the contextual frames discussed in this book. In Goffman's (1975: 144–9) discussion of radio dramas, however, there are some more direct parallels with contextual frames. As already indicated, media which do not convey information visually are particularly dependent on contextual monitoring. Goffman outlines the conventions used to establish a context in a medium in which contexts can only be built through sound, both linguistic and non-linguistic. Country scenes, for example, may be introduced by the radio characters talking about their surroundings or by rural background noises, such as birdsong, which are subsequently faded out. Obviously, this information will need to be monitored from then on and anyone turning on the radio during the scene may find it difficult to identify the full context immediately.

(d) Probability-Based Interpretation of Text

The discussion of frame switches, repairs, and belief frames has shown that interpreting a text often involves weighing probabilities rather than there being a clear-cut deduction. This section gives some examples where a reader may use probability to decide on a referent for a noun or pronoun. Consider the following example:

EXAMPLE 5.14

It happened on the day of Steerpike's second daylight visit to the Library. He was on his return journey and had reached the edge of the pine woods and was awaiting an opportunity to run unobserved across the open ground, when, away to his left, he saw <u>a figure</u> moving in the direction of Gormenghast Mountain.

The invigorating air, coupled with his recognition of the distant figure, prompted him to change his course, and with
quick, birdlike steps he moved rapidly along the edge of the
wood. In the rough landscape away to his left, the tiny figure
in its crimson dress sang out against the sombre background
like a ruby on a slate.

(Mervyn Peake, *Titus Groan* (1985), 269; my emphasis)

Here, it is possible for the reader to infer that the figure in the crimson dress is Fuchsia, since Fuchsia is the only one of the central
directory characters who was known to wear crimson. This inference depends on our remembering that Fuchsia wears crimson, a
piece of information which will probably have been built into her
entity representation. The inference excludes the possibilities
that it is a new character who has not so far been mentioned in
the novel who also happens to wear crimson, and that one of the
other central directory characters happens to be wearing crimson
on this particular occasion. The extent to which the reader ignores
the possibility of the figure being a completely new character will
depend on a number of factors. First, it will depend on the plot. If
the reader is awaiting the reappearance of one of the central characters, then this may be a good reason to believe that it might be
this particular person and not someone new. Secondly, it will
depend on the genre and the author's personal style. In Peake's
Titus Groan (1985) and *Gormenghast* (1985), for example, the
reader is often presented with unidentified people and they generally turn out to be familiar. Previous experience builds expectations. Thirdly, it will depend on the stage that has been reached in
the story. A story which is near completion is less likely to introduce new characters, so the mystery person is more likely to be a
central directory character.

The possibility that the character in crimson may be one of the
already mentioned characters in the novel can be seen as more or
less likely for similar reasons. *Titus Groan* and *Gormenghast* are
novels where most of the characters are caricatures. The twins,
for example, always speak together and always wear purple. In
this type of novel there is a firm correlation between character
and characteristic. The inference that the unidentified woman in
Example 5.14 is Fuchsia seems fairly probable in these circumstances, but the reader cannot be certain from this amount of

evidence. There is, therefore, the possibility of readers changing their minds subsequently. By contrast, if an outright statement has been made and this later proves to be wrong, it is usually necessary for the text to retract it. Such retractions are acceptable if information has been mediated through the subjective perspective of one of the characters and there has been some misunderstanding on the part of this character, as shown below:

EXAMPLE 5.15

She [Stella] turned to the bird with her hand extended as though asking it to contradict her, and noticed for the first time that beyond it the door of the studio was swinging open and that a man was standing silently behind the carving, along the line of her outflung arm.

9

Robert! she thought, in the split second before her eyes focused properly. But the next instant she saw that he was not at all like Robert. He was much taller for a start, and heavier ...

(Susanna Mitchell, *The Token* (1985), 88–9[8])

Stella sees Robert but then realizes that it is not Robert at all but someone who she does not at first recognize but who is known to the reader. The reader first builds Robert into the contextual frame and then, on the retraction, has to remove him from the frame. Robert is then eliminated as a possible referent of 'a man'.

In interpreting the above-mentioned *Titus Groan* example (5.14), however, there is no need for a retraction because the interpretation is not based on an outright statement but on the weighting of probabilities. Reference is often likely to be probability-based when clues rather then names are given. Readers may, for example, be presented with a mention of a particular person's office in which 'someone is working'. Although this 'someone' is likely to be the person whose office it is (a frame independent connection), it may just be an individual who is using the room on that occasion (a frame specific connection).

The twist in a story may rely on our reinterpreting the evidence

---

[8] In the original text, the number '9' is printed in large typeface on a new page and marks the beginning of a new chapter.

at hand. The reader may be forced in one direction and then the fallacy of this interpretation revealed.

EXAMPLE 5.16

'And you knew the Gibbs. Next door. A—kind—couple with an adopted daughter.'

He said, 'She weren't adopted. I remember the day she were born. She once smashed my rabbit dish.'

'Oh, I knew the Gibbs,' he said, 'I knew them all right.'

I said, 'Could you tell me—what happened?'

He scratched his ear for a while and continued to look past me at the sea. 'Well, of course she died,' he said.

'When was that?'

'Oh, years back. Years back.'

I said, 'Poor things. Poor Mr Gibb.'

'Aye,' he said. 'But he was soon over it. Sold up the shop and went off. Went off with another woman, matter of fact, six months later. All over her he was. A poor-looking thing. Lost track of him.'

I said, 'But poor Mrs Gibb. Whatever did she do?'

'I tell't you. Mrs Gibb died.'

'*Mrs Gibb* died! Was that before or after?'

'Before or after what?'

'Helen dying?'

'Oh, Helen didn't die. That Helen didn't die. She's done well. Married rich. She's got half a dozen kids . . .'

(Jane Gardam, 'A Seaside Garden', in *The Pangs of Love and Other Stories* (1984), 129–30; Gardam's italics)

The narrator interprets 'she died' to mean that the daughter, Helen, died. The reader's interpretation will depend on weighting probabilities, taking into account what is already known about both Helen and Mrs Gibb. This accumulated knowledge is as follows. On first meeting Helen many years earlier we have been told that 'She was so thin you feared for her' (p. 113). Her lips are bluish due to a heart condition and she constantly misses school. When the narrator meets her parents she is told by them that Helen 'has about a year' (p. 124), and the parents fuss over her and worry neurotically. Since the whole story has been about Helen's serious ill-health, Helen seems to be the most obvious referent for the phrase 'she died'. Although much evidence seems to be weighted in favour of Helen as the referent, the text has not until this point committed itself to a particular interpretation by actually saying that Mrs Gibb died or Helen died. A character who has been ill and supposedly dying need not die and, conversely, another character, however healthy previously, may have died. Indeed, on hearing that it is Mrs Gibb who has died we can make sense of what has happened because there were some small indications that Helen was stronger than supposed. It had, after all, been predicted that she would not reach school-age and yet she had done this. She tells the narrator that 'In my view I'm not exactly ill at all. It's just they're nurses. A couple of born nurses. They had nothing to nurse so they got me. They're sick. Sicker than I am' (pp. 124–5). There is a suggestion too that Helen, although seriously ill, torments her parents by leading them to believe that she is more ill than she actually is. On the last occasion that we see her as a child she pretends, when out with the narrator, to be too weak to walk home immediately. The narrator runs to tell Helen's parents what has happened and the mother, thinking that something must have happened to Helen, faints. When Helen arrives the narrator observes that 'it seemed to me that she was there quite fast' (p. 126), and even accuses Helen of having planned the incident.

The reader of Example 5.16 must weigh the probabilities of different interpretations in order to decode a pronoun. In the detective novel the entire plot may revolve on such an identification. The skill behind writing such novels seems to lie in weighting the interpretation in a particular direction and then reversing this weighting. In other words the reader is often encouraged to think that a certain person cannot be the murderer and then later we find that we are mistaken. Since the hypothesis about the identity of the murderer was based only on the weighting of probabilities a reversal is normally acceptable. All of this requires some skill on the part of the author. Example 5.17 provides an illustration which is of special interest because part of the weighting of evidence is due to a frame switch and subsequent frame recall.

EXAMPLE 5.17

'The train is due at Woodleigh Road at four-thirty-five. It should arrive in a few minutes now. Then it will take her about five minutes to walk up the hill.'

[One page of text omitted]
'There goes the train,' said Kennedy.
'Coming into the station?'
'No, leaving it.' He paused. 'She'll be here any minute now.'
But the minutes passed and Lily Kimble did not come.

II

Lily Kimble got out of the train at Dillmouth Junction and walked across the bridge to the siding where the little local train was waiting . . .
Presently the train started—puffing its way importantly along a winding valley. There were three stops before the terminus at Lonsbury Bay; Newton Langford, Matchings Halt (for Woodleigh Camp) and Woodleigh Bolton. . . .
She was the only person to alight at the tiny station of Matchings Halt. . . . A little way along the road a signpost with 'To Woodleigh Camp' indicated a footpath leading up a steep hill.
Lily Kimble took the footpath and walked briskly uphill. . . .
Someone stepped out from the trees and Lily Kimble jumped.

'My, you did give me a start,' she exclaimed. 'I wasn't expecting to meet you here.'
'Gave you a surprise, did I? I've got another surprise for you.'
It was very lonely in among the trees. . . . there was no cry and the struggle was very soon over. . . .

III

'What can have become of the woman?' demanded Dr Kennedy irritably.
The hands of the clock pointed to ten minutes to five.
'Could she have lost her way coming from the station?'

(Agatha Christie, *Sleeping Murder* (1977), 154 and 155–6)

The opening of Example 5.17 gives the precise time—4.35. The example closes at 4.50 ('ten minutes to five'). The time of the murder is not stated. The frame in which the murder occurs is set between the frames timed at 4.35 and 4.50, which seems to suggest that the murder took place between these times. If this is the case, it gives Dr Kennedy a perfect alibi. The group can be assumed to have remained together in the same location between the frame switch to the Lily Kimble scene and the frame recall. This is a fair assumption because, since Dr Kennedy is talking to the hero and heroine of the story, it would alert their suspicions if he left, and the reader would expect to hear them discussing his mysterious disappearance the next time that they are alone. Indeed, the reader would be right in making this assumption—Dr Kennedy did remain with Gwenda and Giles from 4.35 to 4.50. The assumption that, if made, is wrong (and, after all, it is founded on no explicit statement of time in the text) is that the murder occurred between 4.35 and 4.50. In fact, the intervening scene is a flashback. Not only may the structure of the narrative mislead the reader, the mention of the train both at the end of Section I and at the beginning of Section II provides a spurious cohesion. On careful reading, it is clear that it is not the same train.

If the narrative structure misleads the reader at this point, the conclusion will be formed that Dr Kennedy cannot be the mysterious 'someone' who murders Lily Kimble. This interpretation is reinforced subsequently by the fact that Gwenda and Giles do not suspect Dr Kennedy because he is an old friend.

The text subsequently reveals that the murder actually took place much earlier and that Dr Kennedy was the 'someone' who killed Lily Kimble. The juxtaposing of the three sections and the coincidental mention of the train, which superficially suggests the 'same time' interpretation, may lead the reader to make an inference based on narrative structure. It is, nevertheless, only an inference and so subsequently Agatha Christie can draw the reader in a different direction, with the result that this earlier assumption has to be rejected. In the meantime, Agatha Christie may have prevented the reader from guessing the identity of the murderer.

Without the orthographic breakers 'II' and 'III', Agatha Christie would have had to have switched frame by such phrases as 'at the same time at the station', (or 'just then') or conversely 'earlier that afternoon'. The first of these switch markers would have meant that Christie could not subsequently time the murder earlier and so would be providing Dr Kennedy with an irrefutable alibi. However, the second type of marker would indicate that she would be leaving Dr Kennedy without any supposed alibi at all. Avoiding the use of explicit time markers means that the reader can be misled into thinking that Dr Kennedy has an alibi but still accept a reversal when it is found that Dr Kennedy is in fact the murderer. Example 5.17, therefore, shows that information may be assigned to an entity representation on the basis of probability and that the reader may subsequently need to re-evaluate this interpretation.

Summary

This chapter has discussed the dynamic nature of contexts in full, real narratives. Contexts are frequently modified and the focus of the action may suddenly switch to a new context which is distant in time and/or space. The reader must balance the need to make assumptions of continuity with a recognition of cues to change the mental frame being used to monitor a particular context.

This chapter has summarized the different types of context change that occur in narratives and which must be taken into account in a model of narrative processing. The term *'frame modification'* was used to describe changes to a context which caused the contextual configuration to be altered in some way but left the rest of the context intact. When a character enters or leaves a location, the remainder of the group can still be assumed to remain. By contrast, the term *'frame switch'* was used to describe how the reader's attention may move from one context to another. A frame switch generally leaves the context completely intact, so it may be reinstated at a later stage by a *frame recall*. The interesting thing about a frame recall is that a mention of one part of the context is often used as a cue to recall the whole context. If this cue is responded to, it provides evidence that the reader does monitor information about contextual configurations and indicates the extent to which this knowledge is required to supplement the words of the text.

In addition to describing the different types of context change in narrative and hypothesizing about the cognitive handling of these changes, this chapter has also commented on other factors which need to be taken into account if a model of narrative processing is to describe a variety of text types and explain how readers respond differently to textual cues to context change. These observations included a consideration of fictional worlds which have different characteristics from the real world. Since contexts are monitored by making assumptions based on how the real world works, these assumptions may need to be modified when a science-fiction text is read. Nevertheless, some contextual continuity is normally assumed even in radically different fictional worlds. The remainder of the chapter examined the way in which readers respond to textual cues. Narrative-processing models need to include a repair mechanism for when readers overlook cues to switch contexts and need subsequently to revise the mental frame they have been operating with. Some provision also needs to be made for readers to change their beliefs and to reinterpret a long stretch of narrative in the light of a new belief frame. In general, narrative processing is, on many occasions, more a matter of weighing probabilities than of decoding a text by a process of rule application and deduction. Narratives may sometimes exploit the indeterministic nature of reading by cueing a reader to make a particular interpretation and then forcing a different interpretation on the reader at a later stage.

Chapters 4 and 5 have presented a summary of the demands which narrative text places on a reader to monitor fictional contexts and to change from one context to another. The reader must constantly be balancing assumptions of continuity against the need to update these assumptions as a result of change. Chapter 4 examined how, within any particular context, a reader must assume a certain amount of continuity whilst updating mental representations as a result of explicit and inferred change. Chapter 5 discussed how the contextual configuration itself might be modified and how one context might be suddenly replaced by another.

The following two chapters turn to the implications of these observations about context management for linguistic theory, looking specifically at reference theory. Chapter 7 is a theoretical discussion which argues that reference theory must take account of narrative frames, entity representations, and the consciousness of the reader. Chapter 6 looks specifically at frame switches which involve the same character in the main frame and the flashback frame, considering how information must be stored in entity representations if the reader is to process these switches.

6

Characters and Contexts

Chapters 4 and 5 have argued that characters are 'episodically' linked to the other individuals in particular locations at particular times. Assumptions can be made on the basis of these episodic contextual links, such as the inference that a character in a context is still present even when not explicitly referred to and the inference that the action of one character in a context can affect the others in that context. For this reason, readers need to keep track of the current context, changing their assumptions if there is a switch of context.

This chapter looks particularly at narrative flashbacks and how they change the reader's assumptions about characters. Flashbacks often result in the same character being juxtaposed in past and present contexts. A reader, therefore, needs not only to be able to identify and monitor the context, but to identify which 'version' of the character is being referred to at any particular point in the text. There has to be some means of separately accessing those facts which are true of entities in the past as opposed to those facts which are true of the same entities in the present. This has implications for the way that information is stored in entity representations. This chapter looks particularly at entity representations of characters, but the same observations apply to objects and locations affected by flashbacks.

Section 1 explores the way in which narrative flashbacks affect the reader's interpretation of references to characters. Section 1a summarizes some of the observations made in Chapters 4 and 5 about the link between characters and contexts and then explains why flashbacks need particular consideration. Section 1b looks at previous research which has indicated that there is a need to view referents as existing in different 'versions'. Section 1b then explores this possibility for characters in narrative flashbacks, labelling the different 'versions' of the characters 'enactors'. Section 2 examines how the reader keeps track of the current enactor. Section 2a suggests that monitoring is necessary because flashback time is not signalled in every sentence by verb aspect (as is often supposed). Section 2b looks at the different types of clues that can be used to identify enactors.

I. CONTEXTS, CHARACTERS, AND REFERENCE THEORY

(a) Overview: Links between Characters and Contexts

Chapters 4 and 5 focused primarily on contexts. Contextual information provides the reader with knowledge about the grouping of characters and individual characters. The main hypotheses that were made in these earlier chapters are as follows:

1. Within a primed context, a character that is 'bound' into that context is assumed to be present even when not being referred to. This character is 'covertly' part of the contextual frame even when other aspects of the frame (e.g. other characters or the location) are being 'overtly' referred to. In Example 4.3, therefore, Stella was assumed to be present even when only the train was mentioned. Likewise, in Example 4.1, Lord Groan was assumed to be present when Dr Prunesquallor spoke.

2. Within a context, the action of one character that is 'bound' into that context can be assumed to affect other characters in the context, even if only in terms of the others seeing and hearing the action. Such assumptions (and the parallel assumptions in 3 and 4 below) are made on the basis of knowledge about the real world (and any special knowledge about the fictional world). In Example 4.1, therefore, Lord Groan was assumed to hear what Dr Prunesquallor said.

3. Within a context, information about the location can be assumed to affect characters in the context. In Example 4.3, the fact that the weather is not 'particularly warm' can lead the reader to assume that Stella is not particularly warm.

4. Within a context, the action of a character or other entity can be assumed to have an effect on the location, even when the location is 'covert'. For example, a bomb exploding can be assumed to cause some destruction within the location.

5. The consequence of 2, 3, and 4 is that an entity representation (of a character or of the location) can be updated even when the entity is 'covert' (i.e. not being referred to). So in Example 4.3, the entity representation of Stella can be updated when we learn that it is not 'particularly warm'.

6. The mention of one character can re-prime the whole contextual frame (i.e. all the characters and the location). In Example 5.9, the mention of Harriet brought the action back to the present (and would have automatically reintroduced the other characters if there had been no explicit statement that they had left).

7. The mention of location or objects in the location can re-prime the whole participant grouping. In Example 5.10, the noun phrase 'the piano' reintroduced the cocktail party frame.

All of these connections have already been discussed in the previous chapters. In this chapter, I consider the implications of these observations for the way in which information is stored in entity representations, looking particularly at the effect of flashbacks.

Flashbacks are interesting because they are a type of context-shifting which can place contexts from two quite different times adjacent to each other in a text. One consequence of this is that the same person can appear in past and present forms in quick succession. Moreover, if one of the contextual frames is temporarily unprimed whilst the other is read, a reader can be monitoring different versions of the same character, one in the primed context and one in a bound but unprimed context. In Winston Graham's *After the Act* (Examples 5.9 and 5.10), for example, whilst the narrator in flashback encounters the girl at the party, a reader can still be aware that the narrator in the present is thinking these thoughts. In this particular text, the two versions of the character are not radically different, since the flashback only takes the reader back to the previous evening, but in other texts there may be a much greater time difference (such as when an adult narrator recalls his/her childhood). This means that when one of these frames is re-primed (e.g. when the narrative returns from flashback), not only does the context have to be reinstated (i.e. the participant grouping, the location, and the time), but the appropriate information within the entity representation(s) needs to be recalled. When, for example, a narrator ceases to think of his/her childhood, not only does the present need to be re-primed but the adult version of the character needs to be rein-stated. This has implications for reference theory because although in one sense the text is referring to the same person, in another sense quite different information within the mental representation is being focused on.

(b) Referents and Contexts

(i) Previous Research

The idea that different versions of a referent may exist is rarely mentioned in the artificial intelligence literature, although it has been observed by Noble (1988: 35–6). Noble constructs the example:

> Draw a triangle p q r.
> Move the triangle upwards by 10 units.
> Now make it blue.   (p. 35)

The triangle looks quite different after the last instruction. Noble comments that: 'We have therefore not one, but many objects which are all separate manifestations or incarnations of a single object at different moments in time. ... We shall refer to this phenomenon as "the multiplicity of a reference object" ' (p. 36). Nevertheless, Noble argues that:

> ... the identity of the triangle persists in spite of a change to the values of the coordinates of its vertices ... This phenomenon—the notion that the identity of an object remains (or persists) even when the values of its parameters change—we shall call 'the persistence of a reference object'.   (p. 36)

Goffman and Quirk, within sociology and linguistics respectively, have also both commented on the way that referents change over time. In 'The Frame Analysis of Talk', the final chapter of Goffman's (1975: 519) *Frame Analysis*, Goffman makes the following point about the use of pronouns in everyday conversation.

> Although certainly the pronoun, 'I,' refers to the speaker, and although certainly the speaker is a specific biographical entity, that does not mean that the whole of this entity in all of its facets is to be included on each occasion of its being cited. For he who is a speaker might be considered a

whole set of somewhat different things, bound together in part because of our cultural beliefs regarding identity. Thus, the referent of 'I' in the statements: 'I feel a chill,' 'I will take responsibility,' and 'I was born on a Tuesday' shifts, although in no easily describable way.

Goffman (1975: 521) illustrates this as follows:

Take this bit of melodrama:

> 'There is no excuse. You are right to hate me. I am coming to do so myself.'

Warmly animated, this utterance is something of a paradox. After all, anyone who identifies himself with the standards against which the culprit is being judged (and is found wanting) can't himself be all bad—and isn't, and in the very degree that he himself feelingly believes he is. A self-deprecator is, in a measure, just that, and in just that measure is not the self that is deprecated. He secretes a new self in the process of attesting to the appraisal he is coming to have of himself.

Quirk (1986: 64), likewise, points out that: ' . . . every "I" has a longitudinal dimension determined by time and the changes that time brings with it' and that therefore: ' . . . every "I" is conscious of a multiple personality . . . as though there were a long regression of *I*'s, one behind another' (Quirk's italics). Quirk (1986: 64) illustrates this with the following hypothetical example:

> Mrs Kim seemed very austere when I met her first some ten years ago, but now I find her warm-hearted and sympathetic.

He comments that: ' . . . here we need to appreciate that it was to *me*, with *my* eyes of ten years ago, that Mrs Kim seemed austere. She may have changed or my outlook on people may have changed (or both), between then and now' (ibid.; Quirk's italics).

The notion of different versions of the same referent has been more widely acknowledged in philosophy, where 'counterparts' of a referent are seen to exist in different possible worlds. This means that a fact may be true of one counterpart of the referent in one possible world, but not true of another counterpart of the referent in another possible world (Lewis 1968). This philosophical idea has been adopted by linguists, most notably Fauconnier (1994) in his theory of 'mental spaces' (see also Dinsmore 1987). Dinsmore (1987: 15) illustrates the notion with the example:

> If J. Edgar Hoover had been born a Russian, then he would have been a Communist.

In this example, the antecedent refers to a real person, whereas the pronoun refers to a hypothetical referent. Much of this research deals with hypothetical worlds, but there is also some discussion of the related issue of how a referent may exist at different points in time. Fauconnier (1994: 29–30) looks particularly at examples of the type:

> In 1929, the president was a baby.   (p. 30)

Here, the designation of the referent in present time (the president) is incompatible with the facts that were true of the referent at that earlier period (he was not the president then). This problem does not arise when the individual has the same designation in past and present or when a narrative retells events using the designation which was appropriate at the time.

Within text linguistics, Werth (MS *a*, *b*, 1995) has linked the philosophical notion of counterparts with discourse observations and considered the implications for anaphoric theory. Werth observes that a pronoun within one 'world' can co-refer with an antecedent from another 'world', arguing that anaphora is not affected by 'cross-world' context shifts. Although this may generally be true of the referring expressions used (i.e. of the link between the pronoun and its antecedent), I would argue that the 'world' or context does have an effect on the information which is accessed within the mental representation of the entity (i.e. the link between the referring expressions and the referent). These different versions of the entity representation are discussed further in the following section.

(ii) *Enactors: Past and Present 'Versions' of Characters*

Quirk and Goffman put particular emphasis on possible psychological changes to entities over time, but there will be other differences too, such as an increase in knowledge. As an example, in Ngaio Marsh's *Clutch of Constables* (1968), the narrative repeatedly alternates between Inspector Alleyn solving a case and, subsequently, telling a lecture theatre of students about how he solved it. Clearly the Inspector Alleyn who is lecturing has a greater knowledge than the Inspector Alleyn who was in the process of solving the case. In Winston Graham's *After the Act* (1965) (Examples 5.9 and 5.10), the flashback is only to the previous evening. Nevertheless, at the opening of the flashback the narrator's knowledge state is different because he does not know Alexandra's name or that he will succeed in meeting her. Over longer periods of time the circumstances of individuals may also change. A character may be new to a city on a past occasion and will not be new on a subsequent occasion (Doris Lessing, *The Four Gated City* (1972), 34; see discussion in Emmott 1989, 1992: 223–4) or may be married in flashback and widowed in the main narrative (Robert Edric, *A Lunar Eclipse* (1989), 39). In addition to this, of course, there are physical differences arising from the ageing of a character and other changes to the character's appearance.

Only a subset of the total information that we know about a character is true at any one time. This needs to be held in the entity representation of that character so that it can be separately drawn on. This suggests that entity representations are not just monolithic structures but have a more complex organization. It is not just a matter of the information being compartmentalized, since information which is not true at a particular time may still be relevant to our overall assessment of a character. A character may not currently be rich and yet the fact that he/she was once rich is still relevant. Likewise, when an individual is dead, we are still able to remember the person he/she once was. These observations suggest that accessing information within the entity representation is more a matter of foregrounding one subset of information against another, rather than treating subsets as mutually exclusive. This foregrounding is complicated by the fact that in flashback a reader may have knowledge of what is to happen next, but must also judge events on the basis that the characters do not have this knowledge.

For fictional narrative, Quirk's 'long regression' of 'personalities' will be limited according to how much is known about the character. As a narrative progresses, time is always moving onwards and new events are occurring, so the character representation is constantly changing, with new past 'personalities' being constantly added.

It is useful to draw a distinction between points at which information about these 'personalities' is explicitly mentioned by the text and points at which the information may be known to the reader but unmentioned in the text. In Susanna Mitchell's *The Token* (1985: 22), Barrie visits Mary when she is ill with flu and makes an impression on her mother Stella. Later, this event forms part of the past histories of all three characters and can, therefore, be added into the entity representations of all three. For the majority of the time the information is just stored away in memory, providing a fuller picture of the background history of the current 'personalities'. On one subsequent occasion, however, the narrative refers to this event. Stella meets Barrie and thinks:

EXAMPLE 6.1

He was that friend of Mary's who had come to see her when she was ill.

(Susanna Mitchell, *The Token* (1985), 89)

Within the relative clause, the references to Barrie ('who') and Mary ('her', 'she') refer to past 'personalities'. The text prompts the reader to access the information in their entity representations which is relevant to this earlier period, as well as recalling the incident as a whole.

The information that is available to a reader in the entity representation is like the 'growth history' in the rings of a tree, for this information comes from different times. Trees only grow outwards, but a narrative can fill in missing details about a character's past as the story progresses. Furthermore, a narrative does not only point our attention to what has happened previously, but can bring these past events 'back to life' by means of a flashback. I refer to a character who appears at the main narrative level and is also 'brought to life' in flashback, as existing as two **enactors** (Emmott 1989, 1992). The remainder of this chapter discusses how the reader needs to keep track of which enactor is being referred to at any one time and how the reader must respond to linguistic signals which indicate a switch of enactors.

2. KEEPING TRACK OF FLASHBACK ENACTORS

(a) *Signals and Monitoring*

Chapter 4 discussed how a reader needs an awareness of which context is being described at any point in a narrative. This is particularly the case with flashbacks since the same character or characters may appear in both contexts. If the reader misses the signal of a context shift, this can lead to confusion. This is most likely to occur when the flashback and main narrative not only contain the same characters but have similar settings, as in the following passage from P. D. James's *A Taste for Death* (1989). In this example, Barbara Berowne is, at main narrative level, watching the television in bed. A narrative flashback then occurs in which Barbara imagines herself as a child in bed overhearing her parents argue about herself and her brother Dicco:

EXAMPLE 6.2

'All right, we'll share. I'll take Barbie, you have Dicco. A boy's place is with his father.'

'Then we're in a difficulty. You'd better consult the father, that is if you know which one it was. By all means let him have Dicco. ...

'My God, Donald, you bastard!'

'Oh no, my dear, I'm not the bastard in this family.'

She thought: I won't listen, I won't remember, I won't think about it, and pressed the volume button, letting the rancorous voices batter at her ears. She didn't hear the door open, but suddenly there was an oblong of pale light and Dicco stood there, wrapped in his knee-length dressing gown, his springing hair a tangled halo. He stood watching her in silence, then moved barefooted across the room and the bedsprings bounced as he settled himself close against her.

(P. D. James, *A Taste for Death* (1989), 182)

To interpret this passage, the reader needs to recognize the signals of a switch of context, the mention of the volume button (referring to the television at main narrative level, mentioned several pages earlier) and the words 'I won't remember'. These could be missed[1] due to inattentive reading or to a failure to see the significance of these context-switch cues. The subsequent description of the tangled-haired Dicco in his dressing gown sounds like that of a child, although in fact it describes the adult Dicco. The subsequent conversation between Barbara and Dicco, however, makes it clear that the narrative has returned to the main level in 'present'

[1] These observations are based on my own reading of this passage as a first-time reader of the novel. On this occasion, I missed the signal of the return to the main narrative level and had to subsequently 'repair' my interpretation. Obviously not all readers would miss the signal as I did in this particular example. The point I am making here is that for any flashback switch, the reader needs (a) a mechanism for switching contexts and switching enactors and, if this mechanism fails, (b) a method of 'repairing'.

time. A reader who has overlooked the significance of the volume button will be forced to employ a repair strategy, looking back for the precise point at which the main narrative frame was recalled. Up until that point the 'wrong' enactor information will have been foregrounded and will be utilized until the incompatibility with the narrated events becomes so obvious that the reader is alerted to the misreading. Obviously, not all readers will misread this passage in this way, but misreadings of this type suggest that identifying the appropriate enactor is as important as identifying the referent. There is no potential for **referent ambiguity** here—the characters are clearly Barbara and Dicco—but there is some possibility of **enactor ambiguity.**

In fact, a reader not only needs to recognize when a switch of enactors has taken place, but also needs to make the simple assumption that, whilst a context remains in force, the same enactor (past or present) is the one that is being referred to. Since past and present versions of a character can be referred to by the same names, this assumption is an important way of identifying the appropriate enactor. Of course, the 'correct' frame and enactor can sometimes be signalled by a switch of aspect, from simple past to past perfect. This may not only be the case at the point of switching but also as the events of a flashback unfold. Nevertheless, the past perfect aspect is not as pervasive as we might think, particularly in lengthy flashbacks. In Example 6.3 the past perfect ('had happened', 'had appeared') is used at the beginning of the flashback, as Gwenda imagines the earlier events of the morning. The aspect, however, fluctuates throughout the flashback. Giles, for example, is said to have 'told' the Inspector rather than to have 'had told' him.

EXAMPLE 6.3

The events of the morning, when she [Gwenda] reviewed them, seemed to be chaotic and impossible. Everything had happened too quickly and too improbably.

Inspector Last had appeared early—at half past nine. With him had come Detective Inspector Primer from head-quarters and the Chief Constable of the County. The latter had not stayed long. It was Inspector Primer who was now in charge of the case of Lily Kimble deceased and all the ramifications arising therefrom. It was Inspector Primer, a man with a deceptively mild manner and a gentle apologetic voice, who had asked her if it would inconvenience her very much if his men did some digging in the garden. . . .

[One paragraph omitted]

Giles had spoken up then. He had said: 'I think, perhaps, we could help you with a suggestion or two.'

And he told the Inspector about the shifting of the steps leading down to the lawn, and took the Inspector out on to the terrace.

The Inspector had looked up at the barred window on the first floor at the corner of the house and had said: 'That would be the nursery, I presume.'

And Giles said that it would. . . .

[Five pages of flashback omitted]

'But I nearly had some brandy yesterday,' said Gwenda. 'Only it makes me think of Channel steamers, so Giles opened a new bottle of whisky.'

'That was very lucky for you, Mrs Reed. If you'd drunk brandy yesterday, I doubt if you would be alive today.'

'Giles nearly drank some—but in the end he had whisky with me.'

Gwenda shivered.

Even now, alone in the house, with the police gone and Giles gone with them after a hasty lunch scratched up out of tins (since Mrs Cocker had been removed to hospital), Gwenda could hardly believe in the morning turmoil of events.

(Agatha Christie, *Sleeping Murder* (1977), 174, 180)

In narrative generally it seems to be quite common for the past perfect, having occurred at the opening of a flashback, to be used intermittently thereafter or for there to be a permanent reversion to the simple past for the remainder of the flashback. This means that the verb form of the flashback in Example 6.3 is indistinguishable in many sentences from the verb form of the main narrative. When these sentences are read, therefore, it is necessary to monitor the fact that the action is set in a flashback and that a flashback enactor, the Gwenda of the morning, is being referred to. Occasionally flashback can be signalled throughout by typesetting, such as the italics in the example below. The reader still, however, has to remember what the italics signify.

EXAMPLE 6.4

She seemed to see his face as if it were carved from marble, impervious to the water pouring over it, all its thoughts locked impenetrably inside, never to be extracted. His eyes would never look into hers. Her tears flowed into the darkness. She began to imagine him alive.

There came a knock on her door. He had blue eyes. Something roughly wrapped in newspaper was held in his hands.

—I caught a couple of trout. Will I cook them for us?

(Jeremy Leland, 'The Lake', in *The Last Sandcastle* (1983), 11; Leland's italics)

In this example, the verb is in the simple past prior to the return from flashback to main narrative. This means that the return from the flashback cannot be signalled by a shift in aspect and must be indicated by other means. Likewise, in Example 6.3, in which it is the words 'Even now' that cause a reversion to the time of the main narrative and signal to the reader that the only participant present is Gwenda, since Giles has left with the police. Even when an aspect shift does occur at the end of a flashback, it cannot alone provide conclusive evidence of a return to the narrative present because such shifts can occur within flashbacks too.

As a result of there being no aspect shift at the close of the flashback, there is the possibility of enactor ambiguity for the reader of Example 6.3. The sentence 'Gwenda shivered' could be taken as occurring within the flashback, an immediate response to the conversation about the poisoned brandy. Alternatively, the timeshift adjunct 'Even now' could be taken to cover the 'Gwenda shivered' action, so that Gwenda is shivering as she thinks back to this incident. The potential ambiguity exists because Gwenda is an enactor in both frames and because there is no other clue to the frame in the sentence. The ambiguity is not referent ambiguity, for there is no doubt that Gwenda is being referred to, it is enactor ambiguity, since it is unclear whether the text means the Gwenda of the flashback or the Gwenda of the main narrative.

Confusion over enactors will sometimes be only temporary but may be more disorientating for the reader, as shown in the following example.

EXAMPLE 6.5

—I'm surprised you've any paint left, said Dolly as Avis
fetched the roll of lining-paper, tore off a length and carefully
unpinned the wet painting before pinning on the fresh sheet.
The small naked girl [Emma] set to at once, a brush in either
hand, kneeling in paint, leaning over the paper. Her mother
patted the small upturned bottom.

—You'd better make the best use of your time, my girl. It's a
good job Dolly's here to distract him or your father'd go off his
rocker when he gets home and sees all this mess.

—You'd drive anyone spare. Why have I got to come home to
this mess every day? No way am I going to stay here a moment
longer, it's a mad-house, came the voice from the doorway. I
just can't stand it. Emma spun round, paintbrush in each
hand, cigarette between her lips.

—But Siggy, you didn't mind when I started, she exclaimed.

(Jeremy Leland, 'In a Suburban Sitting-Room',
in *The Last Sandcastle* (1983), 40)

There is lexical cohesion and textual coherence across the orthographic break, with mess, paint, and anger being mentioned and
the arrival of a character who could be the father. Despite this,
and despite the fact that the same referent, Emma, is primed
before and after the break, the enactors are different. The Emma
of the first section is a small child who has just covered herself
from head to toe in paint. The reader can infer that the Emma of
the second section is older because she is smoking a cigarette.
This is not a frame recall as there has been no mention of an older
enactor until this point. Emma is now painting a mural and the
complaint comes not from her father but from her husband,
Siggy. If the reader interprets the second section as a continuation
of the first, there will be confusion over referents (Siggy and the
father) and over enactors (Emma the child and Emma the adult),
necessitating a repair strategy when it becomes clear that there
has been a frame switch.

(b) Referent and Enactor Identification

Although referents mentioned in a story are sometimes called by the same name (for example, several characters are called 'Brangwen' in Lawrence's *The Rainbow*), characters generally do have different names, enabling the reader to distinguish between one referent and another. By contrast, enactors, since they are past and present realizations of the same referent, will often have the same name. Hence, identification of a particular enactor will not always be as easy as identifying the referent.

Sometimes, of course, a character's name will have altered over time, so that the two enactors might have different names. For example, a female character may have changed her name on marriage, but this will only be relevant if the flashback takes the reader back to before the point at which the new name was adopted. In Example 6.3 Gwenda is married in both the flashback and the main narrative, so her maiden name is irrelevant. Furthermore, since her surname is rarely used in the book, a change of surname would be of little use even if the flashback did take us back further in time.

In the common situation in which there is a need to distinguish between referents of different names and enactors of the same name, the only potential for ambiguity between referents comes when a pronoun is used. In many cases this will be resolved by a nearby antecedent (see the discussion of focusing in Chapter 7). Sometimes additional clues will be needed to identify the referent. The enactors in these circumstances cannot, by contrast, be identified by the use of a name. Since the name does not distinguish between enactors, the name cannot usefully serve as an antecedent for a pronoun in terms of specifying enactors. Additional clues are of particular importance therefore in identifying enactors. These clues are of two basic types—frame independent clues and frame specific clues.

(i) Frame Independent Clues

Frame independent clues are distinguishing pieces of information about a referent or enactor that can be assumed to be relevant beyond the frame in which the information is first presented.

Names and gender are common frame independent clues, as is occupation (see Example 7.2 in which the referent can be identified by the mention of his patient) and descriptive information such as appearance or often-worn clothes (see Example 5.14 in which the referent can be identified because she wears crimson). In films, of course, appearance is the main way in which both referents and enactors can be identified. Flashback characters are often identified, for example, by means of a different hairstyle, period clothes, or their age. In narrative it would, however, be cumbersome to keep on repeating descriptive information when referring to a particular referent or enactor.

Habitual behaviour, associated locations, or known companions may also provide clues. In the following example the information that the referent is female helps to narrow down the field of potential referents but still points to several characters. The reader may instead use two other pieces of frame independent information. The text mentions that the referent is approaching the studio. Stella is the only character to have a studio, so it is probable that it is she who is going there. This is, however, not conclusive as any other female characters in the novel could be climbing the stairs to visit Stella. If the unidentified character was working in the studio, it would be possible to say with more certainty that it was Stella. In this particular case, though, the reader may draw on the information that the referent is struggling up the stairs. The reader knows that Stella is dying and that she is already having trouble performing simple tasks and the reader also knows that this is true of no other character in the story.

EXAMPLE 6.6

The stairs to the studio had grown steeper since <u>she</u> last saw them—had grown steeper and multiplied, rising upwards like Jacob's ladder, without visible end, but <u>she</u> had grown used to such phenomena.

(Susanna Mitchell, *The Token* (1985), 147; my emphasis)

Of course, the reader cannot rely on frame independent features remaining constant forever, but in everyday life, as in reading, it can often be assumed that things will remain the same until there is some indication of change. The strategies that blind or partially sighted people use to identify people are of relevance here, since, in the absence of visual or clear visual input, they too will operate on the basis of probability. For example, blind people do not always wait until an individual speaks, nor do they constantly ask that individual who he or she is. A blind person will frequently, on entering a room, address an individual without having checked that that individual is there or indeed that anyone is there at all. The blind person works on the assumption that, because that individual is regularly in that place at that time, the individual will therefore be present. The partially sighted may likewise use frame independent information to identity individuals. They may see an outline of a person sitting in a certain corner of the room in a certain distinctive position and guess their identity because they know of someone who always sits in that place in that position. Such assumptions are not always correct[2] and may lead to a blind person inadvertently addressing someone by the wrong name. Sighted people make similar assumptions when they cannot rely on vision to identify someone. If, for example, the postman always comes at a certain time in the morning and the doorbell rings at that time, it is a reasonable assumption that it is the postman there.

(ii) *Frame Specific Clues*

Frame specific clues are short-term distinguishing pieces of information which cannot be assumed to apply to a referent outside of the context in which the information is first mentioned.

Real-life disambiguation can be by frame specific clues. Chapter 4 discussed how a blind person would need to monitor the identities of the people around them. Since the blind person cannot check their identities visually, he or she must remember who is there. This still leaves the blind person with the problem of distinguishing between those present when there are no vocal clues. This can be overcome by remembering not only who is there but their positions in the room on a specific occasion. When a noise, such as the dropping of a book, comes from a certain corner of the room, the blind person may attribute it to the individual who was most recently there. Such assumption-making is of course subject to error.

The knowledge of where a person is in a room is frame specific information. On a particular occasion a person can be identified

---

[2] A similar example that I observed was of a blind person misidentifying someone because they arrived at work at exactly the same time that another colleague usually arrived.

by the fact that they are in a certain place. That person may, on another occasion, be in a quite different place and again be identified on a frame specific basis. This is very different from a frame independent interpretation which identifies a person on the basis of where they habitually sit or stand (as discussed in the previous section).

A reader may utilize frame specific features when reading narrative. In Example 6.7, below, the 'She' in 'She rose to her feet' can be interpreted because we know that Stella is sitting down and the nurse is standing. Hence it can only be Stella that is rising to her feet. Again, this is a frame specific interpretation, for on another occasion Stella might be identified by the fact that she happens to be standing.

EXAMPLE 6.7

Yes, at least she [Stella] could have caused the nurse a passing inconvenience.

She rose to her feet . . .

(Susanna Mitchell, *The Token* (1985), 7; my emphasis)

This example shows how the reader can distinguish between two referents within the same frame by means of their positions. Information about their behaviour within the frame might also be used. Enactors rarely both appear in the same frame, although it is sometimes possible for a character to speak to their past self in dreams or in their imagination. Usually, therefore, it is at frame boundaries that we need to identify an enactor, for the relevant enactor can be monitored once introduced and identified.

The actions of one enactor can sometimes be used to identify that enactor. In Jeremy Leland's 'The Lake' (in *The Last Sandcastle* (1983), 8–9), Eilís is in the process of rowing towards an island. The frame switches to a flashback frame in which Eilís and Mrs O'Murphy are talking together in the shop where they work. The first enactor and the whole lake frame are recalled by the words 'Turning her head to check her direction, Eilís noticed . . . ' (p. 9). Since the flashback involved conversation rather than navigation, we can assume that when Eilís 'check[s] her direction' it is the Eilís from the main narrative that is being referred to. In 'The Lake', therefore, an enactor is identified by her frame specific behaviour and the whole frame is recalled. Conversely, the frame can be recalled by a mention of one or more of the participants or the time or location and the appropriate enactor inferred from this. Often a minor piece of frame specific information about the surroundings is used to recall the frame. In Jeremy Leland's 'Intrusion' (in *The Last Sandcastle* (1983), 28) another 'lake frame' is recalled by the words 'Somewhere an invisible moorhen gurgled.' The moorhen had not been previously mentioned as being a part of the 'lake frame', but is appropriate to an outdoor scene.[3] Often, the frame specific clue will have been previously mentioned. In P. D. James's *A Taste for Death* (1989), 179, discussed above, the frame recall cue is 'the volume button', presumably the volume button of the television she is watching in the main narrative (p. 182).

Obviously, if either frame specific or frame independent information is to distinguish between two referents or distinguish between two enactors, it must be distinctive rather than shared. The information, for example, that one enactor is standing by a tree can only identify that enactor if the other enactor is not standing by a tree. Whether information is distinctive or shared often depends more on narrative presentation than on real differences. At one point in Doris Lessing's *The Four Gated City* (1972), Martha stands in the main narrative poised ready to enter the door of a restaurant, whilst she remembers as a flashback an occasion when she had accidentally opened a door of a private room elsewhere in London.[4] A subsequent sentence 'She went in' is potentially ambiguous. Although the buildings are not the same and although a distinction could be made between them, at this point the narrative does not make a distinction and so the description of Martha's entry contains only shared information. The mention of Martha herself is also insufficient to identify the enactor because the pronoun only tells us that the enactor is female and this is applicable to both 'Martha enactors'.

The following example illustrates how a narrative can attempt to make information distinctive, although whether it is interpreted in this way or not depends on the reader:

---

[3] This involves drawing on our general knowledge and using 'frames' in Minsky's (1977) sense of the word (see Ch. 2).

[4] See Emmott (1989: 180–2, 207–9) for a full discussion of this example; also Emmott (1992: 223–4).

EXAMPLE 6.8

[Rachel] stopped by a table of cacti and held her hands an inch from the spikes of the largest. She lit a cigarette and almost immediately a capped and uniformed attendant appeared and asked her to put it out. He watched her to ensure she didn't drop it into the pond. She pinched it out between her fingers without taking her eyes from him. He screwed up his face at the imagined pain.

There was a film of Rachel and Colin in the hothouse, and on the grass outside, chasing each other, behaving like teenagers, one being careful with the hand-held camera, the other being careful to remain in frame. Another shot of Rachel stealing cuttings by pinching off the tips of the plants with her fingernails and palming them into her pocket, in which there was a plastic bag, proof of predetermination.

She lifted the heads of some of the plants beside the cacti and studied them. She disarmed the attendant by apologising to him and then asking him about the plant he held.

(Robert Edric, *A Lunar Eclipse* (1989), 39; my emphasis)

In the first paragraph of this example, Rachel is with the narrator of the story in a hothouse in the park. The narrator has, on previous occasions, been watching home movies dating back to the time when Rachel's husband, Colin, was alive, and in the second paragraph the narrator tells us about one film in which Rachel and Colin were in the same hothouse. The third paragraph could in theory be either a continuation of the film frame or a return to the main narrative. The hothouse appears in both frames in past and present forms. Our general knowledge of hothouses leads us to expect cacti and an attendant in both cases. Since, however, the main narrative text has explicitly mentioned the presence of the cacti and the attendant, whereas the film flashback has not, there seems a greater likelihood that the third paragraph refers to the main narrative frame and the fact that it does is subsequently confirmed by the content of the conversation between Rachel and the attendant. The cacti and the attendant could, therefore, be said to be distinctive pieces of information which identify the main narrative frame. Nevertheless, there is the possibility of confusion, since the two frames are very similar in many respects, especially as in both cases Rachel has performed an action which justifies her apology to the attendant in the third paragraph. The clues about the cacti and the attendant may be distinctive, but the interpretation of the third paragraph depends on whether the reader can remember the information and link it with the appropriate frame. This example suggests that clues to a recalled context can be fairly subtle and that if the contexts of the flashback and main narrative are similar, the reader may miscue and then need to 'repair'.

Summary

This chapter has continued the discussion of context shifts begun in Chapter 5, looking particularly at how information in entity representations would have to be segmented in order to provide the appropriate information about enactors (characters appearing both in present and past times).

Although the reader needs all of the information in the entity representation, some of this information will be more highly activated when one enactor is focused on rather than another. The reader needs to monitor which enactor is being referred to over a stretch of text, since linguistic clues such as verb aspect are not always available in every sentence.

The fact that enactors often share the same name means that ambiguity is possible even when the referent is clear. The reader needs to use both frame independent and frame specific clues to determine which enactor is intended. Frame independent clues are pieces of information about a character which can be expected to be true over a long period of time. Frame specific clues, by contrast, describe the character or the frame itself on a specific occasion. Frame independent and frame specific clues are only useful when they are distinctive rather than shared.

As far as cognitive modelling is concerned, this discussion suggests that entity representations are not just monolithic stores, but that their structure is more complex than this. As far as reference theory is concerned, the implications are that identifying a character (the referent) may not be the final stage in the interpretation process, since the appropriate enactor information needs to be determined too.

PART THREE

Implications: Linguistic Theory and
Narrative Theory

Mental Representations, Inference-Making, and Reference Theory

Previous chapters have argued that the notion of mental representations is needed to explain how information that has been provided at an earlier point in a text is available at subsequent points to supplement the literal words of the text. For narrative text, important mental representations are entity representations, which provide information about particular characters, and contextual frames, which monitor which characters are together in a location at any particular time. These representations explain the behaviour of characters and provide information which enables 'shorthand' forms such as pronouns to be interpreted.

In this chapter, I turn to the implications of these observations for a linguistic theory of reference. In Section 1, I look at theoretical arguments which have been put forward to justify the incorporation of mental representations into linguistic models (such arguments being necessary because linguistic models have not always included these representations). Section 2 considers the altered role of the antecedent in those models that do take account of a 'cognitive layer'.

After considering why linguists need to incorporate this 'cognitive layer' in their models, I look in Section 3 at how the idea of contextual frames can add to the ability of reference theory to explain how participants are identified in full, real narrative texts. Section 4 then examines how my own notion of priming can be linked with artificial intelligence's 'focusing theory' (Grosz 1978; Sidner 1979*b*; Grosz and Sidner 1986) to provide a fuller account of how pronominalization operates in narrative. Priming provides the overall context—supplying the reader with knowledge of the time, location, and participant set—but focusing draws attention to one or more participants within the group.

This discussion argues that focusing is based on the reader's anticipation of what will be mentioned next and that the frequently used expression 'refer back' is not therefore an appropriate way to talk about anaphoric reference.

I. THE ROLE OF MENTAL REPRESENTATIONS IN LINGUISTIC MODELS

It seems little more than common sense to say that the mind collects information about entities, situations, and events as it reads. This is particularly the case when studying narrative data, since observations about creating characters and fictional contexts are taken for granted in narratology and literary criticism. The importance of the notion of mental representations to linguistic study only becomes clear when it is recognized that they are a relatively new innovation as far as text linguistics is concerned (as discussed in Chapter 1). Influential models of reference have not in the past included mental representations. Mental representations are now more widely accepted as an essential part of text theory, but linguists are still battling with the implications of including these representations in their models of how language works.

(a) Working without Mental Representations

As a prelude to discussing the role of mental representations in reference theory, I begin by looking at one particular model of textual reference which has ignored the need for these representations, namely Halliday and Hasan (1976). In the following section, I then contrast this work with G. Brown and Yule's (1983) reference model which includes simple mental representations. Although other disciplines, such as psychology, take mental representations for granted, it is only by showing the relatively recent inclusion of representations in text theory that the significance of current cognitive modelling within text linguistics can be appreciated.

Halliday and Hasan's *Cohesion in English* (1976)[1] is a book

---

[1] Halliday and Hasan's model of reference theory has been reworked since *Cohesion in English* (1976) (e.g. Halliday and Hasan 1989). This book is, nevertheless, their most influential discussion of the subject and is widely cited by linguists (e.g. G. M. Green 1989: 102; Tannen 1989: 59; M. McCarthy 1991) and those in

which has been extremely influential in text analysis and is still frequently cited by text linguists and by those in other fields such as psychology. Halliday and Hasan's book does not, however, make any mention of mental representations, or cognitive matters generally, and as a result there are a number of theoretical and practical problems with the way these authors handle reference theory.

Halliday and Hasan's book operates primarily[2] on what I will call the 'referent in the text' notion. Halliday and Hasan (1976) see pronoun resolution as a search for a 'presupposed' item in the 'sentence' (p. 14) or in a previous 'sentence' (p. 14), in other words a search for something which is part of the text itself. This 'presupposed' item is what is traditionally termed the antecedent, which is generally the last co-referential full noun phrase (i.e. a noun phrase containing either a proper noun or a common noun, but not just a pronoun[3]). For Halliday and Hasan, the task is complete when the antecedent is located, with no further stages being included in their model. So, the antecedent is, by their analysis, the referent, as illustrated by the following extract:

> . . . *he* refers back to *Henry* . . .
>
> (Halliday and Hasan 1976: 14; their italics)

The italicizing of *Henry*, by linguistic convention, suggests that the referent is the antecedent noun 'Henry', so that the referent is in the text (indeed Halliday and Hasan explicitly say elsewhere in their book (p. 49) that the referent is in the text). Halliday (1985: 291) likewise states that anaphoric items 'point . . . to the preceding text'.

In the 'referent in the text' model, reference is seen as the

related disciplines such as educational psychology (e.g. Oakhill and Garnham 1988; Yuill and Oakhill 1991; Peterson and McCabe 1991) and artificial intelligence (e.g. Carter 1987). (This does not, however, mean that all of these writers agree with Halliday and Hasan's reference theory. These books and articles are mentioned to show how influential *Cohesion in English* is both in linguistics and other disciplines.)

[2] Halliday and Hasan's position within *Cohesion in English* (1976) is not consistent. Often they tell us that a pronoun refers to a noun (see subsequent discussion), but on occasion they say that a noun and a pronoun both refer to 'the same thing' (e.g. p. 3).

[3] In fact, some full noun phrases (e.g. 'the woman') give little more information than a pronoun and may be insufficient to identify a particular referent. To interpret a pronoun, what is generally required is a unique full noun phrase.

relationship between a pronoun and its antecedent, this antecedent being a recent full noun phrase. The question of what a noun refers to is a non-issue in the 'referent in the text' model (for the noun is itself regarded as the referent), but is important in the 'referent in the mind' model described below.

Although the 'referent in the text'[4] notion has been particularly evident in discourse analysis, it can also be found in other disciplines such as artificial intelligence (e.g. Carbonell and Brown 1989: 96). Strangely, some writers who appear to believe in mental representations do sometimes talk about reference items using 'referent in the text' descriptions. The psychologists Yuill and Oakhill (1991: 87), for example,[5] say that: 'Anaphors refer to other words elsewhere in the text, but these words may be at some distance from the anaphor'. A response to this criticism might be that this is just a manner of expression, but it does suggest that there is some underlying theoretical confusion which is fairly common in work on anaphora.

(b) Working with Mental Representations

Criticisms of what I have termed 'the referent in the text' model are made by writers such as van Dijk and Kintsch (1983: 163), Morgan (1978), G. M. Green (1989: 27), and Werth (1995, MS *a*, *b*). Not all text linguists ignore the distinction between a word and its referent. The contributors to Chafe (1980*a*) take the notion of mental representations for granted, although without generally using the term 'mental representation'. Hence, within this volume, Chafe (1980*b*) assumes that communicators must be conscious of referents, Downing (1980: 96–7) argues that a refer-

---

[4] Grammarians (e.g. Quirk *et al.* 1985: 347; Givón 1989: 198–203) have sometimes avoided the 'referent in the text' notion by saying that a pronoun and its antecedent co-refer, i.e. that they both refer to the same thing. Co-reference is also a common expression in generative grammar (e.g. Reinhart 1983; E. K. Brown and Miller 1982: 167–8). Halliday and Hasan (1976: e.g. 3) use this terminology sporadically in addition to (and in theoretical conflict with) the 'referent in the text' notation, although again without postulating mental representations of characters. In general, co-reference is a useful notion but the problem is that some writers do not specify what a pronoun and its antecedent are co-referring to (particularly in fictional texts).

[5] See also Grosz (1977: 29) who speaks of 'the use of pronouns whose referents lie far back in the previous discourse'.

ence to an individual recalls all the accumulated information about that individual, Clancy (1980: 128) talks of the 'idea, and perhaps also mental image, of a particular referent', and Du Bois (1980: 221) discusses 'cognitive files'.

One of the few attempts to provide theoretical justification for mental representations of characters can be found in G. Brown and Yule (1983). Brown and Yule argue that a pronoun refers not to its antecedent but to a mental representation. They support their case with the following made-up example (discussed briefly in Chapter 3).

Kill an active, plump chicken. Prepare it for the oven, cut it into four pieces and roast it with thyme for 1 hour.

(Brown and Yule 1983: 202; my emphasis)

If this example were interpreted using the 'referent in the text' notion, the antecedent, 'an active, plump chicken', would be regarded as being the referent of the first pronoun 'it'. This would, however, as Brown and Yule point out, make nonsense of the passage for it would then mean 'Prepare an active, plump chicken for the oven', whereas it is clearly a plump, dead chicken that is being prepared.

Brown and Yule suggest that the reader must build a mental representation of a plump, dead chicken by amalgamating the antecedent noun phrase 'an active, plump chicken' with the verb 'kill'. This entity representation is then the referent of the pronoun 'it'. The model would also need to take account of the fact that the antecedent noun phrase may be amalgamated with any information from its surrounding text, not just the verb.

For every reference that is made in the text to a particular character, whether by a noun or a pronoun, the reader needs to access the mental representation. Nouns, since they are not themselves referents but words denoting referents, need interpreting as much as pronouns. Both nouns and pronouns might be more accurately termed 'pro-referents' and, therefore, in fiction at least,[6]

---

[6] Many researchers would also argue that real-life referents are also perceived by means of mental representations. Except when communication is metalinguistic, words are generally regarded as referring not to other words but to real-world people or objects (with mediating mental representations sometimes being postulated too) (e.g. Ogden and Richards 1985; Lyons 1977: ii. 670; Judge 1985; Kempson 1988; Kronfeld 1990).

'pro-representations'. The proper noun 'Lady Chatterley', therefore, refers technically to a mental representation[7] made up from
all previous mentions of Lady Chatterley plus information in the
accompanying text plus inferences. This makes sense because it
means that reference is to a representation of a character with
whom we can empathize rather than just a word or words in the
text.

The idea that fictional names refer to mental representations
breaks with the philosophical tradition of regarding reference as
being simply a relationship between words and real objects.[8] If
this tradition is followed, it would mean that reference theory
would be inapplicable to narrative fiction, except when stories
incorporate individuals from real life. Some academics do restrict
the term 'reference' in this way. For example, in linguistics, Widdowson (1984) distinguishes between the processes of fictional
'representation' and real-world 'reference'. Likewise, within artificial intelligence, Sidner (1979b) differentiates between 'specifica-
tion' and 'reference'.

Alternatively, the term 'reference' can be used for both fictional
and real-world mentions of an individual (e.g. Sag and Hankamer
1984; Ryan 1991: ch. 1). This use of the term might be objected
to by some philosophers, but linguists and artificial intelligence
researchers have different concerns than philosophers and ' . . . it
is only to be expected that what the one discipline considers to be
crucial the other will regard as being of secondary importance,
and conversely.' (Lyons 1977: i. 184). Philosophers concentrate
on reference to real-world objects because they are primarily
interested in truth and existence. However, linguists and artificial
intelligence researchers, who are mainly concerned with the
mechanisms by which language is interpreted, may use the term
more broadly (Lyons 1977: i. 184; Werth 1984: 170)[9] because

---

[7] Some philosophers (e.g. Rescher 1973) and text linguists (Ryan 1991; Werth
MS *a*, *b*) effectively take this position by drawing on (and developing) the terminology and concepts of possible worlds theory and yet also regarding the possible
worlds as mental constructs.

[8] Some philosophers take account of entities which are non-existent in the real
world by assuming that they exist in some possible world (Leibniz 1953: 12–27;
Russell 1937: 66–9, 210; Lewis 1968, 1973: 84–95; see also discussions in Lyons
1977: 161–7; Allwood, Andersson, and Dahl 1977: 22–3, 54–62; Johnson-Laird
1983: 172–4; S. Allén 1989; and Ishiguro 1990: 175–9, 186–91).

[9] Lyons (1977: i. 184) points out that ' . . . philosophers are professionally concerned with the explication of the notions of truth, knowledge, belief and existence.

the processing of real-world and fictional nouns and pronouns seems to be similar. In reading fictional text, identifying the mental representation is the goal of interpreting a referring expression such as a pronoun. Some academics may, however, in view of the philosophical tradition,[10] prefer to use some other term, such as Sidner's 'specify', for the relationship between names and mental representations of fictional characters. This terminological difference does not, however, affect the major question of whether we need to postulate mental representations in the first place. Furthermore, as cognitive researchers are increasingly viewing 'real-world' reference as itself being mediated by mental representations, the need to view fictional and non-fictional reference as distinct may no longer be relevant.

2. THE ROLE OF THE ANTECEDENT IN A COGNITIVE MODEL OF REFERENCE

The introduction of mental representations into linguistic models of reference has led to some confusion over the role of the antecedent. Ariel (1990), for example, uses the term 'antecedent' indiscriminately for both textual antecedents (e.g. pp. 18, 27) and

---

The fundamental problem for the linguist, as far as reference is concerned, is to elucidate and to describe the way in which we use language to draw attention to what we are talking about. In many situations, it may be unclear, and of little consequence, whether a speaker is implicitly committed, by the word he utters, to a belief in the truth of particular existential propositions; and it is rarely the case that a speaker uses a referring expression for the purpose of ontological commitment. Philosophy and linguistics undoubtedly converge in the study of reference, and each can benefit from their joint discussion of the notions involved. But their primary concerns remain distinct.' Likewise, Werth (1984: 169–70) argues that '... writers ... manage to write about non-existing states of affairs quite convincingly, and without apparently mystifying their readership. ... We take it to be obvious that it is this sort of fact about linguistic behaviour, and not centuries of philosophical problems with the notion of 'existence', that should guide us in our treatment of reference.' (See also Werth (MS *a*, *b*)).

[10] Some academics might argue that it is 'wrong' to use the term 'reference' in a way that differs from traditional philosophy. This, however, ignores the fact that philosophers themselves use terms such as 'reference' and 'sense' in different ways. Linguists and artificial intelligence researchers should be quite used to the idea that a single term can be used in different ways by different writers (providing each writer makes clear their own meaning), as it is common for grammatical metalanguage to vary in meaning in this way. Although differing terminology can be a nuisance, flexibility over terms enables researchers to develop new descriptions, sometimes for different purposes.

mental representations (e.g. pp. 6, 17, 29, 57, 60). This may reflect a belief that readers just store a copy of a textual antecedent in their minds, for Ariel does not discuss the possibility that readers build complex mental representations such as entity representations. Assuming that the label 'antecedent' is used simply for textual items, it needs to be considered what role the antecedent plays in the 'referent in the mind' model.

Although in the 'referent in the mind' model the antecedent is no longer the referent, the antecedent still usually plays a role in assisting the reader to comprehend a pronoun. Generally a pronoun is judged to be co-referential to one of the nearest potential antecedents,[11] with the reader drawing on clues derived from the environment of the antecedent and pronoun where necessary. In sentences of the type 'John hit Henry. He fell to the ground' the likelihood is that Henry falls, since he has been hit. If we accept Brown and Yule's arguments, mental representations are not just the result of the interpretation process, they play an active role in interpretation. The antecedents 'John' and 'Henry' can be regarded as activating the entity representations of the two characters and the information about who has hit and who has been hit is stored within these representations. The reader then draws on this information in the mental representations to supply clues to interpret the pronoun, rather than looking at the text of the previous sentence. The argument that the mental representations themselves often provide the clues to interpretation is more evident when these clues have not been recently mentioned in the text. Example 3.4 was used earlier to make this point and is cited again below:

EXAMPLE 7.1

Esther had forced herself to stay cheerful and strong, to go to Debby's room always with a smile. She was pregnant again and worried because of the earlier stillbirth of twin sons, but to

---

[11] See e.g. Bloomfield's definition of anaphora, '*he* implies, in nearly all its uses, that a substantive designating a species of male personal objects has recently been uttered and that *he* means one individual of this species' (1935: 251; Bloomfield's italics, my underlining). Yule (1981) refers to the most recent item as the 'current entity' and notes the high probability of the current entity being referred to by a pronoun or by ellipsis. See also van Dijk and Kintsch (1983: 165–7); H. H. Clark and Sengul (1979); Corbett and Chang (1983); and Chang (1980).

the hospital staff, the family, and Deborah, her surface never varied, and she took pride in the strength she showed.

(Hannah Green, *I Never Promised You a Rose Garden* (1985), 33; my underlining)

In this example, the fact that only Esther is an adult (and therefore, obviously, the only one able to be pregnant) is known from the mental representations and can be used as a clue to interpret the pronoun.

If clues from mental representations assist in the interpretation of pronouns, the antecedent has a lesser role than in non-cognitive models, quite apart from the fact that it is no longer viewed as the referent. The antecedent is generally still an important key to interpretation, but it does not necessarily function alone.

Moreover, in some cases a pronoun can be interpreted even though there is no antecedent at all,[12] as illustrated in the example below. This is comparatively rare, but since it is possible it should be taken into account in reference theory.

EXAMPLE 7.2

It was not quite true that this was the only connecting link. The other, of course, was the body, the young woman's body. Shiva thought, I must wait for more news, I must bear it and wait.

His patient was getting on for fifty, a handsome, tall woman, very well-dressed. Her expensive clothes—Jasper Conran, he guessed—she had put on again and, while behind the screen, a little more lipstick.

(Barbara Vine, *A Fatal Inversion* (1987), 26; my emphasis)

The words 'His patient' begin a new section of the story and the pronoun can be inferred to refer to a doctor. As Shiva, the last named character, is not a doctor, 'Shiva' cannot be the antecedent.

---

[12] A number of studies (e.g. Haviland and Clark 1974; Rieger 1974: 117; Du Bois 1980; Sanford and Garrod 1981; G. Brown and Yule 1983; Cornish 1986; Givón 1989: 207) have discussed examples in which a pronoun or definite article is used after a schema-related noun phrase (e.g. 'a car' ... 'the driver' or 'he'). In the examples given in this section there is no immediately preceding noun phrase of any kind. See also related discussions in Bolinger (1979); Yule (1982); and Sanford *et al.* (1984).

Although subsequent text provides the name 'Rufus', the pronoun does not, however, need to be interpreted cataphorically, for once the reader realizes that a doctor is being referred to, it is possible to guess immediately that it is Rufus. This involves accessing the entity representation directly using a clue in the environment of the pronoun, but no antecedent. Presumably, readers draw on their mental record of all the entity representations, finding the one which matches this description. This type of direct access may be more common with certain lexical referring expressions than with pronouns. Expressions like 'a figure' need interpretation since, as they do not specify sex, they often carry less identifying information than pronouns. Example 5.14 provided an example from Mervyn Peake's *Titus Groan* (1985: 269). The discussion of this example suggested that the lexical mention of a 'figure in its crimson dress' could be interpreted as Fuchsia on the basis that Fuchsia is the only character in the story that wears crimson. This means that the reader can access the character representation of Fuchsia without an antecedent, matching information in the co-text of the general noun 'figure' with stored information in the mental representation.

The most striking examples of pronouns which can be interpreted without antecedents are found in examples of frame recall. In such cases, it is the reinstatement of the context that supplies the key to interpreting a pronoun, rather than the antecedent functioning as a key. Such examples are discussed in the following section, with the role of the antecedent being considered throughout this chapter.

3. THE ROLE OF CONTEXTUAL FRAMES IN REFERENCE THEORY

Reference theory has originated largely from observations made about decontextualized sentences rather than from a consideration of how reference actually operates in full, real texts. Work within artificial intelligence and discourse analysis has managed partly to redress this balance (e.g. Grosz 1978; Reichman 1985; Fox 1987*a*, *b*), but there is still a need for detailed study of the mechanisms of reference across a range of genres. In particular, discourse contributions to linguistic theory need to be sufficiently well acknowledged that they find their way into the grammar textbooks. This section discusses the role of contextual frames in a linguistic theory of reference, arguing that such frames not only account for comparatively infrequent examples, such as pronominalization after a frame recall, but also explain much more common pronoun usage. This discussion draws partly on points that have been made about text examples in previous chapters, but also makes additional points about the need for readers to have contextual information available when interpreting narrative texts.

(a) *Interpreting Pronouns across Context Boundaries*

A number of examples have already been presented to show how pronouns may occur without antecedents after the recall of a contextual frame. In Example 1.1, the two characters, Jim and Peter, were reintroduced, but only Jim's name was given before the pronoun 'they' was used. Likewise, in Example 5.10 the girl at the party was reintroduced with only the pronoun 'she'. Whilst this type of example only occurs at context boundaries, their interpretation depends on a recognition of context which is also necessary to interpret some of the more common examples discussed below.

When a contextual frame is recalled, the entire participant group is reinstated, regardless of whether they are mentioned or not. This means that an antecedent is not necessary, except as a possible means of recalling the contextual frame. This phenomenon needs to be recognized in reference theory, since the result is that a series of pronouns which look, on the surface, as if they refer to the same character (such as the 'she' pronouns in Example 5.10), actually refer to two different characters in two different contexts.

Apart from forcing the analyst to reconsider the need for an antecedent in all cases, such examples also have implications for the dividing line between anaphora and deixis as discussed in Section 3c below. These frame recall examples also place a question mark over the distinction between anaphora and cataphora. Antecedentless pronouns look cataphoric, since the reader has to wait for a full mention of the character. However, if we assume that the reader has the information available to interpret the antecedentless pronoun, then it can be classed as anaphoric. This does, nevertheless, have the consequence that the meaning of the terms 'anaphora' and 'cataphora' is based on whether the reader has the information available to interpret a pronoun, rather than the order of the pronoun and the nearest co-referential noun phrase. This means replacing a formal explanation with a cognitive one.

(b) Narrowing the Current Reference Set

Contextual frames can also help to clarify a reference to a character by narrowing down the number of potential referents from all those that have previously been mentioned in the book to just those who are present in a particular context (as discussed in Chapter 3, Section 1e). In cases where there is only one character in a context or only one character of a particular sex, the reader can simply assume all pronouns of the appropriate sex to refer to this character. In rare cases where two characters have the same name, they may sometimes be distinguished on the basis of which one is in the primed context. In Example 7.3 below, it is frame narrowing that enables the reader to identify the referent. Although both Tom Brangwen (the father) and Will Brangwen (his nephew) share a surname, when the two are together (as at the beginning of the example) the name 'Brangwen' often refers to Tom, with Will being called just 'Will' or 'the youth'. If, however, Will is the only one of the two in a frame, 'Brangwen' can then be used to refer to Will. The frame therefore narrows the reference set, supplementing the information provided by the antecedent. Although 'Brangwen' at the end of the first paragraph refers to Tom, the frame switch (as Will and his cousin go outside) makes the 'Brangwen' in the second paragraph of the extract a reference to Will, for Will is now the only Brangwen in the frame.

EXAMPLE 7.3

'Come with me, Will,' she said to her cousin. 'I want to see if I put the brick over where that rat comes in.'

'You've no need to do that,' retorted her father [Tom Brangwen]. She took no notice. The youth [Will Brangwen] was between the two wills. The colour mounted into the father's face, his blue eyes stared. The girl stood near the door, her head held slightly back, like an indication that the youth must come. He rose, in his silent, intent way, and was gone with her. The blood swelled in Brangwen's forehead veins.

It was raining. The light of the lantern flashed on the cobbled path and the bottom of the wall. She came to a small ladder, and climbed up. He reached her the lantern, and followed. Up there in the fowl-loft, the birds sat in fat bunches on the perches, the red combs shining like fire. Bright, sharp eyes opened. There was a sharp crawk of expostulation as one of the hens shifted over. The cock sat watching, his yellow neck feathers bright as glass. Anna went across the dirty floor. <u>Brangwen</u> crouched in the loft watching.

(D. H. Lawrence, *The Rainbow* (1949), 118; my emphasis)

Although it is fairly rare to have two characters of the same name in a novel, it is common to have to distinguish between two participants designated by phrases such as 'the woman' or 'the girl'. In the following example, the frame switch is partly responsible for cancelling the 'girl with upswept lacquered hair' as a potential antecedent in the second paragraph, so that 'the girl' in the third paragraph refers to the daughter instead.[13]

EXAMPLE 7.4

He passed a low building, incongruously new, a sign of the New South, with a sign reading PALMETTO MOTOR-IN; he reversed down the street back to the building.

<u>A girl</u> with upswept lacquered hair and candy-pink lipstick gave him a meaningless, dead smile and a room with twin beds

---

[13] Another factor, though, is the reader's awareness that the receptionist is a minor participant whose only role is in the context in which she is introduced, this type of participant being termed a 'scenario-dependent character' by A. Anderson, Garrod, and Sanford (1983). Even when characters are not scenario-dependent, they may have different degrees of prominence in the story. Sometimes long stretches of a book will concentrate on one character rather than another, looking at events unfolding from that character's point of view (see Kuno and Kaburaki (1977) and Kuno (1976) for a discussion of 'empathy'). In some languages, such as Mambila (spoken in Nigeria) and Chitwan Tharu (spoken in Nepal), the relative prominence of characters in a story is a key factor in pronoun interpretation. Major participants may be introduced in distinct ways (sometimes with special morphological markers) and may be more likely to be referred to by pronouns (see Wise 1968; Grimes 1975: 261–71; Grimes 1978b: 107; Newman 1978; Perrin 1978; Sheffler 1978; Ennulat 1978; Taylor 1978; Toba 1978; Leal 1978: 192; Hunt 1978; Schottelndreyer 1978; Levinsohn 1978; Clancy 1980: 185, 193; 1992; Morrow 1986; Givón 1989: 182). Givón (1989: 189–92) has suggested that in informal English, the key character in a story may be introduced by the indefinite 'this' rather than 'a' in phrases such as 'There's *this guy*' (Givón 1989: 190) (see also H. Sacks 1992f: 444–5).

'for myself and my daughter'. In the register he wrote: Lamar Burgess, 155 Ridge Road, Stonington, Conn. After he handed <u>her</u> a night's payment in cash, <u>she</u> gave him a key.

Their cubicle contained two single beds, an iron-textured brown carpet and lime-green walls, two pictures—a kitten tilting its head, an Indian looking into a leafy gorge from a clifftop—a television set, a door into a blue-tiled bathroom. He sat on the toilet seat while <u>the girl</u> undressed and got into bed.

(Peter Straub, *Ghost Story* (1979), 18–19;
Straub's capitals, my emphasis)

Frame narrowing can also reduce the possibilities when an initially unidentified character enters a context (see discussion in Section 3d of 'frame participant ambiguity'). We know, for example, that if someone rings the doorbell, it cannot be one of the people already primed into the current context and we also know that it is unlikely to be someone who is bound into a distant context (such as a character who is abroad). Of course, such assumptions can sometimes have significance to the overall plot, such as when alibis are being established in detective stories.

(c) Interpreting 'Group' Pronouns with Distant Antecedents

Certain pronouns will refer to the entire group of characters in a primed frame or to all the characters in the frame except those specifically excluded. In the following example 'We' refers to everyone in the frame and 'the rest of us' denotes everyone except Tim Dickinson. Such references may be in the first person ('we', 'us') or the third person ('they', 'them') depending on whether they are uttered by a first-person narrator, a third-person narrator, or by characters speaking about the others present.

E X A M P L E 7 . 5

<u>We</u> talked and wrangled amiably for a time. Tim Dickinson, the amateur, had of course far more theories than <u>the rest of us</u> put together.

(Winston Graham, *After the Act* (1965), 10; my emphasis)

These 'primed participant set' pronouns will often have distant antecedents, which occur sentences, paragraphs, or perhaps pages before. Since the characters may not have all been mentioned at the same time, the antecedents will often be scattered too. The interpretation of these pronouns is difficult to explain using linguistic models which involve looking back in the text for an antecedent or antecedents. The reader would not only have to look back a long way for disparate antecedents, but would not know when the search was complete. If, for example, the reader has recovered four antecedents for the pronoun 'We' in Example 7.5 how docs he or she know whether this is the full participant set or whether it is necessary to go back further and look for more? It is easier to regard the information about the participants as being monitored by a contextual frame and being readily available as the pronoun is read. The frame, therefore, brings the appropriate information to these pronouns rather than the pronouns signalling the need for a backward search. The frame, similarly, can account for how location and time adverbs such as 'here' and 'now' can be interpreted even when the place and time have not been recently mentioned.[14]

A major implication of these observations is that in narrative text the dividing line between anaphora and deixis begins to break down. Usually deixis means that there is a reference to the extra-linguistic context (i.e. the physical context surrounding the speaker), with there being no need for an antecedent, since the listener can see the participants in that context. Anaphora, by contrast, normally means that a linguistic antecedent is necessary in the text, since the listener is not able to draw on the extra-linguistic context. In narratives, the distinction is not so clear. The reader builds a representation of the fictional context and then draws on this context to interpret subsequent pronouns. In a sense, this is parallel to drawing on a real-world context and is hence deictic (or pseudo-deictic). The writer cannot, however, physically point out specific characters in the fictional context to the reader, since the writer and reader are separated in time and space. Without an antecedent, therefore, the writer can only point out the whole group in the contextual frame, but he/she needs to use an antecedent to indicate one member of this group.

[14] Bühler's (1990: 140–57) discussion of 'imagination-oriented deixis' ('*Deixis am Phantasma*') raises this issue, suggesting that the language interpreter draws on ' "imagined space" . . . the realm of the somewhere or other of pure phantasy, the realm of the here and there of memory' (p. 142).

Referring to the full primed participant set can, therefore, be done in this deictic (or pseudo-deictic) fashion, but focusing on one participant (as described later in this chapter) must generally be done anaphorically.[15] Relying on the primed context to identify a participant group is deictic in so far as no antecedent is needed. It nevertheless has anaphoric properties, since the context is only created in the first place by earlier mentions of the fact that the characters are bound into that context, which means that a full noun phrase is required at an earlier stage in the text (even though it is not functioning as an antecedent at this point).

(d) *Accounting for Different Types of Ambiguity*

Contextual frames are important because there is a distinction between knowing who is present in a context and identifying which particular character is being referred to at any one point. This distinction is highlighted by the fact that it possible to differentiate between two quite different types of ambiguity, which I term **frame participant ambiguity** and **overt participant ambiguity**. Example 7.6 provides an example of overt participant ambiguity, the type of ambiguity that reference theorists are normally interested in:

EXAMPLE 7.6

From the shadows of the centre table somebody suddenly said very high and clear, 'The soup is cold.' The mother pushed hers away.

'I think,' said the father, 'that it must nevertheless be drunk, don't you?'

Two or three of the children put down their spoons. Elizabeth went on with the soup until it was finished.

'Shall we all finish the soup?' asked the father slowly, turning his head about. The children one by one picked up their spoons again, getting the soup down somehow with the help of the hard bread. The mother turned sideways and looked at the floor.

'Come along now, Elizabeth, eat your bread.'

---

[15] If, however, there is only one participant of a particular sex in a context, priming the full participant set will automatically identify that specific character.

'I have drunk the soup,' said Elizabeth, 'but the bread is too hard.'

'Then we shall hope that you can eat it later, shall we not?'

(Jane Gardam, 'An Unknown Child' in *The Pangs of Love and Other Stories* (1984), 64–5)

The reader cannot be sure who tells Elizabeth to eat her bread. It is probably someone who is sitting at the centre table. It is also, on the basis of general knowledge, presumably an adult. It is possible to list the adults sitting at the centre table: Elizabeth's father and mother. The reader knows who is in the frame, but does not necessarily know whether the mother is the speaker and the father the listener, or vice versa. The reader does not, therefore, know definitely which of these two is the overt participant and which is covert.

Example 7.6, then, demonstrates overt participant ambiguity. Frame participant ambiguity is quite different, occurring when the reader cannot even be certain which characters are in the frame, as illustrated in the following example:

EXAMPLE 7.7

Looking down, along the new embankment in Chelsea, there arc traces of snow on the ground. Yet there is also, if only in the sunlight, the first faint ghost of spring. *I am ver* . . . I am sure the young woman whom I should have liked to show pushing a perambulator (but can't, since they did not come into use for another decade) had never heard of Catullus . . .

(John Fowles, *The French Lieutenant's Woman* (1977), 358; Fowles's italics)

Fowles does not identify this woman until later. The character could be Sarah Woodruff, whose whereabouts the reader is eager to know, or it could be one of the minor female characters in the novel. Alternatively, it could be a completely new character being introduced, although this seems unlikely at this late stage in the story. The reader cannot, in such circumstances, name the full primed participant set, since there is uncertainty about who has been primed into the frame. However, the reader still knows when the mystery woman is overt and when she is covert.

These two types of ambiguity are illustrated in Figures 7.1 and

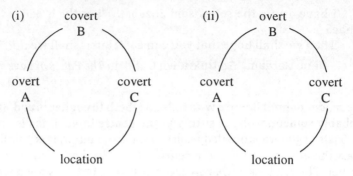

FIG. 7.1. Overt participant ambiguity

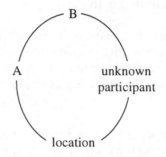

FIG. 7.2. Frame participant ambiguity

7.2. Figure 7.1 illustrates overt participant ambiguity, where the question is whether the participant set takes the form of the right or left hand configuration. The reader knows that the primed participant set consists of A, B, and C, but cannot be sure who is overt and who is covert. This type of ambiguity will often affect just one sentence. In frame participant ambiguity, on the other hand, as shown in Figure 7.2, the reader is not sure of the identity of one of the characters in the frame. Unless the identity is disclosed, this type of ambiguity may last for the whole frame, regardless of which characters are overt and which are covert in any one sentence.

(e) *Monitoring Covert Participants*

Chapter 4 suggested that an important reason for hypothesizing that the reader is aware of contextual information is that characters are assumed to be present even when they are not overtly referred to in a particular sentence. Chapter 4 also argued that the entity representation can be updated even at a point when the character is a covert participant, on the basis of a contextual inference. This is possible because an action of an overt character can often be inferred to affect a covert character. In a narrative representation of a conversation, therefore, each time an overt character speaks, the covert participants can be inferred to hear. In the following example, a physical movement by an overt entity can be assumed to affect a covert entity:

E X A M P L E   7 . 8

> [Lewis] knew, as passive as <u>he</u>'d ever been in his life, that the car had left the road: everything was happening with unbelievable slowness, almost lazily, and the Morgan was floating.
>
> It was over in a moment. The car stopped with a boneshaking jolt in a field, its nose pointed toward the road. The woman <u>he</u> might have struck was nowhere in sight.
>
> (Peter Straub, *Ghost Story* (1979), 167; my emphasis)

In this example, Lewis is not mentioned in the first two sentences of the second paragraph, so he is a covert participant at that point. The reader is, nevertheless, monitoring the fact that Lewis is in the car. Therefore, when the car flies off the road into the field, the reader can infer that Lewis has also flown through the air into the field. This information can be added into the entity representation of Lewis even though Lewis has not been referred to in the first two sentences of the second paragraph. Since entity representations are nowadays generally regarded as an essential part of reference theory, and since they can be updated in this way as a result of priming characters into a contextual frame, priming needs to be included in reference theory.

4. CONTEXTUAL FRAMES AND 'FOCUSING THEORY'

(a) Levels of Awareness

The previous section has argued that a reader of a narrative needs to monitor the presence of the full group of participants in a narrative context. This knowledge will enable the reader to assume the presence of these participants when they are covert and will also allow overt references to the whole group to be interpreted. Reference theory needs to acknowledge the importance of this contextual information, but priming characters into a contextual frame is only one part of the overall picture. As well as building up a representation of the full group of participants, a reader needs some means of identifying specific individuals within the group. The term **focusing** (Grosz 1978; Sidner 1979b;[16] Grosz and Sidner 1986) is used here to describe the process by which a reader refers to one (or more)[17] of the set of primed participants in a context.

This 'two-level' approach is common in artificial intelligence. Indeed, the term 'focusing' itself was originally used by Grosz (1978) to differentiate between two levels, global and immediate focus. As Grosz was describing non-narrative, global focus meant a task or topic, as discussed in Chapter 5. Priming is parallel to this notion of global focus, since contexts in narrative are as much a discourse unit as tasks or topics are in other genres. Grosz's term 'immediate focus' was used mainly to describe ellipsis, but Sidner took the term 'focusing' and applied it to the local relationship between pronouns and their antecedents. Subsequently (Grosz and Sidner 1986), this term 'focusing' has been reapplied to global discourse processing, with the term 'centering'[18] being used for what was previously 'immediate focusing'. I will, however, continue to use the term 'focusing' for local processing here.

---

[16] See also Bullwinkle (1977); Sidner (1979a); Sidner (1983a); and Sidner (1983b).

[17] In fact, it is common for two participants to be focused on, as will be discussed later in the chapter. For ease of discussion, I will, however, assume at this point that focusing selects one participant from the group.

[18] The term 'centering' is discussed later in this chapter.

Whereas the full group of primed participants can be referred to by just a pronoun, focusing generally involves the use of an antecedent before a pronoun (or series of pronouns) can be employed. To build on a metaphor used by Chafe (1974: 120–1), priming is like characters standing on a stage in front of us,[19] whereas focusing is like someone drawing our attention towards one of these characters. The reason that references to the primed group can be by antecedentless pronominals is that within a particular context a 'group pronoun', such as 'they' or 'we', can be inferred to refer to all those that are 'bound' into that context (just as 'here' and 'now' automatically refer to the location and time of that context). Focusing on an individual often requires an antecedent because there would otherwise be the possibility of ambiguity. If, for example, a contextual frame comprises three female characters, 'they' can clearly refer to the primed group but 'she' would be ambiguous unless our attention was first drawn to one of the characters by an antecedent. In a film, focusing could be achieved by pointing, but in the non-visual medium of written narrative a verbal antecedent is normally required. Of course, if there is only one character in a context (or only one character of a particular sex in a context), the character can be identified without repeated use of antecedents, the distinction between priming and focusing then becoming less obvious.

Priming, therefore, relies largely on the reader's common-sense assumptions about a context. The basis of this assumption-making is the inference that the same characters remain 'bound' into a particular context and that if that particular context is 'primed' then 'group pronouns' refer to the characters within it. In fact, once the context is primed, overt references are not necessary for the reader to assume the presence of the characters. Characters may be primed over long stretches of text, remaining covert when unmentioned. Focusing, by contrast, serves to draw our attention repeatedly to different members of a group, so characters generally remain in focus for only a small portion of the time that they are primed. As the text draws the reader's attention

---

[19] Chafe uses this metaphor to show how information is held in consciousness, although he is writing about local 'given' information (i.e. focusing rather than priming, in my terms). Chafe does not make a two-stage distinction with this particular metaphor, although he does elsewhere distinguish between information held in focal and peripheral consciousness, using the metaphor of focal and peripheral vision.

towards a different character, the focus switches. Both priming and focusing rely on certain textual conventions. With priming, the reader expects that there will be contextual continuity until there is some indication to the contrary, such as a signal of a frame modification or frame switch. With focusing, the reader assumes that if an antecedent has been used to draw attention to a character, subsequent pronouns will generally be co-referential with the antecedent.

The following example illustrates the distinction between priming and focusing, showing how priming accounts for a reader's 'background' assumptions about the presence of characters in a context and how focusing periodically shifts the reader's attention from one character to another, repeatedly switching each character from overt to covert status.

EXAMPLE 7.9

[1] Miss Dangerfield's spoon screeched in her cup as she stirred her coffee.

[2] The new assistant, Lizzie, didn't seem to be making any attempt to join in the fun with the others. [3] She was gnawing at a nail, and barely concealing a scowl.

(Lucy Whitman, 'A Dangerous Influence', in The Sheba Collective (ed.), *Everyday Matters: New Short Stories by Women* (1982), 126; my numbering and emphasis)

In this example, a group of women have been primed at the beginning of the story and remain primed throughout the extract cited, even though their names are not given here. In other words, the reader can assume the presence of the group throughout, whether or not they are overtly mentioned. In the first sentence, however, only Miss Dangerfield is in focus. In the second sentence Lizzie is in focus and she remains in focus during the third sentence with the assumption being that any subsequent female third-person singular pronoun will refer to her. In fact the group is also focused on, by the overt expression 'the others', which can be interpreted as meaning everyone in the primed group except Lizzie (and, perhaps, also except Miss Dangerfield).[20]

---

[20] Since Miss Dangerfield is perceiving 'the others' she may be regarded as distinct from the group. This assumes that the reader is able to recognize the current 'point of view', a topic which has been extensively studied in stylistics and literary

The terms 'focus' and 'overt' are related but not synonymous. Focusing is a mental process, since it describes the reader's awareness of a character, whereas overtness is a textual characteristic, since it means that a character is being referred to in a particular sentence. Focusing is triggered by an overt lexical reference to a character, but focusing also continues until the next lexical reference even if the character is, in the meantime, covert. For example:

EXAMPLE 7.10

[1] <u>Ricky</u> turned dismissively away from the cinema and faced a prospect far more pleasing. [2] The original high frame houses of Milburn had endured, even if nearly all of them were now office buildings: even the trees were younger than the buildings. [3] <u>He</u> walked, his polished black shoes kicking through crisp leaves . . .

(Peter Straub, Ghost Story (1979), 38;
my numbering and emphasis)

Throughout the extract, Ricky is primed (because he is bound into the current context) and in focus (because he has been mentioned in the first sentence and, as no other characters are referred to in the remainder of the passage, any subsequent third-person pronouns can automatically be assumed to refer to him). He is, however, only overt in the first and the third sentences for there is no mention of him in the second sentence.

The two main levels of assumption-making that I have been describing are priming and focusing, but in fact the number of levels needs to be extended beyond this to account more fully for narrative interpretation. A reader may also hold assumptions about the presence of characters in unprimed frames. A classic scenario would be a description of two lovers together (the primed frame), when we know that the spouse of one of the lovers is elsewhere (an unprimed bound frame). Whether or not the spouse is present in another context makes a difference to the behaviour of the characters and to the tension felt by the reader about whether or not they will be discovered. It could be argued that the reader is monitoring the unprimed frame at a lower level

work, but has only recently been considered by cognitive scientists (e.g. Wiebe and Rapaport 1988; Duchan, Bruder, and Hewitt 1995b). This means that both the focalizer and focalized have to be tracked, as well as the overall context.

of awareness, but this perhaps overlooks the fact that this awareness of an unprimed frame can make a material difference to our interpretation of events occurring in the primed frame. Even when the action in the primed and unprimed frame is quite independent, a reader might still be thinking about the unprimed frame because of a desire to know how the storyline will develop in that context or because the two contexts provide a thematic contrast or comparison to each other. Of course, there may also be more than two contexts 'active' at any one time. This is the case in most television 'soap operas', where unfinished action in a number of contexts constantly keeps the viewer in suspense.

The reader of a narrative also needs knowledge (although probably not continued awareness) of characters who have already been introduced into the story but are not currently in any specific context. As these characters are part of the 'fictional world', some record must be kept of them. The reader therefore needs to keep a 'central directory' of all the participants, whether they are contextually bound or not. This information is needed to make generalizations, such as that most of the main characters in a narrative are children or that most are women.[21] The central directory can also be used when a reader is attempting to solve a puzzle. In a detective novel, for example, each fresh piece of evidence may cause the reader to run through their mental listing of the suspects to determine whether this evidence makes each character more or less likely to be the guilty person. The central directory also helps the reader to guess the identity of any unnamed or 'mystery' characters who are primed into a frame, enabling the reader to guess that the character might be one of the participants that has appeared earlier in the story. The central directory also leads the reader to wonder when a character will be reintroduced into the action and can create a feeling of 'loose ends' if major characters are not properly accounted for.[22]

This account provides a picture of the mind working at a number of different 'levels'. This has also been suggested by Chafe

---

[21] This is sometimes an important factor in a story. In Muriel Spark's *Memento Mori* (1961), for example, the reader needs to recognize that all the major characters are over the age of 65.

[22] According to Ennulat (1978), narratives in Fali (a language spoken in the north of Cameroun) 'close off' their central directory at the end of the story by introducing dogs who attack and eat all of the participants. This ritual ending need bear no connection to the foregoing story.

(1994: 53–6, 86–7, 201–5) who utilizes the notions of active, semi-active, and inactive information in his descriptions of text processing, pointing out that finer distinctions are probably necessary since consciousness is 'almost certainly' a continuum (Chafe 1994: 55). In my own model, some of the levels may have an influence on the reader even when they are not pushed to the forefront of attention by the text. The reader will need, therefore, to retain an awareness of the primed context as a whole and may also be held in suspense about other, unprimed, contexts and perhaps even about characters who are not bound into any frame. Some of the information may remain temporarily 'dormant' and only be accessed at points at which there is some need for it, as when a 'mystery' participant appears or there is some other puzzle to solve. Throughout the narrative, the reader's consciousness of any one character is constantly changing, as a result of these shifts in the narrative.

(b) Forward-Oriented Anaphora

Sidner's notion of 'immediate focusing', often referred to simply as 'focusing' (and termed 'centering'[23] in later work), is interesting because it offers an account of the link between a pronoun and its antecedent which can more easily be integrated into a cognitive model than traditional ideas about pronominalization.

The traditional description of anaphora is that the pronoun 'refers back' to or via the antecedent (depending on whether mental representations are incorporated in these traditional models). However, Grosz and Sidner's work (in its earlier forms at least) suggests that it is more appropriate to look at anaphora from the opposite perspective, assuming the process to be forward-oriented,[24] with the antecedent anticipating a co-referential pronoun.

[23] 'Centering' (e.g. Grosz, Joshi, and Weinstein 1983; Grosz and Sidner 1986; Gordon, Grosz, and Gillion 1993) in fact argues that each sentence requires the reader to 'look back' and 'look forward'. This work is similar to the linguistic notion of distinguishing between 'given' and 'new' information in a sentence, although I would not use the directional terms in this way. 'Centering' is discussed later in this chapter.

[24] This is quite different from cataphora, where the pronoun precedes the antecedent. In both forward-oriented and backward-oriented anaphora, the pronoun follows the antecedent, but the method of processing is viewed from opposite perspectives.

The fact that the process of anaphoric interpretation has traditionally been viewed as a backward search can be seen from works such as Halliday and Hasan (1976), who state that: 'This form of presupposition, pointing BACK to some previous item, is known as ANAPHORA' (p. 14, their capitals). Some people might argue the expression 'refers back' (or 'pointing back' in this case) is merely a figure of speech, but Halliday and Hasan's (1976) description of anaphoric reference does seem literally to mean a backwards search: ' . . . it is necessary to go back three, four or more sentences, stepping across a whole sequence of [pronouns], before finding the substantial element' (p. 15). Indeed, this explanation is not surprising, since, as Halliday and Hasan (1976) do not include mental representations in their model, they have no mechanism for 'carrying forward' information about the referent. The expression 'refer back' is still very common even since mental representations have been included in models of reference, in linguistics, psychology, and artificial intelligence.[25] Some writers may just be using the expression 'refers back' as a convention, but it nevertheless suggests that there is a need for further discussion about what pronoun processing involves.

The alternative to viewing anaphora as backward-oriented is to see it as forward-oriented. A forward-oriented model of anaphora assumes that the reader is particularly aware of whichever character has been recently mentioned and that on subsequently meeting a pronoun of the same gender the reader automatically assumes the pronoun to refer to this character. If this were not the case a full noun would be used. As Clancy (1980: 178) explains:

By using an inexplicit form of reference, such as a pronoun or ellipsis, the speaker is, in effect, telling the listener that he should be able to identify the referent in question without further information. If the speaker is sufficiently skilled in taking the listener's needs into account, use of inexplicit reference forms represents a shared agreement as to the correct interpretation, that is, which character's identity can be taken for granted at this point in the narration.

---

[25] For example, McTear (1987: 136); M. McCarthy (1991: 36); Garnham (1985: 105, 119, 163); Smyth *et al.* (1987: 171); Peterson and McCabe (1991: 30); Carbonell and Brown (1989: 96); and Schuster (1989: 602).

The idea of anaphora as a forward-oriented process, which has been pointed out by a number of writers,[26] is in line with the theory of focusing advocated by Grosz (1977) and Sidner (1979*b*). Concentrating on pronominalization, Sidner adopts the computing notion of a 'default', which means that a machine adopts particular pre-specified strategies or parameters in the absence of instructions to the contrary. In the focusing model of anaphora in English, the most recently mentioned entity of the same number and gender is the default referent.[27]

Although the intention of Grosz (1977) and Sidner (1979*b*) seems to be to argue for a forward-oriented model, artificial intelligence writers are not always very clear about the direction of processing. Many writers who cite Grosz and Sidner use expressions like 'refer back' when discussing anaphora.[28] This could just represent a misunderstanding of the focusing literature, but Grosz[29] (1977: 42, 118) and Sidner (1978: 86; 1979*b*: 12) do occasionally use the expression 'refer back' themselves, alongside forward-oriented expressions such as 'default' (e.g. Sidner 1983*a*: 122) and 'tracking' (c.g. Sidner 1983*a*: 114). Sidner's mention of 'look[ing] for an antecedent' (1978: 87) is particularly puzzling, since if tracking is taking place it should pre-empt any need to look for an antecedent. In later work, Grosz and Sidner (1986) speak of 'searching' for a referent and describe reference as a process of 'looking forward' and 'looking back' (see discussion of 'centering' in the following section).

[26] See also Chafe (1974, 1980*b*); Grimes (1975: 358); Ballmer (1979, 1981, 1985, 1988); Rieger (1974: 67); Kantor (1977: 3, 48); Bloom and Hayes (1978); Hinds (1978: 148–52); J. B. N. Harris (1980); Hirst (1981: 7–9); Emmott (1985, 1989); Tomlin (1987*b*); Ventola (1990: 224–9); and Sinclair (1992: 9–10).

[27] See also Reichman (1985) and Alshawi (1987) for later discussions of focusing.

[28] For example, McTear (1987: 136); Carbonell and Brown (1989: 96); and Schuster (1989: 602).

[29] Elsewhere, Grosz does seem to suggest that processing is not backward-oriented. She says that 'When the resolution of definite references is considered from the perspective of focus, questions like how far back in a discourse to look for a referent are no longer relevant. Instead, the problem is how long an item stays in focus and what can cause a shift in focus' (1977: 7–8). A later statement, however, suggests that Grosz may perhaps not be arguing against the backward direction, but against the problem of 'how far' back to go. ('A problem of particular interest in resolving references is determining where to search for referents: how far back in the dialogue is it necessary to go?' (1977: 43).) These two statements, together with the use of the expression 'refer back' do, in my opinion, make Grosz's views on this aspect of focusing rather unclear.

The reason that artificial intelligence researchers use expressions like 'refer back' in their discussions of focusing may be because, although they do analyse full real texts, they are primarily involved in producing models of how a computer processes text rather than of how the mind processes text. Some artificial intelligence researchers aim to do both, but the computer still remains the dominant model for hypothesizing about how the mind works. When artificial intelligence researchers discuss how pronouns are interpreted, they need only match a pronoun with a computer file on the character. The mind, however, must not only identify the characters but also think about them in order to comprehend the story fully. A computational model such as Sidner's may use the terms 'tracking' and 'default' simply to mean that the computer has kept a record of the last-mentioned character that can be accessed (or 'referred back' to) on reading the pronoun. This is not the same as remaining conscious of the character after reading the antecedent. Indeed, if computers and minds are fundamentally different, it is likely that the two types of 'tracking' will be different. Computer files may store information as the mind does when priming and focusing, but storing information in files does not automatically make the computer conscious.

Focusing, in my terms, means bringing the entity representation of a character forward as we read and remaining conscious of it as the focus of attention during processing of the intermediate text. An entity representation remains in focus until another noun switches the focus to a new character. The assumption of co-referentiality between two close items is there, as in the traditional notion of anaphora, but the reader now makes this assumption in anticipation rather than in retrospect. The antecedent no longer functions as a key to the pronoun, for the reader does not need to make contact with it at the moment of interpreting the pronoun. In forward anaphora, the antecedent is a trigger. It focuses the reader's attention on the appropriate entity representation and once it has done this it plays no further role. This would mean that a reader would not only be carrying forward knowledge of the full primed participant set, but also carrying forward knowledge of which character had been most recently focused on by means of a recent antecedent.

The main exception to this forward processing would be when a 'repair strategy' is necessary (e.g. H. Sacks, Schegloff, and Jefferson 1974; Schegloff, Jefferson, and Sacks 1977; Schegloff 1979; Schegloff 1987a),[30] which will involve checking back over the preceding text. Repairs become necessary when a reader becomes aware that they have misread the text either through lack of attention or because the text itself is potentially ambiguous.[31] Repair strategies are quite different from normal reading. Readers do have to look back through the text when they misread. If readers had to look back during ordinary processing, they would be turning back the pages whenever a pronoun and its antecedent were separated by a page break or whenever there was no recent antecedent. Experienced readers do not, however, seem to do this and if they did, as already suggested, it would seem to defeat the object of using pronouns.

There has been a fair amount of debate in psychology over how inferences are made. This was discussed briefly in Chapter 2 and is explored in more detail here. H. H. Clark (1977) and H. H. Clark and Haviland (1977) proposed a form of interpretation termed 'bridging', which is essentially backward-oriented. Their work describes the listener having to 'compute' the meaning of a pronoun or definite noun phrase and argues that the reader 'builds a bridge to the intended antecedent'. Neither of these expressions suggest that the mental representation is triggered by the antecedent, then being readily available as the reader reaches the item which needs interpreting. However, any debate about the direction of processing needs to take account of the type of linguistic data being interpreted, for the processing strategy involved in one type of inference-making might be quite distinct from that employed in another type of inference-making. As one illustration of bridging, Clark and Haviland cite Lakoff's (1971: 64) example:

John is a Democrat. Bill is honest too.

In this particular example, I do not debate that some 'computing' and 'backward-oriented' processing may occur, since the listener needs to re-evaluate the first sentence, adding the information that, in the speaker's opinion, Democrats are honest and that

---

[30] The term 'repair' is normally applied to the rectification of conversational communication problems. Here, I use it to mean a reader's rereading of a stretch of text to locate the point at which they have misunderstood or been confused by the text.
[31] See Emmott (1995a).

John is honest by virtue of being a Democrat. One of Clark and Haviland's (1977: 21) own examples[32] is as follows:

> Horace got some picnic supplies out of the car. The beer was warm.

Again, the notion of a backward inference has some intuitive appeal here. A listener or reader could not necessarily assume that the picnic supplies included beer. The beer may therefore be completely new information to the listener (even though it is being treated as 'given' by the speaker) and therefore on reading about it the reader may at that point need to create the link with the previously mentioned supplies. Clark and Haviland attempt to confirm this empirically and find that this 'backward computation' is reflected in an increased reading time of the above sentences compared with the control sentences which replace 'some picnic supplies' with 'some beer'.

This seems like conclusive evidence against forward-oriented inferences, but it is important to remember that not all inferences are of this type. Sanford and Garrod (1981: 101) propose that, in some cases, a prior sentence will lead the reader to expect certain information: '[In certain cases,] decisions, and sometimes potential inferences which could relate to the event, may be made even before the critical sentence is encountered.' An example of the data that Sanford and Garrod (1981: 101) investigate is as follows:

> Mary dressed the baby.
> The clothes were made of pink wool.

They argue that in this example, unlike the Clark and Haviland example, the reader can assume from reading the first sentence that there are clothes, since this is integral to the notion of 'dressing'. The mention of clothes does not, therefore, come as a surprise and the reader does not need to 'compute' a bridge at this point, since a bridge has already been constructed. Sanford and Garrod suggest that on any occasion there will be a 'pay-off' between the effort required to infer a mental link (between stated and connected entities) at the outset and the effort required to 'compute' the link when a connected entity is actually mentioned. Obviously, this depends on the likelihood of the connection.

[32] See Chafe (1994: 169–74) for a detailed discussion of H. H. Clark and Haviland's work on related examples.

Although picnic supplies need not include beer, dressing (in the sense used here) must include clothes. This theory is supported by the fact that reading time experiments conducted by Sanford and Garrod for their own data did not show that additional reading time was needed for the second sentence and therefore suggested that no backward-oriented inference was made.

Sanford and Garrod's work supports the idea that some inferences can be forward-oriented and is a useful reminder that not all inferences should be assumed to be made in the same way. In fact, the debate about these particular examples is only of indirect relevance to the argument about narrative anaphora. The experimental work discussed above describes 'indirect' relations, where an entity has to be inferred from a related entity, the link being made by virtue of general knowledge. The assumptions that I am describing under the heading of focusing are completely different. These assumptions concern the same entity, not two related entities. The inference is simply that a subsequent pronoun form will co-refer and only requires that the reader keep thinking about an entity explicitly mentioned until the next sentence either continues referring to the entity with a pronoun or changes the focus with a non-co-referential noun. In fact, this type of inference is like one of Clark and Haviland's control sentences ('the beer . . . the beer'),[33] which reflected 'direct' rather than 'indirect' antecedence and did not cause any increase in reading time. Priming inferences are also generally 'direct'. A character is mentioned within a particular context and is then assumed to stay there, whether or not mentioned. This does not involve inferring the existence of the character in the first place. The 'frame recall' examples that I have discussed look more like 'indirect antecedence', since the mention of one character can enable the reader to identify another (e.g. in Example 1.1, the name 'Jim' recalls Peter). However, what is really happening is that the assumption of continued presence only applies within a particular context and that the mention of Jim reinstates that context. The contextual link has already been established within the preceding text, rather than being inferred for the first time from general knowledge. To draw empirical conclusions about narrative anaphora,

---

[33] In the experiment discussed above, H. H. Clark and Haviland use the control sentences containing 'some beer . . . the beer'. As a further control, they then compare 'some beer . . . the beer' with 'the beer . . . the beer'.

therefore, priming and focusing would need to be investigated in their own right. Morrow, Bower, and Greenspan's (1990) work is an attempt to show that background situational information is used to make forward inferences during narrative processing, although, as discussed in Chapter 2, their materials and methodology make it difficult to say whether these results would be the same for naturally occurring narrative texts.

In general, the debate over the nature of inferencing can be difficult to follow because of the ambiguity of much cognitive terminology. In this book, I am using terms such as 'activated' to mean that a reader continues to be aware of an entity from when the antecedent is read until when a subsequent pronoun is read. The label is, however, used in a rather different way in the psychology literature. This can be seen from papers such as Dell, McKoon, and Ratcliff (1983) and Chang (1980), in which the term 'activation' is not forward-oriented. Dell, McKoon, and Ratcliff (1983: 121–2), for example, say that:

> When a reader encounters an anaphor, what are the concepts that then become activated, and when, and for how long, are they activated? Presumably, at some point after the anaphor is read, its referent becomes activated, reflecting successful retrieval.

They illustrate this as follows:

A car sped around the corner out of control.
The vehicle smashed into some empty boxes.

and provide this analysis: 'The anaphor *vehicle* should activate the referent *car* and its companions *corner* and *sped around* . . .' (p. 121). This is clearly a backward-oriented model. There is a problem throughout cognitive science over vocabulary. There is a paucity of words to describe the operations of the human mind and so terms like 'activate', 'focus', and 'prime' can be used in very different ways. Psychology has generally established its own meanings for some of these words, but in other disciplines (such as artificial intelligence and linguistics) the meaning of these terms may fluctuate from writer to writer, not always being clearly defined in a particular work. There is no real solution to this except an awareness of the differences (existing outside psychology, at least) and a willingness to explain what the terminology means rather than simply assuming that the meaning is clear.

In this section I have discussed empirical work on inference-making[34] which involves measuring reading times and thereby gives an indication of the point at which the inferences are made. Sanford and Garrod's work suggested that forward-oriented inferences were a possibility for certain types of data, although this concentrated mainly on 'indirect' relations. Another branch of psychology research involves observing the eye movements of a reader. Since some of this work appears to undermine a forward-oriented hypothesis, I will consider it briefly here. Carpenter and Just (1977) (see also Just and Carpenter 1978) found that subjects in their experiments made 'regressive saccades' (i.e. looked back) to the antecedent of a pronoun in 50 per cent of cases. Even if we accept these findings, an explanation is still needed of how pronouns are interpreted in the other 50 per cent of cases. Carpenter and Just's findings have, moreover, been contradicted in subsequent eye-movement experiments by K. Ehrlich (1983), K. Ehrlich and Rayner (1983), and Kerr and Underwood (1983). These later experiments found that it was very rare for subjects to look back through the text for the antecedent of a pronoun. Indeed, in Ehrlich's experiments, the only text example which caused the subjects to look back was a 'trick' passage in which a feminine pronoun was used to refer to someone called 'Tom Norman' (p. 263).

The conflict of evidence in eye-movement research can be explained by the difference in the data. Just and Carpenter (1978: 160) use sentences like:

> The one who the guard mocked was the arsonist. He had been at the prison for only one week.

In this example, there are no semantic clues to tell us who the pronoun 'He' refers to. The pseudo-cleft fronting (i.e. 'The one who') may suggest that the referent is the arsonist, but this is far from clear. It is hardly surprising, therefore, that readers did look back in the text to try to resolve the ambiguity. In real text, such ambiguity would be unusual. As has been shown, there will often be an indication of the referent in the co-text of the pronoun or else the referent can be inferred from our stored knowledge about the

---

[34] There is a large amount of research within psychology on this topic. I have only been able to summarize some of the major contributions here in order to give an indication of the main issues.

characters. Ehrlich's results may be different because her data (apart from the 'trick' example mentioned earlier), although not real, is more like real text, providing more context and being less ambiguous (Shebilske and Fisher (1983) make similar comments on the nature of Carpenter and Just's (1977) data). Ehrlich's (1983: 265) explanation of her data appears similar to the for-ward-oriented model of anaphora which has been argued for in this chapter. She says that:

If readers do not select referents by looking back in the text then they must select them from the representation of the text. As people read a story, they keep track of what the current topic is. The topic can change many times in a story. These dynamic changes in the representation of the text could easily form the basis on which referents are selected, such that enti-ties that form part of the current topic are preferred as referents.

The results of eye-movement research may also be affected by the fact that their referents are not properly formed characters and are not therefore easy for the reader to monitor. Of course, evi-dence that readers do not physically look back in the text itself (except in confusing examples) does not mean that they do not hunt back through their memory of what they have read, so this eye-movement research is inconclusive about the nature of the inference-making.

The remainder of this section provides some arguments in favour of viewing the interpretation of narrative pronouns as a forward-oriented process, although obviously this hypothesis would need to be backed up by empirical work by psychologists. Forward-oriented inferencing can be an efficient form of process-ing because it is unidirectional. The stages involved in interpret-ing a pronoun in the traditional backward-oriented model are cumbersome. Backward-oriented anaphoric models typically start with the pronoun and put the analyst in the position of won-dering how to interpret it. This, however, is really stage two of the model, since a real reader will have recently encountered the noun in the normal process of reading the text. According to the backward-oriented anaphoric model, the reader reads the noun, passes on to the pronoun, wonders to whom the pronoun refers, and looks back for an antecedent. The antecedent recalls an entity representation and the reader then takes this to the pronoun slot and interprets the pronoun with it. A backward-oriented model involves the reader in moving over the same ground several times, apparently forgetting information which has only just been presented. This is not necessary if a forward-oriented model of anaphora is used to account for the processing of pronouns. In this case, a reader begins by first encountering the noun and at that point focuses on the entity representation which the noun denotes, hence activating the entity representation. The reader then automatically slots the appropriate information into the next pronoun slot and continues to do this for whichever pronouns come next. Only when the reader meets a noun denoting a different character does the reader cancel the activation of the first character and focus on the character denoted by the new noun.

Ease of processing may be a good basis on which to build a computer model, but the question is whether the brain works in this way too. It does seem likely that the human mind would use an efficient form of processing, for if pronouns were difficult to interpret, speakers and writers would, presumably, keep reiterating the original noun phrase. There is no point in having a shorthand form if it slows down reading. This becomes particularly obvious when chains of pronouns are considered rather than just individual pronouns. G. Brown and Yule's (1983: 202) example about the active, plump chicken, cited earlier in this chapter, provides a good illustration of this, since at consecutive stages in the recipe the chicken is referred to by pronouns (although Brown and Yule themselves only analyse the first pronoun in the chain). If a backward-oriented model was used, it would suggest that as readers move back along the pronoun chain they pick up the information that it has been cut up, then note that it has been prepared, then find out that it is a dead, plump chicken. This is rather like watching a film in reverse, except that we do not even find out who the character is until the end (see also Charniak and McDermott 1985: 597 for a similar criticism). Although odd, it does, nevertheless, seem to be what is proposed in Halliday and Hasan (1976: 330; their numbering and italics): ' . . . the *she* in ([sentence] 5) has as the target of its presupposition another instance of *she*, that in ([sentence] 4); and in order to resolve it we have to follow this through to the occurrence of *Alice* in sentence (3)'.

G. Brown and Yule (1983) discuss how an entity representation needs to be updated whenever there is an overt reference to a character, but if a character is primed, there will need to be covert updating too, at points when the character is not even mentioned. In the backward-oriented model illustrated in Figure 7.3 (in which the numbers signify the stages of processing), the pronoun functions as a signal which initiates a backward search for the antecedent noun phrase. The antecedent then provides a key to the entity representation, which can be used to interpret the pronoun. The entity representation in Figure 7.3 is, however, out-of-date because in the sentences between the antecedent and the pronoun there has been a covert update. The backward-oriented model does not, therefore, account for this type of data. The alternative is a forward-oriented model of anaphora as shown in Figure 7.4. In this case, the reader is aware of the entity representation throughout, having focused on it. The antecedent triggers this focusing. The entity representation is, therefore, carried forward for subsequent use and so there is no need to search for it. New information is added to the representation as it is carried forward so it is always up-to-date.

The discussion in this chapter has, until now, assumed that there is just one antecedent, but of course the situation is more

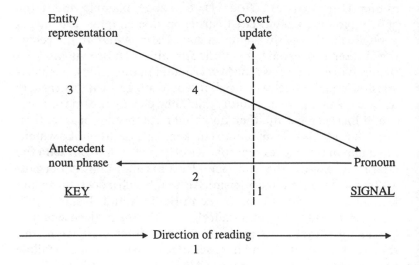

F I G . 7.3. Backward-oriented model of anaphora

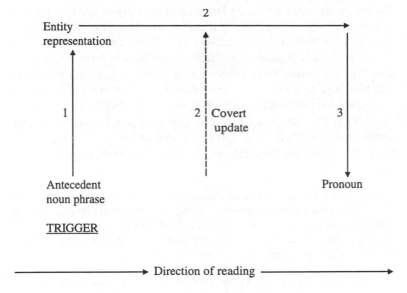

F i g . 7 . 4 . Forward-oriented model of anaphora

complex when two characters have been mentioned immediately prior to a pronoun. In sentences of the type 'John hit Henry. He fell to the ground', there are two potential antecedents and the reader needs to draw additional clues (in this case the verbal link between 'hit' and 'fall') to identify the appropriate referent. Another explanation is that the individual who was referred to as 'new information' in the first sentence (i.e. Henry) is mentioned as the subject of the second sentence, although this is not always the pattern that is followed (see Emmott (1989) for a fuller discussion).[35] Indeed, the switch by artificial intelligence researchers to using the term 'centering' in place of '(immediate) focusing' offers a solution to this problem based on the distinction between given and new information (Grosz, Joshi, and Weinstein 1983; Grosz and Sidner 1986; Gordon, Grosz, and Gillion 1993). They describe

[35] Enkvist's (1989) notion of 'pragmatic judgements of plausibility' may be useful here. Enkvist contrasts 'Susie gave Betty an aspirin because she had a headache' (p. 163) with 'Susie gave Betty an aspirin because she had just been to the drugstore' (p. 163). He says that readers interpret these sentences on the basis of real-world knowledge. A person who has a headache is in need of an aspirin and a person who has just been to the chemist may be in a position to provide one.

the 'given' information in a sentence (generally in initial, subject position) as a 'backward looking center' and the 'new' information (generally in non-initial position) as a 'forward looking center'. The directional terms are, perhaps, unfortunate here. They suggest that the reader or listener is searching for information (and indeed Grosz and Sidner (1986) do speak of a 'search'). This is not, however, compatible with the idea of ongoing consciousness. Chafe (1974: 120–1) points out the inappropriateness of the common suggestion that 'given information is "recoverable" from the preceding context, while new information is not'. He claims that if:

... [this] explanation in terms of consciousness is correct, it is misleading to speak as if the addressee needs to perform some operation of recovery for given information. The point is rather that such information is already on stage in his mind, while new information is that which the speaker brings on stage by uttering the sentence in question.

The notion of given and new information is a useful addition to focusing theory, since it provides a method of handling cases where two referents are competing for the focus, as in the example 'John hit Henry. He fell to the ground'. Here, the pronoun 'He' picks up on the information in 'new' position in the first sentence, treating it as being 'given' by the time the second sentence is read. This can still be explained using forward-oriented terminology, however. Each new piece of information can be regarded as anticipating the given information in the next sentence, with the reader remaining conscious of this information until the next sentence is reached. There is no need to make a forward-oriented link when the first sentence is read and to duplicate this with a backward-oriented link when the second sentence is read. If clues are necessary, they too can be kept activated mentally, rather than being found on a backward search. Both economy of processing effort and the need to keep entity representations updated favour a forward-oriented model, even when there are two potential antecedents.

Summary

This chapter has argued that contextual frames play an important part in pronoun interpretation, providing the information to enable a reader to understand an antecedentless pronoun after a frame recall. Within a particular context, these frames provide information about the context which narrows the set of potential referents, thereby allowing 'group' pronouns with no recent antecedents to be decoded. Contextual frames also constantly supply information about the covert participants, allowing their mental representations to be updated even when they are not mentioned. One indication that the priming of contextual participants is distinct from focusing is that there are these different types of ambiguity: frame participant ambiguity and overt participant ambiguity.

After discussing the role of contextual frames in reference theory, I showed how the notion of priming needs to be supplemented by the notion of focusing. When a contextual frame is primed, the reader has an awareness of the presence of all the participants, but there still needs to be a mechanism, focusing, to enable the reader to concentrate on particular characters within the contextual frame. Focusing brings a participant to the forefront of consciousness and allows pronominal references to that character to be made. The antecedent triggers this consciousness (over and above priming), until a shift in focus cancels it, and is, therefore, quite different from the traditional view that a pronoun is a signal for a search for the last-mentioned referent.

8

Distinguishing Narrative Text Types

Narrative is usually defined as a succession of events but another important feature of narrative texts is that some or all of the events are described as they take place within a particular context. As a result, these events are 'brought to life' for the reader, being 'acted out' rather than presented in summary form. This type of presentation I term *'framed'* text, since the reader needs to monitor the context by means of a contextual frame (see Chapter 4). Another type of presentation, termed here *'unframed'* text, is when events are summarized and presented as background to the main action. It is important for the reader to be aware of these different types of text because for events-in-context, assumptions need to be made about the continuity of the participant set, place and time, whereas the same assumptions do not need to be made for background summaries. Since one type of text can be embedded within another, readers must be able to recognize signals of a switch between text types.

Section 1 provides a background discussion, including an overview of the distinction between framed and unframed text types and an examination of related research (e.g. Labov and Waletzky 1967; Genette 1980) and linguistic work on 'foreground' and 'background' (e.g. Hopper 1979; Hopper and Thompson 1980) and 'event-lines' (Fox 1988).

Section 2 further explores framed and unframed text, providing justification for this distinction. Section 2a shows the transition between the text types, exemplifying the markers used at the boundaries. Section 2b demonstrates that these shifts are often accompanied by breaks in reference chains, meaning that the text types need to be recognized in order to interpret reference items. Section 2c suggests features which might distinguish a framed sentence from an unframed sentence, although points out that some sentences have no distinct properties and therefore take their interpretation from whether the surrounding text is framed or unframed. Section 2d examines a hybrid text type, having properties of both framed and unframed text.

In Section 3, I briefly consider the implications of this analysis of framed and unframed text for genres other than narrative fiction. I suggest that the terms 'framed' and 'unframed' text can also be used to describe non-fictional narratives and that these categories might be a useful way of distinguishing between narratives and non-narratives.

I. BACKGROUND

(a) Introduction: Different Text Types

This book has, so far, focused on text which describes a succession of events in a particular context. I will term this **framed** text, since it is characterized by the fact that the reader must continue to monitor the same context over a stretch of text by means of a mental frame. The characteristics of framed text were discussed in Chapter 4 and can be summarized as follows:

1. Individual sentences each refer to an event occurring on a specific occasion, rather than to an habitual action or generalization.

2. The reader can infer that a group of sentences all refer to the same occasion, assuming continuity of time and place. This inference is based on the conventions of narrative text. The reader also assumes that the writer is being 'cooperative' (Grice 1975, 1978) and not presenting fragments from different contexts without signalling to this effect.[1]

3. During a stretch of framed text, the reader can assume the same characters to remain 'present' unless there is an indication to the contrary. In other words, although not all of the participants will be mentioned overtly in any one sentence, the covert participant set, monitored by the frame, remains constant.

---

[1] See H. Sacks (1992c); Rieger (1974: 149–50); and Fillmore (1982: 258–9) for similar observations about narrative.

The following example is a typical piece of framed text:

EXAMPLE 8.1

Manfred put his head round the drawing-room door. 'Hello, Count, all alone?'

'Hello, Manfred,' said the Count jumping up, 'Gertrude is in with Guy.'

'I could do with a drink,' said Manfred, 'I've had an awful day, and my God it's cold outside.' He helped himself from the tray on the marquetry table.

(Iris Murdoch, *Nuns and Soldiers* (1981), 29)

To understand this passage, the reader must create a fictional context in which Manfred and the Count are together in the drawing room, keeping this information in mind even when individual sentences do not explicitly mention it. This can be done by monitoring the context by means of a contextual frame, so this type of text is referred to as 'framed text'.

By contrast, a stretch of **unframed** text does not require monitoring by a contextual frame, since the narrative does not describe one specific occasion. A text often presents its readers with generalizations rather than events in context, particularly in the introductory paragraphs of a story.[2] The following example, which is the opening paragraph of a novel, provides an illustration:

EXAMPLE 8.2

Kitty Maule was difficult to place. She had a family, that was known, and she disappeared every weekend, so it was assumed that she lived in the country, although her careful appearance belonged to the town. When asked about her background Kitty usually simplified, for her family history was perhaps a little colourful. She found it too tiring to recount, for so much additional explanation was needed, footnotes on alien professions, habits, customs that most people could not be expected to understand and which were to her as native as the colour of her own hair. She usually said, 'My father was in the army. He

---

[2] Bloom and Hayes (1978: 36–7) point to this notion in comparing the examples 'John eats apples' and 'John ate an apple yesterday'. They say that in the first example 'the only inference we can make, ignorant as we are of context, is to indefinite localization (anytime, anywhere)'. Whereas in the second example 'John is limited to some manifestation of given date'.

died before I was born.' This was the exact truth, but it was not all the truth, for the father to whom she delegated the prominent role in her family history had never even registered in her consciousness as absent. Quite simply, he had never been there. Her mother was there ...

(Anita Brookner, *Providence* (1983), 5)

A statement like 'She usually said, "My father was in the army. He died before I was born." ' denotes an habitual action rather than one occurring on a specific occasion. This statement could not be condensed into a single stretch of continuous staged action. Since the reader has not been presented with a particular context there is no need to build a frame for monitoring context.[3] There is no follow-up in the next sentence to what Kitty says from any of her listeners. There is, instead, more information about her father. The text is linked topically rather than on the basis of what happened next in a particular context.

The consequences of this lack of contextual continuity are that in unframed text there is no covert participant continuity of the type exhibited in the framed text of Example 8.1. In Example 8.1 the reader can infer the Count still to be present when Manfred helps himself to a drink, even though the Count is not mentioned in the 'drink' sentences. The Count is, therefore, a covert participant in the 'drink' sentences. Unframed text is different. As in framed text, there may be overt continuity with the same character being mentioned more than once in an unframed stretch, as is the case with Kitty and her father in Example 8.2. There is, however, no covert continuity. This means that there is no assumption that a character who is mentioned in one unframed sentence is 'present' in a subsequent sentence. Indeed, when the framed text consists simply of generalizations, the characters are not 'present' at all. This can be seen in the extract of unframed text given below:

EXAMPLE 8.3

Jim Braddon was a high-grade salesman employed by a breakfast cereal company in Philadelphia: a placid honest man who would never have injured anything larger than a fly. He had a wife and two children whom he spoilt. The 1941 war had

---

[3] Entity representations will, however, still need to be updated.

affected him little for he was over forty and his employers claimed that he was indispensable. But he took up German—he had a German grandmother—because he thought that one day this might prove useful, and that was the only new thing that happened to him between 1941 and 1945. Sometimes he saw in the paper the picture of Schreiber, the Nazi Inspector-General of the concentration camps, but except that one of his children pretended to see a likeness to this Nazi, nobody else even commented on the fact.

(Graham Greene, 'Jim Braddon and the War Criminal', in *The Tenth Man* (1986), 12)

There is overt continuity in this passage (Jim Braddon is mentioned repeatedly) but there is no covert continuity. In the second sentence of this extract Jim Braddon's wife and children are mentioned overtly. There is, however, no assumption that they are present when Jim's employers claim him to be indispensable or when he learns German, so they cannot be inferred to be covert participants on these occasions. No one specific occasion is described at any point, so no frame needs to be set up to monitor it, and no frame assumptions are carried across sentences. The mind focuses on these characters but does not prime them into a context. Example 8.4 provides a more extreme illustration of this:

EXAMPLE 8.4

Had they not all agreed when they left Ecalpemos and went their separate ways that it was to be as if they had never met, known each other, lived together, that in future they must be strangers and more than strangers? Adam, no doubt, adhered to this. So, probably, did Rufus and the girl. There was something, some quality, more fatalistic, more resigned, in Shiva. He might deceive others but he was incapable of deceiving himself, of pretending, of denying thoughts.

(Barbara Vine, *A Fatal Inversion* (1987), 20)

The sentences which name Adam, Rufus, and Shiva are unframed generalizations and hence there is no covert continuity. In this particular example an assumption of continued presence would be nonsensical because what the characters are doing here is ensuring that they never meet.

In the following section, I compare these observations about framed and unframed text with previous research on narrative text types. Having set the work in the context of previous research, I then go on to explore framed and unframed text further, showing how the text switches from type to type and showing the effect on pronoun chains. I also discuss the characteristics of the different text types further and look at a text type which seems to be a hybrid of the two.

(b) Previous Research on Narrative Text Types

There are, of course, depending on the objects of any particular study, other criteria than contextual continuity for dividing up narrative text into text types and these other criteria will give different results. It is common, for example, within linguistics and literary studies to draw a distinction (e.g. Labov and Waletzky 1967; Labov 1972*a*) between text which is sequenced and text which is not, with the sequenced text being regarded as the 'narrative proper'. Framed text is generally sequenced and unframed text is often unsequenced, but this is not always the case. The following piece of unframed text includes in the second paragraph a list of events ordered in time, the text being unframed because it does not place us in any one context:

EXAMPLE 8.5

He had phoned her every day for years. That kind of statement is never quite true. How could it be? He had *tried* to phone her every day. Most days he reached her. It was a kind of challenge for him or quest, a labour of love.

When she was at University she said she didn't like his daily phone calls, they embarrassed her. He never took that very seriously. In her holidays he phoned her at Tessa's or at Anthony's, wherever she happened to be living. She went on to teacher training college and he tried to phone her every day at the students' hall of residence. Quite often he didn't reach her but he persisted. He phoned her when she went to live with Anthony and Susannah and when she moved into that room with Rachel Lingard and when she got the flat with Rachel and Maeve Kirkland.

(Ruth Rendell, *Going Wrong* (1991), 21; Rendell's italics)

Context analysis and sequence analysis do not conflict as they focus on different aspects of text. Sequences are a defining characteristic of stories because something has to happen in a story; there is a beginning, a middle, and an end. Framed text may not be a defining characteristic of narrative, but frames nevertheless play an important part in interpreting a great deal of fictional storytelling. Framed text locates the action in a specific context. In everyday life, individuals can never avoid being in a specific context and so framed text reflects these real-life experiences.

Within literary studies, one of the best-known works on different text types is Genette (1980). Genette's observations about the duration of narrative action divide the text up into categories such as 'summary' and 'scene'. Framed text and 'scene' seem to be similar, since 'scene' is the acting out of events so that the length of the text supposedly correlates with the duration of the action described. For Genette, direct speech is the most clear-cut instance of 'scene', since the convention is that the length of time it takes to read the speech can be roughly equated to the length of time it would have taken the characters to say it. Regardless of the similarity, however, the criterion for deciding whether something is framed is contextual continuity, whereas the criterion for deciding whether something is 'scene' is duration. Events within a single context may occur at different speeds, not all at the same speed as direct speech. In fact to represent every detail of a conversation in direct speech and to try to represent every action would generally make for lengthy narrative and tedious reading. Duration is a gradient (and therefore difficult to use as a basis for dividing up the text), whereas actions are more clearly either in or out of context (depending on whether there is contextual continuity across a stretch of text).

Unframed text also bears similarities to Genette's 'summary' and 'pause'. Summary is 'the narration in a few paragraphs or a few pages of several days, months, or years of existence, without details of action or speech' (pp. 95–6) and 'pause' halts the action to provide description. Nevertheless, a piece of description may be either about the current context (in which case it may be assumed to have some relevance for the primed characters) or an out-of-context generalization, hence it may be framed or unframed.

The framed/unframed distinction also looks similar at first sight to Genette's notion of narrative 'distance' (which he describes under the heading 'mood') but is in fact rather different. Genette draws on Plato's distinction between 'mimesis' and 'diegesis', later termed 'showing' and 'telling' by Henry James (1962). 'Mimesis' means that events are represented without narratorial intervention (as for direct speech), whereas 'diegesis' means that there is an obvious narrator. Again this distinction works well for speech (and has led to the linguistic distinction between direct speech and indirect speech (Leech and Short 1981)), but is more difficult to apply to other events. As far as speech is concerned, this can be direct ('he said, "I love you" ') or indirect ('he said that he loved her') within a particular context, both being framed.

Within linguistics, the notion that narrative can be divided into different discourse types is currently found in research on 'foreground' and 'background' text in a number of different languages (e.g. Grimes 1975; Grimes 1978a; Hopper 1979; Hopper and Thompson 1980; Tomlin 1987a; Givón 1989: 92; Berman and Slobin 1994). Sometimes these terms are used to indicate a distinction between sequenced and unsequenced text (e.g. Thompson 1987), sometimes they differentiate between important and peripheral clauses (e.g. Erbaugh 1987), or main storyline as opposed to explanations (e.g. Grimes 1975: 55–60), or actions rather than descriptions (e.g. Du Bois 1980). Some writers (e.g. Hopper 1979) list a number of these factors when defining 'foreground', whilst others are rather unspecific about how they are using the terms (e.g. Grimes 1978a). Although there is a lot of overlap between these different definitions of 'foreground' and 'background', the factors just listed are all rather different when it comes to applying them to actual stretches of discourse, as some of the researchers working on this topic have acknowledged (e.g. Thompson 1987: 436; Givón 1987: 177; Fleischman 1990: 168–214). I have already indicated how 'events in context' may be a different category than 'events in sequence'. The important/peripheral division of 'grounding' research is different too. Although framed text is likely to contain the important story events, it will also include a lot of minor detail (such as the description of Maurice lowering his spoon into his lemon pudding in Example 8.14). This sort of detail needs to be taken into account as it not only sets the scene but helps us to understand individual characters and the relationship between characters. Detail of this type may be more prominent in the novel than in the oral stories that have been examined by many of those working on 'grounding'.

Grimes's distinction between main storyline and explanatory text is interesting because it includes flashbacks as a type of 'background'. Framed flashbacks often provide a comment on the main narrative and so may have a similar function to the type of text that I have termed 'unframed'. In terms of form, however, flashbacks are very different from unframed text, as flashbacks are generally located in a specific context.

The distinction between actions and descriptions in 'grounding research' is also useful. Du Bois (1980: 227) describes his 'descriptive mode' as 'a cover term which includes categorizations, descriptions of clothing, statements of relation to other discourse participants and so on'. Descriptions like this are classed as unframed text, but there are other types of unframed text that Du Bois does not take account of within his categorization, perhaps because he is studying oral storytelling.

All of the above distinctions may be regarded as valid ways of dividing up a text. The 'foreground/background' researchers justify their divisions by pointing to the way in which they correlate in some languages with aspect (e.g. in French, see Hopper 1979), word order (e.g. in Old English, see Hopper 1979), voice (e.g. in Malay, see Hopper 1979), and transitivity (e.g. Hopper and Thompson 1980), although the correlation is never absolute (Delancey 1987). Erbaugh (1987) has also shown that oral narrators seem to hesitate more when speaking about foreground material than about the background. These observations may well support the claim that there are markedly different text types (with a corresponding psychological awareness of them), but when 'foreground' and 'background' seem to mean slightly different things to different researchers, statistics of this sort are not very helpful. These grammatical indicators may also, perhaps, be signalling different discourse features in different languages.

Also within linguistics, the work of Fox (1987*b*, 1988) is, on the surface, very similar to the discussion of the framed/unframed distinction in this chapter, particularly as she concentrates on anaphoric reference chains. She looks at examples in which the narrative action is suspended whilst one of the character's thoughts are presented and finds that a pronoun can still be used for the character when the action is resumed, even if other individuals are referred to in the embedded passage. Fox's explanation of her examples is that there is an 'off-event-line gap' (Fox 1987b: 164), meaning a suspension of the action. This would also be the case in most of the examples of embedded unframed text that I look at (in the next section). The term would not be so applicable to the stretches of unframed text at the beginning of stories or particular sections of stories, since there is often no action to interrupt at these points. It is also difficult to say whether Fox would class events which are habitual (e.g. Example 8.16) or 'above' the level of a single context (e.g. Example 8.17) as 'on or off event-line'. In addition to this, Fox's notion of 'on/off event-line' does not appear to account so well for flashbacks and other context shifts, since both the embedded stretch and the main narrative are 'on-event-line' (albeit different event-lines) and Fox (1987b, 1988) does not really consider such examples.

Although Fox's idea of event-line and my notion of context could sometimes yield different analyses, the important point is that the explanations are rather different. Fox is looking only at what is overtly expressed and accounts for her examples in terms of a suspension and resumption of focus. My argument is that what is covert is also important and that readers make assumptions about who is and who is not present in addition to the characters overtly referred to, suspending and resuming a primed context as well as the overt focus. This distinction is particularly relevant for examples of flashback and other context shifts, but is applicable to the framed/unframed distinction too (as discussed in the next section). Even though Fox does talk about focus of attention, her model is more linguistic than cognitive. In Fox (1987a) she comments that 'this study focuses on the *distribution* of anaphoric devices, rather than on their production or resolution' (p. 157; Fox's italics) (although she is looking at genres other than narrative in this work). Fox does not consider how known information might be mentally represented and so does not recognize some of the topics discussed earlier in this book, such as the need to access information about different enactors separately and the possibility of viewing reference as a two-stage process of priming and focusing. These hypotheses only arise when mental representations of characters and contexts are considered.

2. EXPLORING NARRATIVE TEXT TYPES

(a) *The Transition between Narrative Text Types*

Chapter 3 described in general terms how discourse analysts recognize that texts can be subdivided into units and that these units are often embedded within one another. Chapter 5 began to examine this embedding in narrative texts, looking particularly at switches from one context to another, such as the switch into and out of flashbacks. These switches can be described as transitions from one stretch of framed text to another stretch of framed text. To comprehend these switches, the reader needs to activate one contextual frame in place of another in his/her mind. By contrast, the switches described in this chapter are from framed to unframed text, with no contextual continuity being assumed during the unframed stretch. Despite this difference, transitions between text types have much the same effect as frame switches on the overall structure of a text, since text types are frequently embedded within each other and therefore create breaks in the local cohesion of a text, such as interruptions of the reference chains. This section explores these switches looking at both changes from framed to unframed text and vice versa.

It is common for a text to switch from describing a particular context to providing background information that the reader needs either to make sense of the events or to provide more information about the participants. The link between the two segments of text seems often to be a topical one. In the following passage, in which Jack and Stella discuss the baby, there is, immediately after the direct speech (framed text), some general information about the baby (unframed text):

EXAMPLE 8.6

> 'How's the baby?'
> 'Little bleeder never sleeps, he's wearing us out, but he's fine.'
> <u>The baby was six weeks old. Having the baby was a definite</u>
> <u>achievement: getting it safely conceived and born had taken a</u>
> <u>couple of years.</u>
>
>> (Doris Lessing, 'A Man and Two Women', in *A Man and Two Women* (1965), 91; my emphasis on unframed text)

Description may also be offered at strategic points in the action. The description below of Stella is not provided at the start of the story (even though other information about Stella, such as her profession, is given there) or at the start of this particular episode. Instead it occurs when another character looks at her.

EXAMPLE 8.7

The train was empty. The little station seemed stranded in a green nowhere. She got out, cumbered by bags full of food. A porter and a station-master examined, then came to succour her. She was a tallish, fair woman, rather ample; her soft hair, drawn back, escaped in tendrils, and she had great helpless-looking blue eyes.

(Doris Lessing, 'A Man and Two Women', in *A Man and Two Women* (1965), 90–1; my emphasis on unframed text)

At the point at which the station-master 'examines' Stella, it becomes relevant to provide information about what he sees. Stella's appearance also helps to explain the actions of the other characters. The narrative goes on to describe how the porter and station-master rush to help her and how she stands 'smiling, accustomed to men running to wait on her, enjoying them enjoying her' (p. 91).

On resuming framed text after an unframed interlude, the action may simply be continued without linguistic marking. The switch from unframed to framed text may, however, be marked by words such as 'Now', as illustrated below:

EXAMPLE 8.8

'What's it like here, shopping?'
'Vegetables all right, I suppose.'
Jack was still Northern in this: he seemed brusque, to strangers; he wasn't shy, he simply hadn't been brought up to enjoy words. *Now* he put his arm briefly around Stella's waist, and said: 'Marvellous, Stell, marvellous.'

(Doris Lessing, 'A Man and Two Women', in *A Man and Two Women* (1965), 91; unframed text underlined, my italics)

In this example, the word 'Now' signals the move from generalizations about Jack to a specific action by Jack, his putting his arm around Stella. The move is from embedded unframed text back to the main text. Example 8.9 takes the reader from an unframed passage to embedded framed text. The move this time is marked by the word 'once'.

EXAMPLE 8.9

> <u>If life tripped him up, on the other hand, failed to provide him with those essential opportunities, he would go all the way down, ruin his health, drink too much, make do sadly with substitutes.</u> 'What did you do in the vacation?' she had *once* asked him. 'Well, I was going to Grenoble to do my Stendhal stuff,' he had answered. 'But I met someone on the train and got off when he did . . .'
>
> (Anita Brookner, *Providence* (1983), 45; unframed text underlined, my italics)

Markers[4] such as these suggest that the distinction between (framed) events in context and (unframed) decontextualized generalizations is important and has a textual realization which needs to be taken into account in developing a cognitive model.

The following section discusses how switches between text types result in disruption of reference chains, which (assuming that readers can disentangle these chains) also needs to be included in hypotheses about processing strategies.

(b) Text Types and Reference Theory

The previous sections have shown that unframed text may appear embedded within framed text, serving as a comment on the action of the framed text (Examples 8.6, 8.7 and 8.8), in addition to occurring at the beginning of a narrative before the 'story proper' begins. This embedding has implications for reference theory, as illustrated by the following example:

EXAMPLE 8.10

> 'Actually we could have walked,' he said, as they shot down a narrow lane, 'but with these groceries, it's just as well.'
>
> 'If the baby's giving you a tough time, there can't be much

---

[4] See Schiffrin (1987*b*) for a discussion of discourse markers.

time for cooking.' <u>Dorothy was a wonderful cook</u>. But now again there was something in the air as he said: 'Food's definitely not too good just now. You can cook supper, Stell, we could do with a good feed.'

<u>Now Dorothy hated anyone in her kitchen, except, for certain specified jobs, her husband; and this was surprising.</u>

> (Doris Lessing, 'A Man and Two Women', in *A Man and Two Women* (1965), 92; unframed text underlined)

Here the statements 'Dorothy was a wonderful cook' and 'Now Dorothy hated anyone in her kitchen' are unframed generalizations embedded within framed text. They give additional information about what is happening in the frame. At this point in the story, only Jack and Stella are present. They are on their way to Jack's home where they will see Dorothy and the baby. Because the statements about Dorothy are unframed generalizations they do not introduce Dorothy into the frame, as would a framed statement. The reader does not begin to monitor Dorothy's presence in the frame for Dorothy is simply being mentioned by the narrator in passing. Dorothy is not, therefore, a covert participant in the narrative that follows. She does not hear and see what goes on between Jack and Stella after the unframed mention of her. The narrative focuses on her without priming her.

These observations can be taken further when pronominalization is considered. A character mentioned only in an unframed statement cannot normally be a potential referent for pronouns and non-unique nouns in subsequent framed text. Consider the following example:

EXAMPLE 8.11

> In her blue dress, in which she had not taken Paris by storm, and her wool coat, Ruth felt shabby and obedient. The girl wore trousers and a pullover, the man a well-cut suit of tweed. A great desire for change came over Ruth and a great uncertainty as to how this might be brought about. For she knew, obscurely, that she had capacities as yet untried but that they might be for ever walled up unless her circumstances changed. Love, she supposed, might do it, but there was no one with whom she might fall in love. Nobody even looked at her, except <u>Humphrey</u>. She shuddered at the thought. At that moment the

bus arrived and in her abstracted move to board it she hit <u>the young man's</u> elbow with her shoulder bag.

(Anita Brookner, *A Start in Life* (1982), 94–5)

In theory, the phrase 'the young man' could be co-referential with 'Humphrey', for 'Humphrey' is the last male name. Humphrey, however, is not present in the frame. Since the young man is present, for Ruth is able to hit him, Humphrey cannot be the young man. (Also, the reader of the whole novel knows from their entity representation of Humphrey that he is not young.)

The following example provides another illustration:

EXAMPLE 8.12

Now he put his arm briefly around Stella's waist, and said: 'Marvellous, Stell, marvellous.' They walked on, pleased with each other. <u>Stella had with Jack, her husband [Philip] had with Dorothy, these moments, when they said to each other wordlessly: If I were not married to my husband, if you were not married to your wife, how delightful it would be to be married to you. These moments were not the least of the pleasures of this four-sided friendship.</u>

    'Are you liking it down here?'

    'It's what we bargained for.'

    There was more than his usual shortness in this, and she glanced at him to find him frowning. They were walking to the car, parked under a tree.

    'How's the baby?'

(Doris Lessing, 'A Man and Two Women', in *A Man and Two Women* (1965), 91; unframed text underlined)

The habitual wordless observations, 'these moments', of the four characters, Stella, Jack, Dorothy, and Philip, are unframed. Again the frame consists only of Jack and Stella. They are the only characters who are present. The unframed references to Philip and Dorothy are not sufficient to add them into the frame, so the reference to them is simply a passing mention. The subsequent framed actions—the direct speech and the phrase 'she glanced at him'—can only be attributed to characters in the frame, either Jack or Stella, despite the fact that there is no obvious cohesion between what is said and done here and what

Jack and Stella have been saying and doing earlier in the frame. It is just that the conversation is framed and Dorothy and Philip are not in the frame. In theory the questions 'Are you liking it down here?' and 'How's the baby?' could just as well be asked by Philip to Dorothy as by Stella to Jack. However, on this occasion Dorothy and Philip are not 'present' to speak to each other. Only Jack and Stella can fill the elided tag slots and the subsequent pronoun slots.

So far in this section, I have argued that framed text places characters in the context, whereas unframed text does not. Generally, this seems to be true, but the framed/unframed distinction is complicated by the fact that there are occasions when framed text mentions a character who is not there, as in the following example:

EXAMPLE 8.13

It was after they had finished entrecote steaks, and she was gazing fondly across the table at him, revolving her half-empty glass of burgundy, that she suddenly thought of the painting of the naked milkman that he had not noticed, and paled, her other hand striking her sternum.

(Jeremy Leland, 'In a Suburban Sitting Room', in *The Last Sandcastle* (1983), 46; my emphasis)

In this example, the naked milkman is not present in the frame except as an image in a painting. It is the painting that is present not the milkman. The sentence, although framed, does not add the milkman into the frame as would a sentence such as 'The milkman coughed.' The milkman is not, therefore, a potential antecedent for any subsequent male pronoun or non-unique noun phrase which requires the character to be present in the frame. In this particular case, the explanation, in grammatical terms, is that the mention of the milkman simply adds extra information about the head of the noun phrase 'the painting', postmodifying it rather than referring directly to the milkman. Likewise, a sentence such as 'He picked up Julie's diary' does not specify whether Julie is present or not, since the name merely premodifies 'diary' Human readers make such assumptions automatically, but a computer would need to be programmed with rules to determine whether such references add a person into the context or not. In addition to this, there is the weightier question of whether an individual or object exists only in the thoughts of one of the characters. Werth (1995, MS *a*, *b*) provides a detailed discussion of this topic. In the above example, the painting that is occupying the thoughts of the character also exists in the physical context (which is why the character is worried), but there will be many occasions when entities are referred to in this way but are not present in the context. In such cases, the contextual frame would not change when the entity was mentioned, although a separate mental record would need to be kept of the entity and any embedded frame that it occurred in.

(c) *Identifying Different Types of Text*

I have suggested that over a stretch of framed text the reader monitors the same context, setting up a frame for this purpose. In order to decide whether or not to set up a frame in the first place, the reader has to know whether particular sentences are framed or unframed.

The first sentence of Example 8.14 is at the beginning of a chapter. It is necessary for the reader to decide at this point whether to set up a frame to monitor the characters as being 'present' for the rest of the passage and beyond.

EXAMPLE 8.14

> Kitty watched Maurice lower his spoon into his lemon pudding. She watched him until he had finished it, and as he helped himself to some more. He ate seriously, his eyes cast down.
> 'Is it all right?,' she asked.
> 'Everything you do is all right,' he said, scraping his plate.

> (Anita Brookner, *Providence* (1983), 56)

The opening sentence can be regarded as framed. The reader knows from the sentence that two characters are together in the same location at the same time, for one is watching the other. Even if the sentence had just read 'Maurice lowered his spoon into his lemon pudding', the reader could still infer the text to be framed, for even if Maurice was alone, the action must still take place in one place at one time. More importantly, the opening sentence is characterized by the fact that it describes a fairly trivial event which is not of its own accord newsworthy (or, as Sperber and Wilson (1986) would term it, 'relevant'). A reader can therefore expect more narrative about this situation. This expectation can be handled by the reader setting up a frame to monitor the presence of Kitty and Maurice, whether or not they are mentioned in subsequent sentences.

In contrast to framed text, unframed text often takes the form of generalizations which are not rooted in any particular context. Many of these generalizations are descriptions, such as the description of the baby in Example 8.6 and the description of Stella in Example 8.7. An unframed statement may also describe an action which extends in duration beyond a single occasion, as in Example 8.15 below, or an action which is repeated on several occasions, as in Example 8.16.

EXAMPLE 8.15

The boy ... was given a considerably superior education to that his father had enjoyed ...

(Barbara Vine, *A Dark Adapted Eye* (1986), 28)

EXAMPLE 8.16

... and the four went about for some weeks, sharing meals, hotels, trips.

(Doris Lessing, 'A Man and Two Women', in *A Man and Two Women* (1965), 88)

In Example 8.15 it can be inferred that the action lasted longer than one occasion because we know from our real-world knowledge that it takes many years to acquire an education. In Example 8.16 the duration is signalled by the phrase 'for some weeks' and a reader also knows from general knowledge that such things as trips must take place on a number of different occasions.

Certain statements could, if taken in isolation, be read as either framed or unframed. These I will describe as being **indeterminate** as far as text type is concerned. Although such statements are not linguistically marked as belonging to a particular text type, their meaning is usually clear from reading the surrounding text. The following examples, which will be discussed both in isolation and with their surrounding text, illustrate this:

EXAMPLE 8.17

He painted, she drew.

(Doris Lessing, 'A Man and Two Women',
in *A Man and Two Women* (1965), 88)

This example is potentially ambiguous. It could be a generalization meaning that he is a painter and she is someone who draws. As a generalization the statement is true even when the characters are not at their respective easels. Alternatively, the sentence could describe a particular situation when he is in the process of painting and she is drawing. The same observation applies to the following sentence:

EXAMPLE 8.18

When she spoke her voice was harsh and brittle.

(Agatha Christie, *Sleeping Murder* (1977), 64)

This could mean that the character always has a 'harsh and brittle' voice and hence could serve as a general description. Alternatively, it could mean that she is speaking in this way on this particular occasion.

In their textual context, statements such as Examples 8.17 and 8.18 are rarely ambiguous, for a reader's interpretation is controlled by the statements that have come earlier. Normally, if the preceding statements are unframed this will yield an unframed interpretation for the indeterminate statement and if the preceding statements are framed this will yield a framed interpretation. Some additional context for Examples 8.17 and 8.18 is provided below:

EXAMPLE 8.19 (EXPANSION OF EXAMPLE 8.17)

There were a great many people she might have seen, but it was the Bradfords she saw most often, two or three times a week, at their flat or hers. They were at ease with each other. Why were they? Well, for one thing they were all artists in different ways. Stella designed wallpapers and materials; she had a name for it. The Bradfords were *real* artists. He painted, she drew.

(Doris Lessing, 'A Man and Two Women', in *A Man and Two Women* (1965), 88; Lessing's italics, my underlining)

The sentence 'He painted, she drew' follows on from a number of generalizations. In particular, it adds extra detail to the description 'The Bradfords were *real* artists.' The unframed co-text forces an unframed interpretation onto the sentence.

In its textual context, Example 8.18 can be interpreted as framed:

EXAMPLE 8.20 (EXPANSION OF EXAMPLE 8.18)

When Giles came back from seeing Dr Kennedy off, he found Gwenda sitting where he had left her. There was a bright red patch on each of her cheeks, and her eyes looked feverish. <u>When she spoke her voice was harsh and brittle.</u>

'What's the old catchphrase? Death or madness either way? That's what this is—death or madness.'

(Agatha Christie, *Sleeping Murder* (1977), 64; my emphasis)

This example describes Gwenda's reaction to a disturbing piece of news. The information that Gwenda's voice is 'harsh and brittle' is not a general fact about her but is specific to this particular occasion. This means that the statement is functioning as framed. Were the reader to interpret it as unframed it would be difficult to explain why a description of Gwenda's everyday manner of speaking is being introduced at this late stage in the novel.

Another example of an indeterminate statement was given in Example 8.11. 'Nobody even looked at her, except Humphrey' could, taken out of the context of the novel, refer to a particular occasion and so be framed. However, as already mentioned, the reader knows that Humphrey is not currently present. The reader also knows from earlier in the novel that Humphrey is an old man who regularly observes Ruth through a crack in the bathroom door (Anita Brookner, *A Start in Life* (1982), 92). The statement can, therefore, be taken as a generalization about Humphrey and is, therefore, unframed.

Indeterminate statements are therefore, in theory, ambiguous, but in practice their interpretation is resolved by framed or unframed co-text. Occasionally, however, there may be ambiguity about how a statement is to function. This occurs particularly at the boundary of unframed and framed text. Example 8.21 provides an illustration. The passage should be read before the analysis in order not to prejudge the issue.

EXAMPLE 8.21

[1] 'Can I just drop in to the studio?'
[2] 'Help yourself.' [3] Stella walked into the long, glass-roofed shed. [4] In London Jack and Dorothy shared a studio. [5] They had shared huts, sheds, any suitable building, all around the Mediterranean. [6] They always worked side by side. [7] Dorothy's end was tidy, exquisite, Jack's lumbered with great canvases, and he worked in a clutter. [8] Now Stella looked to see if this friendly arrangement continued, but as Jack came in behind her he said: 'Dorothy's not set herself up yet, I miss her, I can tell you.'

(Doris Lessing, 'A Man and Two Women', in *A Man and Two Women* (1965), 93–4; my numbering)

My own interpretation of this passage (as a first-time reader of the story rather than as an analyst) was as follows. Sentences 1–3 are framed sentences describing a specific situation, whereas sentences 4–6 are unframed. Sentence 7 is, however, more problematic. I initially interpreted the first two clauses as referring to the particular studio in which Stella is standing, the long, glass-roofed shed. This was because of the degree of detail which seemed more appropriate to a description of a specific occasion than as a general comment. However, the final clause of sentence 7 seems to cast a new light on this initial interpretation. Jack cannot be working in the studio at present. He has only a minute ago been standing with Stella outside the studio and we have not even been told yet that he has entered the building with her. This seems to suggest that the preceding clauses in the sentence may also be generalizations, still governed by the 'always' of the preceding sentence. This interpretation is confirmed by the word 'Now' in sentence 8 which contrasts the present framed situation with the unframed sentence 7.[5] My own reading of Example 8.21, therefore, forced me to employ a repair strategy, reinterpreting the first two clauses of sentence 7. This happened because the unframed generalization in sentence 7 was taken at first to be a return to the Stella–Jack frame, whereas the frame recall in fact occurs in sentence 8.

---

[5] However, note that 'Now' in Example 8.10 ('Now Dorothy hated anyone in her kitchen') is used quite differently in an unframed statement.

The difficulty of equating a particular linguistic structure with a particular text type can also be seen by considering the function of direct speech. Direct speech is generally characteristic of framed text. Two or more characters are together in one location (or are, for example, communicating on the telephone) and each is assumed to be present as the other speaks. Direct speech can, though, in certain circumstances function as unframed. In everyday conversation, people often quote extracts of direct speech without necessarily being interested in or even aware of the original context of the quotation. For example, in citing Dr Johnson's 'When a man is tired of London, he is tired of life', the speaker may well not be aware of whether Johnson originally said this in speech or in writing, exactly when it was said or written, or even that Dr Johnson was the originator. Often this lack of awareness of the original context of such sayings is unimportant because the statement is functioning as a comment on the current context. A speaker may, for example, use the citation from Dr Johnson in answer to a friend's observation that they dislike London. This use of the saying would focus attention on the current attractions of London rather than on those of Dr Johnson's day. The intention in making the comment might also be different than the original intention. Made to the friend who disliked London it would be a criticism, implying that he or she was not acknowledging London's potential. Made to a friend who had just been talking enthusiastically about London it would serve to reinforce what the friend had said. Dr Johnson's actual meaning would in either case be irrelevant.

In narrative text, there is a parallel to this real-life quoting of direct speech. Characters may cite Dr Johnson, but they may also cite other characters in the fictional world even if the reader has not already been presented with the piece of speech in its original context. When direct speech is cited in this way it is unframed, as shown below:

EXAMPLE 8.22

But she [Dorothy] was not at all, as Jack was, a great success. There was a strain here, in the marriage, nothing much, it was kept in check by their scorn for their arbitrary rewards of 'the racket'. But it was there, nevertheless.

Stella's husband had said: 'Well, I can understand that, it's like me and you—you're creative, whatever that may mean, I'm just a bloody TV journalist.' There was no bitterness in this. He was a good journalist, and besides he sometimes got the chance to make a good small film. All the same, there was that between him and Stella, just as there was between Jack and his wife.

(Doris Lessing, 'A Man and Two Women', in *A Man and Two Women* (1965), 89; my emphasis)

Example 8.22 continues on from a page and a half of unframed text which provides an introduction to the short story. The topic has been the relationship between the couples, Dorothy and Jack, and Stella and her husband. Stella's husband's remark, 'Well, I can understand that . . . ' is 'quoted' as part of the argument that is being put forward, rather than being presented in its original context as part of a conversation.

Unframed direct speech is characterized by the fact that it often occurs in isolation from other direct speech. The speaker does not have to be one of the characters who is being talked about: it is the content of what is said that is important. There is no expectation, as in framed text, of a response from the listener in the subsequent sentence. No frame monitoring is initiated.

(d) Context Summarizers: A Hybrid Text Type

The previous section argued that certain indeterminate sentences are not linguistically marked as framed or unframed but that in their textual context they function clearly as one particular text type (except in cases of ambiguity over the text type boundary). This section discusses, by contrast, a hybrid type of sentence which has properties of both framed and unframed text types, the **context summarizer**.

Context summarizers can, in a single sentence, summarize everything that happened in a particular context,[6] as illustrated below:

---

[6] Bernado (1980: 297) has a similar idea. He says that in the sentence 'I spent last weekend in Yosemite', 'the entire memory is represented here as a single event and so it has been expressed as a single clause'. This for me raises the problem of how we define a single event. Most events can be broken into component parts, even the filling of a kettle with water (James Joyce, *Ulysses* (1969), 591–3). My own cut-off point for frames is the line between occasions when we can assume continuity of the participant set and occasions when we cannot.

EXAMPLE 8.23

She [Miss Marple] was seen in the High Street at eleven o'clock. She called at the Vicarage at ten minutes to twelve. That afternoon three of the gossipy ladies of the village called upon her and obtained her impressions of the gay Metropolis and, this tribute to politeness over, themselves plunged into details of an approaching battle over the fancywork stall at the Fête and the position of the tea tent.

(Agatha Christie, *Sleeping Murder* (1977), 36; context summarizers underlined)

The statements 'She was seen in the High Street at eleven o'clock' and 'She called at the Vicarage at ten minutes to twelve' are context summarizers, each describing a separate context. The people who saw Miss Marple on the High Street are not necessarily present at the Vicarage and, likewise, the people at the Vicarage are not necessarily present when the gossipy ladies call. Context sumarizers are like framed text in view of the fact that each sentence describes a specific context. However, they are also like unframed text because there is no contextual continuity across a sequence of sentences. If the reader creates a contextual frame, it has no further use after the sentence is read and assumptions cannot be made about the continued co-presence of participants.

Context summarizers function in a way identified by van Dijk (1980: 156–7). He provides the following example:

(a) Dorothy went to the bank.
(b) She entered the bank.
(c) She walked to the counter.
(d) She had to wait a long time.
(e) Then it was her turn.
(f) She filled out a check.
(g) She showed her identification card.
(h) She obtained the money.
(i) She left the bank.
(j) She went home.

Van Dijk points out that the statement 'Dorothy went to the bank' can, as well as being used in position (a), also be used to summarize the action sequence (a)–(j). In position (a), 'Dorothy went to the bank' means, roughly, that she 'travelled to the bank'. The actions in the bank are outlined in statements (b)–(j). When statements (b)–(j) are missing, 'Dorothy went to the bank' fills their space. It no longer means just 'Dorothy travelled to the bank' but 'Dorothy travelled to the bank and performed a financial transaction'. It is then, in my terms, a context summarizer.

The underlined sentences in Example 8.23 are like 'Dorothy went to the bank', for as well as standing on their own as context summarizers, they could be followed by more detail about the same context and, therefore, be framed. The first clause of the third sentence, 'That afternoon three of the gossipy ladies of the village called upon her', could also function as a context summarizer, although here it is framed. In contrast to these actual or potential context summarizers, it is difficult to imagine a framed sentence like 'Kitty watched Maurice lower his spoon into his lemon pudding' (Example 8.14) existing in isolation from other statements about the same context.

The context summarizers in Example 8.23 are followed by statements which reset the time and place parameters and so prevent a reader from carrying a frame forward. There is overt continuity in these opening sentences, for Miss Marple is referred to several times by pronouns. There is, however, no covert continuity, so, for example, it cannot be inferred that characters who saw Miss Marple in the High Street are also present at the Vicarage.

Context summarizers are characterized by the fact that the verb is often one which has little lexical content and so, therefore, generally has a range of possible meanings which can only be narrowed down in actual use. In van Dijk's example, 'went' could mean either 'travelled' or 'visited'. In theory, 'called at' in the second sentence of Example 8.23 could mean either 'arrived at the door' or 'visited'. The fact that there is a very precise time marker at ten minutes to twelve does, however, cast some doubt over the notion that this sentence describes the whole visit.

The second sentence of Example 8.23 could instead be seen as summarizing the context by mentioning a salient part of it, the arrival, and allowing us to infer the remainder. This technique is seen more clearly in the following example, which was cited earlier as Example 4.4.

E X A M P L E 8 . 2 4

Time had passed and Guy Openshaw was dead. He lived longer than had been expected, but obliged the doctor's prediction by dying on Christmas Eve. <u>His ashes had been scattered in an anonymous garden</u>. It was now early April in the following year, and Gertrude Openshaw, *née* McCluskie, was looking out of a window at a cool cloudy sunlit scene.

(Iris Murdoch, *Nuns and Soldiers* (1981), 103; my emphasis)

The statement 'His ashes had been scattered in an anonymous garden' describes one specific action. The salience of the action, however, means that it can stand alone as the only piece of information about the funeral ceremony, summarizing the ceremony by symbolizing it.

Context summarizers are different from unframed text because they describe a specific context, albeit in a single sentence. Unframed text consists either of generalizations, such as descriptions (as in Example 8.7), which are not tied to a specific context, or of events which are above the level of a specific context, in terms of duration (as in Example 8.15), or frequency (as in Example 8.16). Context summarizers are also, however, different from framed text, since a single context is not maintained over a series of sentences.

3. BEYOND NARRATIVE FICTION: TEXT TYPES IN OTHER GENRES

This book has looked mainly at examples from fictional narratives. In this section I extend the discussion to texts which are either non-narrative or narrative non-fiction, considering how the framed/unframed distinction applies to such text types. This section provides some suggestions, but further study is necessary to provide a more comprehensive picture.

So far, I have argued that narrative fiction can be both framed and unframed (as well as containing hybrid context summarizers), although framed text is probably most central to storytelling. Non-fictional narratives would appear generally to be similar in this respect, as in the following extract from an autobiography:

EXAMPLE 8.25

Ten minutes later we were lost in the white-out. There was no wind, and the snow fell silently in large heavy flakes. It was about two-thirty and we knew it would snow until late evening. We stood in silence, staring around us, trying to make out where we were.

'I think we should head down.'

'I don't know . . . no, not down. We must keep in touch with the ridge. Didn't you see those flutings on this side. We'd never get back up again.'

(Joe Simpson, *Touching the Void* (1989), 46)

In this extract we monitor the presence of the two characters whether or not they are mentioned. This particular story is largely framed. It makes sense for it to be set in a specific context because it is a detailed account of physical endurance. The distribution of text types will, nevertheless, vary according to the type of autobiography. In James Watson's autobiographical *The Double Helix* (1970), which tells of the discovery of the structure of DNA, the narrative fluctuates between framed and unframed text because of the need to focus on ideas as well as actions (see G. Myers (1990) for a discussion of this text as narrative).

Academic writing is, in contrast to storytelling, often unframed, as shown below:

EXAMPLE 8.26

The world of 'Them' is the world of the bosses, whether those bosses are private individuals, or as is increasingly the case today, public officials. 'Them' may be, as occasion requires, anyone from the classes outside other than the few individuals from those classes whom working-people know as individuals. A general practitioner, if he wins his way by his devotion to his patients, is not, as a general practitioner, one of 'Them'; he and his wife, as social beings, are. A parson may or may not be regarded as one of 'Them', according to his behaviour. 'Them' includes the policemen and those civil servants or local-authority employees whom the working-classes meet—teachers, the school attendance man, 'the Corporation', the local bench.

(Richard Hoggart, *The Uses of Literacy* (1958), 72)

The above text is unframed because it consists of a series of generalizations, in which there is no covert continuity. There is no suggestion, for example, that the parson and the school attendance man are present together in a single context. Example 8.26 is both unframed and unsequenced. Not all academic writing is like this, however. History texts are often sequenced, becoming framed when they describe a series of events which occur in a specific context. Procedural texts (recipes, instruction manuals, etc.) are likewise framed, although they are not describing events which have actually happened. A recipe might for example give the instruction to 'Add salt' which means to add it to whatever is currently in the context if the instructions are followed.

Academic writing quite often describes generic contexts. Like 'procedural' contexts, these also require assumptions of contextual continuity. The following example is set in a generic context with generic participants,[7] but it is nevertheless a context which needs to be monitored by a frame. In the last sentence, although the guest is not mentioned, he is still a covert participant. The host is behaving in this way because of the guest's presence.

EXAMPLE 8.27

In social situations, the classic Intention Movement is the 'chair-grasp'. Host and guest have been talking for some time, but now the host has an appointment to keep and must get away. His urge to go is held in check by his desire not to be rude to his guest. If he did not care about his guest's feelings, he would simply get up out of his chair and announce his departure. This is what his body wants to do, but his politeness glues his body to the chair and refuses to let him rise.

(Desmond Morris, *Manwatching: A Field Guide to Human Behaviour* (1978), 173)

Framed text which is incorporated within academic writing is often rather different from the framed text of novels and short stories. In the above example the characters are not actual people, which becomes clear when the text starts offering us alternatives for how the character might behave:

---

[7] See Ozieblowska (1994) for an interesting discussion of the generic pronouns in such texts.

EXAMPLE 8.28

The guest, if he is engrossed in the conversation, may fail to notice the change in his host's body posture, or he may see it but ignore it. A sensitive guest will, however, usually respond fairly quickly.

(Desmond Morris, *Manwatching: A Field Guide to Human Behaviour* (1978), 173)

Characterization is often irrelevant, the only information given being that which is needed to illustrate the academic point being made. In the following legal case history, for example, we do not find out how the plaintiff escaped, what her injury was or whether she eventually recovered from it.

EXAMPLE 8.29

The plaintiff visited a public lavatory owned by the defendants, and having put a penny in the slot she went in. The door having closed behind her she found that she could not get out, and for ten to fifteen minutes she tried to attract attention. She then thought that she could get out by climbing over the door and she stood with her right foot on the seat of the lavatory, holding with one hand a pipe and the other the top of the door, and put her left foot on the toilet roll and its attachment. Having got into this position she realized that she could not in fact get over the door, and in trying to get down she put some weight onto the toilet roll which revolved causing her to slip, fall and sustain injury. The county court judge found that the defendants had been negligent, but dismissed the plaintiff's case on the ground that the damage to the plaintiff was too remote . . .[The Court of Appeal, however, found] that she was entitled to succeed, but that she had, on the facts, been guilty of some contributory negligence and she must bear one quarter of the blame.

(Summary; for original text see Sayers v. Harlow Urban District Council, *The Weekly Law Reports*, 1958, i. 342)

Academic framed text can often lack the essential qualities of a story:

EXAMPLE 8.30

Person A sits at a desk, working on a psychological test. Person B sits opposite him, watching his progress. In front of B is a push button. B has been told that pushing the button causes A to receive an excruciatingly painful electric shock (though no permanent injury). Periodically, Professor Jones walks over to A's desk, notes an incorrect answer, and instructs B to press the button.

(William Poundstone, *Labyrinths of Reason: Paradox, Puzzles and the Frailty of Knowledge* (1991), 126)

In the above example, the text goes on to inform the reader that A is actually Professor Jones's confederate and that the two are playing a trick on B, seeing whether B can be coerced into inflicting pain. The reader then discovers that, unknown to Professor Jones, he too is the subject of an experiment to explore whether an authoritarian figure is more likely to coerce someone like B to inflict pain than a non-authoritarian figure. The full text, therefore, involves two examples of reframing, in Goffman's (1975) sense of 'twists in the tale', but it describes a situation rather than a sequence of events (see also Ryan's (1991: 2) discussion of mathematics problems). It is not, therefore, a very good example of a story, since it does not have a clear beginning, middle, and end, but it is set within a single context and is therefore framed text, in the sense that the word 'frame' is used in this book.

Summary

This chapter has drawn a distinction between framed and unframed text. Framed text describes a particular context and causes the reader to assume participant continuity even when characters are textually covert. For unframed text, no contextual frame needs to be set up by the reader, as there is no such covert continuity.

Framed and unframed text can be distinguished in a number of ways. Some sentences contain linguistic signalling of the text type, but others are indeterminate and their function has to be determined from the surrounding text. The transition between text types may be signalled by markers such as 'now' and 'once', as well as being reflected by disruption to reference chains. The distinction between framed and unframed text types accounts for the majority of narrative text, since most sentence groups are either in a specific context or are not set in a context at all. Context summarizers are, however, a hybrid form, since a single sentence describes a context and there is no contextual continuity across sentences.

The final section of the chapter explored other genres beyond narrative fiction. Framed text occurs in true stories where the techniques of storytelling are often the same as in fictional stories. Although other genres such as academic writing are characteristically unframed, framed descriptions can still be found, although they may lack the specificity of storytelling and may sometimes describe static situations rather than event sequences.

9

SUMMARY

The interpreter's experience always has a clear dynamic aspect,[1] to which our work has to pay close attention. We need to show, for example, that a text can create expectations in the reader's mind at one point which it then satisfies or subverts at a later point . . . In order to present the dynamic aspect of a reader's experience with a text, we have developed a method of text analysis which takes the text one segment at a time, asking ourselves at each point in this unrolling of the text something like, 'Having read this far, what would [the reader] have figured out, or be puzzled by, or be expecting?'

(Fillmore 1982: 254)

What is obvious from a consideration of naturally occurring narratives is the amount of text-specific knowledge that a reader needs in order to have even the most basic understanding of a text. The reader must work at a number of discourse levels. He or she must not only monitor the events overtly specified in recent sentences, but also remain conscious of the full context and be aware of any on-going action in other 'temporarily suspended' contexts. Obviously, representations of the characters must also be built up and updated as events occur. At the same time, the significance of events in relation to the overall plot and themes of a story has to be assessed. All of this requires not only stores of information, but assumption-making about the continuity of contexts and the ability to respond to linguistic signals of context changes.

This can be demonstrated by looking briefly at a short extract of text and considering how much mentally stored information the reader has to add. The sentences are deliberately presented out of

---

[1] See also Hasan (1981); Sinclair (1983: 71–5, 1985, 1992: 10–11); and Ravelli (1991) for discussions of the 'dynamic approach' to text analysis.

context here to highlight the amount of knowledge the reader
needs to bring forward from the previous text.

EXAMPLE 9.1

She said: 'Until recently Jack and I were always with people
who took it for granted that getting pregnant was a disaster,
and now suddenly all the people we know have young children
and baby-sitters and . . . perhaps . . . if . . .'
Jack said: 'You'll feel better when it's born.'

(Doris Lessing, 'A Man and Two Women', in *A Man and Two
Women* (1965), 92)

Some of the 'gap-filling' needed is immediately obvious. The reader
must have a referent available to interpret the pronouns 'She', 'I',
and 'You'. To do this, the reader needs to have kept the last-mentioned character, Dorothy, *in focus* from the previous paragraph,
assuming the pronoun 'She' to refer to her and hence also the pronoun 'I'. The reader also needs to assume the continued co-presence of Dorothy and Jack during the conversation, so that Jack's
mention of 'You' can be taken to mean Dorothy. This inference
and assumptions about the presence of other characters in the
contextual frame require *priming* inferences. Establishing the
identity of the characters involves having *entity representations*
available, to interpret both the pronouns and the name 'Jack'.
These entity representations supply information which make
sense of the passage. The reader already knows that Dorothy is
pregnant, so her remark can be taken as a comment on her own
situation. Conversely, characters' conversation provides us with
extra information to update their entity representations.

There is also processing work resulting from the hierarchical
structure of the text, signalled before this extract begins and after
it finishes. The reader, therefore, needs to know that this dialogue
is occurring in flashback time, not the present time, even though
there is no indication of this in these particular sentences. Hence
the characters are flashback *enactors* and the appropriate information has to be accessed from their entity representations. Keeping
track of the flashback involves observing the signals of a *frame
switch*, setting up a new frame, monitoring the flashback context,
and eventually responding to clues to leave it. At the same time,
the reader needs to retain an awareness of the temporarily aban-

doned action occurring at the main narrative level, in which Stella and Jack are talking as they walk towards their car. This awareness is necessary, as the subsequent *frame recall* is achieved solely by a pronoun, 'They', and a mention of the car. Furthermore, an awareness of both frames is necessary because this flashback (and a stretch of *unframed* text which precedes it), serve as a commentary on the main text, in which Jack and Stella are talking about the baby. This passage also has relevance for the story as a whole. The pressures of parenthood are the major *theme* of the story. Also, the *plot* requires Stella (and the reader) to have some knowledge of Dorothy's circumstances and some sympathy for her, since Stella later rejects a sexual advance by Jack on this basis.

This analysis may be confusing to someone who has not read the story, but it serves as an illustration of the extent to which naturally occurring sentences depend for their interpretation on a knowledge of the full text. All of this discourse-level interpretation occurs in addition to the orthographic, semantic, and syntactic processing at sentence level. Although the demands on the reader are most obvious at frame boundaries, the reader is making contextual assumptions continually. Whenever events are set in a fictional context, the reader has to make priming and focusing inferences and repeatedly update entity representations. Whenever there is a flashback, the reader needs to keep the appropriate enactor at the forefront of consciousness and monitor the appropriate contextual frame. Whenever the main action of a narrative is temporarily suspended, the reader needs to remember that particular context and be prepared to return to it in response to often relatively subtle signals. When reading about any context, the reader also needs to be alert to stretches of embedded unframed text, since a different text type can introduce different characters.

Experienced readers achieve all this processing with remarkable ease. These observations about the creation of a fictional context, identification of characters, and management of context shifts seem obvious to those of us with these literacy skills. However, not everyone achieves advanced literacy, or even basic literacy, and not every child learns at a speed in line with their intelligence. Clearly, there are often political and social reasons for this, but there is also a lack of real understanding on the part of academics and educationalists about what reading involves, as can be seen from the uncertainty in recent years about the best way to teach reading. Indeed, only very recently have educational psychologists begun to suggest that an overall model of a textual world is necessary to read a text (Oakhill and Garnham 1988; Yuill and Oakhill 1991; Oakhill and Yuill 1995).

It is easy to overlook the demands discourse processing places on the unskilled reader. The immensity of the task is more obvious when, as skilled readers of our own native language, we try to read a novel in a less familiar foreign language. If our competence is low, we may, as we stumble over individual words and struggle to tie sentences together, lose track of our overall orientation, particularly if the system of discourse cues is also unfamiliar to us. We do, nevertheless, have our previous reading experience to draw on. Children do not have the same familiarity with textual conventions. They have to learn to distinguish a fictional world from the real world, they have to realize that they may need to make continuity assumptions, they need to become familiar with the fact that a text may contain hierarchical shifts, and they must learn to recognize the signals which mark such shifts. All this is supposed to happen without explicit teaching of the conventions of narrative and then, ironically, at the stage when many children have begun to master these skills, they are presented with non-narrative texts which require quite different skills (Hoey 1986), again with no real explanation or training.

Although this book is a theoretical study rather than an applied one, the aim is to highlight the extent to which a global representation of a textual world is necessary to make basic inferences. This seems to be the 'forgotten' level of processing as far as the teaching of reading is concerned. Children are taught to read simple stories and are later, as young adults, taught to interpret literary works, but there is a long stage of development which seems to occur more by chance than by design. It is hardly surprising therefore that many potential readers fall by the wayside and fail to acquire advanced literacy skills (Tucker 1981: 131; Bettelheim and Zelan 1991: 46).

Implications

Cognitive study has recently added a new dimension to discourse analysis and one of my main aims has been to provide a justification of this approach to those within my own subject area. To explain how a text is processed, it is not enough to say simply that information is available in the prior text, there also needs to be some explanation of how the reader has access to this information at the appropriate point. An examination of naturally occurring texts can give an indication of the amount and type of information that needs to be retained to make basic coherence inferences. It can also indicate the distances over which such information needs to be held, the extent to which we need to keep track of different levels of the textual world, and the subtlety of signals of discourse structure.

Another aim of this book has been to make discourse analysts aware of the implications of adding mental representations to linguistic models. Adding a major new component to any model has an effect on the other components. In reference theory, the role of the antecedent has altered as mental representations have been added. In addition, mental representations place new demands on the analyst in terms of explanatory work, for the information in these representations needs to be kept updated as the text is read. Theoretical categories are also subject to challenge, such as the borderline between anaphora and deixis, and the definitions of core terms sometimes need reworking, as in the case of anaphora and cataphora. These topics are still being explored, but the results also need to be communicated,[2] via textbooks, to the general linguist who has to teach grammar and discourse analysis.

This book has also attempted to highlight properties of narrative which make this genre interesting as a topic of study in its own right within text-processing research. The need to accumulate text-specific information becomes very clear from a study of narrative, because of the creation of a fictional world which is independent of the real world. Narrative contexts are interesting to the analyst because they are continually requiring the reader to make continuity assumptions and to make inferences about covert entities (also placing a question mark over the nature of reference itself). Narrative flashback is particularly worthy of study, since it requires sudden major reorientations, which can be signalled in subtle ways and which have implications for the way that information is stored in entity representations.

---

[2] See Emmott (1996) for further discussion of this issue.

In addition to these objectives, I have tried to explain the importance of a 'discourse perspective'. Discourse analysts generally assume that the distinction between a real text and an artificially constructed 'sentence pair' is glaringly obvious and that there is no need to point this out. It is a shock to discover that the distinction is not at all obvious to many of those in other disciplines. Although psychology has begun to recognize the need for 'ecological validity', there is still a long way to go to establish this in text-processing research and the cognitive discourse analyst can provide a contribution in this respect. Cognitive discourse analysts also need to justify their own research. Psychologists sometimes judge textual study as a half-hearted attempt to 'do' psychology—since the data is there, but it is not empirically tested. However, as far as discourse analysts are concerned, there is much to discover from the texts themselves. Studying texts to gauge the demands they place on readers is a valuable contribution to text-processing research, but it may be a while before it is recognized in this way.

Future Research

This book is, of course, only a beginning and there are many areas in which the research could be extended either within discourse analysis or by other researchers such as psychologists.

One obvious extension would be a more systematic collection of some of the linguistic features discussed, such as antecedentless pronouns and frame switch indicators. My aim here has been to illustrate these features of texts rather than to provide a comprehensive analysis of a corpus. Some indication of the complexity of textual structure in different levels of childhood reading materials would also be useful, such as the number of flashbacks and the complexity of signalling, as well as the balance between framed and unframed text. There is also an important place for psychological testing of frame switch processing by both skilled and unskilled readers. This might be done by traditional experimental means (assuming that the materials reflect these textual complexities) or by protocol analysis.

As far as knowledge representation is concerned, there needs to be a more thorough analysis of the extent to which different types of knowledge, such as general knowledge and text-specific knowledge, are used to read naturally occurring narratives. This book suggested a categorization of knowledge types in Chapter 2, but a more comprehensive typology is needed and the interaction between the types needs to be studied. Much of the text-specific contextual knowledge discussed in this book assumes a general knowledge of probabilities associated with time and space. Conversely, the text itself weights probabilities by forcing the reader to take into account the ongoing situation in the fictional world, rather than making decontextualized judgements about stereotyped characters in stereotyped situations.

As far as narrative structure is concerned, an area which needs extensive linguistic research is the distinction between framed and unframed text. In this book I have identified the categories by both an appeal to intuition and by pointing out verb forms and the markers of a switch from one text type to another. It is likely that further insights can be found from applying Clause Relational Analysis or Rhetorical Structure Theory to these text types. My comments about non-fiction narratives and non-narratives are only initial speculations.[3] Clearly, the analysis of text types is central to our understanding of genre distinctions.

From the point of view of linguistic theory, this work has raised questions about the nature of reference and the borderline between deixis and anaphora, at least as far as fictional contexts are concerned. My concern here has been to present a model which is able to handle narrative data. These observations, however, need to be compared and contrasted with observations that have been made from a cognitive linguistic perspective about other genres. This research has focused primarily on third-person singular anaphoric pronouns, but there is an obvious need for a similar analysis of other pronouns, such as the first-person pronoun and plural pronouns, as well as time and place adverbs. A fair amount of work has already been done on the definite article in narrative, but there is a need to provide a theoretical model which integrates observations about definiteness and pronominalization.

---

[3] See Emmott (forthcoming *c*) for a further exploration of this topic.

Conclusion

> ...[the mind] will not give up its secrets to psychology alone;
> nor is any other isolated discipline—artificial intelligence,
> linguistics, anthropology, neurophysiology, philosophy—
> going to have any greater success.
>
> (Johnson-Laird 1988: 7)

> Any a priori decision about which line of analysis 'gets things
> right' or 'has the last word' prejudges the question of whether
> different analyses might be legitimate for different explana-
> tory purposes and thus compatible with each other, or at
> least capable of peaceful coexistence.
>
> (Flanagan 1992: 11)

Discourse analysis, cognitive psychology, and artificial intelligence are all currently at an important stage of development. Discourse analysis has recently recognized the need to include a
'cognitive layer' in its work, but is still struggling to come to
terms with the implications. Cognitive psychology is beginning
to move towards what it terms 'ecological validity', although in
text-processing research there is still a need for recognition of the
complex structure and linguistic patterning of naturally occurring texts. Artificial intelligence probably faces the greatest obsta-
cle, since it is being forced to consider the role of consciousness in
mental processing whilst having little idea of what consciousness
actually is. It is not easy to build a working replica of something
when the most important component is unavailable.

Text-processing researchers are on the point of making substantial discoveries, but time invested in research is being squandered
because of the unwillingness of some researchers to even consider
work from other disciplines. In theory, cognitive science exists as
a new field, since it has its own academic departments, journals,
and conferences. In reality, the divisions seem almost insur-
mountable. Cognitive psychology and neuroscience are two
obvious polarizations, but as more disciplines become interested
in mental processing, the differences are multiplied.[4] However,
although other methodologies and objectives are sometimes
quite alien to us, there is usually some insight to be gained from
another approach. Probably one of the greatest scientific over-

---

[4] See Sharkey (1986: 13–14) for a summary.

sights of recent times has been to ignore human consciousness, a topic which received serious consideration by William James back in the 1890s but was subsequently thought not worthy of study until the last quarter of this century. We know so little about how the human mind works that we have much to learn from other disciplines. This book is an attempt to bridge some of the gaps between linguistics and psychology, but we will make no real progress in text-processing research whilst these divisions remain.

SUGGESTED FURTHER
READING FOR STUDENTS

(A Note to the 1999 Paperback Edition)

For students requiring a general linguistic introduction to narrative, two very useful textbooks are Leech and Short (1981) and Toolan (1988). Chafe (1980a) provides an important study of the cognitive effort involved in story-telling. Although focusing on production rather than comprehension, Chafe (1980a) is of particular relevance to the current work since it provides a model for examining the hierarchical shifts in a narrative and for analysing the chains of referring items used to denote characters. In literary studies, Genette (1980) is a classic analysis of time shifts in narrative that provides a useful framework for linguistic analysis.

One major new direction in recent years has been the development of cognitive models of text processing by researchers from literary linguistics. Werth (1995) gives a summary of the 'text worlds' approach which has developed out of cognitive linguistic theory (see also Werth (forthcoming)). Duchan, Bruder, and Hewitt (1995b) offers interdisciplinary perspectives on deixis in narrative, focusing particularly on the influence of shifting points of view on references to characters (see also Green (1995)). Semino (1997) draws on schema theory, building on earlier work by Cook (1994). Although Semino's analysis focuses primarily on poetry, the book also contains a useful discussion of narrative. Stockwell (1999) develops the model of 'frame switches' presented in *Narrative Comprehension* to account for the special features of science fiction. Gerrig (1993) offers a psychologist's perspective on 'narrative worlds'.

Narrative Comprehension emphasizes the importance of a discourse-based approach to narrative processing. Coulthard (1985), Schiffrin (1994), and van Dijk (1997) are good general introductions to discourse analysis. Although much work within discourse analysis has been on spoken text, Coulthard (1994) applies the same principles to written texts. van Dijk and Kintsch (1983) is an important and still very influential psycholinguistic study of text processing.

For students who wish to read further on discourse anaphora, Cornish (1999) provides an excellent survey and critique of current theories. Sanford and Garrod (1981) formulates one of the major psychological approaches to discourse anaphora. Grosz (1977), Sidner (1979b), Reichman (1985), and Walker, Joshi, and Prince (1998) provide major contributions from the field of artificial intelligence. Halliday and Hasan (1976) is still an influential and important study of reference in texts, although this work takes little account of cognitive processing. Fauconnier (1994) and Langacker (1987, 1991) provide the basis for much current cognitive linguistic work on anaphora.

Additional references (see the main bibliography for all other works cited above):

CORNISH, F. (1999), *Anaphora, Discourse, and Understanding: Evidence from English and French* (Oxford: Oxford University Press).

COULTHARD, M. (1994) (ed.), *Advances in Written Text Analysis* (London: Routledge).

GREEN, K. (1995) (ed.), *New Essays in Deixis: Discourse, Narrative, Literature* (Amsterdam: Rodopi).

SEMINO, E. (1997), *Language and World Creation in Poems and Other Texts* (London: Longman).

STOCKWELL, P. (1999), *The Poetics of Science Fiction* (London: Longman).

WALKER, M. A., JOSHI, A. K., and PRINCE, E. F. (1998) (eds.), *Centering Theory in Discourse* (Oxford: Oxford University Press).

WERTH, P. (forthcoming), *Text Worlds: Representing Conceptual Space in Discourse* (London: Longman). (An earlier draft of this book is referred to as Werth (MS a) in the main text.)

VAN DIJK, T. A. (1997) (ed.), *Discourse as Structure and Process* (London: Sage).

C.E.

Glasgow
January 1999

BIBLIOGRAPHY

ABELSON, R. P. (1987), 'Artificial Intelligence and Literary Appreciation: How Big is the Gap?', in L. Halász (ed.), *Literary Discourse: Aspects of Cognitive and Social Psychological Approaches* (Berlin: de Gruyter), 38–48.

ADAMS, D. (1988), *Dirk Gently's Holistic Detective Agency* (London: Pan).

ADAMS, R. (1973), *Watership Down* (Harmondsworth: Puffin/Penguin).

ADLER, J. E. (1984), 'Abstraction is Uncooperative', *Journal for the Theory of Social Behavior*, 14: 165–81.

ALEXANDER, L., and GUENTHER, R. K. (1986), 'The Effect of Mood and Demand on Memory', *British Journal of Psychology*, 77: 343–50.

ALEXSANDER, I., and BURNET, P. (1987), *Thinking Machines: The Search for Artificial Intelligence* (Oxford: Oxford University Press).

ALLBRITTON, D. W., and GERRIG, R. J. (1991), 'Participatory Responses in Text Understanding', *Journal of Memory and Language*, 30: 603–26.

ALLEN, J. (1983), 'Recognizing Intentions from Natural Language Utterances', in M. Brady and R. C. Berwick (eds.), *Computational Models of Discourse* (Cambridge, Mass.: MIT Press), 107–66.

ALLÉN, S. (1989) (ed.), *Possible Worlds in Humanities, Arts and Sciences: Proceedings of Nobel Symposium 65* (Berlin: de Gruyter).

ALLWOOD, J., ANDERSSON, L.-G., and DAHL, O. (1977), *Logic in Linguistics* (Cambridge: Cambridge University Press).

ALSHAWI, H. (1987), *Memory and Context for Language Interpretation* (Cambridge: Cambridge University Press).

ANDERSON, A., GARROD, S. C., and SANFORD, A. J. (1983), 'The Accessibility of Pronominal Antecedents as a Function of Episode Shifts', *Quarterly Journal of Experimental Psychology*, 35A: 427–40.

ANDERSON, J. R. (1978), 'The Processing of Referring Expressions within a Semantic Network', in D. Waltz (ed.), *Theoretical Issues in Natural Language Processing 2* (Urbana: University of Illinois), 51–6.

—— (1987), 'Methodologies for Studying Human Knowledge', *Behavioural and Brain Sciences*, 10: 467–505.

ANDERSON, R. C., and FREEBODY, P. (1985), 'Vocabulary Knowledge', in H. Singer and R. B. Ruddell (eds.), *Theoretical Models and Processes of Reading* (Newark, Del.: International Reading Association), 343–71.

—— and PICHERT, J. W. (1978), 'Recall of Previously Unrecallable Information Following a Shift of Perspective', *Journal of Verbal Learning and Verbal Behavior*, 17: 1–12.

APPELYARD, J. A. (1991), *Becoming a Reader: The Experience from Childhood to Adulthood* (Cambridge: Cambridge University Press).

ARIEL, M. (1990), *Accessing Noun Phrase Antecedents* (London: Routledge).

ATKINSON, J. M., and DREW, P. (1979), *Order in Court* (London: Routledge).

AUSTIN, J. L. (1975), *How to do Things with Words* (Oxford: Oxford University Press; first published 1962).

BADDELEY, A. (1981), 'The Cognitive Psychology of Everyday Life', *British Journal of Psychology*, 72: 257–69.

—— (1985), 'Domains of Recollection', in A. M. Aitkenhead and J. M. Slack (eds.), *Issues in Cognitive Modeling* (London and Hillsdale, NJ: Lawrence Erlbaum; article first published 1982), 209–27.

BAKHTIN, M. M. (1981), 'Discourse in the Novel', in M. Holquist (ed.), *The Dialogic Imagination: Four Essays* [by M. M. Bakhtin] (Austin: University of Texas Press), 259–425.

BALLMER, T. T. (1979), 'Context Change, Truth and Competence', in R. Bäuerle, U. Egli, and A. von Stechow (eds.), *Semantics from Different Points of View* (Berlin: Springer-Verlag), 21–31.

—— (1981), 'Context Change and its Consequences for a Theory of Natural Language', in H. Parret, M. Sbisà, and J. Verschueren (eds.), *Possibilities and Limitations in Pragmatics* (Amsterdam: Benjamins), 17–55.

—— (1985), 'The Psychology of Context Change', in T. T. Ballmer (ed.), *Linguistic Dynamics: Discourse Procedures and Evolution* (Berlin: de Gruyter), 322–56.

—— (1988), 'Context and Context Change', in J. S. Petöfi (ed.), *Text and Discourse Constitution—Empirical Aspects, Theoretical Approaches* (Berlin: de Gruyter), 317–76.

BANFIELD, A. (1982), *Unspeakable Sentences: Narration and Representation in the Language of Fiction* (Boston: Routledge & Kegan Paul).

BANKS, L. R. (1966), *An End to Running* (Harmondsworth: Penguin).

BAR-HILLEL, Y. (1954), 'Indexical Expressions', *Mind*, 63: 359–79.

BARNES, J. (1990), *A History of the World in $10\frac{1}{2}$ Chapters* (London: Picador/Pan).

BARTLETT, F. C. (1932), *Remembering: A Study in Experimental and Social Psychology* (Cambridge: Cambridge University Press).

BARWISE, J., and PERRY, J. (1983), *Situations and Attitudes* (Cambridge, Mass.: MIT Press).

BATESON, G. (1955), 'A Theory of Play and Fantasy: A Report on Theoretical Aspects of the Project for Study of the Role of Paradoxes of Abstraction in Communication', *Psychiatric Research Reports 2, American Psychiatric Association*, 39–51 (subsequently reprinted in G. Bateson, *Steps to an Ecology of Mind* (New York: Ballantine, 1972), 177–93).

BAXTER, J. S., MANSTEAD, A. S. R., STRADLING, S. G., CAMPBELL, K. A., REASON, J. T., and PARKER, D. (1990), 'Social Facilitation and Driver Behaviour', *British Journal of Psychology*, 81: 351–60.

BEECH, J. R., and COLLEY, A. M. (1987) (eds.), *Cognitive Approaches to Reading* (Chichester: John Wiley).

BERMAN, R. A. (forthcoming), 'Narrative Competence and Storytelling Performance: How Children Tell Stories in Different Contexts'.

—— and SLOBIN, D. I. (1994) (eds.), *Relating Events in Narrative: A Cross-Linguistic Developmental Study* (Hillsdale, NJ: Lawrence Erlbaum).

BERNADO, R. (1980), 'Subjecthood and Consciousness', in Chafe (1980a), 275–99.

BETTELHEIM, B., and ZELAN, K. (1991), *On Learning to Read* (Harmondsworth: Penguin).

BHARUCHA, J. J., OLNEY, K. L., and SCHNURR, P. P. (1985), 'Detection of Coherence-Disrupting and Coherence-Conferring Alterations in Text', *Memory and Cognition*, 13(6): 573–8.

BLACK, A., FREEMAN, P., and JOHNSON-LAIRD, P. N. (1986), 'Plausibility and the Comprehension of Text', *British Journal of Psychology*, 77: 51–62.

BLACK, J. B., and WILENSKY, R. (1979), 'An Evaluation of Story Grammars', *Cognitive Science*, 3: 213–30.

BLAKEMORE, C., and GREENFIELD, S. (1987) (eds.), *Mindwaves: Thoughts on Intelligence, Identity and Consciousness* (Oxford: Basil Blackwell).

BLEICH, D. (1978), *Subjective Criticism* (Baltimore: Johns Hopkins University Press).

BLOOM, D., and HAYES, D. G. (1978), 'Designation in English', in J. Hinds (ed.), *Anaphora in Discourse* (Edmonton: Linguistic Research Inc.), 1–69.

BLOOMFIELD, L. (1935), *Language* (London: George Allen & Unwin).

BODEN, M. (1987), *Artificial Intelligence and Natural Man* (London: MIT Press; first published 1977).

—— (1988), *Computer Models of Mind* (Cambridge: Cambridge University Press).

BOLINGER, D. (1979), 'Pronouns in Discourse', in T. Givón (ed.), *Syntax and Semantics*, xii. *Discourse and Syntax* (New York: Academic Press), 289–309.

BOOTH, W. (1983), *The Rhetoric of Fiction* (Chicago: Chicago University Press; first published 1961).

BOWER, G. H., BLACK, J. B., and TURNER, T. J. (1979), 'Scripts in Memory for Text', *Cognitive Psychology*, 11: 177–220.

BRANSFORD, J. D., and FRANKS, J. J. (1971), 'The Abstraction of Linguistic Ideas', *Cognitive Psychology*, 2: 331–50.

—— BARCLAY, J. R., and FRANKS, J. J. (1972), 'Sentence Memory: A Constructive versus Interpretive Approach', *Cognitive Psychology*, 3: 193–209.

BREWER, W. F. (1987), 'Schemas versus Mental Models in Human Memory', in P. E. Morris (ed.), *Modelling Cognition* (Chichester: John Wiley), 187–97.

—— and TREYENS, J. C. (1981), 'Role of Schemata in Memory for Places', *Cognitive Psychology*, 13: 207–30.

BRITTON, B. K., and PELLEGRINI, A. D. (1990) (eds.), *Narrative Thought and Narrative Language* (London: Lawrence Erlbaum).

BROOKNER, A. (1982), *A Start in Life* (London: Triad/Panther Books).

—— (1983), *Providence* (London: Triad/Panther Books).

BROWN, A. L., and CAMPIONE, J. C. (1978), 'The Effects of Knowledge and Experience on the Formation of Retrieval Plans for Studying from Texts', in M. M. Gruneberg, P. E. Morris, and R. N. Sykes (eds.), *Practical Aspects of Memory* (London: Academic Press), 378–84.

BROWN, E. K., and MILLER, J. E. (1982), *Syntax: Generative Grammar* (London: Hutchinson).

BROWN, F. M. (1987), *The Frame Problem in Artificial Intelligence: Proceedings of the 1987 Workshop* (Los Altos, Calif.: Morgan Kaufmann).

BROWN, G., and YULE, G. (1983), *Discourse Analysis* (Cambridge: Cambridge University Press).

BRUCE, B. (1980), 'Analysis of Interacting Plans as a Guide to the Understanding of Story Structure', *Poetics*, 9: 295–311.

BRUDER, G. A. (1995), 'Psychological Evidence that Linguistic Devices are used by Readers to Understand Spatial Deixis in Narrative Text', in Duchan, Bruder, and Hewitt (1995*b*), 243–60.

—— and WIEBE, J. M. (1995), 'Recognizing Subjectivity and Identifying Subjective Characters in Third-Person Fictional Narrative', in Duchan, Bruder, and Hewitt (1995*b*), 341–56.

—— DUCHAN, J. F., RAPAPORT, W. J., SEGAL, E. M., SHAPIRO, S. C., and ZUBIN, D. A. (1986), *Deictic Centers in Narrative: An Interdisciplinary Cognitive-Science Project*, internal report (Buffalo: Department of Computer Science, SUNY Buffalo).

BRUNER, J. S. (1986), *Actual Minds, Possible Worlds* (Cambridge, Mass.: Harvard University Press).

—— and KENNEY, H. J. (1974), 'Representation and Mathematics Learning', in J. S. Bruner, *Beyond the Information Given: Studies in the Psychology of Knowing*, ed. J. M. Anglin (London: George Allen & Unwin), 426–36.

BÜHLER, K. (1990), *Theory of Language: The Representational Function of Language*, translated by D. G. Goodwin (Amsterdam: John Benjamins; first published (in German) 1934).

BULLWINKLE, C. L. (1977) [See also SIDNER, C. L.], 'Levels of Complexity in Discourse for Anaphora Disambiguation and Speech Act Interpretation', *Proceedings of the Fifth International Conference on Artificial Intelligence* (Cambridge, Mass.: MIT Press), 43–9.

CAENEPEEL, M., and MELLOR, M. (1992), 'Moving Backwards in Time: A Linguistic Perspective on Martin Amis's Novel *Time's Arrow*', paper presented by M. Mellor at the XII Poetics and Linguistics Association Conference (Gent: University of Gent).

CAMPBELL, J. (1989), *Winston Churchill's Afternoon Nap: A Wide-Awake Inquiry into the Human Nature of Time* (London: Paladin).

CARAMAZZA, A., GROBER, E., GARVEY, C., and YATES, J. (1977), 'Comprehension of Anaphoric Pronouns', *Journal of Verbal Learning and Verbal Behavior*, 16: 601–9.

CARBONELL, J. G., and BROWN, R. D. (1989), 'Anaphor Resolution: A Multi-Strategy Approach', in D. Vargha (ed.), *COLING 88 BUDAPEST: Proceedings of the 12th International Conference on Computational Linguistics*, i (Budapest: John von Neumann Society for Computer Sciences), 96–101.

CARPENTER, P. A., and JUST, M. A. (1977), 'Reading Comprehension as Eyes see it', in M. A. Just and P. A. Carpenter (eds.), *Cognitive Processes in Comprehension* (Hillsdale, NJ: Lawrence Erlbaum), 109–39.

CARROLL, J. B. (1985), 'The Nature of the Reading Process', in H. Singer and R. B. Ruddell (eds.), *Theoretical Models and Processes of Reading* (Newark, Del.: International Reading Association), 25–34.

CARTER, D. (1987), *Interpreting Anaphors in Natural Language Texts* (Chichester: Ellis Horwood).

CHAFE, W. L. (1972), 'Discourse Structure and Human Knowledge', in J. B. Carroll and R. O. Freedle (eds.), *Language Comprehension and the Acquisition of Knowledge* (Washington: Winston), 41–69.

—— (1973), 'Language and Memory', *Language*, 49 (2): 261–81.

—— (1974), 'Language and Consciousness', *Language*, 50 (1): 111–33.

—— (1976), 'Givenness, Contrastiveness, Definiteness, Subjects, Topics, and Point of View', in C. N. Li (ed.), *Subject and Topic* (New York: Academic Press), 27–55.

—— (1979), 'The Flow of Thought and the Flow of Language', in T. Givón (ed.), *Syntax and Semantics*, xii. *Discourse and Syntax* (New York: Academic Press), 159–81.

—— (1980a) (ed.), *The Pear Stories: Cognitive, Cultural and Linguistic Aspects of Narrative Production* (Norwood, NJ: Ablex).

—— (1980b), 'The Deployment of Consciousness in the Production of a Narrative', in Chafe (1980a), 9–50.

—— (1987), 'Cognitive Constraints on Information Flow', in Tomlin (1987a), 21–51.

—— (1990), 'Some things that Narratives tell us about the Mind', in Britton and Pellegrini (1990), 77–98.

—— (1994), *Discourse, Consciousness and Time: The Flow and Displacement of Conscious Experience in Speaking and Writing* (Chicago: University of Chicago Press).

CHANG, F. R. (1980), 'Active Memory Processes in Visual Sentence Comprehension: Clause Effects and Pronominal Reference', *Memory and Cognition*, 8 (1): 56–64.

CHARNIAK, E. (1972), 'Towards a Model of Children's Story Comprehension', Ph.D. thesis, AI-TR-266 (Cambridge, Mass.: MIT Press).

—— (1973), 'Context and the Reference Resolution Problem', in R. Rustin (ed.), *Natural Language Processing* (New York: Algorithmics Press), 311–31.

—— (1978), 'With a Spoon in Hand this must be the Eating Frame', in D. Waltz (ed.), *Theoretical Issues in Natural Language Processing 2* (Urbana: University of Illinois), 187–93.

—— (1983), 'Passing Markers: A Theory of Contextual Influence in Language Comprehension', *Cognitive Science*, 7: 171–90.

—— (1986), 'Jack and Janet in Search of a Theory of Knowledge', in B. J. Grosz, S. J. Karen, and B. L. Webber (eds.), *Readings in Natural Language Processing* (Los Altos, Calif.: Morgan Kaufman), 331–7.

—— and McDERMOTT, D. (1985), *Introduction to Artificial Intelligence* (Reading, Mass.: Addison-Wesley).

CHATMAN, S. (1978), *Story and Discourse* (Ithaca, NY: Cornell University Press).

CHOMSKY, N. (1957), *Syntactic Structures* (The Hague: Mouton & Co.)

—— (1965), *Aspects of the Theory of Syntax* (Cambridge, Mass.: MIT Press).

—— (1972), *Language and Mind* (New York: Harcourt Brace Jovanovich; first published 1968).

CHRISTIE, A. (1957), *The Murder of Roger Ackroyd* (London: Fontana).

—— (1959), *Murder on the Orient Express* (London: Fontana).

—— (1977), *Sleeping Murder* (London: Fontana).

CLANCY, P. M. (1980), 'Referential Choice in English and Japanese Narrative Discourse', in Chafe (1980a), 127–202.

—— (1992), 'Referential Strategies in the Narratives of Japanese Children', *Discourse Processes*, 15: 441–67.

CLARK, A. (1989), *Microcognition: Philosophy, Cognitive Science and Parallel Distributed Processing* (Cambridge, Mass.: Bradford/MIT Press).

CLARK, H. H. (1977), 'Bridging', in P. N. Johnson-Laird and P. C. Wason (eds.), *Thinking: Readings in Cognitive Science* (Cambridge: Cambridge University Press), 410–20.

CLARK, H. H. (1992), *Arenas of Language Use* (Chicago: University of Chicago Press and CSLI).

—— and HAVILAND, S. E. (1977), 'Comprehension and the Given–New Contract', in R. O. Freedle (ed.), *Discourse Production and Comprehension*, i. (Norwood, NJ: Ablex), 1–40.

—— and MARSHALL, C. R. (1978), 'Reference Diaries', in D. Waltz (ed.), *Theoretical Issues in Natural Language Processing 2* (Urbana: University of Illinois), 57–63.

—— (1981), 'Definite Reference and Mutual Knowledge', in A. K. Joshi, B. L. Webber, and I. A. Sag (eds.), *Elements of Discourse Understanding* (Cambridge: Cambridge University Press), 10–63.

—— and SENGUL, C. J. (1979), 'In Search of Referents for Nouns and Pronouns', *Memory and Cognition*, 7 (1): 35–41.

CLIFFORD, B. R., and BULL, R. (1978), *The Psychology of Person Identification* (London: Routledge & Kegan Paul).

COHEN, G. (1983), *The Psychology of Cognition* (London: Academic Press; first published 1977).

—— EYSENCK, M. W., and LE VOI, M. E. (1986), *Memory: A Cognitive Approach* (Milton Keynes: Open University Press).

COLBY, B. N. (1973), 'A Partial Grammar of Eskimo Tales', *American Anthropologist*, 75: 645–62.

COOK, G. (1990), 'Transcribing Infinity: Problems of Context Presentation', *Journal of Pragmatics*, 14: 1–24.

—— (1994), *Discourse and Literature: The Interplay of Form and Mind* (Oxford: Oxford University Press).

CORBETT, A. T., and CHANG, F. R. (1983), 'Pronoun Disambiguation: Accessing Potential Antecedents', *Memory and Cognition*, 11 (3): 283–94.

CORNISH, F. (1986), *Anaphoric Relations in English and French: A Discourse Perspective* (London: Croom Helm).

COULTHARD, R. M. (1985), *An Introduction to Discourse Analysis* (London: Longman).

CRICK, F., and KOCH, C. (1990), 'Towards a Neurobiological Theory of Consciousness', *Seminars in the NeuroSciences*, 2: 263–75.

—— (1992), 'The Problem of Consciousness', *Scientific American, Special Issue: Mind and Brain*, 111–17.

D'YDEWALLE, G., and ROSSELLE, H. (1978), 'Test Expectations in Text Learning', in M. M. Gruneberg, P. E. Morris, and R. N. Sykes (eds.), *Practical Aspects of Memory* (London: Academic Press), 609–17.

DAHL, R. (1990), 'Genesis and Catastrophe: A True Story', in *The Best of Roald Dahl* (New York: Vintage), 259–65.

DALE, R. (1992), *Generating Referring Expressions* (Bradford, Mass.: MIT Press).

DANEMAN, M. (1987), 'Reading and Working Memory', in Beech and Colley (1987), 58–86.

DAVIDSON, C. (1993), 'I Process, Therefore I Am', *New Scientist*, 137 (1866): 22–6.

DE BEAUGRANDE, R. (1980), *Text, Discourse, and Process: Towards a Multi-disciplinary Science of Texts* (London: Longman).

—— and DRESSLER, W. (1981), *Introduction to Text Linguistics* (London: Longman).

DELANCEY, S. (1987), 'Transitivity in Grammar and Cognition', in Tomlin (1987), 53–68.

DELL, G. S., MCKOON, G., and RATCLIFF, R. (1983), 'The Activation of Antecedent Information during the Processing of Anaphoric Reference in Reading', *Journal of Verbal Learning and Verbal Behavior*, 22: 121–32.

DENNETT, D. C. (1987), 'Cognitive Wheels: The Frame Problem in A. I.' in Pylyshyn (1987), 41–64.

—— (1990), 'Cognitive Wheels: The Frame Problem of A. I.', in M. Boden (ed.), *The Philosophy of Artificial Intelligence* (Oxford: Oxford University Press), 147–70.

—— (1991), *Consciousness Explained* (Harmondsworth: Penguin).

DINSMORE, J. (1987), 'Mental Spaces from a Functional Perspective', *Cognitive Science*, 11: 1–21.

DONALDSON, M. (1978), *Children's Minds* (London: Fontana).

DOWNING, P. (1980), 'Factors influencing Lexical Choice in Narrative', in Chafe (1980a), 89–126.

DREYFUS, J. H. (1979), *What Computers Can't Do: The Limits of Artificial Intelligence* (New York: Harper & Row; first published 1972).

DU BOIS, J. W. (1980), 'The Trace of Identity in Discourse', in Chafe (1980a), 203–74.

DUCHAN, J. F., BRUDER, G. A., and HEWITT, L. E. (1995a), 'Prologue: A Simple Exercise in Narrative Understanding', in Duchan, Bruder, and Hewitt (1995b), pp. xi–xix.

—— —— —— (1995b) (eds.), *Deixis in Narrative: A Cognitive Science Perspective* (Hillsdale, NJ: Lawrence Erlbaum).

DUFFY, S. A. (1986), 'Role of Expectations in Sentence Integration', *Journal of Experimental Psychology: Learning, Memory and Cognition*, 12 (2): 208–19.

DYER, M. G. (1983a), *In-Depth Understanding: A Computer Model of Integrated Processing for Narrative Comprehension* (Cambridge, Mass.: MIT Press).

—— (1983b), 'The Role of Affect in Narratives', *Cognitive Science*, 7 (3): 211–42.

EAGLETON, T. (1983), *Literary Theory: An Introduction* (Oxford: Basil Blackwell).

Eco, U. (1979), *The Role of the Reader: Explorations in the Semiotics of Texts* (Bloomington: Indiana University Press).

Edric, R. (1989), *A Lunar Eclipse* (London: Heinemann).

Ehrlich, K. (1980), 'Comprehension of Pronouns', *Quarterly Journal of Experimental Psychology*, 32: 247–55.

—— (1983), 'Eye Movements in Pronoun Assignment: A Study of Sentence Integration', in K. Rayner (ed.), *Eye Movements in Reading: Perceptual and Language Processes* (New York: Academic Press), 253–68.

—— and Johnson-Laird, P. N. (1982), 'Spatial Descriptions and Referential Continuity', *Journal of Verbal Learning and Verbal Behavior*, 21: 296–306.

—— and Rayner, K. (1983), 'Pronoun Assignment and Semantic Integration during Reading: Eye Movements and Immediacy of Processing', *Journal of Verbal Learning and Verbal Behavior*, 22: 75–87.

Ehrlich, S. (1990), *Point of View: A Linguistic Analysis of Literary Style* (London: Routledge).

Einstein, G. O., McDaniel, M. A., Owen, P. D., and Cote, N. C. (1990), 'Encoding and Recall of Texts: The Importance of Material Appropriate Processing', *Journal of Memory and Language*, 29: 566–81.

Ellis, H. C., and Hunt, R. R. (1989), *Fundamentals of Human Memory and Cognition* (Dubuque, Ia: Wm. C. Brown).

Emmott, C. (1985), 'Expanded Nominals. A Computer-Assisted Stylistic Study', MA thesis (Birmingham: University of Birmingham).

—— (1989), 'Reading between the Lines: Building a Comprehensive Model of Participant Reference in Real Narrative', Ph.D. thesis (Birmingham: University of Birmingham).

—— (1992), 'Splitting the Referent: An Introduction to Narrative Enactors', in M. Davies and L. J. Ravelli (eds.), *Advances in Systemic Linguistics: Recent Theory and Practice* (London: Pinter), 221–8.

—— (1994), 'Frames of Reference: Contextual Monitoring and Narrative Discourse', in R. M. Coulthard (ed.), *Advances in Written Text Analysis* (London: Routledge), 157–66.

—— (1995a), 'Consciousness and Context-Building: Narrative Inferences and Anaphoric Theory', in K. Green (ed.), *New Essays in Deixis: Discourse, Narrative, Literature* (Amsterdam: Rodopi), 81–97.

—— (1995b), 'Lexical Density and Narrative Intensity: Some Problems with Using Computer Concordances in Stylistic Analysis', paper presented at the European Society for the Study of English (Glasgow: University of Glasgow).

—— (1996), 'Real Grammar in Fictional Contexts', *Glasgow Review*, 4, 9–23; also http://www.arts.gla.ac.uk/www/english/comet/comet.html

—— (forthcoming a), 'Situated in a Fictional World: Contextual Knowledge, Inference-Making, and Narrative Text Types', in M. Fludernik (ed.), *Strange Bedfellows: Linguistic Theory and Practice in Current Literary Scholarship*, European Journal of English Studies (special issue).

—— (forthcoming *b*), 'On the Complexity of Participant Reference: Designating the Major Characters in Written Narrative Fiction'.

—— (forthcoming *c*), 'Narration Across Genres: Fictional Narrative, "Factional" Narrative, and the Use of Stories and Pseudo-Stories in Discursive Writing'.

—— (forthcoming *d*), *Textual Cohesion and Coherence: Exploring Recent Theory and Applications*.

ENKVIST, N. E. (1989), 'Connexity, Interpretability, Universes of Discourse and Text Worlds', in S. Allén (ed.), *Possible Worlds in Humanities, Arts and Sciences: Proceedings of Nobel Symposium 65* (Berlin: de Gruyter), 162–86.

ENNULAT, J. H. (1978) 'Participant Categories in Fali Stories', in Grimes (1978*a*), 143–56.

ERBAUGH, M. S. (1987), 'A Uniform Pause and Error Strategy for Native and Non-Native Speakers (Psycholinguistic Evidence for Foregrounding and Backgrounding)', in Tomlin (1987), 109–30.

ERICSSON, K. A., and SIMON, H. A. (1985), 'Protocol Analysis', in T. A. van Dijk (ed.), *Handbook of Discourse Analysis*, ii. *Dimensions of Discourse* (London: Academic Press), 259–68.

EYSENCK, M. W., and KEANE, M. T. (1990), *Cognitive Psychology: A Student's Handbook* (Hove/London: Lawrence Erlbaum).

FAUCONNIER, G. (1994), *Mental Spaces* (Cambridge: Cambridge University Press; first published in French 1984, in English 1985).

—— (1995), 'Cognitive Dynamics of Language', paper presented at the International Cognitive Linguistic Association Conference (Albuquerque: University of New Mexico).

FAULKNER, W. (1966), *The Sound and the Fury* (London: Chatto and Windus).

FELDMAN, C. F., BRUNER, J. S., RENDERER, B., and SPITZER, S. (1990), 'Narrative Comprehension', in Britton and Pellegrini (1990), 1–78.

FILLMORE, C. J. (1982), 'Ideal Readers and Real Readers', in D. Tannen (ed.), *Analyzing Discourse: Text and Talk*, Georgetown University Round Table on Languages and Linguistics 1981 (Washington: Georgetown University Press), 248–70.

FIRBAS, J. (1986), 'On the Dynamics of Written Communication in the Light of the Theory of Functional Sentence Perspective', in C. R. Cooper and S. Greenbaum (eds.), *Studying Writing: Linguistic Approaches* (London: Sage), 40–71.

—— (1992*a*), 'On Some Basic Problems of Functional Sentence Perspective', in M. Davies and L. J. Ravelli (eds.), *Advances in Systemic Linguistics: Recent Theory and Practice* (London: Pinter), 167–88.

FIRBAS, J. (1992*b*), *Functional Sentence Perspective in Written and Spoken Communication* (Cambridge: Cambridge University Press).

FISH, S. (1980), 'Is there a Text in this Class?', in S. Fish (ed.), *Is there a Text in this Class?: The Authority of Interpretive Communities* (Cambridge, Mass.: Harvard University Press), 303–21.

FLANAGAN, O. (1992), *Consciousness Reconsidered* (London: MIT/Bradford).

FLEISCHMAN, S. (1990), *Tense and Narrativity: From Medieval Performance to Modern Fiction* (London: Routledge).

FLETCHER, C. R. (1984), 'Markedness and Topic Continuity in Discourse Processing', *Journal of Verbal Learning and Verbal Behavior*, 23: 487–93.

FLIK, E. (1978), 'Dan Tense-Aspect and Discourse', in Grimes (1978*a*), 46–62.

FLUDERNIK, M. (1993), *The Fictions of Language and the Languages of Fiction: The Linguistic Representation of Speech and Consciousness* (London: Routledge).

FORSTER, E. M. (1963), *Aspects of the Novel* (Harmondsworth: Penguin; first published 1927).

FOWLER, R. (1977), *Linguistics and the Novel* (London: Methuen).

—— (1986), *Linguistic Criticism* (Oxford: Oxford University Press).

FOWLES, J. (1977), *The French Lieutenant's Woman* (Bungay: Triad/Granada).

FOX, B. A. (1987*a*), *Discourse Structure and Anaphora. Written and Conversational English* (Cambridge: Cambridge University Press).

—— (1987*b*), 'Anaphora in Popular Written English Narratives', in Tomlin (1987*a*), 157–74.

—— (1988), 'Anaphora in Popular Stories: Implications for Narrative Theory', *Empirical Studies of the Arts*, 6 (2): 149–69.

FRANCIS, D. (1981), *Whip Hand* (London: Pan).

—— (1994), *Decider* (London: Pan).

FREDERIKSEN, C. H. (1986), 'Cognitive Models and Discourse Analysis', in C. R. Cooper and S. Greenbaum (eds.), *Studying Writing: Linguistic Approaches* (London: Sage), 227–67.

FREEMAN, D. C. (1992), ' "According to my Bond": King Lear and Re-Cognition', *Language and Literature*, 2 (1): 1–18.

—— (1993), 'To Catch the Nearest Way: Cognitive Metaphor in *Macbeth*', plenary paper presented at the XIII Poetics and Linguistics Association Conference (Åbo: Åbo Academy).

—— (1995), 'Metaphorical Systems in Poetry', paper presented at the XV Poetics and Linguistics Association Conference (Granada: University of Granada).

FREEMAN, M. H. (1995), 'Reflexives, Emphatics, and Deixis: Does Dickinson Violate the-*Self*?', video presentation at the International Cognitive

Linguistic Association Conference (Albuquerque: University of New Mexico).

FREUND, E. (1987), *The Return of the Reader: Reader-Response Criticism* (London: Methuen).

GALBRAITH, M. (1995), 'Deictic Shift Theory and the Poetics of Involvement in Narrative', in Duchan, Bruder, and Hewitt (1995*b*), 19–59.

GARDAM, J. (1984*a*), 'A Seaside Garden', in *The Pangs of Love and Other Stories* (London: Abacus), 113–30.

—— (1984*b*), 'An Unknown Child', in *The Pangs of Love and Other Stories* (London: Abacus), 55–68.

GARDNER, H. (1985), *The Mind's New Science: A History of the Cognitive Revolution* (New York: Basic Books).

GARFINKEL, H. (1967), *Studies in Ethnomethodology* (Englewood Cliffs, NJ: Prentice-Hall).

—— and SACKS, H. (1970), 'On Formal Structures of Practical Actions', in J. C. McKinney and E. A. Tiryakian (eds.), *Theoretical Sociology* (New York: Appleton-Century-Crofts), 337–66.

GARNHAM, A. (1981), 'Mental Models as Representation of Text', *Memory and Cognition*, 9 (6): 560–5.

—— (1985), *Psycholinguistics: Central Topics* (London: Methuen).

—— (1988), *Artificial Intelligence: An Introduction* (London: Routledge & Kegan Paul).

—— and OAKHILL, J. (1988), 'On-Line Resolution of Anaphoric Pronouns: Effects of Inference-Making and Verb Semantics', *British Journal of Psychology*, 76: 385–93.

GARROD, S. (1990), 'Reconciling the Psychological with the Linguistic in Accounts of Text Comprehension', in A.-C. Lindeberg, N. E. Enkvist, and K. Wikberg (eds.), *Nordic Research on Text and Discourse* (Åbo: Åbo Academy Press), 27–43.

GENETTE, G. (1980), *Narrative Discourse* (Oxford: Blackwell).

—— (1988), *Narrative Discourse Revisited* (Ithaca, NY: Cornell).

GERNSBACHER, M. A. (1985), 'Surface Information Loss in Comprehension', *Cognitive Psychology*, 17: 324–63.

—— (1989), 'Mechanisms that Improve Referential Access', *Cognition*, 99–150.

—— (1990), *Language Comprehension as Structure Building* (Hove: Lawrence Erlbaum).

GERRIG, R. J. (1986), 'Process Models and Pragmatics', in N. E. Sharkey (ed.), *Advances in Cognitive Science*, 1 (Chichester: Ellis Horwood), 23–42.

—— (1993), *Experiencing Narrative Worlds: On the Psychological Activities of Reading* (New Haven: Yale University Press).

GIBSON, E. J. (1985*a*), 'Trends in Perceptual Development: Implications for the Reading Process', in H. Singer and R. B. Ruddell (eds.), *Theoretical Models and Processes of Reading* (Newark, Del.: International Reading Association), 144–73.

—— (1985b), 'Learning to Read', in H. Singer and R. B. Ruddell (eds.), *Theoretical Models and Processes of Reading* (Newark, Del.: International Reading Association), 222–38.

GIVÓN, T. (1987), 'Beyond Foreground and Background', in Tomlin (1987), 175–88.

—— (1989), *Mind, Code and Context: Essays in Pragmatics* (Hillsdale, NJ: Lawrence Erlbaum).

GOFFMAN, E. (1975), *Frame Analysis: An Essay on the Organization of Experience* (Harmondsworth: Penguin).

GOLDING, W. (1961), *The Inheritors* (London: Faber & Faber).

GOLDMAN, S. R., and VARNHAGEN, C. K. (1986), 'Memory for Embedded and Sequential Story Structures', *Journal of Memory and Language*, 25 (4): 401–18.

GOODWIN, C. (1984), 'Notes on Story Structure and the Organization of Participation', in J. M. Atkinson and J. Heritage (eds.), *Structures of Social Action: Studies in Conversation Analysis* (Cambridge: Cambridge University Press), 225–46.

GORDON, P. C., GROSZ, B. A., and GILLION, L. A. (1993), 'Pronouns, Names and the Centering of Attention in Discourse', *Cognitive Science*, 17: 311–47.

GRAESSER, A. C. (1981), *Prose Comprehension beyond the Word* (New York: Springer Verlag).

—— LANG, K. L., and ROBERTS, R. M. (1991), 'Question Answering in the Context of Stories', *Journal of Experimental Psychology*, 120 (3): 254–77.

—— MILLIS, K. K., and LONG, D. L. (1986), 'The Construction of Knowledge Structures and Inferences during Text Comprehension', in Sharkey (1986), 125–57.

—— ROBERTSON, S. P., and ANDERSON, P. A. (1981), 'Incorporating Inferences in Narrative Representations: A Study of How and Why', *Cognitive Psychology*, 13 (1): 1–26.

GRAHAM, W. (1965), *After the Act* (London: The Bodley Head).

GREEN, G. M. (1989), *Pragmatics and Natural Language Understanding* (Hillsdale, NJ: Lawrence Erlbaum).

GREEN, H. (1985), *I Never Promised You a Rose Garden* (London: Pavanne/ Pan).

GREENE, G. (1986), 'Jim Braddon and the War Criminal', in *The Tenth Man* (Harmondsworth: Penguin), 12–17.

GREENE, J. (1986), *Language Understanding: A Cognitive Approach* (Milton Keynes: Open University Press).

GREIMAS, A. J. (1971), 'Narrative Grammar: Units and Levels', *Modern Language Notes*, 86: 793–806.

GRICE, H. P. (1975), 'Logic and Conversation', in P. Cole and J. L. Morgan (eds.), *Syntax and Semantics*, iii. *Speech Acts* (New York: Academic Press), 41–58.

—— (1978), 'Further Notes on Logic and Conversation', in P. Cole (ed.), *Syntax and Semantics*, ix. *Pragmatics* (New York: Academic Press), 113–28.

GRIMES, J. E. (1975), *The Thread of Discourse* (The Hague: Mouton).

—— (1978a) (ed.), *Papers on Discourse* (Dallas: Summer Institute of Linguistics).

—— (1978b), 'Topic Levels', in D. Waltz (ed.), *Theoretical Issues in Natural Language Processing 2* (Urbana: University of Illinois), 104–8.

GROSZ, B. J. (1977), 'The Representation and Use of Focus in Dialogue Understanding', Ph.D. thesis (Berkeley: University of California, Berkeley).

—— (1978), 'Focusing in Dialog', in D. Waltz (ed.), *Theoretical Issues in Natural Language Processing* (Urbana: University of Illinois), 96–103.

—— (1981), 'Focusing and Description in Natural Language Dialogues', in A. K. Joshi, B. L. Webber, and I. A. Sag (eds.), *Elements of Discourse Understanding* (Cambridge: Cambridge University Press), 84–105.

—— (1986), 'The Representation and Use of Focus in a System for Understanding Dialogs', in B. J. Grosz, S. J. Karen, and B. L. Webber (eds.), *Readings in Natural Language Processing* (Los Altos, Calif.: Morgan Kaufman), 353–62.

—— and SIDNER, C. L. (1986), 'Attention, Intentions, and the Structure of Discourse', *Computational Linguistics*, 12 (3): 175–204.

—— JOSHI, A. K., and WEINSTEIN, S. (1983), 'Providing a Unified Account of Definite Noun Phrases in Discourse', *Proceedings of the Association of Computational Linguistics*, 21: 44–50.

GUNDEL, J. K., HEDBERG, N., and ZACHARSKI, R. (1993), 'Cognitive Status and the Form of Referring Expressions in Discourse', *Language*, 69 (2): 274–307.

HALLIDAY, M. A. K. (1967), 'Notes on Transitivity and Theme in English', Part 2, *Journal of Linguistics*, 3: 199–244.

—— (1971), 'Linguistic Function and Literary Style: An Inquiry into William Golding's *The Inheritors*', in S. Chatman (ed.), *Literary Style: A Symposium* (Oxford: Oxford University Press), 330–65.

—— (1985), *An Introduction to Functional Grammar* (London: Edward Arnold).

—— and HASAN, R. (1976), *Cohesion in English* (London: Longman).

—— —— (1989), *Language, Text and Context: Aspects of Language in a Social-Semiotic Perspective* (Oxford: Oxford University Press).

HARRIS, J. B. N. (1980), 'Suprasentential Organisation in Written Discourse with Particular Reference to Writing by Children in the Lower Secondary School', MA thesis (Birmingham: University of Birmingham).

HARRIS, P. L. (1978), 'Developmental Aspects of Memory', in M. M. Gruneberg, P. E. Morris, and R. N. Sykes (eds.), *Practical Aspects of Memory* (London: Academic Press), 369–77.

HASAN, R. (1981), 'What's Going On: A Dynamic View of Context in Language', in J. E. Copeland and P. W. Davis (eds.), *The 7th Lacus Forum 1980* (Columbia: Hornbeam Press), 106–21.

HASTIE, R., OSTROM, T. M., EBBESEN, E., WYER, R. S., HAMILTON, D. L., and CARLSTON, D. E. (1980) (eds.), *Person Memory: The Cognitive Basis of Social Perception* (Hillsdale, NJ: Lawrence Erlbaum).

HAUGELAND, J. (1987), 'An Overview of the Frame Problem', in Pylyshyn (1987), 77–94.

HAVILAND, S. E., and CLARK, H. H. (1974), 'What's New? Acquiring New Information as a Process in Comprehension', *Journal of Verbal Learning and Verbal Behavior*, 13: 512–21.

HAYES, P. J. (1971), 'A Logic of Actions', in B. Meltzer and D. Mitchie (eds.), *Machine Intelligence 6* (New York: Wiley), 495–520.

HERITAGE, J. (1984), *Garfinkel and Ethnomethodology* (Cambridge: Polity Press).

HERRMANN, D. J., and NEISSER, U. (1978), 'An Inventory of Everyday Memory Experiences', in M. M. Gruneberg, P. E. Morris, and R. N. Sykes (eds.), *Practical Aspects of Memory* (London: Academic Press), 35–51.

HEWITT, L. E. (1995), 'Anaphor in Subjective Contexts in Narrative Fiction', in Duchan, Bruder, and Hewitt (1995*b*), 325–39.

HICKS, S. D. (1995), 'Cultural Worlds in the Contemporary Novel', workshop presented at the XV Poetics and Linguistics Association Conference (Granada: University of Granada).

HINDS, J. (1978), 'Anaphora in Japanese Conversation', in J. Hinds (ed.), *Anaphora in Discourse* (Edmonton: Linguistic Research Inc.), 136–80.

HIRST, G. (1981), *Anaphora in Natural Language Understanding: A Survey* (Berlin: Springer-Verlag).

HJELMQUIST, J. (1984), 'Memory for Conversations', *Discourse Processes*, 7: 321–36.

HOCKETT, C. F. (1963), 'The Problem of Universals in Language', in J. H. Greenberg, *Universals of Language* (Cambridge, Mass.: MIT Press), 1–52.

HOEY, M. P. (1979), *Signalling in Discourse* (Discourse Analysis Monograph, 6; Birmingham: English Language Research Group, University of Birmingham).

—— (1983), *On the Surface of Discourse* (London: George Allen & Unwin).

—— (1986), 'Undeveloped Discourse: Some Factors Affecting the Adequacy of Children's Non-Fictional Written Discourses', in J. Harris and J. Wilkinson (eds.), *Reading Children's Writing: A Linguistic View* (London: Allen & Unwin), 74–92.

—— (1991), *Patterns of Lexis in Text* (Oxford: Oxford University Press).

HOGGART, R. (1958), *The Uses of Literacy* (Harmondsworth: Penguin).

HOLLAND, N. (1975), *5 Readers Reading* (New Haven: Yale University Press).

HOLUB, R. C. (1984), *Reception Theory: A Critical Introduction* (London: Methuen).

HOPPER, P. J. (1979), 'Aspect and Foregrounding in Discourse', in T. Givón (ed.), *Syntax and Semantics*, xii. *Syntax and Semantics* (New York: Academic Press), 213–41.

—— (1991), 'Dispersed Verbal Predicates in Vernacular Written Narrative', in L. A. Sutton, C. Johnson, and R. Shields (eds.), *Proceedings of the Seventeenth Annual Meeting of the Berkeley Linguistics Society: General and Parasession on the Grammar of Event Structure*, 402–13.

—— (1995), 'The Category "Event" in Natural Discourse and Logic', in W. Abraham, T. Givón, and S. A. Thompson (eds.), *Discourse Grammar and Typology: Papers in Honor of John W. M. Verhaar* (Amsterdam: John Benjamins), 139–50.

—— and THOMPSON, S. A. (1980), 'Transitivity in Grammar and Discourse', *Language*, 56: 251–99.

HULME, C. (1987), 'Reading Retardation', in Beech and Colley (1987), 245–70.

HUNT, G. F. (1978), 'Paragraphing, Identification and Discourse Types in Hanga', in Grimes (1978a), 237–47.

ISER, W. (1978), *The Act of Reading: A Theory of Aesthetic Response* (Baltimore: Johns Hopkins University Press).

ISHIGURO, H. (1990), *Leibniz's Philosophy of Logic and Language* (Cambridge: Cambridge University Press; first published 1972).

JACKSON, F. (1982), 'Epiphenomenal Qualia', *Philosophical Quarterly*, 32: 127–36.

—— (1986), 'What Mary Didn't Know', *Journal of Philosophy*, 83 (5): 291–5.

JAEGER, M. E., and ROSNOW, R. C. (1988), 'Contextualism and its Implications for Psychological Inquiry', *British Journal of Psychology*, 79: 63–75.

JAMES, H. (1962), *The Art of the Novel* (New York: Charles Scribner).

—— (1967), *The Turn of the Screw* (Airmont: Airmont Publishing).

JAMES, P. D. (1989), *A Taste for Death* (Harmondsworth: Penguin).

JAMES, W. (1890), *The Principles of Psychology* (New York: Dover Publications).

JEFFERSON, G. (1972), 'Side Sequences', in D. Sudnow (ed.), *Studies in Social Interaction* (New York: Free Press), 294–338.

—— (1978), 'Sequential Aspects of Story-Telling in Conversation', in J. Schenkein (ed.), *Studies in the Organization of Conversational Interaction* (New York: Academic Press), 219–48.

JOHNSON, M. (1987), *The Body in the Mind: The Bodily Basis of Meaning, Imagination and Reason* (Chicago: Chicago University Press).

JOHNSON, M. K. (1988), 'Reality Monitoring: an Experimental Phenomenological Approach', *Journal of Experimental Psychology: General*, 117 (4): 390–4.

—— and RAYE, C. L. (1981), 'Reality Monitoring', *Psychological Review*, 88: 67–85.

—— BRANSFORD, J. D., and SOLOMON, S. (1973), 'Memory for Tacit Implications of Sentences', *Journal of Experimental Psychology*, 98: 203–5.

JOHNSON, R. E. (1986), 'Remembering Prose: Holistic or Piecemeal Losses?', *Journal of Memory and Language*, 25: 525–38.

JOHNSON-LAIRD, P. N. (1980), 'Mental Models in Cognitive Science', *Cognitive Science*, 4: 71–115.

—— (1981), 'Mental Models of Meaning', in A. K. Joshi, B. L. Webber, and I. A. Sag (eds.), *Elements of Discourse Understanding* (Cambridge: Cambridge University Press), 106–26.

—— (1983), *Mental Models* (Cambridge: Cambridge University Press).

—— (1988), *The Computer and the Mind: An Introduction to Cognitive Science* (London: Fontana).

—— (1993), *Human and Machine Thinking* (Hillsdale, NJ: Lawrence Erlbaum).

—— and GARNHAM, A. (1980), 'Descriptions and Discourse Models', *Linguistics and Philosophy*, 3: 371–93.

—— and STEVENSON, R. (1970), 'Memory for Syntax', *Nature*, 227: 412.

—— and WASON, P. C. (1977), 'A Theoretical Analysis of Insight into a Reasoning Task', in P. N. Johnson-Laird and P. C. Wason (eds.), *Thinking: Readings in Cognitive Science* (Cambridge: Cambridge University Press), 143–57.

—— LEGRENZI, P., and SONINO-LEGRENZI, M. (1972), 'Reasoning and a Sense of Reality', *British Journal of Psychology*, 631: 395–400.

JONES, P. (1994), 'The Great Anaphora Hoax: A Radical Critique of Syntactic and Pseudo-Pragmatic Approaches to Co-Reference Phenomena', paper presented at the XIV Poetics and Linguistics Association Conference (Sheffield: Sheffield Hallam University).

JORDAN, M. P. (1984), *Rhetoric of Everyday English Texts* (London: George Allen & Unwin).

JOYCE, J. (1969), *Ulysses* (Harmondsworth: Penguin).

JUDGE, B. (1985), *Thinking about Things: A Philosophical Study of Representation* (Edinburgh: Scottish Academic Press).

JUST, M. A., and CARPENTER, P. A. (1978), 'Inference Processes during Reading: Reflections from Eye Fixations', in J. W. Senders, D. F. Fisher, and R. A. Monty (eds.), *Eye Movements and the Higher Psychological Functions* (Hillsdale, NJ: Lawrence Erlbaum), 157–74.

KAMP, J. A. W. (1979), 'Events, Instants and Temporal Reference', in R. Bäuerle, U. Egli, and A. von Stechow (eds.), *Semantics from Different Points of View* (Berlin: Springer-Verlag), 376–417.

—— (1981), 'A Theory of Truth and Semantic Representation', in J. Groenendijk, T. Janssen, and M. Stokhof (eds.), *Formal Methods in the Study of Language*, i (Amsterdam: Mathematical Centre Tracts), 277–322.

KANTOR, R. N. (1977), 'The Management and Comprehension of Discourse Connection by Pronouns in English', Ph.D. thesis (Ohio: Ohio State University).

KARTTUNEN, L. (1976), 'Discourse Referents', in J. D. McCawley (ed.), *Syntax and Semantics*, vii. *Notes from the Linguistic Underground* (New York: Academic Press, first produced 1969), 363–85.

KATZENBERGER, I. (1994), 'Cognitive, Linguistic, and Developmental Factors in the Narration of a Picture Series', Ph.D. thesis (Tel Aviv: Tel Aviv University, published in Hebrew (English summary)).

KEMPSON, R. M. (1988) (ed.), *Mental Representations: The Interface between Language and Reality* (Cambridge: Cambridge University Press).

KENNEDY, A. (1987), 'Eye Movements, Reading Skill and the Spatial Code', in Beech and Colley (1987), 169–86.

KERR, J. S., and UNDERWOOD, G. (1983), 'Fixation Time on Anaphoric Pronouns Decreases with Congruity of Reference', in A. G. Gale and F. Johnson (eds.), *Theoretical and Applied Aspects of Eye Movement Research: Selected/Edited Proceedings of The Second European Conference on Eye Movements* (Amsterdam: North Holland), 195–203.

KINTSCH, W., and VAN DIJK, T. A. (1978), 'Toward a Model of Text Comprehension and Production', *Psychological Review*, 85: 363–94.

—— MANDEL, T. S., and KOZMINSKY, E. (1977), 'Summarizing Scrambled Stories', *Memory and Cognition*, 5 (5): 547–52.

KNUF, J. (1994), 'Deixis and Paradeixis in the Talk of Alzheimer's Patients', paper presented at the First International Colloquium on Deixis (Lexington: University of Kentucky).

KORIAT, A., BEN-ZUR, H., and SHEFFER, D. (1988), 'Telling the Same Story Twice: Output Monitoring and Age', *Journal of Memory and Language*, 27: 23–39.

KOSSLYN, S. M. (1975), 'Information Representation in Visual Images', *Cognitive Psychology*, 7: 341–70.

KOSSLYN, S. M. (1980), *Image and Mind* (Cambridge, Mass.: Harvard University Press).

KRONFELD, A. (1990), *Reference and Computation: An Essay in Applied Philosophy of Language* (Cambridge: Cambridge University Press).

KRUSI, P. (1978), 'Mumuye Discourse Structure', in Grimes (1978*a*), 267–72.

KUNO, S. (1976), 'Subject, Theme, and the Speaker's Empathy: A Re-Examination of Relativization Phenomena', in C. Li (ed.), *Subject and Topic* (New York: Academic Press), 417–44.

—— and KABURAKI, E. (1977), 'Empathy and Syntax', *Linguistic Inquiry*, 8: 627–72.

LABERGE, D., and SAMUELS, S. J. (1985), 'Toward a Theory of Automatic Information Processing', in H. Singer and R. B. Ruddell (eds.), *Theoretical Models and Processes of Reading* (Newark, Del.: International Reading Association), 689–718.

LABOV, W. (1972*a*), *Language in the Inner City* (Pennsylvania: University of Pennsylvania Press).

—— (1972*b*), *Sociolinguistic Patterns* (Oxford: Basil Blackwell).

—— and WALETZKY, J. (1967), 'Narrative Analysis: Oral Versions of Personal Experience', in J. Helm (ed.), *Essays on the Verbal and Visual Arts: Proceedings of the 1966 Annual Spring Meeting of the American Ethnological Society* (Seattle: American Ethnological Society), 12–44.

LAKOFF, G. (1971), 'The Role of Deduction in Grammar', in C. J. Fillmore and D. T. Langendoen (eds.), *Studies in Linguistic Semantics* (New York: Holt, Rinehart & Winston), 62–70.

—— (1972), 'Structural Complexity in Fairy Tales', *The Study of Man*, 1: 128–90.

—— (1987), *Women, Fire and Dangerous Things: What Categories Reveal about the Mind* (Chicago: University of Chicago Press).

—— and JOHNSON, M. (1980), *Metaphors We Live By* (Chicago: University of Chicago Press).

LANGACKER, R. W. (1986), 'An Introduction to Cognitive Grammar', *Cognitive Science*, 10: 1–40.

—— (1987), *Foundations of Cognitive Grammar*, i (Stanford, Calif.: Stanford University Press).

—— (1991), *Foundations of Cognitive Grammar*, ii (Stanford, Calif.: Stanford University Press).

LÁSZLÓ, J. (1987), 'Understanding and Enjoying: An Information Processing Approach to Reception', in L. Halász (ed.), *Literary Discourse: Aspects of Cognitive and Social Psychological Approaches* (Berlin: de Gruyter), 113–24.

LAWRENCE, D. H. (1949), *The Rainbow* (Harmondsworth: Penguin).

LE NY, J. F. (1980), 'Selective Activities and Elective Forgetting in the

Process of Understanding and in the Recall of Semantic Contents', in F. Klix and J. Hoffman (eds.), *Cognition and Memory* (Amsterdam: North Holland), 76–81.

LEAL, W. M. (1978), 'Who's Where in Chitwan Tharu Narratives', in Grimes (1978a), 190–207.

LEAVIS, F. R. (1962), *The Great Tradition* (Harmondsworth: Penguin; first published 1948).

LEE, H. (1960), *To Kill a Mockingbird* (New York: Popular Library).

LEE-SAMMONS, W. H., and WHITNEY, P. (1991), 'Reading Perspectives and Memory for Text: An Individual Differences Analysis', *Journal of Experimental Psychology: Learning, Memory and Cognition*, 17 (6): 1074–81.

LEECH, G. N. (1983), *Principles of Pragmatics* (London: Longman).

—— and SHORT, M. H. (1981), *Style in Fiction: A Linguistic Introduction to English Fictional Prose* (London: Longman).

LEHNERT, W. G. (1981), 'Plot Units and Narrative Summarization', *Cognitive Science*, 5 (4): 293–331.

LEIBNIZ, G. W. (1953), *Discourse on Metaphysics*, translated by P. G. Lucas and L. Grint (Manchester: Manchester University Press; written 1686).

LELAND, J. (1983a), 'In a Suburban Sitting Room', in *The Last Sandcastle* (Dublin: O'Brien Press), 38–69.

—— (1983b), 'Intrusion', in *The Last Sandcastle* (Dublin: O'Brien Press), 25–37.

—— (1983c), 'The Lake', in *The Last Sandcastle* (Dublin: O'Brien Press), 6–19.

LESSING, D. (1965), 'A Man and Two Women', in *A Man and Two Women* (St. Albans: Granada Publishing), 88–107.

—— (1972), *The Four-Gated City* (London: Grafton Books).

—— (1979), 'A Woman on a Roof', in *Collected Short Stories I: To Room Nineteen* (St Albans: Granada Publishing), 248–57.

LÉVI-STRAUSS, C. (1968/1977), *Structural Anthropology*, i and ii (London: Allen Lane).

LEVINSOHN, S. H. (1978), 'Participant Reference in Inga Narrative Discourse', in J. Hinds (ed.), *Anaphora in Discourse* (Edmonton: Linguistic Research Inc.), 69–136.

LEVINSON, S. C. (1983), *Pragmatics* (Cambridge: Cambridge University Press).

LEWIS, D. (1968), 'Counterpart Theory and Quantified Modal Logic', *Journal of Philosophy*, 65: 113–26.

—— (1973), *Counterfactuals* (Oxford: Basil Blackwell).

LINDE, C. (1974), 'The Linguistic Encoding of Spatial Information', Ph.D. thesis (Columbia: University of Columbia).

LINDE, C. (1979), 'Focus of Attention and the Choice of Pronouns in Discourse', in T. Givón (ed.), *Syntax and Semantics*, xii. *Discourse and Semantics* (New York: Academic Press), 337–54.

—— (1993), *Life Stories: The Creation of Coherence* (Oxford: Oxford University Press).

—— and LABOV, W. (1975), 'Spatial Networks as a Site for the Study of Language and Thought', *Language*, 51 (4): 924–39.

LINDSAY, D. (1987), *The Haunted Woman* (Edinburgh: Canongate).

LODGE, D. (1992), *The Art of Fiction* (Harmondsworth: Penguin).

LOFTUS, E. F. (1975), 'Leading Questions and the Eye-Witness Report', *Cognitive Psychology*, 7: 560–72.

—— MILLER, D. G., and BURNS, H. J. (1978), 'Semantic Integration of Verbal Information into Visual Memory', *Journal of Experimental Psychology: Human Learning and Memory*, 4: 19–31.

LONG, D. L., GOLDING, J. M., GRAESSER, A. C., and CLARK, L. F. (1990), 'Goal, Event, and State Inferences: An Investigation of Inference Generation During Story Comprehension', in A. C. Graesser and G. H. Bower (eds.), *Inferences and Text Comprehension* (London: Academic), 89–103.

LONGACRE, R. E. (1974), 'Narrative Versus Other Discourse Genre', in R. M. Brend (ed.), *Advances in Tagmemics* (Amsterdam: North Holland), 357–76.

—— (1983), *The Grammar of Discourse* (New York: Plenum Press).

LORMAND, E. (1990), 'Framing the Frame Problem', *Synthese*, 82: 353–74.

LOVELACE, E. A., and SOUTHALL, S. D. (1983), 'Memory for Words in Prose and their Locations on the Page', *Memory and Cognition*, 11 (5): 429–34.

LUCAS, M. M., TANENHAUS, M. K., and CARLSON, G. N. (1990), 'Levels of Representation in the Interpretation of Anaphoric Reference and Instrument Inference', *Memory and Cognition*, 18 (6): 611–31.

LURIA, A. R. (1975), *The Man with a Shattered World* (Harmondsworth: Penguin).

—— (1979), *The Making of a Mind: A Personal Account of Soviet Psychology*, ed. M. Cole and S. Cole (Cambridge, Mass.: Harvard University Press).

—— (1987), *The Mind of a Mnemonist* (Cambridge, Mass.: Harvard University Press; first published 1968).

LYONS, J. (1977), *Semantics*, i and ii (Cambridge: Cambridge University Press).

McCABE, A., and PETERSON, C. (1991) (eds.), *Developing Narrative Structure* (London: Lawrence Erlbaum).

McCARTHY, J. (1968), 'Programs with Common Sense', in M. L. Minsky (ed.), *Semantic Information Processing* (Cambridge, Mass.: MIT Press; first distributed/published 1958/1963), 403–418.

—— and HAYES, P. J. (1969), 'Some Philosophical Problems from the Standpoint of Artificial Intelligence', in B. Meltzer and D. Michie (eds.), *Machine Intelligence 4* (Edinburgh: Edinburgh University Press), 463–502.

McCARTHY, M. (1991), *Discourse Analysis for Language Teachers* (Cambridge: Cambridge University Press).

McCLELLAND, J. L., and RUMELHART, D. E. (1985), 'An Interactive Activation Model of Context Effects in Letter Perception: Part I. An Account of Basic Findings', in H. Singer and R. B. Ruddell (eds.), *Theoretical Models and Processes of Reading* (Newark, Del.: International Reading Association), 276–322.

—— —— and HINTON, G. (1986), 'The Appeal of PDP', in D. E. Rumelhart, J. L. McClelland, and the PDP Research Group (eds.), *Parallel Distributed Processing: Explorations in the Microstructure of Cognition*, i (Cambridge, Mass.: MIT Press), 3–44.

MACDONALD, M. C., and MacWHINNEY, B. (1990), 'Measuring Inhibition and Facilitation from Pronouns', *Journal of Memory and Language*, 29: 469–92.

McKOON, G., and RATCLIFF, R. (1980), 'The Comprehension Processes and Memory Structures Involved in Anaphoric Reference', *Journal of Verbal Learning and Verbal Behavior*, 19: 668–82.

—— —— (1981), 'The Comprehension Processes and Memory Structures Involved in Instrumental Inference', *Journal of Verbal Learning and Verbal Behavior*, 20: 671–82.

MACLEAN, I. (1986), 'Reading and Interpretation', in A. Jefferson and D. Robey (eds.), *Modern Literary Theory: A Comparative Introduction* (London: B. T. Batsford), 122–44.

MACLEOD, C. M. (1989), 'Word Context During Initial Exposure Influences Degree of Priming in Word Fragment Completion', *Journal of Experimental Psychology: Learning, Memory and Cognition*, 15 (3): 398–406.

McTEAR, M. (1987), *The Articulate Computer* (Oxford: Basil Blackwell).

MALT, B. L. (1985), 'The Role of Discourse Structure in Understanding Anaphora', *Journal of Memory and Language*, 24: 271–89.

MANDLER, J. M. (1984), *Stories, Scripts, and Scenes: Aspects of Schema Theory* (Hillsdale, NJ: Lawrence Erlbaum).

—— and JOHNSON, N. S. (1977), 'Remembrance of Things Parsed: Story Structure and Recall', *Cognitive Psychology*, 9: 111–51.

MANI, K., and JOHNSON-LAIRD, P. N. (1982), 'The Mental Representation of Spatial Descriptions', *Memory and Cognition*, 10 (2): 181–7.

MANN, W. C., and THOMPSON, S. A. (1987), *Rhetorical Structure Theory: A Framework for the Analysis of Texts* (University of Southern California and Information Sciences Institute Research Report, RR-87-190).

MANN, W. C., and THOMPSON, S. A. (1988), 'Rhetorical Structure Theory: Toward a Functional Theory of Text Organization', *Text*, 8 (3): 243–81.

—— MATTHIESSEN, C. M. I. M., and THOMPSON, S. A. (1992), 'Rhetorical Structure Theory and Text Analysis', in W. C. Mann and S. A. Thompson (eds.), *Discourse Description: Diverse Linguistic Analyses of a Fund-Raising Text* (Amsterdam: John Benjamins), 39–78.

MARCHESE, L. (1978), 'Time Reference in Godie', in Grimes (1978a), 63–75.

MARR, D. (1985), 'Vision: The Philosophy and the Approach', in A. M. Aitkenhead and J. M. Slack (eds.), *Issues in Cognitive Modeling* (London and Hillsdale, NJ: Lawrence Erlbaum), 103–26.

MARSH, N. (1968), *Clutch of Constables* (London: Hamlyn).

MARTIN, M. (1978), 'Assessment of Individual Variation in Memory Ability', in M. M. Gruneberg, P. E. Morris, and R. N. Sykes (eds.), *Practical Aspects of Memory* (London: Academic Press), 354–65.

MELLISH, C. S. (1985), *Computer Interpretation of Natural Language Descriptions* (Chichester: Ellis Horwood).

MERRITT, M. (1976), 'On Questions Following Questions in Service Encounters', *Language in Society*, 5: 315–57.

MINSKY, M. L. (1977), 'Frame-System Theory', in P. N. Johnson-Laird and P. C. Wason (eds.), *Thinking: Readings in Cognitive Science* (Cambridge: Cambridge University Press), 355–76.

MITCHELL, D. C. (1987), 'Reading and Syntactic Analysis', in Beech and Colley (1987), 87–112.

MITCHELL, S. (1985), *The Token* (London: Futura).

MORGAN, J. L. (1978), 'Toward a Rational Model of Discourse Comprehension', in D. Waltz (ed.), *Theoretical Issues in Natural Language Processing 2* (Urbana: University of Illinois), 109–14.

MORRIS, D. (1978), *Manwatching: A Field Guide to Human Behaviour* (London: Grafton).

MORROW, D. G. (1986), 'Places as Referents in Discourse', *Journal of Memory and Language*, 25: 676–90.

—— BOWER, G. H., and GREENSPAN, S. L. (1990), 'Situation-Based Inferences during Narrative Comprehension', in A. C. Graesser and G. H. Bower (eds.), *Inferences and Text Comprehension* (London: Academic), 123–36.

MORTON, J., and BEKERIAN, D. (1986), 'Three Ways of Looking at Memory', in Sharkey (1986), 43–71.

MURDOCH, I. (1981), *Nuns and Soldiers* (Harmondsworth: Penguin).

—— (1986), *The Good Apprentice* (Harmondsworth: Penguin).

MURPHY, G. L. (1984), 'Establishing and Accessing References in Discourse', *Memory and Cognition*, 12 (5): 489–97.

MYERS, G. (1990), 'Making a Discovery: Narratives of Split Genes', in C. Nash (ed.), *Narrative in Culture* (London: Routledge), 102–26.

MYERS, J. L., and DUFFY, S. A. (1990), 'Causal Inferences and Text Memory', in A. C. Graesser and G. H. Bower (eds.), *Inferences and Text Comprehension* (San Diego: Academic), 159–73.

NAKHIMOVSKY, A., and RAPAPORT, W. J. (1989), 'Discontinuities in Narrative', in D. Vargha (ed.), *COLING 88 BUDAPEST: Proceedings of the 12th International Conference on Computational Linguistics*, ii (Budapest: John von Neumann Society for Computer Sciences), 465–70.

NEISSER, U. (1976), *Cognition and Reality* (San Francisco: W. H. Freeman).

—— (1978), 'Memory: What are the Important Questions?', in M. M. Gruneberg, P. E. Morris, and R. N. Sykes (eds.), *Practical Aspects of Memory* (London: Academic Press), 3–24.

NEWMAN, J. F. (1978), 'Participant Orientation in Longuda Folk Tales', in Grimes (1978a) 91–104.

NOBLE, H. M. (1988), *Natural Language Processing* (Oxford: Basil Blackwell).

O'BRIEN, E. J. (1987), 'Antecedent Search Processes and the Structure of Text', *Journal of Experimental Psychology: Learning, Memory and Cognition*, 13 (2): 278–90.

—— DUFFY, S. A., and MYERS, J. L. (1986), 'Anaphoric Inferences during Reading', *Journal of Experimental Psychology: Learning, Memory and Cognition*, 12 (3): 346–52.

—— PLEWES, P. S., and ALBRECHT, J. E. (1990), 'Antecedent Retrieval Processes', *Journal of Experimental Psychology: Learning, Memory and Cognition*, 16 (2): 241–9.

—— SHANK, D. M., MYERS, J. L., and RAYNER, K. (1988), 'Elaborative Inferences during Reading: Do They Occur On-Line?', *Journal of Experimental Psychology: Learning, Memory and Cognition*, 14 (3): 410–20.

OAKHILL, J. (1986), 'Effects of Time of Day on the Integration of Information in Text', *British Journal of Psychology*, 77: 481–8.

—— and DAVIES, A.-M. (1991), 'The Effects of Text Expectancy on Quality of Note-Taking and Recall of Text at Different Times of Day', *British Journal of Psychology*, 82: 179–89.

—— and GARNHAM, A. (1988), *Becoming a Skilled Reader* (Oxford: Basil Blackwell).

—— and YUILL, N. (1995), 'Learning to Understand Written Language', in E. Funnell and M. Stuart (eds.), *Learning to Read: Psychology in the Classroom* (Oxford: Basil Blackwell), 161–85.

—— GARNHAM, A., and VONK, W. (1989), 'The On-Line Construction of Discourse Models', *Language and Cognitive Processes*, 4, (3/4): 263–86.

OGDEN, C. K., and RICHARDS, I. A. (1985), *The Meaning of Meaning* (London: Ark Paperbacks; first published 1923).

OZIEBLOWSKA, B. (1994), 'Generic Pronouns in Current Academic Writing', M.Phil. thesis (Glasgow: University of Glasgow).

PAGE, N. (1973), *Speech in the English Novel* (London: Longman).

PAVEL, T. G. (1986), *Fictional Worlds* (Cambridge, Mass.: Harvard University Press).

PEAKE, M. (1985*a*), *Gormenghast* (London: Methuen).

—— (1985*b*), *Titus Groan* (London: Methuen).

PEIRCE, C. S. (1932), *Collected Papers of Charles Sanders Peirce*, ii. *Elements of Logic*, ed. C. Hartshorne and P. Weiss (Cambridge, Mass.: Harvard University Press).

PENROSE, R. (1987), 'Minds, Machines and Mathematics', in Blakemore and Greenfield (1987), 259–76.

—— (1989), *The Emperor's New Mind: Concerning Computers, Minds and the Laws of Physics* (Oxford: Oxford University Press).

—— (1995), *Shadows of the Mind: A Search for the Missing Science of Consciousness* (London: Vintage).

PERRIN, M. (1978), 'Who's Who in Mambila Folk Stories', in Grimes (1978*a*), 105–18.

PETERSON, C., and McCABE, A. (1991), 'Children's Connective Use and Narrative Macrostructure', in McCabe and Peterson (1991), 29–53.

PETROS, T. V., BECKWORTH, B. E., and ANDERSON, M. (1990), 'Individual Differences in the Effects of Time of Day and Passage Difficulty on Prose Memory in Adults', *British Journal of Psychology*, 81: 63–72.

PIAGET, J. (1955), *The Language and Thought of the Child* (New York: World Meridian).

—— (1966), *The Growth of Logical Thinking* (London: Routledge & Kegan Paul).

PITRAT, J. (1988), *An Artificial Intelligence Approach to Understanding Natural Language* (London: North Oxford Academic).

PLATO, 'The Republic', in *Plato: The Collected Dialogues*, ed. E. Hamilton and H. Cairus (Princeton, NJ: Princeton University Press, 1963).

POLANYI, L. (1985*a*), *Telling the American Story: A Structural and Cultural Analysis of Conversational Storytelling* (Norwood, NJ: Ablex).

—— (1985*b*), 'Conversational Storytelling', in T. A. van Dijk (ed.), *Handbook of Discourse Analysis*, iii. *Discourse and Dialogue* (London: Academic Press), 183–201.

POLLINA, L. K., GREENE, A. L., TUNICK, R. H., and PUCKETT, J. M. (1992), 'Dimensions of Everyday Life in Young Adulthood', *British Journal of Psychology*, 85: 305–21.

POUNDSTONE, W. (1991), *Labyrinths of Reason: Paradox, Puzzles and the Frailty of Knowledge* (Harmondsworth: Penguin).

PRINCE, E. F. (1981), 'Toward a Taxonomy of Given–New Information', in P. Cole (ed.), *Radical Pragmatics* (New York: Academic), 223–55.

PRINCE, G. (1973), *A Grammar of Stories: An Introduction* (The Hague: Mouton).

—— (1982), *Narratology: The Form and Functioning of Narrative* (Berlin: Mouton).

PROPP, V. (1968), *Morphology of the Folktale*, ed. L. A. Wagner (Austin: University of Texas Press).

PYLYSHYN, Z. W. (1973), 'What the Mind's Eye Tells the Mind's Brain: A Critique of Mental Imagery', *Psychological Bulletin*, 80: 1–24.

—— (1987) (ed.), *The Robot's Dilemma: The Frame Problem in Artificial Intelligence* (Norwood, NJ: Ablex).

QUILLIAN, M. R. (1968), 'Semantic Memory', in M. L. Minsky (ed.), *Semantic Information Processing* (Cambridge, Mass.: MIT Press), 227–70.

QUIRK, R. (1986), *Words at Work: Lectures on Textual Structure* (London: Longman).

—— GREENBAUM, S., LEECH, G., and SVARTVIK, J. (1985), *A Comprehensive Grammar of the English Language* (London: Longman).

RABBITT, P., and ABSON, V. (1990), ' "Lost and Found": Some Logical and Methodological Limitations of Self-Report Questionnaires as Tools to Study Cognitive Ageing', *British Journal of Psychology*, 81: 1–16.

RAVELLI, L. J. (1991), 'Language from a Dynamic Perspective: Models in General and Grammar in Particular', Ph.D. thesis (Birmingham: University of Birmingham).

REASON, J. T., and MYCIELSKA, K. (1982), *Absent Minded? The Psychology of Mental Lapses and Everyday Errors* (Englewood Cliffs, NJ: Prentice-Hall).

REDEKER, G. (1995), 'Voices in Journalistic Discourse', paper presented at the International Cognitive Linguistic Association Conference (Albuquerque: University of New Mexico).

REICHMAN, R. (1985), *Getting Computers to Talk Like You and Me: Discourse Context, Focus and Semantics (An ATN Model)* (Cambridge, Mass.: Bradford/MIT Press).

REINHART, T. (1983), *Anaphora and Semantic Interpretation* (London: Croom Helm).

RENDELL, R. (1991), *Going Wrong* (London: Arrow).

RESCHER, N. (1973), 'The Ontology of the Possible', in M. K. Munitz (ed.), *Logic and Ontology* (New York: New York University Press), 213–28.

RIEGER, C. J. (1974), 'Conceptual Memory: A Theory and Computer Program for Processing the Meaning Content of Natural Language Utterances', Ph.D. thesis (Palo Alto, Calif.: Stanford University).

—— (1975), 'Conceptual Memory', in R. C. Schank (ed.), *Conceptual Information Processing* (New York: Elsevier), 157–288.

RIEGER, C. J. (1976), 'An Organization of Knowledge for Problem Solving and Language Comprehension', *Artificial Intelligence*, 7: 89–127.

—— (1977), 'Spontaneous Computation in Cognitive Models', *Cognitive Science*, 1: 315–54.

—— (1979), 'Five Aspects of a Full Scale Story Comprehension Model', in N. V. Findler (ed.), *Associative Networks: Representation and Use of Knowledge by Computers* (New York: Academic Press), 425–62.

RIESBECK, C. K. (1982), 'Realistic Language Comprehension', in W. G. Lehnert and M. H. Ringle (eds.), *Strategies for Natural Language Processing* (Hillsdale, NJ: Lawrence Erlbaum), 37–54.

RIMMON-KENAN, S. (1983), *Narrative Fiction: Contemporary Poetics* (London: Methuen).

ROCHESTER, S., and MARTIN, J. R. (1979), *Crazy Talk: A Study of the Discourse of Schizophrenic Speakers* (New York: Plenum).

ROSCH, E. (1977), 'Linguistic Relativity', in P. N. Johnson-Laird and P. C. Wason (eds.), *Thinking: Readings in Cognitive Science* (Cambridge: Cambridge University Press), 501–19.

RUMELHART, D. E. (1975), 'Notes on a Schema for Stories', in D. G. Bobrow and A. Collins (eds.), *Representation and Understanding: Studies in Cognitive Science* (New York: Academic Press), 211–36.

—— and NORMAN, D. A. (1983), 'Representation in Memory', in R. C. Atkinson, R. J. Herrnstein, G. Lindzey, and R. D. Luce (eds.), *Stevens' Handbook of Experimental Psychology* (New York: John Wiley), 511–87.

RUSSELL, B. (1937), *A Critical Exposition of the Philosophy of Leibniz* (London: George Allen & Unwin; first published 1900).

RYAN, M.-L. (1991), *Possible Worlds: Artificial Intelligence and Narrative Theory* (Bloomington and Indianapolis: Indiana University Press).

SACHS, J. S. (1967), 'Recognition Memory for Syntactic and Semantic Aspects of Connected Discourse', *Perception and Psychophysics*, 2 (9): 437–42.

SACKS, H. (1976), 'On Formulating Context', *Pragmatics Microfiche*, 1 (7–8): F5–G8.

—— (1989), 'An Analysis of the Course of a Joke's Telling in Conversation', in R. Bauman and J. Sherzer (eds.), *Explorations in the Ethnography of Speaking* (Cambridge: Cambridge University Press), 337–53.

—— (1992a), *Lectures on Conversation*, i, ed. G. Jefferson (Oxford: Basil Blackwell).

—— (1992b), *Lectures on Conversation*, ii, ed. G. Jefferson (Oxford: Basil Blackwell).

—— (1992c), 'The Baby Cried. The Mommy Picked It Up', lecture presented 1966, in H. Sacks (1992a), 236–42.

—— (1992d), ' "What's Going On" in a Lay Sense; Tracking Co-

Participants; Context Information; Pre-Positioned Laughter; Interpreting Utterances Not Directed To One', lecture presented 1970, in H. Sacks (1992*b*), 269–81.

—— (1992*e*), 'Poetics; Tracking Co-participants; Touched-Off Topics; Stepwise Topical Movement', lecture presented 1971, in H. Sacks (1992*b*), 291–302.

—— (1992*f*), 'Selecting Identifications', lecture presented 1971, in H. Sacks (1992*b*), 444–52.

—— SCHEGLOFF, E. A., and JEFFERSON, G. (1974), 'A Simplest Systematics for the Organisation of Turn-Taking for Conversation', *Language*, 50: 696–735.

SACKS, O. (1985), *The Man who Mistook his Wife for a Hat* (London: Pan Books).

SAG, I. A., and HANKAMER, J. (1984), 'Toward a Theory of Anaphoric Processing', *Linguistics and Philosophy*, 7: 325–45.

SAMUELS, S. J. (1985), 'Word Recognition', in H. Singer and R. B. Ruddell (eds.), *Theoretical Models and Processes of Reading* (Newark, Del.: International Reading Association), 256–75.

SANDERS, J. (1994), 'Perspective in Narrative Discourse', Ph.D. thesis (Tilburg: University of Tilburg).

—— (1995), 'Mental Spaces and Attribution: On Readers' Representation of Perspective in Discourse', paper presented at the International Cognitive Linguistic Association Conference (Albuquerque: University of New Mexico).

SANFORD, A. J., and GARROD, S. C. (1981), *Understanding Written Language: Explorations in Comprehension beyond the Sentence* (Chichester: John Wiley & Sons).

—— —— (1989), 'What, When and How?: Questions of Immediacy in Anaphoric Reference Resolution', *Language and Cognitive Processes*, 4 (3/4): 235–62.

—— —— LUCAS, A., and HENDERSON, R. (1984), 'Pronouns Without Explicit Antecedents?', *Journal of Semantics*, 2 (3/4): 303–18.

SCHANK, R. C. (1972), 'Conceptual Dependency: A Theory of Natural Language Processing', *Cognitive Psychology*, 3: 552–631.

—— (1982), *Dynamic Memory: A Theory of Reminding and Learning in Computers and People* (Cambridge: Cambridge University Press).

—— (1984), *The Cognitive Computer* (Reading, Mass.: Addison-Wesley).

—— and ABELSON, R. P. (1977*a*), *Scripts, Plans, Goals and Understanding: An Enquiry into Human Knowledge Structures* (Hillsdale, NJ: Lawrence Erlbaum).

—— (1977*b*), 'Scripts, Plans, and Knowledge', in P. N. Johnson-Laird and P. C. Wason (eds.), *Thinking: Readings in Cognitive Science* (Cambridge: Cambridge University Press), 421–32.

306   Bibliography

SCHEGLOFF, E. A. (1972), 'Sequencing in Conversational Openings', in J.
J. Gumperz and D. H. Hymes (eds.), *Directions in Sociolinguistics* (New
York: Holt, Rinehart, & Winston), 346–80.
—— (1978), 'On some Questions and Ambiguities in Conversation', in W.
U. Dressler (ed.), *Current Trends in Textlinguistics* (Berlin: de Gruyter),
81–102.
—— (1979), 'The Relevance of Repair to Syntax-for-Conversation', in T.
Givón (ed.), *Syntax and Semantics*, xii. *Discourse and Semantics* (New
York: Academic Press), 261–86.
—— (1982), 'Discourse as an Interactional Achievement: Some Uses of
"Uh Huh" and Other Things that come between Sentences', in D.
Tannen (ed.), *Analyzing Discourse: Text and Talk*, Georgetown University
Round Table on Languages and Linguistics, 1981 (Washington:
Georgetown University Press), 71–93.
—— (1987a), 'Recycled Turn Beginnings: A Precise Repair Mechanism
in Conversation's Turn-Taking Organisation', in G. Button and J. R. E.
Lee (eds.), *Talk and Social Organization* (Clevedon and Philadelphia:
Multilingual Matters), 70–85.
—— (1987b), 'Analyzing Single Episodes of Interaction: An Exercise in
Conversation Analysis', *Social Psychology Quarterly*, 50 (2): 101–14.
—— (1988a), 'Presequences and Indirection: Applying Speech Act
Theory to Ordinary Conversation', *Journal of Pragmatics*, 12: 55–62.
—— (1988b), 'Discourse as an Interactional Achievement II: An Exercise
in Conversation Analysis' in D. Tannen (ed.), *Linguistics in Context: Connecting Observation and Understanding, Lectures from the 1985 LSA/
TESOL and NEH Institutes* (Norwood, NJ: Ablex), 135–58.
—— (1992), 'In Another Context', in A. Duranti and C. Goodwin (eds.),
Rethinking Context: Language as an Interactive Phenomenon (Cambridge:
Cambridge University Press), 191–227.
—— and SACKS, H. (1973), 'Opening Up Closings', *Semiotica*, 7 (4): 289–
327.
—— JEFFERSON, G., and SACKS, H. (1977), 'The Preference for Self-Cor-
rection in the Organization of Repair in Conversation', *Language*, 53:
361–82.
SCHIFFRIN, D. (1987a), *Discourse Markers* (Cambridge: Cambridge University Press).
—— (1987b), 'Toward an Empirical Base in Pragmatics', Review Article
of Stephen Levinson's *Pragmatics*, *Language in Society*, 16 (3): 381–95.
—— (1994), *Approaches to Discourse* (Oxford: Blackwell).
SCHOTTELNDREYER, B. (1978), 'Narrative Discourse in Sherpa', in Grimes
(1978a), 248–66.
SCHUSTER, E. (1989), 'Anaphoric Reference to Events and Actions: A
Representation and its Advantages', in D. Vargha (ed.), *COLING 88*

BUDAPEST: *Proceedings of the 12th International Conference on Computational Linguistics*, ii (Budapest: John von Neumann Society for Computer Sciences), 602–7.

SCRIVEN, M. (1963), 'The Mechanical Concept of Mind', in K. M. Sayre and F. J. Crosson (eds.), *The Modeling of Mind* (South Bend, Ind.: University of Notre Dame Press), 243–54.

SEARLE, J. R. (1969), *Speech Acts: An Essay on the Philosophy of Language* (Cambridge: Cambridge University Press).

—— (1980), 'Minds, Brains and Programs', *Behavioral and Brain Sciences*, 3: 417–24.

—— (1984), *Minds, Brains and Science* (London: BBC).

—— (1987), 'Minds and Brains without Programs', in Blakemore and Greenfield (1987), 209–33.

SEGAL, E. M. (1995a), 'Narrative Comprehension and the Role of Deictic Shift Theory', in Duchan, Bruder, and Hewitt (1995b), 3–17.

—— (1995b), 'A Cognitive Phenomenological Theory of Fictional Narrative', in Duchan, Bruder, and Hewitt (1995b), 61–78.

SELDEN, R. (1989), *A Reader's Guide to Contemporary Literary Theory* (New York: Harvester Wheatsheaf).

SEMINO, E. (1995), 'Schema Theory and the Analysis of Text Worlds in Poetry', *Language and Literature*, 4 (2): 79–108.

SEYMOUR, P. H. K. (1987), 'Word Recognition Processes: An Analysis based on Format Distortion Effects', in Beech and Colley (1987), 31–55.

SHAPIRO, S. C. (1987) (ed.), *Encyclopedia of Artificial Intelligence*, i (New York, and Chichester: John Wiley).

SHARKEY, N. E. (1986) (ed.), *Advances in Cognitive Science*, i (Chichester: Ellis Horwood).

—— and BROWN, G. D. A. (1986), 'Why Artificial Intelligence Needs an Empirical Foundation', in M. Yazdani (ed.), *Artificial Intelligence: Principles and Applications* (London: Chapman & Hall), 267–93.

—— and PFEIFER, R. (1984), 'Uncomfortable Bedfellows: Artificial Intelligence and Cognitive Psychology', in M. Yazdani and A. Narayanan (eds.), *Artificial Intelligence: Human Effects* (Chichester: Ellis Horwood), 163–72.

SHEBILSKE, W. L., and FISHER, D. F. (1983), 'Eye Movements and Context Effects During Reading of Extended Discourse', in K. Rayner (ed.), *Eye Movements in Reading: Perceptual and Language Processes* (New York: Academic Press), 153–79.

SHEFFLER, M. (1978), 'Munduruku Discourse', in Grimes (1978a), 119–42.

SIDNER, C. L. (1978), 'The Use of Focus as a Tool for Disambiguation of Definite Noun Phrases', in D. Waltz (ed.), *Theoretical Issues in Natural Language Processing 2* (Urbana: University of Illinois), 86–95.

308 *Bibliography*

SIDNER, C. L. (1979*a*), 'Disambiguating References and Interpreting Sentence Purpose in Discourse', in P. H. Winston and R. H. Brown (eds.), *Artificial Intelligence: An MIT Perspective*, i. *Expert Problem Solving, Natural Language Understanding, Intelligent Computer Coaches, Representation and Learning* (Cambridge, Mass.: MIT Press), 231–52.

—— (1979*b*), 'Towards a Computational Theory of Definite Anaphora Comprehension in English Discourse', Ph.D. thesis (Cambridge, Mass.: MIT Press).

—— (1983*a*), 'Focusing and Discourse', *Discourse Processes*, 6: 107–30.

—— (1983*b*), 'Focusing in the Comprehension of Definite Anaphora', in M. Brady and R. C. Berwick (eds.), *Computational Models of Discourse* (Cambridge, Mass.: MIT Press), 267–328.

SIMPSON, J. (1989), *Touching the Void* (London: Pan).

SIMPSON, P. (1993), *Language, Ideology and Point of View* (London: Routledge).

SINCLAIR, J. McH. (1983), 'Planes of Discourse', in S. N. A. Rizvil (ed.), *The Twofold Voice: Essays in Honour of Ramesh Mohan, Salzburg Studies in English Literature* (Salzburg: Universitat Salzburg), 70–91.

—— (1985), 'On the Integration of Linguistic Description', in T. A. van Dijk (ed.), *Handbook of Discourse Analysis*, ii. *Dimensions of Discourse* (London: Academic Press), 13–28.

—— (1987*a*) (ed.), *Collins COBUILD English Language Dictionary* (London: Collins).

—— (1987*b*) (ed.), *Looking Up: An Account of the COBUILD Project in Lexical Computing and the Development of the Collins COBUILD English Language Dictionary* (London: Collins ELT).

—— (1990) (ed.), *Collins COBUILD English Grammar* (London: Collins).

—— (1992), 'Trust the Text: The Implications are Daunting', in M. Davies and L. J. Ravelli (eds.), *Advances in Systemic Linguistics: Recent Theory and Practice* (London: Pinter), 5–19.

—— and COULTHARD, R. M. (1975), *Towards an Analysis of Discourse* (London: Oxford University Press).

SINGER, M., HALLDORSON, M., CLEAR, J., and ANDRUSIAK, P. (1992), 'Validation of Causal Bridging Inferences in Discourse Understanding', *Journal of Memory and Language*, 31: 507–24.

SMITH, F. (1985), *Reading* (Cambridge: Cambridge University Press).

SMYTH, M. M., MORRIS, P. E., LEVY, P., and ELLIS, A. W. (1987) (eds.), *Cognition in Action* (London: Lawrence Erlbaum).

SPARK, M. (1961), *Memento Mori* (Harmondsworth: Penguin).

SPEELMAN, C. P., and KIRSNER, K. (1990), 'The Representation of Text-Based and Situation-Based Information in Discourse Comprehension', *Journal of Memory and Language*, 29: 119–32.

SPERBER, D., and WILSON, D. (1986), *Relevance: Communication and Cognition* (Oxford: Basil Blackwell).

STEINBECK, J. (1961), *The Grapes of Wrath* (Harmondsworth: Penguin).

STERELNY, K. (1990), *The Representational Theory of Mind* (Oxford: Basil Blackwell).

STEVENSON, R. L. (1979), 'The Strange Case of Dr Jekyll and Mr Hyde' in *Dr Jekyll and Mr Hyde and Other Stories* (Harmondsworth: Penguin), 27–97.

STRAUB, P. (1979), *Ghost Story* (London: Jonathan Cape).

SUCHMAN, L. A. (1987), *Plans and Situated Actions: The Problem of Human-Machine Communication* (Cambridge: Cambridge University Press).

SULEIMAN, S. R., and CROSMAN, I. (1980) (eds.), *The Reader in the Text: Essays on Audience and Interpretation* (Princeton NJ: Princeton University Press).

TALMY, L. (1978), 'The Relation of Grammar to Cognition: A Synopsis', in D. Waltz (ed.), *Theoretical Issues in Natural Language Processing 2* (Urbana: University of Illinois), 14–24.

—— (1988), 'Force Dynamics in Language and Cognition', *Cognitive Science*, 12: 49–100.

TANNEN, D. (1980), 'A Comparative Analysis of Oral Narrative Strategies: Athenian Greek and American English', in Chafe (1980a), 51–87.

—— (1989), *Talking Voices: Repetition, Dialogue and Imagery in Conversational Discourse* (Cambridge: Cambridge University Press).

TAYLOR, D. (1978), 'Topicalisation in Tamang Narrative', in Grimes (1978a), 149–56.

TEMPLE, C. M. (1987), 'The Alexias', in Beech and Colley (1987), 271–95.

—— (1993), *The Brain: An Introduction to the Psychology of the Human Brain and Behaviour* (Harmondsworth: Penguin).

THOMPSON, S. A. (1987), ' "Subordination" and Narrative Event Structure', in Tomlin (1987), 435–54.

THORNDYKE, P. W. (1976), 'The Role of Inferences in Discourse Comprehension', *Journal of Learning and Verbal Behavior*, 15: 437–46.

—— (1977), 'Cognitive Structures in Comprehension and Memory of Narrative', *Psychology*, 9: 77–110.

TILL, R. E., MROSS, E. F., and KINTSCH, W. (1988), 'Time Course of Priming for Associate and Inference Words in a Discourse Context', *Memory and Cognition*, 16 (4): 283–98.

TOBA, S. (1978), 'Participant Focus in Khaling Narratives', in Grimes (1978a), 157–62.

TOMLIN, R. S. (1987a) (ed.), *Coherence and Grounding in Discourse* (Amsterdam: John Benjamins).

TOMLIN, R. S. (1987b), 'Linguistic Reflections of Cognitive Events', in Tomlin (1987a), 455–79.

TOMPKINS, J. P. (1980) (ed.), *Reader-Response Criticism: From Formalism to Post-Structuralism* (Baltimore: Johns Hopkins University Press).

TOOLAN, M. (1988), *Narrative: A Critical Linguistic Introduction* (London: Routledge).

TUCKER, N. (1981), *The Child and the Book* (Cambridge: Cambridge University Press).

TULVING, E. (1972), 'Episodic and Semantic Memory', in E. Tulving and W. Donaldson (eds.), *Organization of Memory* (New York: Academic Press), 382–403.

—— (1983), *Elements of Episodic Memory* (Oxford: Oxford University Press).

TURING, A. M. (1963), 'Computing Machinery and Intelligence', in E. A. Feigenbaum and J. Feldman (eds.), *Computers and Thought* (New York: McGraw-Hill; article first published 1950), 11–35.

USPENSKY, B. (1973), *A Poetics of Composition: The Structure of the Artistic Text and the Typology of a Compositional Form*, translated by V. Zavarin and S. Wittig (Berkeley: University of California Press; first published (in Russian) 1970).

VAN DIJK, T. A. (1980), *Macrostructures: An Interdisciplinary Study of Global Structures in Discourse, Interaction and Cognition* (Hillsdale, NJ: Lawrence Erlbaum).

—— and KINTSCH, W. (1983), *Strategies of Discourse Comprehension* (New York: Academic Press).

VENTOLA, E. (1990), 'Text and Reference', in A.-C. Lindeberg, N. E. Enkvist, and K. Wikberg (eds.), *Nordic Research on Text and Discourse* (Åbo: Åbo Academy Press), 223–35.

VINE, B. (1986), *A Dark-Adapted Eye* (Harmondsworth: Penguin).

—— (1987), *A Fatal Inversion* (Harmondsworth: Penguin).

WARR, P. B., and KNAPPER, C. (1968), *The Perception of People and Events* (London: John Wiley & Sons).

WATSON, J. D. (1970), *The Double Helix: A Personal Account of the Structure of DNA* (Harmondsworth: Penguin).

WATTERS, D. (1978), 'Speaker-Hearer Involvement in Kham', in Grimes (1978a), 1–18.

WEBBER, B. L. (1978), 'Description Formation and Discourse Model Synthesis', in D. Waltz (ed.), *Theoretical Issues in Natural Language Processing 2* (Urbana: University of Illinois), 42–50.

—— (1979), *A Formal Approach to Discourse Anaphora* (New York and London: Garland; reprinted Ph.D. thesis, Harvard University, 1978).

—— (1983), 'So What Can We Talk About Now?', in M. Brady and R. C. Berwick (eds.), *Computational Models of Discourse* (Cambridge, Mass.: MIT Press), 331–71.

Weekly Law Reports, The (1958), Volume 1 (London: The Incorporated Council of Law Reporting for England and Wales).

WEIZENBAUM, J. (1966), 'ELIZA—A Computer Program for the Study of Natural Language', *Communications of the Association for Computer Machinery*, 9: 36–45.

—— (1984), *Computer Power and Human Reason* (San Francisco: Freeman; first published 1976).

WELDON, F. (1984), *The Life and Loves of a She Devil* (London: Coronet).

WENTWORTH, P. (1977), *Poison in the Pen* (London: Coronet).

WERTH, P. N. (1984), *Focus, Coherence and Emphasis* (London: Croom Helm).

—— (1993), 'Accommodation and the Myth of Presupposition: The View from Discourse', *Lingua*, 89: 39–95.

—— (1994), 'Extended Metaphor: A Text World Account', *Language and Literature*, 3 (2): 79–108.

—— (1995), 'How to Build a World (In a Lot Less than Six Days, and using Only What's in your Head)', in K. Green (ed.), *New Essays in Deixis: Discourse, Narrative, Literature* (Amsterdam: Rodopi), 49–80.

—— (MS *a*), *Text Worlds: Representing Conceptual Space in Discourse*.

—— (MS *b*), 'Who's Who in Discourse: Anaphora as a Tracking Device'.

WESLEY, M. (1986), *Harnessing Peacocks* (London: Black Swan).

WHITMAN, L. (1982), 'A Dangerous Influence', in The Sheba Collective (ed.), *Everyday Matters: New Short Stories by Women* (London: Sheba Feminist Publishers), 125–41.

WIDDOWSON, H. G. (1984), 'Reference and Representation', in H. G. Widdowson (ed.), *Explorations in Applied Linguistics*, ii (Oxford: Oxford University Press), 150–9.

WIEBE, J. M. (1995), 'References in Narrative Text', in Duchan, Bruder, and Hewitt (1995*b*), 263–86.

—— and RAPAPORT, W. J. (1988), 'A Computational Theory of Perspective and Reference in Narrative', *Proceedings of the Association for Computational Linguistics* (Menlo Park, Calif.: Association for Computational Linguistics), 131–8.

WILKS, Y. (1982), 'Some Thoughts on Procedural Semantics', in W. G. Lehnert and M. H. Ringle (eds.), *Strategies for Natural Language Processing* (Hillsdale, NJ: Lawrence Erlbaum), 495–516.

WINOGRAD, T. (1972), *Understanding Natural Language* (New York: Academic Press).

WINTER, E. (1982), *Towards a Contextual Grammar of English* (London: George Allen & Unwin).

WISE, M. R. (1968), 'Identification of Participants in Discourse: A Study of Aspects of Form and Meaning in Nomatsiguenga', Ph.D. thesis (Ann Arbor: University of Michigan).

WOLL, S. B., and GRAESSER, A. C. (1982), 'Memory Discrimination for Information Typical or Atypical of Person Schemata', *Social Cognition*, 1 (4): 287–310.

WRIGHT, E. (1986), 'Modern Psychoanalytic Criticism', in A. Jefferson and D. Robey (eds.), *Modern Literary Theory: A Comparative Introduction* (London: B. T. Batsford), 145–65.

YOUNG, A. W., HAY, D. C., and ELLIS, A. W. (1985), 'The Faces that Launched a Thousand Slips: Everyday Difficulties and Errors in Recognising People', *British Journal of Psychology*, 6: 495–523.

YUILL, N., and OAKHILL, J. (1991), *Children's Problems in Text Comprehension: An Experimental Investigation* (Cambridge: Cambridge University Press).

YULE, G. (1981), 'New, Current and Displaced Entity Reference', *Lingua*, 55: 42–52.

—— (1982), 'Interpreting Anaphora Without Identifying Reference', *Journal of Semantics*, 1 (4): 315–23.

YUSSEN, S., HUANG, S.-T., MATHEWS, S., and EVANS, R. (1988), 'The Robustness and Temporal Course of the Story Schema's Influence on Recall', *Journal of Experimental Psychology: Learning, Memory and Cognition*, 14 (1): 173–9.

ZIMAN, J. (1991), *Reliable Knowledge: An Exploration of the Grounds for Belief in Science* (Cambridge: Canto; first published 1978).

ZUBIN, D. A., and HEWITT, L. E. (1995), 'The Deictic Center: A Theory of Deixis in Narrative', in Duchan, Bruder, and Hewitt (1995*b*), 129–55.

ZWAAN, R. A. (1993), *Aspects of Literary Comprehension* (Amsterdam: John Benjamins).

AUTHOR INDEX

This index contains works cited and principal authors.

Abelson, R. P. 24, 53, 55, 105
Adams, D., *Dirk Gently's Holistic Detective Agency* 123–4, 146
Adams, R., *Watership Down* 29
Allbritton, D. W. 90
Alshawi, H. 223 n.
Anderson, A. 27 n., 150, 209 n.
Anderson, J. R. 37, 92 n.
Ariel, M. 60, 203–4
Austin, J. L. 108

Baddeley, A. 92, 92 n.
Bakhtin, M. M. 109
Ballmer, T. T. 223 n.
Banfield, A. 39
Banks, L. R., *An End to Running* 160–1
Bar-Hillel, Y. 107
Barnes, J., *A History of the World in 10½ Chapters* 164
Bartlett, F. C. 23, 67, 69, 97 n.
Barwise, J. 107
Bateson, G. 164
Berman, R. A. 67 n., 105 n., 117 n., 243
Bernado, R. 9, 37, 59, 88 n., 258 n.
Black, J. B. 24, 32, 33
Blakemore, C. 52 n.
Bloomfield, L. 204 n.
Boden, M. 4 n., 5 n., 53 n., 55 n., 92 n., 95 n., 163
Bolinger, D. 27 n., 205 n.
Booth, W. 39
Bower, G. H. 24, 48–50, 91, 104, 228
Brewer, W. F. 23, 43 n., 91, 92 n.
Brookner, A., *A Start in Life* 249–50, 255
——, *Providence* 238–9, 248, 252
Brown, G. 27 n., 37–8, 97, 198, 201, 205 n., 231
Brown, G. D. A. 54 n.
Bruce, B. 39
Bruder, G. A. 39, 58, 107 n., 127 n., 219 n.
Bruner, J. S. 92 n., 93
Bühler, K. 107, 211 n.
Bullwinkle, C. L. [*See also* Sidner, C. L.] 216 n.

Carpenter, P. A. vi n., 229–30
Carter, D. 199 n.
Chafe, W. L. v, v n., 6 n., 7 n., 9, 10 n., 39, 44 n., 59–63, 59 n., 62 n., 74, 85, 96 n., 114, 116, 119 n., 135 n., 135–6, 200, 217, 217 n., 220–1, 223 n., 226 n., 234
Charniak, E. 4 n., 6, 8 n., 27, 87 n., 140–1, 159, 231

Chatman, S. ix n., 105, 105 n.
Chomsky, N. 9 n., 32
Christie, A., *Murder on the Orient Express* 31
——, *Sleeping Murder* 130–1, 144–5, 170–3, 184–5, 254, 255, 259
——, *The Murder of Roger Ackroyd* 120
Clancy, P. M. 37, 59, 62 n., 201, 209 n., 222
Clark, A. 51 n.
Clark, H. H. 4, 7, 15 n., 27, 27 n., 97 n., 204 n., 205 n., 225–6, 226 n., 227 n.
Cook, G. 10 n., 31
Cornish, F. 27 n., 205 n.
Coulthard, R. M. 9 n., 78
Crick, F. 52 n., 53 n.

Dahl, R., 'Genesis and Catastrophe: A True Story' 30
Dale, R. 38
de Beaugrande, R. 26, 67, 86, 90, 104, 110–12
Dennett, D. C. x n., 51, 52 n., 53, 54, 119, 119 n.
Downing, P. 59, 200
Dressler, W. 110
Dreyfus, J. H. 55, 55 n.
Du Bois, J. W. 27 n., 37, 59, 113, 201, 205 n., 243–4
Duchan, J. F. 39, 58, 107 n., 127 n., 219 n.
Dyer, M. G. 39

Eagleton, T. 3, 68 n., 69 n., 69–70
Eco, U. 68 n.
Edric, R., *A Lunar Eclipse* 181, 193–4
Ehrlich, K. 43 n., 88 n., 229–30
Emmott, C. 11 n., 14, 14 n., 58, 61, 61 n., 76, 86, 121 n., 181, 182, 192 n., 223 n., 225 n., 233, 271 n., 273 n.
Enkvist, N. E. 233 n.

Fauconnier, G. 10 n., 56, 56 n., 179–80
Faulkner, W., *The Sound and the Fury* 30
Fillmore, C. J. 8, 237 n.
Firbas, J. 59 n.
Fish, S. 70
Flanagan, O. x n., 51, 52 n., 54–5, 111, 274
Fleischman, S. 243
Fludernik, M. 39
Forster, E. M. 12 n., 105, 105 n.
Fowler, R. 29, 118 n.
Fowles, J., *The French Lieutenant's Woman* 213

Fox, B. A. 78, 86, 139–40, 206, 236, 244–5
Francis, D., *Whip Hand* 34
——, *Decider* 165–6
Frederiksen, C. H. 106 n.
Freeman, D. C. 56 n.
Freeman, M. H. 56 n.

Galbraith, M. 58
Gardam, J., 'A Seaside Garden' 169–70
——, 'An Unknown Child' 212–13
Gardner, H. 92 n.
Garfinkel, H. 7, 107
Garnham, A. vi n., ix n., 43 n., 64 n., 88 n.,
    89, 95 n., 109, 113, 199 n., 222 n., 270
Garrod, S. 8 n., 8–9, 27, 27 n., 62, 69, 86,
    88 n., 89, 89 n., 97, 97 n., 150, 205 n.,
    209 n., 226, 227
Genette, G. 135, 150, 236, 242
Gernsbacher, M. A. 40, 42 n., 89 n., 97 n.
Gerrig, R. J. 57–8, 90, 97
Gillion, L. A. 60 n., 221 n., 233
Givón, T. 27 n., 108, 159, 165, 200 n.,
    205 n., 209 n., 243
Goffman, E. 164, 166, 178–9, 265
Golding, W., *The Inheritors* 30
Gordon, P. C. 60 n., 221 n., 233
Graesser, A. C. 6 n., 44 n., 88 n., 89 n., 92 n.
Graham, W., *After the Act* 151–4, 177, 180–
    1, 210
Green, G. M. 107, 198 n., 200
Green, H., *I Never Promised You a Rose Garden*
    84–5, 204–5
Greenbaum, S. 14, 14 n., 200 n.
Greene, G., 'Jim Braddon and the War
    Criminal' 239–40
Greenfield, S. 52 n.
Greimas, A. J. 32
Grice, H. P. 7, 34, 79, 120, 237
Grimes, J. E. 135, 135 n., 150, 209 n., 223 n.,
    243–4
Grosz, B. J. x n., 4, 8 n., 60 n., 78, 87 n., 93 n.,
    98, 133, 136, 197, 200 n., 206, 216,
    221 n., 223, 223 n., 233, 234
Gundel, J. K. 27 n., 60

Halliday, M. A. K. 30, 59, 59 n., 85, 198 n.,
    198–9, 199 n., 200 n., 222, 231
Hankamer, J. 44 n., 202
Hasan, R. 85, 198 n., 198–9, 199, 199 n.,
    200 n., 222, 231, 267 n.
Haugeland, J. 115
Haviland, S. E. 7, 27 n., 97 n., 205 n., 225–6,
    227 n.
Hayes, P. J. 113, 113 n., 119
Hedberg, N. 27 n., 60
Heritage, J. 108
Hewitt, L. E. 39, 58, 107 n., 118 n., 127 n.,
    219 n.
Hinds, J. 223 n.

Hinton, G. 51
Hirst, G. 223 n.
Hockett, C. F. ix n.
Hoey, M. P. 33, 76–7, 79, 80, 81
Hoggart, R., *The Uses of Literacy* 262
Holland, N. 67, 69 n.
Hopper, P. J. 93 n., 105 n., 236, 243, 244

Iser, W. 7, 68 n.

James, H. 243
——, *The Turn of the Screw* 165
James, P. D., *A Taste for Death* 183, 192
James, W. 52, 275
Jefferson, G. 77, 77 n., 78, 160, 224–5
Johnson, M. 10 n., 56
Johnson, N. S. 32
Johnson-Laird, P. N. x, x n., 4, 4 n., 5 n., 21,
    42 n., 43 n., 43–48, 52 n., 55 n., 88 n.,
    89 n., 91, 92 n., 95 n., 109, 163, 202 n.,
    274
Jones, P. 86
Jordan, M. P. 33, 76
Joshi, A. K. 221 n., 233
Joyce, J., *Ulysses* 258 n.
Just, M. A. vi n., 229–30

Kamp, J. A. W. 37
Kantor, R. N. 223 n.
Karttunen, L. 37
Katzenberger, I. 117 n.
Kenney, H. J. 92 n.
Kintsch, W. vi n., 21, 37, 42 n., 43–4, 45 n.,
    74, 89 n., 92, 104, 109 n., 109–10, 200,
    204 n.
Koch, C. 52 n., 53 n.
Kosslyn, S. M. 115 n.

Labov, W. 50 n., 79, 91, 105 n., 236, 241
Lakoff, G. 10 n., 32, 56, 225
Langacker, R. W. 10 n., 56
László, J. 42, 91
Lawrence, D. H., *The Rainbow* 188, 208–9
Leavis, F. R. 69
Lee, H., *To Kill a Mockingbird* 30
Leech, G. N. 14, 14 n., 30, 30 n., 94, 107,
    200 n., 243
Lehnert, W. G. 39
Leland, J., 'In a Suburban Sitting-Room' 187,
    251
——, 'Intrusion' 192
——, 'The Lake' 149, 186, 191
Lessing, D., 'A Man and Two Women' 127,
    246–7, 248–9, 250, 253–4, 256, 257–8,
    268
——, 'A Woman on a Roof' 84
——, *The Four-Gated City* 181, 192
Lévi-Strauss, C. 32
Lewis, D. 179, 202 n.

Linde, C. ix n., 50 n., 78, 133, 138
Lindsay, D., *The Haunted Woman* 143
Lodge, D. 12 n.,
Loftus, E. F. 26, 92 n.
Longacre, R. E. 86
Luria, A. R. 35, 64–6, 67 n.
Lyons, J. 43 n., 201 n., 202, 202 n.

Malt, B. L. 93–4
Mandler, J. M. 24 n., 32
Mani, K. 43 n.
Mann, W. C. 33, 76–7, 96
Marsh, N., *Clutch of Constables* 180
Marshall, C. R. 4
Martin, J. R. x n., 66
Matthiessen, C. M. I. M. 33, 77
McCarthy, J. 113, 113 n.
McClelland, J. L. vi n., 51
Minsky, M. L. 23, 192 n.
Mitchell, S., *The Token* 168, 181–2, 189, 191
Morgan, J. L. 200
Morris, D., *Manwatching: A Field Guide to Human Behaviour* 263–4
Morrow, D. G. 48–50, 91, 104, 209 n., 228
Murdoch, I., *Nuns and Soldiers* 129, 238, 261
——, *The Good Apprentice* 145
Nakhimovsky, A. W. J. 87 n.
Neisser, U. 92
Noble, H. M. 178
Norman, D. A. 44 n.

Oakhill, J. ix n., 68, 88 n., 91, 93, 95 n., 199 n., 200, 270
Ozieblowska, B. 263 n.

Pavel, T. G. 58 n.
Peake, M., *Gormenghast* 167
——, *Titus Groan* 114, 126, 155–6, 166–7, 206
Peirce, C. S. 107
Penrose, R. 52, 53
Perry, J. 107
Pfeifer, R. 54 n.
Piaget, J. ix n., 92 n., 117
Polanyi, L. ix n., 67 n., 77 n.
Poundstone, W., *Labyrinths of Reason: Paradox, Puzzles and the Frailty of Knowledge* 265
Prince, E. F. 27 n., 59, 60, 85
Prince, G. 32, 105, 105 n.
Propp, V. 32
Pylyshyn, Z. W. 113, 113 n., 115 n.

Quillian, M. R. 24
Quirk, R. 14, 14 n., 179, 200 n.

Rapaport, W. J. 39, 87 n., 219 n.
Ravelli, L. J. 267 n.
Reichman, R. x n., 8 n., 78, 87 n., 133, 138, 206, 223 n.

Rendell, R., *Going Wrong* 241
Rieger, C. J. 27 n., 28, 37, 97 n., 150, 205 n., 223 n., 237 n.
Riesbeck, C. K. 87 n.
Rimmon-Kenan, S. 105 n., 135
Rochester, S. x n., 66
Rosch, E. 23
Rumelhart, D. E. vi n., 32, 44 n., 51, 134
Ryan, M.-L. 164, 202, 202 n., 265

Sacks, H. 77, 77 n., 93 n., 107, 108, 117 n., 160, 209 n., 224–5, 237 n.
Sacks, O. 66, 116
Sag, I. A. 44 n., 202
Sanders, J. 56 n.
Sanford, A. J. 8 n., 8–9, 27, 27 n., 62, 69, 86, 89, 89 n., 97, 97 n., 150, 205 n., 209 n., 226, 227
Schank, R. C. ix n., 5, 23, 24, 25, 39, 53, 55 n., 64 n., 68, 81, 98, 105
Schegloff, E. A. 77, 77 n., 93 n., 109, 160, 224–5
Schiffrin, D. 10 n., 248 n.
Searle, J. R. 52 n., 53, 53 n., 55, 108
Segal, E. M. 39, 58
Semino, E. 31
Shapiro, S. C. 23 n., 39
Sharkey, N. E. 54 n.
Short, M. H. 30, 30 n., 94, 243
Sidner, C. L. x n., 8 n., 37, 39, 93 n., 136, 197, 202, 216, 216 n., 221 n., 223–4, 233, 234
Simpson, J., *Touching the Void* 262
Simpson, P. 39, 96
Sinclair, J. McH. 9 n., 14 n., 78, 223 n., 267 n.
Slobin, D. I. 67 n., 105 n., 243
Smith, F. vi n.
Spark, M., *Memento Mori* 220 n.
Sperber, D. 78, 253
Steinbeck, J., *The Grapes of Wrath* 30
Stevenson, R. 42 n., 89 n.
Stevenson, R. L., 'The Strange Case of Dr Jekyll and Mr Hyde' 159
Straub, P., *Ghost Story* 11, 82–3, 159, 209–10, 215, 219
Suchman, L. A. 4, 108, 162–3
Svartvik, J. 14, 14 n., 200 n.

Talmy, L. 56
Tannen, D. 59, 67 n., 86, 198 n.
Thompson, S. A. 33, 76–7, 93 n., 96, 105 n., 236, 243, 244
Thorndyke, P. W. 32
Tomlin, R. S. 105 n., 223 n., 243
Toolan, M. 79, 81
Treyens, J. C. 23, 91, 92 n.
Tulving, E. 24, 121, 128 n.
Turing, A. M. 53
Turner, T. J. 24

Uspensky, B. 39, 118 n.

van Dijk, T. A. vi n., 21, 37, 42 n., 43–4,
    45 n., 74, 92, 104, 109 n., 109–10, 200,
    204 n., 259
Ventola, E. 223 n.
Vine, B., *A Dark-Adapted Eye* 253
——, *A Fatal Inversion* 148, 154, 205, 240

Waletzky, J. 79, 105 n., 236, 241
Wason, P. C. 92 n.
Webber, B. L. 8 n., 37
Weekly Law Reports, The 264
Weinstein, S. 221 n., 233
Weizenbaum, J. 54
Weldon, F., *The Life and Loves of a She Devil* 30
Wentworth, P., *Poison in the Pen* 42
Werth, P. N. 24 n., 31, 39, 56 n., 56–7,
    107 n., 180, 200, 202, 202 n., 203 n., 252

Wesley, M. *Harnessing Peacocks* 142, 147
Whitman, L., 'A Dangerous Influence' 218
Widdowson, H. G. 202
Wiebe, J. M. 39, 58, 219 n.
Wilensky, R. 32, 33
Wilks, Y. 55
Wilson, D. 78, 253
Winograd, T. 8 n.
Winter, E. 33, 76

Yuill, N. ix n., 68, 93, 199 n., 200, 270
Yule, G. 27 n., 37–8, 97, 198, 201, 204 n.,
    205 n., 231

Zacharski, R. 27 n., 60
Zubin, D. A. 39, 58, 118 n.
Zwaan, R. A. 42, 42 n.

SUBJECT INDEX

academic text, *see* genres, other than narrative fiction
accessibility scale (Ariel) 60
activation, *see* consciousness
adverbs 211, *see also* discourse markers
Alzheimer's disease, *see* reading problems
ambiguity, *see* referent ambiguity; enactors (enactor ambiguity); frames, contextual (frame participant ambiguity); overt participant ambiguity; narrative (text types: indeterminate text)
anaphora
  anaphoric theory
    backward-oriented theory (arguments against) 222, 230–2
    and discourse structure, *see* pronouns (and discourse hierarchy)
    forward-oriented theory (arguments for) 221–34
    general comments vii, 13–14, 271, 273
    with mental representations (arguments for) 200–35
    without mental representations (arguments against) 198–200
  and cataphora 85, 207–8, 271
  and deixis vii, 13–14, 211–12, 271
  indirect anaphora 227–9
  see also pronouns; definite articles; antecedents; focusing; centering
antecedents
  distant 210–12
  and enactor identification 188
  lack of vii, 13, 16, 66, 153, 155–6, 207, 272
  role of 13–14, 188, 203–6, 221, 224, 232–3
  scattered 210–12
  see also backward/forward inferences; anaphora
antecedentless pronouns, *see* antecedents (lack of)
artificial intelligence
  and consciousness 52–5, *see also* consciousness; human experience; empathy
  context shifts (Charniak) 140–1
  and mental representations 37, 125 n., *see also* mental representations
  and reference/pronouns 8, 178, 200, 202–3, *see also* topic shifts
  research techniques, *see* methodology (artificial intelligence)
  robustness of programs 163, *see also* repairs

and topic shifts, *see* topic shifts
  see also frame problem; situated actions; focusing; centering; cognitive science; robotics
aspect 184–6
autobiography, *see* genres, other than narrative fiction
awareness, *see* consciousness
background, *see* grounding research
backward inferences 15 n., 27, 225–6, 228, *see also* anaphora (anaphoric theory: backward-oriented); bridging
backward-oriented anaphora, *see* anaphora (anaphoric theory: backward-oriented), *see also* backward inferences; bridging
belief frames, *see* frames (Goffman)
binding, *see* frames, contextual (binding)
blindness 54, 118–19, 126, 143, 146–7, 156–7, 158, 162, 163, 189–90
bookkeeping (Charniak) 140–1
brain damage, *see* reading problems
bridging 15, 27, 97, 225–6, *see also* backward inferences

cataphora, *see* pronouns (cataphoric pronouns)
causality 6, 27, 33, 41, 80–1, 97
centering 221 n., 233–4, *see also* focusing
central directory 125, 167, 220
character constructs/representations, *see* entity representations (characters in narrative)
children's reading, *see* literacy; reading differences (age)
Chinese room (Searle) 53
clause relational theory 33–4, 76–7, 80, 138, 273, *see also* causality
COBUILD 14 n., *see also* corpus linguistics
cognitive discourse analysis 10, 96, 272, *see also* Bernado; Chafe; Clancy; Du Bois; Emmott; Grosz; Sidner; Reichman; Linde; Werth; Deictic Shift Theory
cognitive linguistics
  general use of term, *see* cognitive perspective; cognitive discourse analysis
  specific group of researchers 10, 56, *see also* Fauconnier; Lakoff; Langacker; Talmy; M. Johnson; Werth
cognitive perspective on text viii, 9, 95, *see also* mental representations; inference-making; knowledge; dynamic approach
cognitive psychology, *see* psychology

cognitive science 5 n., 37, 43, 45, 50, 228, 274, *see also* disciplines
cognitive terminology, problematic nature of 228
coherence (textual) 9, 22, 28, 95, 97, 271
cohesion
　lexical/grammatical 11, 85–6, 94, 187, 246
　spurious cohesion 172, 187
　see also Halliday/Hasan; pronouns
competence 9, 10
comprehension, *see* mental representations; inference-making; knowledge
computational explosion (Rieger) 28
computer, *see* artificial intelligence; corpus linguistics; parallel distributed processing
connectionism, *see* parallel distributed processing
connectivity 75, 85–7, *see also* cohesion; coherence; given-new
consciousness
　cognitive science research 52–9, 274–5
　focal/peripheral consciousness 63
　forward-oriented anaphora 224–34
　forward inferences 27
　levels of activation 59–61, 63, 125, 216–21
　mental imagery 111
　science research 53–4
　text linguistics 59–63
　see also human experience; Chinese room; Turing test; contextual monitoring; frames, contextual (priming); focusing
constructed text, *see* data (artificially constructed)
context, fictional
　activating contexts, *see* frames, contextual (priming)
　building contexts, *see* frames, contextual (binding)
　changes to current context, *see* frames, contextual (frame modification)
　shifts to different contexts, *see* frames, contextual (frame recall/switch)
context, real life 58, 109 n., 110, 117–19, 129–30, 156–7, 162, 201 n., 202, *see also* contextual monitoring; blindness
context space (Reichman) 138–9
context summarizers, *see* narrative (text types)
contextual consciousness, *see* contextual monitoring
contextual frame theory (Emmott), *see* frames, contextual
contextual monitoring
　in fiction 40, 106, 112–15, 117–18, 120, 160–2
　in real life/robotics research 112–13, 115–19, 163

see also frames, contextual (priming); context, real life
contrastiveness (Chafe) 60–1
controlled experiments, *see* data (artificially constructed); methodology (psychology)
conversation, *see* dialogue, real life, *see also* Conversation Analysis
Conversation Analysis 77–8, 107–9, 160, 225
cooperative principle 7, 237
corpus linguistics 14, 272, *see also* COBUILD
counterparts 179–80, *see also* possible worlds
covert participants 124–7, 142, 146, 155, 176–7, 213–15, 239–40, 245, 260
covert update 177, 215, 232–3

data
　artificially constructed dialogue 94
　artificially constructed narrative 48–50, 79, 93
　artificially constructed sentence pairs v n., x–xi, 10–16, 40, 50, 74, 85–6, 89–90, 92–3, 140–1, 229, 272
　real/natural full-length text v n., xi, 40, 74–9, 85–6, 87 n., 89, 267, *see also* discourse perspective; discourse structure
definite articles 14, 27, 84, 205 n., 273
Deictic Shift Theory 57–58, 107 n., 127, 219 n.
deixis viii, 13, 207, 211–12, 271, 273, *see also* Deictic Shift Theory
detective/crime fiction 31, 41, 106, 170, 210, 220
determiners, *see* definite articles
dialogue, fictional 30 n., 94, 242–3, 257–8
dialogue, real life
　conversation 46–7, 77–8, 107–9, 139, 160 n., 178
　instructional dialogue 78, 98, 136–8
disciplines, *see* interdisciplinary research; artificial intelligence; cognitive science; linguistics; psychology; literary theory; education; philosophy; neuroscience
direct speech, *see* dialogue, fictional
discourse analysis vii, viii, 9–10, 13–14, 59–63, 76–9, 95–6, 206, 271–2, 274, *see also* discourse perspective; discourse structure; data (real/natural full-length text); methodology (discourse analysis)
discourse markers (Schiffrin) 248 n.
discourse perspective xi, 13–14, 74–99, 272, *see also* discourse analysis
Discourse Representation Theory (Kamp) 37
discourse structure (hierarchy/embedding)
　general comments x, 13–14, 16, 40, 75, 90, 136, 141, 270
　narrative

contextual frame theory, *see* frames, contextual (frame recall/switch)
other work on narrative hierarchy 62, 134–6, 244–5
non-narrative, 76–9, 136–40, *see* topic shifts; Conversation Analysis; clause relational theory; Rhetorical Structure Theory
distinctive information 192–4, *see also* frames, contextual (frame specific clues)
dynamic approach viii, 14, 173, 267
dynamic memory (Schank) 25, 98
ecological validity x, 92, 272, 274
education, ix–x, 269–70, *see also* literacy; psychology (educational)
educational psychology, *see* psychology
embedding, *see* discourse structure
embodiment 57, 58, *see also* consciousness; empathy; human experience; situatedness
empathy 16–17, 48, 57, 81, 106, 202, 209 n.
empirical research, *see* data; methodology
enactors 180–2, 268
  enactor ambiguity 184–7
  identification 188–94
  monitoring 182–4, 269
entity representations
  characters in narrative 15–16, 36–9, 81–5, 104, 122, 129, 159, 167, 173, 176–7, 181–2, 201–6, 224, 230–3, 268
  in other genres 37–8
  in real life 37
  general knowledge of entities, *see* schemata
  see also enactors; covert update; updating
ethnomethodology 7, 107–8, *see also* Conversation Analysis
events
  and entity representations 39
  events in context 80–1, 107, 242–3, *see also* frames, contextual
  event-line (Fox) 140, 245
  event sequences ix, 48, 105, 241–3, 260
  habitual events 81, 189, 239, 245, 250, *see also* narrative (text types: unframed text)
  stereotypical sequences, *see* schemata (scripts)
experimental tests, *see* data; methodology
eye movements 88, 229–30

fictional worlds vi–vii, 30, 32, 35–6, 49, 50, 58, 121, 125, 128 n., 129, 149–50, *see also* mental representations; worlds
flashbacks vi–vii, xi, 16, 38, 83, 90, 153, 162, 172, 177, 180–6, 188–9, 191–4, 244–5, 268–9, 271, *see also* frames, contextual (recall/switch); enactors
focusing 39, 197–8, 216–34

global focus (Grosz/Sidner) 137–8, 140, 216
immediate focus (Grosz/Sidner) 216, 221, 223–4
  see also anaphora (anaphoric theory: forward-oriented)
force dynamics (Talmy) 56
forgetting, *see* memory limits
foreground, *see* grounding research
foregrounding, stylistic (lexical reiteration) 6 n., 42, 86, *see also* linguistics (stylistics)
forward inferences 15 n., 27–8, 226–8, *see also* anaphora (anaphoric theory: forward-oriented)
forward-oriented anaphora, *see* anaphora (anaphoric theory: forward-oriented)
frame problem (artificial intelligence) 113, 119
frames, contextual 121–2
  basic notion 103, 121–3, 132
  binding (into frames) 123–4, 125, 142–9, 152
    retrospective binding 145–9
  contextual monitoring of fiction 106–7, 114–20
  fictional context vi n., 103–7, 114, *see also* frames, contextual (contextual monitoring)
  frame independent clues 168, 188–90, *see also* distinctive/shared information
  frame modification
    of primed frames 142–3
    of unprimed frames 134–5
    contrasted with frame switch 147–9
    repairs 160–2
  frame narrowing 208–10
  frame participant ambiguity 212–14
  frame recall 150–4, 227, 269
    and probability-based interpretation 170–2
    progressive/instantaneous 154–7
    and reference theory 207, 227
  frame specific clues 168, 190–4, *see also* distinctive/shared information
  frame switch 147–9, 150, 218, 272
    contrasted with frame modification 147–9
    and probability-based interpretation 170–2
    progressive/instantaneous 154–7
    and reference theory 208–9
    repairs 160–2
  priming 123–6, 142–3, 145–9, 150–2, 155, 176–7, 214–5, 216–20, 268
    and reference theory 206–15, 216–34
    restricted contexts 129–31
    overlapping restricted contexts 130–1, 159
    unbound frames 125, 220

frames, contextual (*cont.*)
  unprimed frames 125–6, 134–5, 143–5,
    151, 177, 219
  see also narrative (text types: framed/
    unframed text); covert/overt partici-
    pants, enactors; contextual monitor-
    ing
frames (Goffman) 164–6, 265
frames (Minsky) 23, 25, 192 n., *see also*
  schemata
framed text, *see* narrative (text types)

general knowledge
  basic inferences 5–6, 26–8, 55, 71, 78,
    192
  overall textual interpretation 28–32
  seminal studies 23–6, 140–1
  and story schemata 33
  and text-specific knowledge 28, 35–6, 83,
    105–7, 112, 272–3
  see also schemata
generalizations 247, 249, 253–6, 261, *see
  also* narrative (text types: unframed text)
genres, narrative, *see* narrative (comments
  on specific genres)
genres, other than narrative fiction
  academic text 77, 139, 262–5
  advertisements 31, 77
  autobiography 262
  history books 263
  legal text 264
  letters 33, 77
  newspaper articles 31, 92, 109–10
  poems 31
  recipes 38, 263
  speech, *see* dialogue, real life
ghost stories 82, 158–9, 165
given-new 56–62, 85–6, 233–4, *see also*
  givenness hierarchy
givenness hierarchy 60, *see also* given-new
global focus, *see* focusing
grammatical theory, *see* anaphora
grounding research 243–4
group pronouns, *see* pronouns

habitual actions, *see* events
hierarchical structure, *see* discourse
  structure
human experience, contrasted with
  computer capabilities 54–9, *see also*
  consciousness, empathy

ideal reader, *see* reader
identifiability (Chafe) 60–1
imagery 45, 47, 52, 62, 66–7, 71, 80, 111,
  115, 118, 138
immediate focus, *see* focusing
implied reader, *see* reader
indeterminate text, *see* narrative (text types)

indexicality 107–9
indirect anaphora, *see* anaphora
inference-making
  general comments viii–ix, xi, 3, 10, 50, 97,
    111, *see also* bridging; backward/for-
    ward inferences
  general knowledge 5–6, 24, 27, 112, *see
    also* schemata
  about overall plot 31, 57, 165–6, 170–2,
    210
  text-specific 16, 28, 36, 83, 123–30, 144,
    167, *see also* anaphora (anaphoric
    theory: forward oriented); priming;
    focusing; covert update; contextual
    monitoring; updating
instantaneous frame recall/switch, *see*
  frames, contextual
intentions 39, 56
interdisciplinary research, vii–viii, 274, *see
  also* disciplines

knowledge
  general, *see* general knowledge, *see also*
    schemata
  mutual/shared knowledge, *see* mutual
    knowledge
  text-specific, *see* text-specific knowledge/
    representations

laboratory data, *see* data (artificially
  constructed)
laboratory reading, *see* methodology
  (psychology)
legal text, *see* genres, other than narrative
  fiction
linguistics
  discourse analysis/text theory, *see* dis-
    course analysis
  generative linguistics 9–10, 96, 200 n., *see
    also* Chomsky
  pragmatics 7, 10, 107–8, 233 n.
  stylistics 6 n., 14 n., 31, 42, 61 n., 86, 96
literacy ix–x, 4, 8, 269–70, 272
literary theory viii, 8, 32, 68–71, 96, 109,
  164, *see also* reader response theory;
  psychoanalytic criticism
location representations 104, *see also* place
logic 45, 48, 56

made-up sentences, *see* data (artificially
  constructed)
memory
  episodic memory 24–5, 64 n., 68, 104,
    121–3, 127, 128 n.
  non-episodic memory 122, 128–9
  semantic memory 24–5
  see also mental representations; memory
    limits; contextual monitoring;
    dynamic memory; knowledge;

frames, contextual (priming);
dynamic memory (Schank)
memory limits 41–2, 63–6, *see also*
mnemonist
mental models (Johnson-Laird) 43–50, 109,
111, 138
mental representations
text-specific representations, *see* text-specific representations
general knowledge, *see* general knowledge; schemata
see also mental spaces; mental models
mental spaces (Fauconnier) 56, 179–80, *see
also* cognitive linguistics
metalinguistic pronouns, *see* pronouns
methodology
artificial intelligence 4–6, 87 n., 98
discourse analysis 62–3, 94–8, 272
psychology
controlled laboratory experiments v n.,
viii, x, 16, 45–50, 74, 79, 87–94, 95,
97, 229–30
protocol analysis 93, 272
mimesis 58, 243
mind, *see* mental representations; inference-
making; knowledge; cognitive science;
artificial intelligence; psychology
mind-style (Fowler) 6 n., 29–30
mnemonist 64–5
monitoring, *see* contextual monitoring
mutual knowledge 4, 6, 22, 76

narrative
characters, *see* entity representations
comments on specific genres, *see* detective/
crime fiction; science fiction; ghost
stories
comprehension *see* mental representations; inference-making; knowledge
contexts, *see* frames, contextual
oral narratives v n., 62–3, 135–6, 244
production v n., 6, 62, 135–6
and reference theory 248–52
structure, *see* discourse structure; flashbacks; frames, contextual
text types
context summarizers 258–61
framed text 237–8, 241–5, 248–56,
262–4, 273, *see also* frames, contextual
indeterminate text 253–6
unframed text 239–52, 253–8, 262–3,
269, 273
see also embodiment; events; mimesis; plot;
style; suspense; themes, literary;
worlds
narrative worlds (Gerrig) 57
narratology ix, 39, 134–5, 198, 241–5
natural discourse, *see* data (real/natural text)

Natural Language Processing, *see* artificial
intelligence
neural networks, *see* parallel distributed
processing
neuroscience 50–2, 95, 122, 274
nouns
general nouns 206
lexical reiteration 86–7, *see also* foregrounding, stylistic
as pro-referents 201–2
see also antecedents

oral narratives/storytelling, *see* narrative
orthographic breaks 148, 172, 187
overlapping restricted context, *see* frames,
contextual
overt participants 124–6, 127, 155, 176,
217–19, 240, *see also* overt participant
ambiguity
overt participant ambiguity 212–14

parallel distributed processing 3, 50–2, 122
participants, *see* entity representations
(characters)
participant continuity, *see* covert
participants; frames, contextual (priming)
participatory response (Gerrig) 57
past perfect, *see* aspect
personal experience, *see* reading differences
philosophy 52–4, 107, 164, 179–80, 202 n.,
203 n.
place 147–9, 176–7, *see also* location
representations
plot, overall 12, 15, 29, 31, 34, 41, 47, 50,
61 n., 106, 167, 210, 267, 269
point of view 39, 58, 107 n., 118–19, 127 n.,
131, 161, 165, 168, 218 n.
possible worlds 56, 164, 179–80, 202 n., *see*
counterparts
pragmatics, *see* linguistics
priming
priming of contextual frames, *see* frames,
contextual (priming)
psychology term 228
probability-based interpretation of text 28,
128, 166–73, 273
process models, *see* mental representations;
inference-making; dynamic approach
production, *see* narrative (production)
progressive frame recall/switch, *see* frames,
contextual (frame recall/switch)
pronouns
anaphoric pronouns, *see* anaphora
antecedentless pronouns, *see* antecedent
(lack of)
avoidance of pronouns (lexical reiteration)
86–7
cataphoric pronouns 85, 206, 207–8,
221 n., 271
and consciousness 224

pronouns (*cont.*)
    difficulties in reading pronouns ix, 66
    and discourse hierarchy vi, 8, 11–16, 40,
        62, 75, 136–41, 155–6, 180, 206–8,
        248–52
    generic pronouns 263
    group pronouns 210–12, 217
    importance in cognitive research 8–9
    in instructional discourse 136–9
    and mental representations 16, 63, 83–5,
        93, 97, 120–1, 201–6, 206–35, 224
    metalinguistic pronouns 42–3
    and probability-based interpretation 166,
        170
    as pro-referents 201–2
    statistical analysis of 61
propositional representations (contrasted
    with mental models) 43–5, 47, 110
psychoanalytic criticism 67, 69, 71, *see also*
    literary theory
psychology
    cognitive viii, x–xi, 8, 9, 37, 86, 87–94, 97,
        225–30, 275, *see also* methodology;
        data; eye movements
    educational ix, 4
    social 37

reader
    actual 8, *see also* reading differences;
        methodology (psychology)
    ideal/implied 7–8
    see also consciousness; mental representa-
        tions; inference-making
reader response theory viii, 68–71, 97, *see
    also* literary theory
reading, *see* reader; reading differences;
    reading problems; literacy; text-
    processing research
reading differences
    age 35, 68, 269–70
    culture 67, 150
    non-native speakers 35, 270
    personal experience 63, 66–8
    see also mnemonist; reading problems;
        reader response theory
reading problems
    due to Alzheimer's disease 66
    due to brain damage 66
    due to schizophrenia x, 66
    mnemonist's problems, *see* mnemonist
    see also reading differences
real text/discourse, *see* data
real world, *see* context, real life
recipes, *see* genres, other than narrative
    fiction
reference theory, *see* anaphora; pronouns;
    antecedents; definite articles
referent ambiguity (versus enactor
    ambiguity) 184–6, 188

referent identification (versus enactor
    identification) 188–92
relevance 78, 80, 253
repairs 160–3, 164, 183 n., 184, 187, 224–
    5, 256
restricted contexts, *see* frames, contextual
    (restricted contexts)
retrospective binding/priming, *see* frames,
    contextual (binding/priming)
Rhetorical Structure Theory 33–4, 76, 138,
    140, 273
robotics, 112–3, 115, 119, *see also* frame
    problem; situated actions
scenario, *see* schemata
scenario-dependent (Anderson *et al.*) 209 n.
schemata
    and mental models 44 n.
    scenarios 23–4, 25–6, 50 n.
    in social psychology 37
    scripts 24, 26–7, 28, 31, 53, 105–6
    see also general knowledge; story sche-
        mata; frames (Minsky)
schizophrenia, *see* reading problems
science fiction 158–9
scripts, *see* schemata
semantic memory, *see* memory
sentence-level theory vi n., 10, 13, 14, 76
sentence pairs, *see* data (artificially
    constructed)
sequence analysis, *see* events
shared information 192, *see* frame specific
    clues
shared knowledge, *see* mutual knowledge
shifts, temporal-spatial, *see* flashbacks;
    frames, contextual (frame recall/switch)
situated actions (in Robotics), *see* Suchman
situatedness (in narrative) 58, *see also*
    frames, contextual; embodiment
situation (Morrow *et al.*) 49–50
situation model (van Dijk and Kintsch) 45,
    109–10
speech, *see* dialogue, real life; narrative
    (oral), *see also* speech in narrative
speech act theory 108
speech in narrative, *see* dialogue, fictional
spoken text, *see* speech, *see also* speech
    in narrative
spurious cohesion, *see* cohesion
stories/storytelling, *see* narrative
story grammars, *see* story schemata
story schemata 32–5, 81, 134, *see also*
    schemata
style, *see* text-specific stylistic
    representations; linguistics (stylistics);
    mind-style; foregrounding, literary
stylistics, *see* linguistics (stylistics)
subjective perspective 58, *see also* point of
    view
subjective readings, *see* memory limits;

reading differences; reader response
theory
suspense 12, 34, 57

Talespin Project 5–6
tests, psychology, *see* data; methodology
text structure, *see* discourse structure
text-processing research, *see* mental
representations; knowledge; inference-
making; disciplines
text-specific knowledge/representations
general comments 7, 28, 34, 35–41, 103
specific types, *see* frames, contextual;
entity representations; location
representations; central directory
see also Deictic Shift Theory
text-specific stylistic representations 41–3
text types, *see* narrative (text types); genres,
other than narrative fiction
text worlds (Werth), 56–7, 180
textual worlds (de Beaugrande) 110–12
textually-covert, *see* covert participants
textually-overt, *see* overt participants
themes, literary 4, 29, 61 n., 66, 267, 269
time 104, 112, 120, 135, 149–50, *see also*
frames, contextual (frame switch/recall);
enactors; flashbacks
topic xi, 77, 134, 137–9, 246

topic shifts xi, 16, 137–9
tracking, *see* contextual monitoring, *see also*
updating
Turing test 53–4, *see also* consciousness,
human experience

unbound, *see* frames, contextual (unbound)
unframed text, *see* narrative (text types:
unframed), *see also* generalizations; events
(habitual events)
unprimed, *see* frames, contextual (unprimed)
updating (of mental representations)
entity representations 15, 37–9, 129, 177,
215, 231–3, *see also* covert update
contextual frames, *see* frames, contextual
(binding/priming)
general comments viii, 112

vision
artificial intelligence 5, 117
everyday vision 26
philosophy 54–5
see also imagery; blindness

worlds, *see* fictional worlds; possible
worlds; narrative worlds (Gerrig); text
worlds (Werth); textual worlds (de
Beaugrande)